CLINICAL PATHS

Tools for Outcomes Management

Patrice L. Spath, editor

AHA books are published by American Hospital Publishing, Inc.,
an American Hospital Association company

The views expressed in this publication are strictly those of the authors and do not necessarily represent official positions of the American Hospital Association.

Library of Congress Cataloging-in-Publication Data

Clinical paths : tools for outcomes management / Patrice L. Spath,
  editor.
      p.   cm.
    Includes bibliographical references.
    ISBN 1-55648-120-9 (pbk.)
    1. Medical care – Quality control. 2. Medical care – Cost
effectiveness. 3. Hospitals – Quality control. 4. Medical
protocols. I. Spath, Patrice.
    [DNLM: 1. Patient Care Planning – organization & administration.
2. Delivery of Health Care – organization & administration – United
States. 3. Clinical Protocols. 4. Outcome and Process Assessment
(Health Care) – organization & administration. 5. Total Quality
Management.   WX 162 C641 1994]
RA399.A1C58   1994
362.1'1'0685 – dc20
for Library of Congress   94-13825
                                                                           CIP

Catalog no. 027101

©1994 by American Hospital Publishing, Inc.,
an American Hospital Association company

Printed in the USA

AHA is a service mark of the American Hospital Association used under license by American Hospital Publishing, Inc.

Text set in Century Textbook
3M—08/94—0374
6M—04/95—0406

Audrey Kaufman, Acquisitions and Development Editor
Nancy Charpentier, Production Editor
Peggy DuMais, Production Coordinator
Susan Edge-Gumbel, Cover Designer
Marcia Bottoms, Books Division Assistant Director
Brian Schenk, Books Division Director

This book is dedicated to all the people I sometimes neglect to thank:

- The authors of these chapters who freely share their successes and failures so others can learn
- Audrey Kaufman, my protagonist at American Hospital Publishing
- Robert O. Brown, my friend and my husband

Now, it is done.

Patrice L. Spath

Contents

List of Figures and Tables

About the Editor

Patrice L. Spath is based in Forest Grove, Oregon, and has extensive experience in hospital and medical staff quality and utilization management and external review activities, with a special interest in clinical paths. She has written several books and articles on these topics for private publishers and also for the American College of Surgeons and American Hospital Publishing, Inc. Ms. Spath currently serves as staff columnist for *Hospital Peer Review* and as an editorial board member for *Topics in Health Record Management* and *Quality Management Update.* During 1992–93 she served on a task group for the Agency for Health Care Policy and Research to develop a model for translating guidelines into medical review criteria. She is a past chairman of the quality assurance section of the American Health Information Management Association and member of the executive board of the National Association for Health-care Quality. Ms. Spath is a private consultant offering awareness training, education, and publications addressing health care quality and resource management issues.

Contributors

Cathy K. Ahern, RN, is coordinator for cardiac rehabilitation at Immanuel-St. Joseph's Hospital in Mankato, Minnesota. She has 23 years experience in cardiovascular nursing, serving in the coronary care unit, the intensive care unit, the coronary step-down unit, and cardiac rehabilitation. Ms. Ahern served as a noninvasive cardiovascular diagnostics nurse for 10 years. Her previous affiliations include Fairview Hospital in Minneapolis, Fairview Southdale Hospital in Edina, and the Minnesota Department of Health.

David T. Allen, MD, MPH, is senior vice-president for quality and medical affairs at Alliant® Health System, Louisville, Kentucky. Dr. Allen brought 20 years experience as an epidemiologist to the challenge of measuring and improving the quality of care delivered in the inpatient arena.

Connie Anton, RNC, is clinical liaison, quality and medical affairs, at Alliant® Health System. Previously she held the position of head nurse, geriatric psychiatry, at Norton Psychiatric Clinic in Louisville. In that position she coordinated the development of critical paths for psychiatric diagnoses.

Stephen Baker, PharmD, is a clinical pharmacist. He is a member of the pharmacy and therapeutics committee, infection control committee, and the pharmacy quality assurance committee reviewing drug utilization, drug protocols, and therapeutic drug monitoring, ASHP, OSHP.

Kathleen A. Bower, DNSc, RN, is a principal in The Center for Case Management, South Natick, Massachusetts. Prior to her current role, Dr. Bower held a series of positions over 17 years at New England Medical Center in Boston, including vice-chairman of nursing, nurse leader, and associate nurse leader. She was also director of research and development for The Center for Nursing Case Management while it was based at New England Medical Center. Dr. Bower pioneered the development of nursing case management and has assisted nursing departments nationwide and in Canada with implementation and refinement of Critical Path/CareMap™ and case management systems. She is a frequent workshop leader and an active member of several nursing organizations. Her most recent publication is a chapter in *The Encyclopedia of Nursing*

Care Quality, edited by Pat Schroeder. She was a contributing author in *Collaborative Care: Nursing Case Management* and author of an American Nurses Association publication, *Case Management by Nurses* (1992). Dr. Bower has a BSN from Georgetown University, a MSN from Boston College, and earned the DNSc from Boston University.

Sonja Bray, RN, is director of the advanced care unit at Douglas Community Hospital in Roseburg, Oregon. She is currently working toward a BSN at OHSU in Portland.

David A. Casey, MD, is an assistant professor in the department of psychiatry and behavioral sciences, University of Louisville (Kentucky) School of Medicine. He is also medical director, geriatric psychiatry program, Edward E. Landis Geriatric Psychiatry Center, Norton Psychiatric Clinic, Louisville.

Kathleen Ciccone, RN, MBA, CPQA, is vice-president of the quality assurance division at the Healthcare Association of New York State, Albany. Ms. Ciccone has extensive experience in quality management and previously served as a consultant for HANYS Services, Inc.

Karen A. Doran, RN, MSN, CCRN, is a clinical nurse specialist at Abbott Northwestern Hospital in Minneapolis.

Carol Fisher, RN, BSN, is manager of nursing systems, Alliant Adult Hospitals. She assisted in defining clinical paths as a med-surg staff nurse and implemented clinical paths and critical management teams at Methodist Evangelical Hospital, Louisville. She also implemented a pneumonia path in adult hospitals in the revised format of daily physician orders.

Tina Gerardi, RN, MSN, CPHQ, is director of professional and quality improvement at HANYS Services, Inc., an affiliate of the Healthcare Association of New York State. She formerly was director of clinical services at Northeastern New York Hospital Council, Albany. Ms. Gerardi is on the board of directors of New York State Nurses Association.

Edward B. Goldman, JD, is medical center attorney at the University of Michigan, Ann Arbor. He is also adjunct professor, University of Michigan School of Public Health. Mr. Goldman formerly was president of the Michigan Society of Health Lawyers and a member of the White House legal audit task force on health care reform.

Christopher Heller, MD, FACS, is chairman and cofounder of MIDS, Inc., where he also is vice-president for research and development and codeveloper of the MIDAS software program. MIDS is the leading vendor of quality management information systems. For 20 years Dr. Heller was a general and vascular surgeon in Tucson and was the medical director at Carondelet St. Joseph's Hospital. He is now a health care consultant for the Carondelet Health Care Corporation and a highly recruited speaker on CQI and the medical staff.

Sharon A. Henry, RN, is the director of cardiovascular services for Health One Mercy and Unity hospitals. She received her RN from Anoka-Ramsey Community College, Coon Rapids, Minnesota, and is completing the bachelor of arts at Metropolitan State University, Minneapolis. Her previous positions include ICU staff nurse and head nurse of the emergency department at Mercy Hospital. Ms. Henry has a high level of nursing knowledge in the critical care area, with emphasis on patient/staff education and expertise in overall product line management and outreach. She is also a consultant for The Center for Case Management in Boston for managed care and case management.

Mike Holbert, RCP, is a staff therapist with cardiopulmonary services at Douglas Community Hospital, Roseberg, Oregon. He graduated from Indiana University of Pennsylvania with a bachelor of arts in 1974; trained for respiratory therapy at Rogue Community College, Grants Pass, Oregon; and became a registered respiratory therapist in 1988. In addition to regular staff duties, Mr. Holbert does pulmonary function testing and cardiac stress testing, and oversees quality control for the blood gas lab. He is a member of the American Association for Respiratory Care.

Carol A. Huttner, RN, BSN, MA, is director of nursing for cardiovascular services with Abbott Northwestern Hospital in Minneapolis and has been a key member of the cardiovascular continuous quality improvement team. She frequently speaks nationwide on improving patient care through integrated teams and implementation of cardiovascular clinical paths and has coauthored articles on these topics.

Kathleen B. Jarrell, MS, RN, CCRN, is cardiac clinical coordinator at Chippenham Medical Center (CMC) in Richmond, Virginia. She chairs the nursing standards committee at CMC and has facilitated the change from nursing care plans to nursing standards. Ms. Jarrell has 14 years experience as a critical care nurse and has been active in staff development and patient education. She is an active member of the Greater Richmond Chapter of AACN. She has also coauthored and authored several critical paths.

Alice B. Keeling, RN, BSN, MA, is on the total quality management staff for Alliant® Health System in Louisville. In her former position, manager of nursing systems, she coordinated the implementation of critical paths for Norton Hospital, also in Louisville.

John T. Kelly, MD, PhD, is chief medical officer, senior vice-president of clinical information of GMIS, a health information services organization, located in Malvern, Pennsylvania. Previously, Dr. Kelly was director of the American Medical Association's office of quality assurance and utilization management, where he coordinated the AMA/Specialty Society Practice Parameters Forum. He has written and spoken extensively on practice parameters and clinical paths.

Mary Jo Kocan, MSN, RN, CNRN, CCRN, is a clinical nurse specialist for neurology/neurosurgery at the University of Michigan Hospitals. She has been active in the implementation of coordinated care on neurology/neurosurgery units and has authored several publications related to care of the neuroscience patient. Past positions include clinical and management roles in neuroscience critical care.

Diane Lavoie, MS, RN, is coordinator of clinical management at Rhode Island Hospital, Providence. She has been at Rhode Island Hospital since 1988 in various administrative and staff development positions. Previously, she was a clinical nurse manager at Charlton Memorial Hospital in Fall River, Massachusetts.

Vicky A. Mahn, RN, MS, CCRN, is cardiovascular nurse case manager at Carondelet St. Joseph's Hospital in Tucson. She is responsible for coordinating care from admission through discharge for patients undergoing open-heart surgery and their families. In addition, she facilitates the development of clinical pathways, continuous quality improvement, and nursing research at St. Joseph's. Previously, she was the nursing manager for St. Joseph's 32-bed telemetry step-down unit, and is an adjunct faculty member to the University of Arizona College of Nursing.

Robert J. Marder, MD, is medical director, quality management, at Rush-Presbyterian-St. Luke's Medical Center in Chicago. He is responsible for medical staff quality improvement programs at Rush (a 900-bed teaching hospital). Previously he was project manager for indicator development at the JCAHO. Dr. Marder frequently speaks on medical staff involvement in quality improvement.

Darlene Martch, RN, BSN, is a case manager at Douglas Community Hospital in Roseburg, Oregon. Her memberships include the Oregon Association of Professionals in Quality Improvement, Association of Practitioners in Infection Control, and Society of Gynecologic Nurse Oncologists. She is a member of the Society's utilization management committee.

Sharon McCartney, RN, BSN, CPHQ, is a manager of nursing quality improvement at the University of Pittsburgh Medical Center, Montefiore University Hospital, and Presbyterian University Hospital, all in Pittsburgh. She previously was a clinical nurse manager at the University of Pittsburgh Medical Center Eye and Ear Hospital.

Hilary Monaghan, ADN, RN, is a case coordinator for cardiac surgery and heart and lung transplant patients at the University of Michigan Hospitals, Ann Arbor. Ms. Monaghan has developed multiple clinical pathways and variance data collection forms.

Mary Beth Pais, MNEd, RN, ONC, is a clinical nurse manager at the University of Pittsburgh Medical Center, Montefiore University Hospital. Ms. Pais is a member of the orthopedic utilization resource committee, and it was largely due to her efforts that work redesign, patient care management, and clinical paths came into use at the UPMC. She is a former clinical instructor of staff development at University of Pittsburgh Medical Center and Presbyterian University Hospital.

Cynthia Pringle, RN, is director of quality improvement and utilization management at Douglas Community Hospital in Roseburg, Oregon. She coordinates both medical staff and hospital department quality improvement and utilization management activities. Ms. Pringle is a member of the Oregon Association of Professionals in Quality Improvement.

Marc R. Pritzker, MD, is director of transplantation, chairman of the department of cardiovascular disease, and president of Minneapolis Heart Institute.

Janet S. Richards, MS, RN, CNA, is assistant director for nursing at University of Michigan Hospital, Ann Arbor. Her responsibilities include coordination and implementation of the coordinated care program. Ms. Richards has held head nurse and director associate positions in units that piloted the development and implementation of clinical pathways in University of Michigan Hospital. She was a member of a hospital committee that developed the implementation process for pathways based on experiences of the pilot units. She has published articles in *Quality Management in Health Care* and *The Quality Letter for Healthcare Leaders*.

Carla Sanders, RN, is manager of nursing systems at Kosair Children's Hospital of Alliant®Health System. She has 24 years of pediatric experience and has coordinated the development and implementation of 86 clinical paths. She developed and implemented employee productivity standards for pediatrics and coordinated QA/QI processes for pediatric hospitals.

Susan E. Simundson, MHA, is director of clinical management at Rhode Island Hospital. Previously she was an administrative fellow at the hospital.

Laura Sullivan, RN, BSN, is manager, product line/critical paths for adult nursing services of Alliant® Health System. Previously she was manager of information support services, a division of corporate information systems. In this position she managed the implementation and support functions of the medical information system.

Susan Wintermeyer-Pingel, MS, RN, OCN, is a clinical nurse specialist at the University of Michigan Medical Center in Ann Arbor. Ms. Wintermeyer-Pingel participates in the center's coordinated care program, working with the hematology/oncology patient population.

Foreword

Over the past decade health care providers have witnessed an evolutionary change in efforts to improve the quality of health care in the United States. Providers have shifted from retrospective analysis of patient records in an effort to identify substandard care delivery systems and practices and take corrective actions, to statistical analysis of the *outcomes* of care based on these systems and practices. This outcomes-focused approach seeks to identify a "best practices" standard and to learn which interventions can be incorporated into day-to-day practices and have a positive impact on patient outcomes. In other words, of those approaches that produce the same or similar outcomes, which ones are cost-effective? In this context, as will be seen throughout this book, cost-effectiveness is measured by length of hospital stay, number of readmissions for the same illness within a certain time, and standardization of physician practice patterns (among other indicators).

AmHS and AHPI/MSC Surveys

To help identify a best practices rule of thumb in patient care management in a changing health care climate, quality improvement activities concentrate increasingly on the clinical aspects of patient care. Many efforts are under way to identify variation in the care processes and outcomes of specific components of health care delivery. These efforts are being initiated by hospitals, managed care organizations, outpatient clinics, and other providers at a rapidly accelerating rate.

To document the diversity of these activities, American Healthcare Systems (AmHS), an alliance of 40 not-for-profit multihospital and/or health care systems, conducted a survey of corporate-level members in April 1993 to learn what they were doing to design guidelines for clinical care. Also, American Hospital Publishing, Inc. (AHPI) and Medicus Systems Corporation (MSC) collaborated in July of that year to conduct a similar survey. The AHPI/MSC questionnaire was mailed directly to leaders at individual hospitals, managed care organizations, and physicians' multispecialty clinics.

Survey Results

The majority of AmHS alliance respondents reported that they began analyzing clinical care processes after nursing, administration, or medical staff expressed a desire to become involved in quality improvement activities. Cost reduction, quality management, and payer pressures were cited as influences on this organizational initiative.

The 328 hospital leaders who responded to the AHPI/MSC survey indicated that a desire to improve quality and efficiency also was the catalyst for their initiatives. Not surprisingly, nearly 100 percent of the 38 managed care and outpatient clinic respondents in the AHPI/MSC survey expressed this same goal.

Although the motivation for initiating improved clinical process management activities is fairly consistent among all organizations, there is considerable diversity in certain specifics that will become apparent from reading this book. The more notable categories of variation (highlighted in both surveys and throughout the book) are touched on briefly in the following subsections.

Terminology

There is significant variability in the name given the tool used to manage clinical care processes. For example, respondents to the AmHS survey referred to it as *critical paths, protocols, clinical paths, case management, collaborative patient care, care plans, clinical guidelines, coordinated care, practice parameters, anticipated recovery paths,* and *clinical progressions.* When asked to name the tool at their institutions, 324 AHPI/MSC survey respondents reported the following breakdown:

Critical paths	137	(42%)
Practice guidelines/parameters	43	(13%)
Clinical guidelines	40	(12%)
Clinical protocols/algorithms	26	(8%)
Clinical benchmarking	19	(6%)
Other names (more than 30)	123	(38%)

This diversity of terminology is echoed throughout the pages of this book. For example, at Rhode Island Hospital (chapter 6), the tool is called *critical paths,* whereas at Douglas Community Hospital (chapter 7), it is referred to as *care tracks.* For purposes of consistency, however, the term used throughout this book is *clinical pathways,* or *paths.*

Specific Elements of the Initiatives

Clinical process management activities in health care organizations encompass a wide variety of initiatives. According to the AHPI/MSC survey findings, data analysis is the most frequent activity performed by hospitals, managed care organizations, and outpatient clinics. In descending order of frequency, other elements include education, development of guidelines/parameters, and physician practice profiling. Findings from both surveys showed a remarkable variety of clinical quality improvement activities being conducted by individual organizations. This book brings to light a number of initiatives, such as cost efficiency, resource utilization management, patient and staff satisfaction, and quality enhancement.

Ownership of the Process

No one department or unit seems to oversee the hospitals' clinical path-related activities. Of the 328 hospitals responding to the oversight question in the AHPI/MSC survey, 77 (24 percent) had not yet designated a particular department for this task. The remaining 251 hospitals stated that responsibilities are shared among several different departments or positions: quality improvement—162 (65 percent); nursing—122 (49 percent); utilization management—102 (41 percent); medical director—43 (17 percent); and risk management—30 (12 percent). Managed care and outpatient clinic participants named their quality improvement or utilization management department as primary owners of these activities.

Extent of Experience

Most organizations are only beginning to use clinical paths to manage their clinical care processes. When asked how many pathways are completed, hospital respondents in the AHPI/MSC survey answered anywhere from 0 to 110. In the 202 hospitals that answered this question, the mean number of completed paths was 7.5.

More hospitals reportedly are in the pathway development (rather than implementation) phase, with 251 (AHPI/MSC survey) reporting an average of 6.5 in development. Only 6 hospitals in the AmHS survey reported more than 10 complete paths.

Managed care organizations appear to be slightly ahead in development. The average number completed in these facilities, according to AHPI/MSC findings, was 10; for physician clinics, only 3.

What should emerge from reading this book is an appreciation for setting realistic goals for the number of clinical paths to design within a specified time frame. The experience at Rhode Island Hospital is enlightening on this point: In January 1991 the hospital set a goal of 20 paths over the next two months; by March 1991, however, only 13 medical paths and 1 surgical path were in use. But two years later, Rhode Island Hospital had 25 medical paths and 50 surgical paths in place.

The development and implementation of path-based inpatient care is still in its infancy. Of the 248 hospitals that provided information about their start dates in the AHPI/MSC survey, 203 reported beginning their initiatives *after* January 1992. Almost 50 percent of the managed care groups and physician clinics reported starting *before* that time.

Impact of Individual Variation on Future Management Efforts

Both AmHS and AHPI/MSC survey results demonstrate clearly that clinical care process management has been embraced by a number of hospitals, managed care organizations, and outpatient clinics. This trend is confirmed by the eight case studies in part two of this book.

As the U.S. health care delivery system continues to be reconfigured and "re-formed" (pun intended) in response to market forces and to regulatory requirements, providers inevitably will have to demonstrate the efficiency and effectiveness of their practices. Improving clinical care by promoting the use of processes *proved* to yield optimal outcomes undoubtedly will become a powerful strategy for documenting and measuring the value of services provided.

The variety of clinical pathway-related activities at all levels of health care delivery is impressive; however, this variety severely inhibits the exchange of ideas because the element of multidisciplinarity through a team approach has not been given center stage. The hospital care route remains somewhat fragmented and structured around daily physician orders. Organizations use such diverse nomenclature for their management tools that one cannot know for certain if all tools are similar in basic design or content.

For example, the clinical path format, content focus, and overall path-based management strategy at Douglas Community Hospital (where the tool is called *care tracks*) may differ significantly from that used at Mercy and Unity Hospitals (where it is called *anticipated recovery pathways*). Likewise, because no one department or unit seems to oversee (or "own") the related activities, even a simple telephone inquiry to learn more about another organization's initiatives becomes a bewildering task.

Another disparity that affects successful application of clinical paths is the wide range of activities that may be ascribed inaccurately to an organization's clinical quality improvement strategy. Specifically, without clear definitions for each component in the care processes, one cannot determine which, if any, led to the reported quality and cost-efficiency improvements. Did the presence of the clinical path in the patient's record result in shorter length of stay? Was reduced LOS merely a reaction to changes in financial reimbursement incentives, stepped-up education efforts, or individualized case coordination activities?

If *all* improvements in quality and cost efficiency are automatically credited to clinical path usage, providers may find themselves blindly and routinely developing more of these tools. This could be an unnecessarily expensive and time-consuming commitment when in fact other catalysts could be at work.

What Is to Be Gained from this Book?

Clinical Paths: Tools for Outcomes Management may seem long overdue, yet health care organizations probably were not ready to hear its message before now. "Practice time" was needed to design, pilot test, and evaluate tools and systems and to manage clinical care processes. In some cases, as shown in the case studies, time was needed to "fail" before succeeding in attempts at engineering improved procedures. This way, learning took place as to what worked and what did not. Now, with most managed care organizations and well over 50 percent of U.S. hospitals and large outpatient clinics implementing clinical measurement and management activities, it is time to bring some uniformity to the process.

This book is a timely effort to help standardize the definitions and applications in a path-based patient care strategy. Standardization is not intended to inhibit creativity or lead to "cookbook" medicine practices. Rather, it is seen as a positive step toward the design of a common language that providers across multiple disciplines can use to communicate collaboratively while engaging in continuous quality improvement and case management strategies.

This book reaffirms the evolutionary character of clinical path-based patient management, a feature typical of the CQI principle of ongoing improvement. Pathways have changed significantly since their early beginnings at New England Medical Center in the mid-1980s. They are continuing to unfold into a powerful and collaborative tool designed and used by *all* members of the health care team throughout the patient's *entire* episode of care. No matter how far along an organization is in implementing clinical paths and clinical process care management, the stories of successes and frustrations that lie between the covers of this book will help advance those efforts.

David N. Sundwall, MD
Vice-President and Medical Director
American Healthcare Systems
Washington, DC

Preface

Health care providers continually search for new ways to improve the quality of patient care services. The past decade witnessed an increase in the number of different strategies used by organizations to achieve their quality objectives. Total quality management, case management, patient-centered care units, outcomes management, and clinical path-based patient care are a sampling of the many practices being adopted by quality-conscious health care organizations. Even though these activities differ slightly in terms of focus, their objectives are similar. At the heart of all quality oriented activities is the desire to reduce system failures, minimize unnecessary variations in patient care practices, and enhance collaboration among the health care team members.

Although a number of books and articles address health care quality, providers and external reviewers remain uncertain about how best to measure and improve clinical quality. Some of this confusion stems from the newness of the different quality methodologies. Health care providers are still experimenting with various clinical quality improvement techniques; many have yet to realize or report benefits. Facilities are also challenged to do more with fewer resources, a factor that influences leadership's decision to direct quality efforts where they will yield the best return. Under siege of increasing reimbursement controls, health care organizations no longer can afford to embrace every quality initiative that comes their way but must select those methods *most likely to succeed.*

One principle that is constant in providers' enduring efforts to measure and improve quality is the need to manage patient outcomes. *Outcomes management* is defined as the analysis, evaluation, and dissemination of the results of medical processes or procedures to improve health care outcomes. Outcomes management can be achieved by concentrating on four elements:

1. *Outcomes specification:* Define expected outcomes and measures to assess outcomes achievement.
2. *Outcomes measurement:* Design valid and reliable assessment tools.
3. *Information systems:* Design automated or manual information systems to support data collection, input, retrieval, and analysis.
4. *Process improvement:* Design continuous quality improvement techniques to improve the processes of care.

One tool that organizations use to manage patient care outcomes is a clinical path (also called, as noted earlier, *critical path, clinical protocol, CareMap™,* among other terminology). Treatment interventions recommended on the path guide clinicians in their patient care decisions. Path recommendations are not a standard of care; rather, they serve as reminders of those interventions the health care team believes most likely to be needed by the "average" patient. Clinical paths can be a framework for outcomes management activities because each of the four elements cited above is inherent in path-based patient care. For example, to design a clinical path, the care team prospectively defines *elected patient outcomes* and details those treatment choices they feel will most likely produce these outcomes. *Measurement instruments* are constructed to assess the impact of treatment interventions on expected outcomes. By correlating clinical path variance data and patient outcomes, clinicians can identify optimal treatment regimens. *Information systems* are designed to support variance reporting and outcomes analysis. Finally, the health care team uses various *process improvement* techniques to design the initial path and to constantly improve performance.

This book is written for health care providers who seek to understand how clinical path-based patient care is being used to manage patient outcomes in different organizational settings. It describes how clinicians use paths to reduce system breakdowns, decrease unwarranted variation in patient care, and improve communication and collaboration among multidisciplinary care givers. Clinical path-based patient care can augment outcomes management activities by providing a systematic methodology for defining, measuring, and improving clinical quality. To give the reader a comprehensive look at clinical paths, the book is divided into three parts. Part one (chapters 2 through 5) discusses the evolution of clinical paths in health care services and issues that affect development and implementation. Part two (chapters 6 through 13) presents case studies of eight organizations and their experiences with developing and implementing clinical pathways. Part three (chapters 14 and 15) discusses how organizations are broadening clinical path boundaries to encompass an entire episode of care.

Implementing clinical paths is not without challenges and unresolved questions. Part one describes some major clinical path strategy issues being confronted by organizations. Chapter 2 addresses the relationship between clinical paths and case management, illustrating how both tactics work in unison to ensure the coordination of patient care activities. Using clinical paths to document patient care and the legal ramifications of this decision are examined in chapter 3. Chapters 4 and 5 discuss clinical paths from the perspective of quality, illustrating how path-based care can promote dissemination of practice parameters and improvements in the processes of care.

In the case illustrations that make up part two of this book, for each organization the authors share a "snapshot" of their ever-evolving clinical path process. An important evolutionary step in this regard is the decision to make the clinical path a permanent part of the medical record. This change, which may on the surface appear innocuous, significantly influences the character of path-based patient care. As a rule, organizations may initiate a clinical path for a patient but do not include it as a permanent patient care record. Currently this is the case at Rhode Island Hospital, Douglas Community Hospital, and Chippenham Medical Center. Until this practice changes, the path is likely to be viewed as an embellishment rather than an indispensable component of the clinical process. Each of these organizations describes their plans to incorporate clinical paths with record documentation at some future date.

Compare the clinical path strategies presented in chapters 6 through 8 to the testimonies offered in chapters 9 through 12. At Norton Psychiatric Clinic, Mercy and Unity Hospitals, University of Pittsburgh Medical Center, and Carondelet St. Joseph's Hospital, the clinical path is used to document patient care activities. It replaces other documentation in the patient's record, thereby lessening the need for clinicians to double-document. At these facilities, the path has been upgraded to become a more integral part of the patient care delivery system. Even so, these organizations still are faced with unanswered questions about what role the path plays in case management and continuous quality improvement initiatives. The authors provide several insights into how their institutions plan to address these interface issues.

In chapter 13, leaders from Alliant®Health System share what they learned from two years' experience in designing and implementing clinical paths. In 1992, Alliant suspended its clinical path initiative in order to rethink initial strategy. This occurred because an introspective analysis, the results of which are shared with the reader, raised several important questions and steered the facility toward a "second generation" clinical path strategy. Alliant executives urge that the most important step in instituting a pathway program is for leaders to be focused clearly on their purposes for doing so.

In chapter 14 Huttner relates Abbott Northwestern's experience in designing a clinical path for myocardial infarction patients from a managed care perspective. Finally, in chapter 15 Ciccone and Gerardi describe a regional approach to the clinical path development effort within a community health care consortium, showing how all member hospitals collaborated in designing broad-based clinical paths that link health care settings. One major outcome was a total hip replacement pathway.

This book should expand readers' understanding of how pathways can be used to manage patient outcomes along the entire continuum of health care services. The issues chapters and the case illustrations also heighten awareness of the challenges, accomplishments, and questions that remain unresolved. The book is replete with sample documentation forms, variance tracking and data analysis tools, and other practical aids to work with in constructing a strategy/action plan. Hopefully the information provided here will help administrators and medical staff leaders work through the ramifications of implementing path-based patient care.

Embarking on clinical paths with only a superficial understanding of the scope of such a project has three negative effects: administrators, physicians, nurses, and other clinicians unaware of the opportunities offered by path-based patient care are more likely to view paths as nothing more than a documentation tool; fear of the unknown is a strong deterrent to change; and incorrect approaches to path-based patient care frequently will fail to produce lasting results.

As is shown by the testimonies of organizations undertaking design and implementation of clinical paths, strategies will vary among institutions. However, two factors appear to contribute to the success of each clinical path process:

- Administrative and medical staff leaders should introduce clinical paths with a clear understanding of leadership objectives and of the barriers to overcome in achieving these objectives.
- Clinical path-based patient care is a process that takes time to implement, one that must be nurtured and whose evolution must be encouraged.

CHAPTER ONE

Clinical Paths: An Outcomes Management Tool

Patrice L. Spath

The belief that collaborative and integrated health care services lead to cost-efficient, high-quality care seems relatively new to the U.S. health care system. However, this philosophy of health care delivery in the country dates back to 1863. In that year, Massachusetts established the nation's first Board of Charities, charged with coordinating public health services and conserving public funds used to care for the poor and sick. Case management became important after World War II, when the notion of a "continuum of care" described extended services for patients discharged from psychiatric institutions. In 1962, the President's Commission on Mental Retardation recommended "program coordination" as a means of reducing hospitalizations at state mental hospitals and ensuring a higher quality of life for patients residing outside these institutions. In 1971, the Allied Services Act, leading to the Services Interaction Targets for Opportunities (SITO) Program, was funded by the U.S. Department of Health, Education and Welfare. Included in SITO was "case management" as a method of integrating social and health services for clients. Previously, case management had been practiced informally by physicians, nurses, social service agencies, and hospitals. The SITO legislation was the first effort to formalize case management as a reimbursable, distinct service.[1]

With the passage of the Omnibus Budget Reconciliation Act of 1981, which included prospective, diagnosis related group (DRG)-based payment for hospitalized Medicare patients, case management became more attractive to providers because of its potential for lowering patient length of stay (LOS), as well as ensuring better service quality. Faced with the mandate to provide cost-efficient health care services, many hospitals began exploring case management strategies and implementing formal programs designed to meet the multiple needs of patients through assessment, planning, service procurement/delivery/coordination, and monitoring.[2] Many programs evolved within the hospital nursing service area because the principles of case management seemed to fit closely with the definition of the nursing process—assessment, diagnosis, outcomes identification, planning, implementation, and evaluation.[3]

This chapter provides a look at the evolution of clinical paths as applied in health care services. Design and implementation strategies have matured in response to internal and external priorities. Not only has the definition of a clinical path changed; the terminology used to describe this patient care tool has become more variable. Growth in the use of clinical paths has promoted an assortment of methodologies as well as insights, many of which are described in subsequent chapters.

This chapter's glimpse at the evolution of clinical paths in health care delivery is intended to provide valuable information that organizations can use in designing (or redesigning) their clinical path-based patient care strategies. The chapter also imparts an appreciation of the future role clinical paths will play in outcomes management and systems redesign.

Introduction of Clinical Paths into Case Management Strategies

The department of nursing at New England Medical Center Hospitals (NEMC) in Boston was one of the first groups to publish information about the components of its managed care strategy. At the core of NEMC's strategy was an instrument it called a *critical path*, which was described as a project management tool based on standards of care for a particular case type.[4] The path was considered a "shorthand version" of a larger patient case management plan that included the following components: nursing diagnoses, clinical outcomes for each diagnosis that were considered achievable within the DRG-allotted length of stay, intermediate goals and estimated dates for each outcome, and nursing and physician interventions that facilitate the patient's movement toward each goal. The critical path (hereafter referred to as clinical path) complemented or replaced the nursing care plan, serving as the focal point for nursing change-of-shift reports and care coordination or intervention. Using the clinical paths as their guide, unit-based nurses assumed the case manager role as a part of their direct patient care responsibilities.

Another early pioneer in nursing case management was Hillcrest Medical Center in Tulsa, Oklahoma. This model selected DRG-related patient groups that were felt to benefit most from nursing case management, developed case management plans and a one-page abbreviated clinical path, implemented and monitored plans, and evaluated results.[5] Unlike the NEMC model, Hillcrest employed nurse case managers to oversee patients' progress along the clinical paths to ensure that case management criteria were achieved and that path variances were justified and well documented. In general, these nurse case managers did not have hands-on patient care responsibilities.

Early case management strategies emphasized the physician's role in designing case management plans and the abbreviated versions, clinical paths. At New England Medical Center every designated patient was admitted to a formally prepared group practice composed of an attending physician and staff nurses from each unit and clinic likely to receive the patients.[6] At Hillcrest, clinical paths were developed by a multidisciplinary committee whose members analyzed information about physician practice patterns. The committee that designed their coronary artery bypass graft with catheterization clinical path, for example, included nurses from all units caring for these patients, one cardiologist, and two cardiac surgeons.

The purpose of the clinical path was to guide patient care. During the hospital stay, the bedside nurse or the case manager monitored the patient's progress each day and noted variances—digressions or detours—from the path.

Path Variances

Specifically, *variances* were considered deviations from the patient's and/or family's intermediate goals, from outcomes, and from staff interventions outlined on the path that might alter the anticipated discharge date, the expected cost, or the expected outcomes.[7] In path-based patient care, every day on each shift case managers and/or unit nurses had to ask and obtain answers to several questions about patient care practice. For example:[8]

- What interventions and outcomes should be happening this shift?
- What is actually happening?
- What did not happen? Why?
- What should be done about it?
- Who will rectify it? When?

At Hillcrest Medical Center, nurse case managers worked closely with the attending physician and unit nurses to understand why path variances occurred and what could be done to get the patient back on track.[9] At New England Medical Center, a unit nurse fulfilled this coordinating role, noting any deviations from the path, exploring their cause with other caregivers, and arranging for specific actions to be taken because of the variances.[10] All detours from the path were recorded concurrently and reported to a central database to enable caregivers to retrospectively analyze the source and cause of path variances. To streamline reporting, many organizations designed variance coding systems such as the one shown below:[11]

400 Series: No Variance

401 Adherence to clinical pathway (including preadmission and postdischarge experience)
410 Cancellations
411 Preadmission testing
412 Physician
413 Institution

420 Series: Preadmission/Postdischarge Variance

421 Emergency/urgent admission
422 Transfer to another institution
423 Patient convenience (that is, out of area)
424 Patient refusal
425 Other

430 Series: Current Stay Variance, Patient-Related

431 Clinical complication
432 Unresponsive/change clinical regimen
433 Psycho/social delay
434 Other

440 Series: Current Stay Variance, Physician-Related

441 Physician ordering delay
442 Nurse delay
443 Support service delay
444 Other

450 Series: Current Stay Variance, Hospital-Related

451 Scheduling delay due to equipment workload
452 Scheduling delay due to equipment breakdown
453 Other

460 Series: Discharge Variance

461 Unavailability/delay of nursing home bed
462 Inadequate home support
463 Other service unavailability
464 Unresolved health concerns
465 Other

Aggregate variance information was displayed and evaluated in hopes of identifying system breakdowns that could be fixed or unwarranted practice variations that could be changed. For example, at New England Medical Center an evaluation of post-operative wound infections in patients undergoing radical vulvectomy surgery suggested a need for more intensive preventive measures. The clinicians changed their wound management practices from betadine soaks starting 48 hours postop to one which began the evening following surgery. Consistent use of this new regimen drastically reduced wound infections and promoted more rapid surgical wound healing.[12]

A Documentation Tool

In some organizations, the clinical path became a nursing documentation tool to record interventions during the patient's hospitalization. Clinical path tools such as standardized treatment records, teaching plans, and discharge instructions were built around patient care elements on the path and became common adjuncts to the case management process.[13-15] Tools were also designed by nonhospital providers for documentation purposes.[16] In most organizations, only patient-related variances were recorded on the path, which was kept as a permanent document in the record. A separate form was required for reporting variances caused by other factors.

Clinical Path Benefits

The clinical path reduced variation in patient management practices by minimizing the range of treatment decisions made by physicians, nurses, and other health care professionals. Furthermore, the treatment plan outlined by the clinical path helped allied health professionals learn what physicians expected during a patient's hospitalization, thereby ensuring that these expectations could be met. Physicians, nurses, and allied professionals found that even when the definition of *optimal care* was unclear, reduction in wide variation allowed the health care team to determine whether one care regimen should be favored over another. Many organizations found that the clinical path development process (physicians working in collaboration with other hospital caregivers) was, in itself, an argument for the merits of clinical paths. Due to reductions in variations, a number of additional benefits were realized such as elimination of system breakdowns, better control over liability risk, reduction in length of stay, and decreased patient charges.

Elimination of System Breakdowns

Once developed, clinical paths were used to continuously refine the processes of care by finding and eliminating system breakdowns and by incorporating new medical knowledge into the treatment plan itself. In this respect, clinical paths had the potential for ongoing improvement in patient care. For example, at the New England Medical Center, patients suffering from cerebrovascular accidents (CVAs) had usually gone from the emergency unit, to the intensive care unit, then to a general neurological unit. Evaluation of this process by the clinical path design team suggested patients could achieve the same clinical outcomes if they went directly from the emergency unit to the general neurological unit. Avoiding the intensive care unit decreased the patients' lengths of stay as well as overall costs. Additional evaluation of CVA patient management demonstrated that maintaining a wider range and greater capacity for diagnostic testing on the weekends would further reduce hospital days of care.[17]

Improved Liability Management and Outcomes

By reducing variation in patient management practices, organizations also found themselves better able to control their liability risk. Because clinical paths were explicit and comprehensive, and because they covered both timing and elements of care, they helped keep patient care on track. The clinical path reduced delays in care and helped focus the health care team's attention on important steps that otherwise might become lost in a wealth of detail. Once the clinical path was made accessible to all caregivers, not just the physician or the nurse, the health care team found that working off the "same program" facilitated communication and collaboration. Clinical path success stories began to appear regularly in professional journals and books as well as in presentations at utilization management conferences:

- *Decreased length of stay:* At Kosair Children's Hospital in Louisville, Kentucky, length of stay for pediatric patients with diabetic ketoacidosis dropped from 5.25 days to 2.9 days after a path was implemented.[18]
- *Reduction in patient charges:* At the University of Michigan Medical Center, average daily charges for patients managed with clinical paths decreased by 13.8 percent, and their ancillary service charges decreased by 2.6 percent.[19]
- *Reduction in complications:* During development of a clinical path for patients undergoing transurethral prostatectomy at InterMountain Health Care in Salt Lake City, Utah, physicians discovered that catheter removal on day 2 postoperatively, rather than on day 1, resulted in fewer complications. This finding prompted that institution to modify practice patterns that in turn were reflected in the design of its clinical path.[20]

Hearing of the positive impact that case management and clinical paths had on hospital length of stay, cost, and quality, many providers reacted quickly to design programs that incorporated one or more of these elements. However, without a clear appreciation of the objectives and scope of such programs, many clinical path efforts foundered.

Common Clinical Path Program Shortcomings

As more health care providers began to design and implement clinical path-based patient care, limitations of the traditional concepts espoused by early developers became evident. By mid-1993, it was not uncommon to find some organizations' efforts failing. The most common causes of program breakdown related to the following observations:

- Lack of involvement among physicians and other clinicians in the design phase of clinical paths
- Lack of leadership education about the scope of path-based patient care and/or delegation of program development to middle management without active administrative and medical staff leadership involvement
- Failure to identify the goals for clinical path-based patient care and the role of this objective in the overall organizational quality and utilization management strategies
- Unrealistic goals for completing development and implementation of the clinical path program
- Seemingly unnecessary paperwork added to the process of patient care
- The collection of information about all variances from the clinical path, without regard to what information was really necessary to identify system problems and to test the hypothesis that staying on the path resulted in better outcomes
- Inability to convince caregivers that clinical paths and variance analysis were integral to the processes of care and not merely an "add-on" without value

These and other shortcomings are discussed more fully in the following subsections.

Absence of Mutual Involvement

Although physician involvement in formulating case management strategies and designing clinical paths was encouraged, many organizations found little enthusiasm among members of the medical staff. For example, nursing leaders at Hillcrest reported that some physicians viewed nursing case management as another attempt to control their business.[21] It was not uncommon to find nurses developing paths without any front-end involvement by physicians. These nurse-driven efforts commonly produced paths that focused largely on the nursing aspects of the patient care process and measured the patient's achievement of nursing care goals.

Whereas nurse-designed paths traditionally included the interventions expected of physicians and other clinicians, the lack of upfront buy-in by these disciplines usually weakened the path's worth as a concurrent case management and process improvement tool. For example, nurses at hospitals in the Alliant® Health System in Louisville began to design clinical paths in 1988. By the end of 1991, more than 200 paths had been developed and implemented systemwide. However, very little physician involvement had been garnered. In early 1992, hospital leaders confirmed that these nursing-driven paths were not being used by physicians to guide patient care. A study at that time showed a compliance rate of less than 20 percent with the physician-related components on the paths.[22] Because physician involvement was seen as crucial to the success of its path-based patient care quality improvement strategy, leadership at Alliant began redirecting its clinical path process to a more physician-driven effort.

Physician Resistance

A survey of hospital clinical path activities sponsored by American Hospital Publishing, Inc. (AHPI), and Medicus Systems Corporation (MSC) in July 1993 revealed physician resistance to be the greatest barrier to successful implementation of path-based patient care.[23] This finding is not surprising, given that most beginning clinical path strategies are aimed at controlling costs, not improving quality. Many practicing physicians perceive that health care administrators, regulators, and payers care *only* about reducing costs and find this outlook to be contradictory to their professional values.[24]

Lack of Multidisciplinarity

Proponents of case management and clinical paths in the 1980s and early 1990s suggested that physicians and nurses should participate in these strategies, but few articles addressed the need to involve other clinical disciplines. Understandably, this shortcoming also inhibited acceptance of paths by the nonnursing clinical disciplines. The AHPI/MSC survey in 1993 showed a lack of acceptance by caregivers (other than physicians and nurses) to be the second-greatest barrier to clinical path implementation.

Lack of Administrative–Medical Staff Leadership

Some organizations seem to have designed and implemented clinical paths as a grassroots effort or without meaningful involvement on the part of administrative and medical staff leadership. This impression was substantiated by answers to the AHPI/MSC survey, wherein 30 percent of the 314 hospital respondents said they assigned clinical path development and/or implementation responsibilities to a middle manager or to a group or an individual even lower in the organizational hierarchy. Without effective leadership from the chief executive officer and key medical staff, the results were suboptimal.[25]

Failure to Identify Goals

Without first knowing what patient care difficulties existed, the health care team was ill equipped to design appropriate paths. This limitation was evident in a research project at the Chicago Rehabilitation Institute (CRI), where clinical paths were developed for patients undergoing stroke rehabilitation. The authors found that path-guided care for stroke patients did not significantly change patient outcomes when compared to those of patients managed with traditional team-planning instruments.[26] In reviewing the results of this experiment, clinicians at CRI discovered the need for enhanced interinstitutional coordination and communication. Had this obstacle been identified *prior to* developing the clinical path for stroke patients, the path could have been designed jointly with facilities that transfer patients to CRI and could have spanned the continuum from acute care to rehabilitation. This type of clinical path would have enhanced interinstitutional coordination and communication.

Unrealistic Goals and Time Frames

Clinical path-based patient care is not a "quick-fix" strategy, and yet many organizations attempted to design and implement paths for a majority of their patients within a very short period. For example, it was not uncommon to hear of administrative directives requiring the development of 10 or more paths in a one-year time frame. In general, these speedy efforts failed because production time of one well-designed, multidisciplinary clinical path ranges from one month to one year. An informal survey of hospitals that used clinical paths in July 1992 revealed a wide variation in path development times, as follows:[27]

- *Barnes Hospital, St. Louis:* Average path development time of 80 to 100 staff/ physician hours
- *Soldiers and Sailors Hospital, Penn Yan, New York:* Forty-five-minute team meetings once a week for five weeks to develop their first path
- *University of Pittsburgh Medical Center, Pittsburgh:* Average path development time—physicians, 300 hours; nursing, 60 hours; administration, 50 hours
- *El Dorado Hospital, Tucson, Arizona:* Three hours for group meetings and 10 hours for project manager to develop one clinical path

The time commitment necessary for clinical path implementation was substantiated by respondents to the AHPI/MSC survey. The respondents who had begun their clinical path initiatives after 1990 reported that only an average of 8.5 paths had been fully designed and were in clinical use as of July 1993. These hospitals expected to have an average of only 80 paths completed by the end of the year 2000.

Ill-Defined Documentation Requirements

The documentation requirements generated by clinical path-based patient care have also overwhelmed many implementation efforts. For example, after implementing paths in home health care services at Gottlieb Memorial Hospital in Melrose Park, Illinois, the nurses felt that pathways added to documentation requirements instead of reducing them.[28] Generally speaking, in most organizations the clinical path did not replace other parts of patient records but unfortunately added new documentation prerequisites.[29] Caregivers' acceptance of the clinical path was very low if they had to document on the path form and record the same information somewhere else in the patient's chart.

Inadequate Variance Reporting Process

It was not uncommon to find bedside nurses responsible for identifying any and all variances from the path, regardless of impact on patient outcomes. This complex variance tracking process was one of the barriers that temporarily halted the clinical path project at Toronto Hospital, Ontario, Canada, in June 1992. After developing and implementing more than 300 clinical paths, leaders found that identifying and reporting every single path variance was time-consuming and failed to yield significant advantages.[30]

While organizations continued to experiment with clinical paths and overcome some of the problems inherent in different development and implementation methodologies, several other changes were occurring in health care. These innovations influenced the way some organizations designed and deployed the clinical path tool.

Link between Clinical Paths and Quality Improvement

While clinical path strategies were evolving in health care, the industrial quality control methods were taking hold in American industry. This movement highlighted the need for organizations to manage their quality through a process of continuous quality improvement. The goal of industrial quality improvement was to eliminate undesirable variations or defects in their processes by removing the causes of the variations. The medical community soon learned that quality improvement techniques could successfully be applied to health care services and started to promote the concepts for health care institutions.[31] Health care professionals began to learn about and apply the process improvement techniques that had proved successful in other industries.

Many health care organizations started their first quality improvement projects in business processes (for example, the patient admission process). As hospital and medical staff leaders began to expand these projects to clinical processes (for example, how patients with myocardial infarctions are managed), the relationship between clinical paths and continuous improvement became apparent. For example, Providence Medical Center in Portland, Oregon, formed a multidisciplinary quality improvement team to study the management of patients undergoing total joint replacements.[32] The project followed three common process improvement steps: (1) understand the process, (2) design improvements, and (3) monitor the gains. In the process-understanding phase, the team analyzed data to determine how patients currently were being managed. They identified ways to improve the clinical process and integrated these improvements into the design of the clinical path for total hip arthroplasty patients. Using path variance data and other sources of outcomes information, the team monitored their gains.

As organizations adopted continuous quality improvement strategies, they began to view the clinical path as an integral part of their clinical process improvement activities and no longer merely a case management tool.[33] The clinical path became their methodology for describing the processes of patient care, just as tools such as flowcharts were being used to illustrate their business processes.[34] They found that the clinical path tool corresponded with the *plan* phase of Deming's plan–do–check–act (PDCA) cycle of continuous improvement.[35] Variance analysis corresponded with the *check* phase of the cycle. The relationship of the clinical path patient management tool to Deming's PDCA cycle is illustrated in figure 1-1.

Health care organizations began to use their knowledge gained from improving business processes and to apply these principles to their improvement of clinical processes. For example, in designing a clinical path (or map) for patients undergoing abdominal hysterectomy, the path design team at one hospital diagrammed the process of care as it currently existed. Once the map was drawn, the team studied the clinical process and asked such questions as: Why do we do this? How do we know whether we are doing it right? Where do inefficiencies occur? Do we need to do this at all? The care map shown in figure 1-2 helped provide some answers to these questions.[36] For example, the map identified nonvalue-added steps and causes of process variation. This information allowed the team to streamline the activities of care as well as improve the clinical process.

Figure 1-1.   The Relationship of Clinical Path-Based Patient Care and Deming's Plan–Do–Check–Act Cycle of Continuous Process Improvement

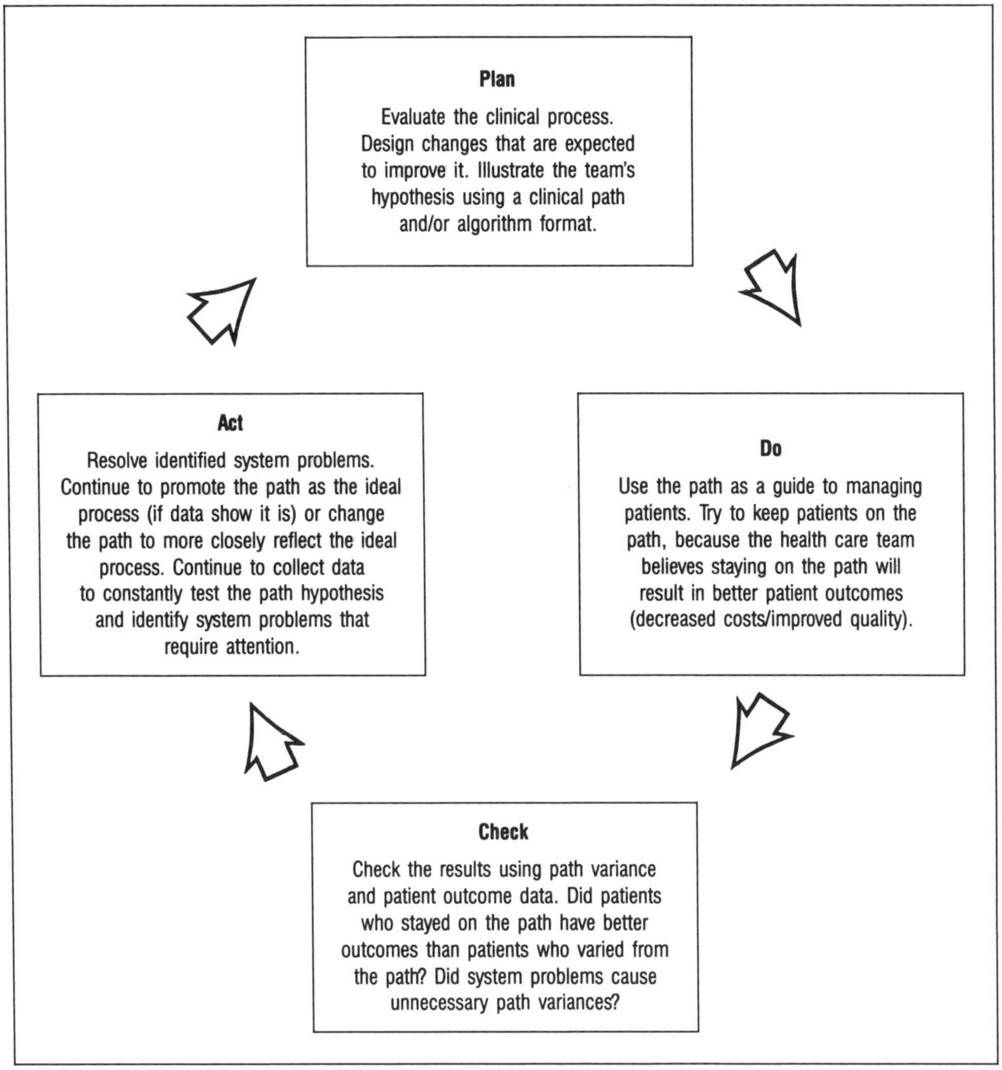

Plan

Evaluate the clinical process. Design changes that are expected to improve it. Illustrate the team's hypothesis using a clinical path and/or algorithm format.

Act

Resolve identified system problems. Continue to promote the path as the ideal process (if data show it is) or change the path to more closely reflect the ideal process. Continue to collect data to constantly test the path hypothesis and identify system problems that require attention.

Do

Use the path as a guide to managing patients. Try to keep patients on the path, because the health care team believes staying on the path will result in better patient outcomes (decreased costs/improved quality).

Check

Check the results using path variance and patient outcome data. Did patients who stayed on the path have better outcomes than patients who varied from the path? Did system problems cause unnecessary path variances?

Link between Practice Guidelines and Clinical Paths

In the 1980s health care providers saw not only the introduction of continuous quality improvement, but also a growth in the number of clinical decision-making tools called *guidelines*. Although patient management models, or protocols, had been used in service delivery since the early 1900s, medical professional societies and allied health professional groups accelerated their guidelines development efforts in the 1980s. Generally speaking, two descriptive terms were used to describe these patient management policies. The Institute of Medicine adopted the term *clinical practice guidelines* to refer to statements systematically developed to assist practitioner and patient decisions about appropriate health care for specific clinical circumstances.[37] The American Medical Association referred to *practice parameters* as educational tools that enable physicians to obtain the advice of recognized clinical experts, stay abreast of the latest clinical research, and assess the clinical significance of conflicting research findings. Practice parameters also provide a rational foundation for quality assurance, utilization review, facility accreditation, and other review activities.[38]

Figure 1-2. Map of Care Elements in the Major Functions of Treatment for Patients Admitted for Abdominal Hysterectomy (including possible nonvalue-added steps and sources of variation)

Preadmission	Day of Surgery	Day 1 Postop	Day 2 Postop	Discharge Goals
• Fleet enema • Betadine douche/shower • Incentive spirometry	• Abdominal prep • Foley insertion • O₂ postanaesthesia • Incentive spirometry	• Discontinue Foley • Change or discontinue wound dressing • Wound care • Incentive spirometry	• Staples out/steri-strip • Change or discontinue dressing • Wound care • Incentive spirometry	Patient is: • Free of signs of infection • Emptying bladder well • Passing flatus
Nonvalue-Added Steps • Incentive spirometry for low-risk patients (e.g., nonsmokers)	**Nonvalue-Added Steps** • Incentive spirometry for low-risk patients • O₂ for low-risk patients	**Nonvalue-Added Steps** • Incentive spirometry for low-risk patients	**Nonvalue-Added Steps** • Incentive spirometry for low-risk patients	**Causes of Variation from Desired Goals** • Patient slow to progress • Goal attainment delayed due to comorbidities/complications • Patient/family not prepared for patient's discharge • Physician does not order discharge
Causes of Variation • Patient unable/unwilling to perform treatments prior to admission • Patient uninformed of treatment needs • Treatment supplies unavailable to patient	**Causes of Variation** • Patient admitted too late for incentive spirometry treatment	**Causes of Variation** • Patient unable to void without Foley • Patient refuses treatment(s) • Physician does not order dressing change/discontinuation • Physician makes rounds too late to order day 2 treatments	**Causes of Variation** • Patient slow to progress • Patient refuses treatment(s) • Physician does not order dressing change/discontinuation • Physician makes rounds too late to order day 2 treatments	

By 1993, more than 80 physician organizations—including specialty societies and state, county, and metropolitan physician organizations—were developing and disseminating clinical practice guidelines. As of January 1993, these entities had developed almost 1,500 guidelines addressing all aspects of health care diagnosis and treatment.[39] A number of nursing and allied health professional groups were also developing standards of practice and related guidelines specific to their area of expertise and clinical experiences.

The U.S. Public Health Service established the United States Preventive Services Task Force (USPSTF) in 1984 to develop evidence-based practice guidelines for preventive care. For five years, this panel of nonfederal experts examined more than 2,000 studies regarding the effectiveness of 169 preventive services. The USPSTF completed its charge in 1989 with the publication of *Guide to Clinical Preventive Services: An Assessment of the Effectiveness of 169 Interventions.*[40] In 1990 a second USPSTF panel was formed to update previous recommendations, to examine important preventive services that the first review did not address, and to issue a revised edition of the guide.

The Agency for Health Care Policy and Research (AHCPR) was established on December 19, 1989, by the Omnibus Budget Reconciliation Act (Public Law 101-239) as one of the agencies of the U.S. Public Health Service. The purpose of the AHCPR was to enhance the quality, appropriateness, and effectiveness of health care services and access to such services. The Office of the Forum on Quality and Effectiveness in Health Care of the AHCPR was charged with facilitating the development and periodic update of clinically relevant guidelines that may be used by physicians, nurses, social workers, educators, and health care practitioners to assist in determining how diseases, disorders, and other health-related conditions can most effectively and appropriately be prevented, diagnosed, treated, and managed clinically.[41] Ten AHCPR clinical practice guidelines had been released as of April 1994.[42]

Several quality measurement efforts, based on clinical practice guidelines, have been initiated. These include Medicare's Cooperative Cardiovascular Project (CCP), expected to be implemented throughout 1994. As a part of the Medicare quality improvement strategy, all Medicare cases of coronary artery bypass graft surgery, acute myocardial infarction, and percutaneous transluminal coronary angioplasty will undergo a clinical path guideline-based method of peer review. Clinical guidelines developed by the American College of Cardiology are being used initially in the CCP, with revisions or modifications to come from medical specialty societies, the American Medical Association, and other professional participants in the project. These guidelines are being converted into computer-based algorithms so that the Uniform Clinical Data Set computer abstracting system can be used to flag cases for physician review.[43]

Third-party payers and business coalitions became interested in guideline-based quality measurements because of their usefulness in evaluating the quality and value of care. Increasingly, third-party payers and employers were focusing on clinicians' use of guidelines as a factor in deciding which providers to form relationships with and also to evaluate the care that their beneficiaries receive. A 1992 survey of regional health purchasing coalitions identified 20 coalitions that had programs whose purpose was to measure and evaluate the quality of medical care purchased by employers, with several specifically geared toward clinical practice guidelines, quality criteria, or performance standards for providers.[44] A new health care purchasing coalition was formed in Minnesota that included payment incentives for those providers using as many as 36 clinical practice guidelines developed by medical societies as well as preventive health screening techniques in their practices.

In 1991 the state of Maine initiated a five-year demonstration project to produce standards of practice for certain physician specialties so as to avoid malpractice claims and strengthen the defensibility of those claims that are pursued. The process was designed by the Maine Medical Association and is defined by state statute. If 50 percent of physicians in the state agree to practice according to the guidelines, then all physicians can cite the guidelines in their defense in malpractice cases.[45]

As providers began understanding the importance of following clinical practice guidelines or documenting their rationale for varying from guidelines, they sought ways to incorporate guidelines into the decision-making process. Clinical paths were identified as a "point-of-service" tool that could remind practitioners of the most current guideline recommendations. The clinical path became a useful vehicle for disseminating and implementing clinical practice guidelines—a new purpose for the tool that was originally designed to complement case management objectives.

Figure 1-3, a clinical path for adult patients undergoing appendectomy, incorporates some of the postoperative pain management recommendations of the AHCPR practice guidelines.[46] By including these recommendations in the path, physicians, nurses, and other clinicians are assured access to the guidelines during the delivery of patient care. They can choose to follow the guidelines or, if a deviation is warranted, be reminded to document their rationale for divergence.

Link between Clinical Paths and Outcomes Management

In the flurry of continuous quality improvement and guidelines development activities in the 1980s, a third concept began to emerge. In 1988 Paul Ellwood wrote about outcomes management as a "technology of patient experience designed to help patients, payers, and providers make more rational medical care-related choices based on better insight into the effect of these choices on the patient's life."[47] Ellwood introduced outcomes management as a comprehensive strategy designed to:

- Provide physicians and other clinicians with widely accepted guidelines and standards to assist in the process of delivering medical care
- Provide the skills and tools necessary to measure the status and well-being of a patient, both clinically and functionally
- Promote the development of large databases of clinical and outcomes information to strengthen decision making

To be effective, outcomes management required the collection of outcome data across the entire continuum of an episode of care. Not only were outcome measures such as morbidity and mortality important, but health care providers had to learn how to evaluate behavioral, physiological, and psychosocial outcomes. This prompted the development of reliable and valid instruments to measure the effect of health care services on a patient's social, physical, and functional status. One such instrument is the Health Status Questionnaire (or SF-36);[48] other methods, such as the Patient Reports on System Performance (PROSPER),[49] evaluate the quality of health care processes.

Some institutions that were using clinical paths to guide inpatient care and achieve specific discharge outcomes expanded the boundaries of their paths and tenor of their outcome measurements (see chapter 14). Other institutions stopped reporting and analyzing every clinical path variance, choosing to focus only on those process variances considered to have the greatest impact on outcomes (see chapters 5 and 13). The introduction of outcomes management added another dimension to health care's quality agenda, and this evolution in thinking is just starting to influence the clinical path strategies in many organizations.

Clinical Path: A Tool Undergoing Transformation

Since it was first introduced as a case management instrument in the mid-1980s, the clinical path has undergone changes in its design and purpose. Health care organizations

Figure 1-3. Adult Appendectomy (without evidence of peritonitis) Clinical Path with Selected Postoperative Pain Management Guidelines Incorporated into the Path Recommendations

	Emergency/preop	First 24 hours postop	48 hours postop/discharge
Consults	Anesthesia		
Tests	Complete blood count with differential Electrolytes Urinalysis		Complete blood count
Treatments	IV fluids Weight	Heparin lock IV Check incision Abdominal dressing change as needed Cough & deep breathe with vital signs	D/C heparin lock Check incision Abdominal dressing change as needed Cough & deep breathe with vital signs
Assessment	Vital signs q 1–2 hours Weight	Vital signs q 2 hours Assess patient's pain q 2 hours, consider patient-reported pain assessment findings	Vital signs q 4–8 hours Assess patient's pain q 4–8 hours, consider patient-reported pain assessment findings
Medications	IV antibiotics, first dose within 2 hours preop After diagnosis established, IV Demerol 100 mg q 3 hours or IV Morphine 10 mg q 3–4 hours	Continue IV antibiotics Continue IV analgesics for 12 hours postop; switch to oral analgesic of choice when patient able to tolerate oral intake Adjust dose of analgesic if pain level is reported by patient as being "3" or higher	D/C antibiotics Continue oral analgesic Adjust dose of analgesic if pain level is reported by patient as being "3" or higher
Activity	Assist with care Out of bed with help	Ambulate with assistance Out of bed with help	Self-care Ambulate independently
Nutrition	Nothing by mouth	Clear liquid to full liquid	Regular diet
Elimination		Check bowel sounds	Check for bowel movement; may take milk of magnesia as needed at home
Teaching	General pre- and postop teaching Provide patient with education and information about pain control Develop with patient plan for pain control	Instruct patient in use of numeric pain self-assessment tool	Review discharge instructions Provide written discharge instructions that include details of pain management, including: • Specific drugs to be taken • Frequency of drug administration • Potential side effects of the medication • Potential drug interactions • Specific precautions to follow when taking the medication (e.g., physical activity limitations, dietary restrictions) • Name of individual to notify about pain problems and other postoperative concerns
Psychosocial	Patient/family support	Patient/family support	Patient/family support
Discharge planning	Admission assessment Continuing care as needed		Home health referral as needed

are beginning to consider the clinical path as one of many tools available for improving health care processes rather than as a stand-alone device used only to advance their case management objectives. Even the definition of a clinical path has changed from "a listing of key nursing and physician processes and corresponding timelines that a patient must undergo to achieve standard outcomes within a DRG-specific length of stay"[50] to "a collaboratively developed hypothesis that describes what the health care team believes is the best way to manage patients."[51]

This change in thinking is occurring at a different pace among organizations. For this reason, some hospitals still apply clinical paths as nurse-driven, case management tools, whereas others incorporate them to varying degrees into their organizationwide quality and utilization management efforts. Some organizations have developed patient versions of the clinical path to promote patient and family involvement in the care process. Still others are evaluating the use of an algorithm format for their paths, rather than the traditional matrix model. As providers become linked with networks, clinical paths are being developed to cover an entire episode of care rather than just the hospital component. All of these evolutionary steps are in response to a growing need to align the clinical path tool with the system of health care, rather than underutilizing it as an accessory with narrow purpose.

One dilemma presented by these new uses for the clinical path tool is that each organization's strategy is in a different phase of evolution. One hospital may claim to have clinical paths, and yet careful inspection of its process shows the paths to be nurse-driven procedures that play a very small role (if any) in managing and improving patient care. Another hospital may have had physicians, nurses, and other clinicians jointly involved in path design, but have yet to initiate variance analysis. Some organizations may attest to developing and implementing in excess of 300 clinical paths; yet their bedside nurses and practicing physicians, when asked privately, know little about how the paths are being used. Other organizations may be using clinical paths as an element in the redesign of all major clinical processes and the paths are crucial to their delivery of high-quality service. This "missynchronization" of clinical path tactics among organizations is evident even among the contributors of this book. The seemingly endless variety of clinical path strategies creates difficulties as one organization dialogues with another about their path-based patient care process.

Elements of a Contemporary Clinical Path Strategy

Although the clinical path is likely to remain a dynamic tool—that is, one in continual flux—it is necessary to establish at least a uniform definition for *path-based patient care*. A consistent definition will make it easier for organizations to communicate about how this tool is (or is not) being used within their delivery system. Such a definition, summarized as a checklist in figure 1-4, describes the elements of a well-rounded clinical path-based patient care strategy as health care providers know it today. Unless all of these essential components are in place, an organization should not presume to have a dynamic path-based patient care process in place. This checklist can be used as a generic model for a definition; if one or more elements are missing from a facility's clinical path strategy, modifications should be made as necessary. This definition is not intended to be stagnant; health care providers should continue to "push the envelope" of the clinical path tool and discover even more essential elements.

Components of a Successful Clinical Path Strategy

Merely fulfilling the criteria for path-based patient care does not ensure success. The probability of success goes up as more and more attributes of a comprehensive, well-designed strategy are identified. Three of these components—planning, deployment,

Figure 1-4. Elements of Clinical Path-Based Patient Care

Do all of the following statements describe your clinical path patient management strategy?

✔ Our clinical paths are designed by a multidisciplinary team of health care professionals representing *all* the disciplines involved in caring for the patient for whom the path is being designed.

✔ Our clinical paths *are not* considered standards of care; they are considered a description of the important interventions of care the health care team believes will achieve the optimal outcomes (maximum quality/minimum cost).

✔ Variances from the path are expected and considered desirable when warranted by the patient's clinical condition.

✔ Our clinical paths are used by all clinicians to guide patient management decisions and are readily accessible to them throughout the episode of care.

✔ Our clinical paths are integral to the process of patient care and add value to the patient care experience for caregivers and patients.

✔ Our clinical path-based patient care process includes (1) a concurrent mechanism that affects changes in the process of care when a patient's response to care varies from the path without valid cause or (2) a system that allows the process of care to be revised when path variances are warranted.

✔ Path variance data *are not* used in evaluating the competency of individual physicians and other caregivers.

✔ Path variance data are used in the aggregate to identify system breakdowns that require improvement to constantly improve patient care activities.

✔ Path variance data are correlated with patient outcome data and used in the aggregate to support the clinical path "best care" hypothesis or to modify the path to reflect improvements in the "best care" hypothesis.

✔ Clinical paths are regularly updated with the publication of new clinical practice guidelines, research studies, and other relevant practice parameters to ensure that they reflect the best available knowledge about patient management practices.

and process improvement—are summarized in figure 1-5 and detailed in the following subsections. They are likely to be found in the approaches of those organizations that have benefited significantly from implementing clinical paths.

Planning

The decision to adopt clinical paths as a patient management strategy for the organization should not be made in a knowledge vacuum. Leaders frequently choose to implement clinical paths without understanding what this decision means to their organizations. Path-based patient care is much more than designing the path itself. It is a long-term commitment to seek out ways of improving clinical processes. What distinguishes clinical paths from "programs of the month" is a fundamental shift in the way patient care is delivered. An appreciation of these subtleties is possible only after administrative and medical staff leadership has been educated in the concepts and practicalities of path-based patient care.

Once leaders understand the scope of their commitment to clinical paths, the planning work proceeds. First, a *multidisciplinary leadership task group* should be formed. Charged with overseeing the design and implementation process, this group should include key administrative personnel, nursing and physician leaders, as well as information management support. At Barnes Hospital, the task group directing their CarePath activities is composed of the hospital president, physicians, directors of quality assurance, directors of clinical services lines, and representatives from all disciplines, including medical records, finance, and pastoral care.[52] This planning group then must set goals, project the resources required, and provide for education and orientation activities once paths are approved.

Setting Goals
Clinical paths will change the way patients are managed, and leaders must define and communicate why this change is necessary. To increase the probability that clinical

paths will benefit patient care, specific goals for the path-based care strategy should be formulated. Ideally, the goals are expressed in measurable terms, allowing for later assessments of goal attainment. Goals could include targeted quality improvements and cost reductions, although an emphasis on quality is more likely to promote cooperation from physicians and other clinicians.[53] The leadership group should also select the patient categories for developing the first paths and set up the ground rules for clinical path design and implementation. A consistent strategy for the entire organization is important, because nonstandard formats and procedures can impede success.[54]

Figure 1-5. Components of a Successful Clinical Path Design and Implementation Strategy

Planning	Deployment	Process Improvement
• Administrative and medical staff leaders are educated in how clinical paths are used in managing patient care. • Administrative and medical staff leaders are personally committed to path-based patient care and are involved in setting the design and implementation strategies for the organization. • Quality improvement, not cost control, is the *primary* goal of path-based patient care. • All goals and objectives are clearly defined in measurable terms. • A mechanism for measuring goal attainment is defined and integrated with the deployment strategies. • The goals and objectives are communicated to all caregivers, and they understand how path-based patient care will improve quality and reduce costs. • Preliminary plans are made to integrate clinical paths into the organization's quality and utilization management program activities. • Adequate resources are provided to initiate the organization's path-based patient care strategies.	• Physicians, nurses, and other health professionals caring for patients are involved in the initial design of the clinical path and subsequent revisions. • The time progression for clinical paths is clinically relevant to the patients' management course. • The clinical path incorporates current knowledge about optimal medical practices and effective treatment approaches. • The clinical path includes elements of patient management *and* expected outcomes during a specified period of patient care. • The clinical path represents optimal quality, not necessarily lowest costs, for a specific provider. • The clinical path design team seeks input from all individuals involved in the care of the patient for whom the path is being designed. • Clinical paths *do not* compel physicians, nurses, and other caregivers to document the same information in more than one place. • Clinical paths are readily accessible to all caregivers throughout the patient's episode of care. • Caregivers are asked to respond concurrently *only* to significant path variances. • Caregivers are asked to report *only* significant path variances. • Preliminary plans are initiated to design an information system that will support "point-of-care" data entry.	• The significance of path variances is reviewed by a multidisciplinary team representing physicians, nurses, and other clinicians caring for patients. • Variance data are used to identify system breakdowns requiring correction. • Variance data are used to test the clinical care hypothesis of the path, that is, following the path will achieve maximum quality at minimum cost. • Variances from the management components on the path are correlated with patient outcomes to identify the impact of management decisions. • Patient outcome data cover an entire episode of care and include information obtained from patients about their function and quality of life following treatment. • Each clinical path is scheduled for regular review and is updated, as necessary. • Physicians, nurses, and other clinicians who are expected to use the clinical path to manage patients are provided the results of variance analysis. • Leaders regularly evaluate attainment of their clinical path strategy goals and give feedback to providers.

Projecting Resource Needs

Leaders also must allocate adequate resources for designing and implementing clinical paths. At the start, a realistic estimate of resource needs may be difficult. Organizations with experience in clinical paths suggest that considerable time, human, and financial resources be available to ensure long-term objectives. The planning component should involve a discussion of how clinical paths will fit into the organization's quality, utilization, and risk management programs. Ideally, the path variance report system can be used as a data-collection mechanism to satisfy the information needs of many different programs. Scripps Memorial Hospital in La Jolla, California, employs five full-time people to support the multidisciplinary clinical paths development teams and to perform related data-collection activities.[55] Scripps began its clinical paths effort in 1991 and currently has about 40 paths covering key inpatient diagnoses and procedures. In addition to staff, other resources needed to support a clinical path strategy include information systems technology and ongoing educational sessions for physicians and other clinicians.

Educating Vested Parties

Once the leadership group has clearly outlined the clinical path strategy and defined what improvements are expected, education begins for medical staff members and middle managers. Physicians, nurses, and other clinical staff who have heard about other institutions' clinical path process may wonder what their leadership is doing to implement similar tools. Orientation sessions at medical staff department meetings and at nursing and other staff meetings give leaders an opportunity to share decisions made thus far and to summarize their one-, two-, and three-year implementation plans. At these educational sessions leaders should provide physicians and staff with convincing information about the benefits of adopting clinical paths; otherwise, the changes may be viewed with skepticism. Briefing sessions also minimize the risk that individual departments will attempt to initiate clinical paths without knowing what is planned for the entire organization.

Deployment

Deployment covers three key elements in devising path strategies. These are the design steps, operational procedures used to merge clinical paths into patient care processes, and variance action and reporting mechanisms.

Design Action Steps

The team designing the path should include representatives from all disciplines involved in relevant patient care activities. When the clinical path is not provider-specific, representatives should include professionals involved throughout the entire episode of care.

Although traditional clinical paths have been day oriented, the design team should select a time line that represents clinically relevant progression steps throughout the episode of care. For ambulatory surgery paths, for example, blocks of hours might be an appropriate time line. Alternatively, for medical patients, levels or phases of care (defined with objective clinical criteria) might be meaningful progression stages for the path. It is important to design a path that illustrates clinically relevant steps in the process of care and if a day-to-day (that is, a day-oriented) progression is not a practical time line, then another should be selected.

Recommendations included on the path can merely summarize current patient management practices within the organization. However, the clinical path may incorporate suggestions from clinical practice guidelines, research studies, and "best practice" organizations. The summary approach is likely to ensure the status quo, whereas the latter approach is more likely to promote optimal patient care management. The leadership oversight committee should champion the development of clinical paths that reflect the best patient care practices. In addition to optimal interventions, the clinical path should describe anticipated patient outcomes. When outcomes are included on the path, it is easier to correlate path variances with patient outcomes during variance analysis.

As providers enter into capitated reimbursement contracts and community health networks, they may assume financial liability for health care services provided outside their institutions. In these instances, it is important to design a clinical path that promotes cost efficiency across an entire continuum of patient care. In developing comprehensive clinical paths, many new questions should be considered: Will an extra day in the hospital decrease the cost of posthospital services? Should patients in skilled nursing care or rehabilitation units be evaluated more often than every 30 days? Is skilled care less costly than home care? Will home visits by a nurse practitioner decrease the likelihood of readmission? Providers working together in a capitated reimbursement system or network need to balance short- and long-term risk or reward of treatment options. Ultimately, choosing the course of treatment that provides the best outcomes over time will be in the best interest of the patient and, often, the least expensive.[56]

The design team will produce a preliminary hypothesis about the optimal way to manage patients. To ensure acceptance by all physicians and other clinicians involved in patient care, they should be given an opportunity to react to this preliminary hypothesis before path deployment is fully under way. Providers expected to use the clinical path to guide patient care should understand how the path was formulated and the quality and/or cost reductions expected.

Operating Procedures Development

The clinical path should enhance, not hinder, caregivers' ability to manage patients. By minimizing path documentation requirements, staff nurses or case managers are not overburdened with the tasks of writing on the path and then rewriting the same information on another form in the patient's record. During a pilot phase, double-documenting might be acceptable, but once the path becomes a permanent part of the patient's chart, redundant charting should be eliminated.

To serve as an effective guideline for patient care, the clinical path must be a visible reminder of the optimal patient management hypothesis. Therefore, the path should be placed in a location convenient for *all* members of the health care team, including physicians. Clinical paths appearing on the nursing Kardex™, the bedside chart, or on a clipboard "somewhere on the unit" are not likely to guide decision making for all clinicians. Each organization must evaluate its current methods of patient care and documentation so as to select the best location at which to post their path recommendations.

Variance Reporting

In the early stages of clinical path implementation, a number of organizations may require that staff nurses or case managers *react to and report all path detours*. Ideally this requirement subsides as the program evolves. Several authors in this book suggest that only selected path variances should require concurrent action and reporting. This caveat is noteworthy, for continuing to respond to every detour will likely weaken clinician enthusiasm for path-based patient care.

The biggest operational barrier to clinical path implementation reported by respondents to the July 1993 AHPI/MSC survey was a lack of information technology to support the variance reporting process. Mary Thomasma, vice-president of sales and marketing for Medicus Systems Corporation, noted that clinical path developers usually need automated tools within six months to a year of starting their initiative.[57] Not only is automation needed to support variance reporting and analysis, but caregivers will need relief from the paperwork requirements. Thomasma urges organizations to plan for automation from day one, even if they do not need it during the planning stages.

Process Improvement

Like the business process improvement project that follows Deming's PDCA cycle, the activity of improving clinical processes is also circular. Either the original multi-disciplinary team that designed the clinical path or a group composed of similar disciplines must *check* the results of their *plan*. One use of variance data is to identify system breakdowns that cause patients to vary from the prescribed path. These problems may include missed treatments due to staffing shortages, unavailability of needed equipment, or miscommunications that delay treatment. Variances due to system problems are the easiest to recognize from variance data reports.

It is more difficult to evaluate the clinical path hypothesis—that is, does staying on the path result in optimal outcomes? To *check* this *plan*, variance data must be correlated with outcome data. Common statistical analysis methods used for these correlations are one-way tables, histograms, pie charts, and comparison analysis using statistical process control techniques. Graphical information displays help the team determine the impact of path variances on patient outcomes. For instance, the graph in figure 1-6 illustrates the impact of increased use of ace inhibitors on patients' lengths of stay.[58] Hard evidence such as this can convince physicians to modify their patient management approaches.[59]

As outcomes management becomes a critical part of performance assessment activities, the organization must begin to gather outcome data from beyond the patient's acute care episode. Variance correlations with the patient's functional status, quality of life, quickness of recovery, need for additional services, and the like are important ways of testing the clinical path hypothesis.

Effective clinical path implementation requires that feedback on compliance, variances, and outcomes be given to physicians, nurses, and other caregivers. System breakdowns are best fixed through process improvement activities. Behavior modifications are best achieved by sharing credible clinical data with providers.[60] Caregivers using clinical paths should also be provided with information about how the paths have (or have not) achieved the organization's strategic objectives. Support of path-based patient

Figure 1-6. Comparison of Average Length of Stay and Percentage of Patients on Ace Inhibitors for Treatment of Systolic Congestive Heart Failure

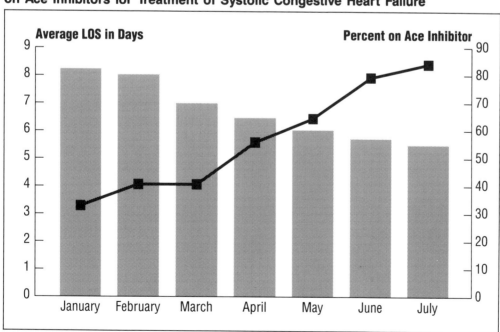

care will be heightened if on a regular basis physicians, nurses, and other clinicians are made aware of its benefits.

Review of path variances and analysis of goal attainment must be performed regularly, and a review schedule should be established toward this end. Likewise, when new clinical practice guidelines are published, all relevant clinical paths should be evaluated and updated as necessary.

Are Clinical Paths Merely a Fad?

As stressed earlier in the chapter, health care providers are likely to see changes in the clinical path as it is known today. Those phenomena that have already inspired modifications will continue to exert their influence. Other factors that will dictate clinical path changes include computerization, outcomes management studies, and patients' involvement in their care. Each of these factors is touched on briefly in the closing sections to this chapter.

Computerization

As information technologies advance, point-of-care computerized data systems will change the format and perhaps the content of clinical paths. With computerization may come an algorithmic description of patient care, in which key decision points rather than specific interventions are the focus.

Computerization also will have an impact on providers' ability to collect and analyze path variance and patient outcome data. Successful clinical path implementation rests on the availability of an adequate information system that reliably correlates path variances with patient outcome data from an entire episode of care.

Outcomes Management Studies

As health care providers learn more about the relationship between the processes of care and outcomes, clinical paths may become more prescriptive. Although clinical judgment will remain important, less variation will be tolerated once specific management parameters are validated by outcome studies as being optimal.

Patient Involvement

As health care consumers become more involved in decisions regarding their care, clinical paths will be expanded to incorporate more patient choice alternatives. Patients' involvement in their health care decisions also will focus more attention on the design of paths intended for use by patients and their families.

The format and function of clinical paths will continue to evolve. However, the basic goals of path-based patient care will remain the same: to promote collaboration among the health care team and to reduce unnecessary variation in patient management practices. If the clinical path tool helps achieve these objectives, it will remain a useful guide in the delivery of health care services. If a better tool comes along, clinical paths will be replaced. The clinical path as it is known today may go away or at least change form and purpose; however, the advancements made by organizations that successfully implemented path-based patient care will not be lost. The physicians, nurses, and other caregivers who learned how to work together to improve the clinical processes of care and discovered how to use data to measure and improve performance will find themselves ahead of those groups who chose not to initiate clinical paths. Path-based patient care is the start of a new realization for health care providers — that collaboration and information are the essence of optimal patient care.

References and Notes

1. Reiley, T. T. Critical pathways: historical perspectives and future directions. *American Society for Quality Control Health Care Division Newsletter* 3(1)1-2, Summer 1993.

2. Fuszard, H., and others. *Case Management: A Challenge for Nurses.* Kansas City, MO: American Nurses' Association, 1988, p. 1.

3. American Nurses' Association. *Standards of Clinical Nursing Practice.* Kansas City, MO: American Nurses' Association, 1991, p. 2.

4. Zander, K. Managed care and nursing case management. In: G. G. Mayer, M. J. Maddin, and E. Lawrenz, editors. *Patient Care Delivery Models.* Rockville, MD: Aspen Publications, 1990, p. 38.

5. McKenzie, C. B., Torkelson, N. G., and Holt, M. A. Care and cost: nursing case management improves both. *Nursing Management* 20(10):30-34, 1989.

6. Zander, 1990, p. 47.

7. Zander, K. Quantifying, managing and improving quality. *The New Definition* 7(4):2, Fall 1992.

8. Zander, K. Critical Paths. In: M. M. Melum and M. K. Sinioris, editors. *Total Quality Management: The Health Care Pioneers.* Chicago: American Hospital Publishing, 1992, p. 310.

9. McKenzie, Torkelson, and Holt.

10. Etheredge, M. L., Zander, K., and Bower, K., editors. *Nursing Case Management: Blueprints for Transformation.* Boston: Center for Nursing Case Management, New England Medical Center Hospital, 1987.

11. Ciccone, K. R., and Lord, J. *IQA-2: Continuous Performance Improvement through Integrated Quality Assessment.* Chicago: American Hospital Publishing, 1992.

12. Zander, K. Managed care: integrating "Q.A." in everyday practice. *Definition* 4(3):1-2, Summer 1989.

13. Zander, 1989.

14. Mosher, C., Cronk, P., Kidd, A., McCormick, P., Stockton, S., and Sulla, C. Upgrading practice with critical pathways. *American Journal of Nursing,* Jan. 1992, pp. 41-44.

15. Giuliano, K. K., and Poirier, C. E. Nursing case management: critical pathways to desirable outcomes. *Nursing Management* 22(3):52-55, Mar. 1991.

16. Goodwin, D. R. Critical pathways in home healthcare. *JONA* 22(2):35-40, Feb. 1992.

17. Giuliano and Poirier.

18. Miller, D. (vice-president, Alliant Health System) speaking at Emerging Trends in Utilization Management seminar sponsored by the American Hospital Association, June 1992, San Antonio, Texas.

19. Coffey, R. J., Richards, J. S., Remmert, C. S., LeRoy, S. S., Schoville, R. R., and Baldwin, P. S. An introduction to critical paths. *Quality Management in Health Care* 1(1):45-54, 1992.

20. The Governance Committee. *Strategies for Redesigning Care.* Washington, DC: The Advisory Board Company, 1991.

21. McKenzie, Torkelson, and Holt.

22. Causey, W. Nursing paths being abandoned as physicians get involved? *Hospital Peer Review* 18(4):49-52, Apr. 1993.

23. Lumsdon, K., and Hagland, M. Mapping care. *Hospitals & Health Networks* 67(20):34-40, Oct. 20, 1993.

24. James, B. C. Implementing practice guidelines through clinical quality improvement. *Frontiers of Health Services Management* 10(1):3-37, Fall 1993.

25. King, J. O. The relevance of practical experience to American hospitals (commentary). *Frontiers of Health Services Management* 10(1):48-50, Fall 1993.

26. Falconer, J. A., Roth, E. J., Sutin, J. A., and others. The critical path method in stroke rehabilitation: lessons from an experiment in cost containment and outcome improvement. *Quality Review Bulletin* 19(1):8-16, 1993.

27. Spath, P. From workbook materials for Critical Path Management seminar sponsored by Medical Management Development Associates, Oct. 1993, Dallas.

28. Olsen, C. A. Building critical pathways for a hospital-based home care program. *Outreach* 14(3):1, 3, May-June 1993.

29. Coffey and others.

30. Causey.

31. Berwick, D. M. Continuous quality improvement as an ideal in health care. *New England Journal of Medicine* 320:53–56, 1989.

32. Miller, D., and Durbin, S. Improving patient recovery following total joint replacement. *The Quality Letter* 4(1):22–26, Feb. 1992.

33. Mangano, J. Clinical pathways seen as opportunity to integrate traditional QA with CQI. *QI/TQM* 2(4):49–51, Apr. 1992.

34. Spath, P. L. Critical paths: a tool for clinical process management. *JAHIMA* 64(3):48–58, Mar. 1993.

35. Deming, W. E. *Out of the Crisis.* Cambridge, MA: Massachusetts Institute of Technology Center for Advanced Engineering Study, 1986.

36. Spath, Mar. 1993.

37. Institute of Medicine, Committee on Clinical Practice Guidelines. *Guidelines for Clinical Practice: From Development to Use.* M. J. Field and K. N. Lohr, editors. Washington, DC: National Academy Press, 1992.

38. Kelly, J. T., and Toepp, M. C. Practice parameters: development, evaluation, dissemination, and implementation. *Quality Review Bulletin* 18:405–9, 1992.

39. Toepp, M. C., and Kuznets, N., editors. *Directory of Practice Parameters: Titles, Sources, and Updates.* Chicago: American Medical Association, 1993.

40. United States Preventive Services Task Force. *Guide to Clinical Preventive Services: An Assessment of the Effectiveness of 169 Interventions.* Baltimore: Williams & Wilkins, 1989.

41. Agency for Healthcare Policy and Research. Clinical Practice Guideline Development. Program Note. Rockville, MD: AHCPR, Aug. 1993 (AHCPR publication no. 93-0023).

42. Clinical practice guidelines released by the AHCPR as of April 1994: Management of Post-Operative Pain (adult and pediatric); Prediction and Prevention of Pressure Ulcers in Adults; Management of Urinary Incontinence in the Elderly; Management of Cataracts in Adults; Detection, Diagnosis and Treatment of Depression in Primary Care; Comprehensive Screening and Management of Sickle Cell Disease in Newborns and Infants; Managing Early HIV Infection; Diagnosis and Treatment of Benign Prostatic Hyperplasia; Managing Cancer Pain; and Diagnosis and Management of Unstable Angina.

43. Jencks, S. F., and Wilensky, G. The health care quality improvement initiative: a new approach to quality assurance in Medicare. *JAMA* 268(7):900–903, 1992.

44. Sundwall, D. N. Quality of care developments. *The Quality Letter* 5(5):supplement, June 1993.

45. *The Wall Street Journal,* May 3, 1993, pp. A1, A9.

46. Acute Pain Management Guideline Panel. Acute Pain Management in Adults: Operative Procedures, Quick Reference Guide for Clinicians. AHCPR pub. no. 92-0019. Rockville, MD: Agency for Health Care Policy and Research, Public Health Service, U.S. Department of Health and Human Services.

47. Ellwood, P. M. Outcomes management: a technology of experience. *New England Journal of Medicine* 318(23):1549–56, 1988.

48. Nash, D. B., and Markson, L. E. Emerging trends in outcomes management. *Frontiers of Health Services Management* 8(2):3–52, 1991.

49. Hargraves, J. L., Palmer, H. R., Zapka, J., and others. Using patient reports to measure health care system performance. *Clinical Performance and Quality HealthCare* 1(4):208–13, Oct.–Dec. 1993.

50. McKenzie, Torkelson, and Holt.

51. Spath, P. *Succeeding with Critical Paths.* Forest Grove, OR: Brown-Spath & Associates, 1993, p. 3.

52. Bean, B. Critical path leads to changes in cardiac cath patient care. *Hospital Case Management* 1(2):29–32, Feb. 1993.

53. James.

54. Causey.

55. Lumsdon and Hagland.

56. King.

57. Lumsdon and Hagland.

58. Wall, D. W., and Joseph, E. Analyzing critical pathways with statistics. *Quality Management Update* 3(6):8–10, June 1993.

59. Todd, J. S. Quest for quality or cost containment (commentary). *Frontiers of Health Services Management* 10(1):51–53, Fall 1993.

60. Caper, P. Population-based measures of the quality of medical care. In: J. Conch, editor. *Health Care Quality Management for the 21st Century.* Tampa, FL: American College of Physician Executives, 1991.

PART ONE

Development and Implementation Issues

Case Management and Clinical Paths: Definitions and Relationships

Kathleen A. Bower, DNSc

Both case management and clinical paths are strategies used to manage patient care. Although discrete approaches, both are related.

This chapter is meant to provide an overview of case management. In doing so, the chapter defines and examines the scope of case management: how to identify prospective case management patients; responsibilities of a case manager; and case manager networks, disciplines, and bases of operations. The chapter then looks at the correlation between case management and clinical paths, closing with a brief word about selecting clinical path and/or case management strategies.

Case Management Definition and Scope

Case management has been defined as "a clinical system that focuses on the accountability of an identified individual or group for coordinating a patient's care (or group of patients) across a continuum of care; ensuring and facilitating the achievement of quality, clinical and cost outcomes; negotiating, procuring and coordinating services and resources needed by the patient/family; intervening at key points (and/or significant variances) for individual patients; addressing and resolving patterns in aggregate variances that have a negative quality-cost impact; and creating opportunities and systems to enhance outcomes."[1] Although case management processes may differ among institutions, generally its goals are these:[2]

1. To provide a well-coordinated care experience for patients/families, who should experience the continuum of care instead of segments or events
2. To ensure that satisfactory clinical outcomes are met
3. To manage length of stay (LOS) and resources effectively
4. To integrate and coordinate the activities of multiple disciplines

As disclosed in the preceding definition, the primary function of a case management program is to enhance the coordination of needed resources for patients and their families. This coordinating function results in enhanced quality of care and cost-efficiency outcomes. Another key feature introduced in the definition is that case management is continuum based or episode based. This means that case managers work with patients and/or families throughout as much of the continuum of care as needed, usually spanning geographic care areas.

There are two major types of case management: external and internal. *External* case management is performed by third-party reimbursers or groups contracted to perform services for the reimbursers. *Internal* case management refers to a provider-based service. This chapter focuses primarily on internal case management, although the two types of case management share many processes and concepts.

The key concerns of case management include the identification of patients, the roles and responsibilities of the case manager, the utilization of networks, the disciplines of case managers, and strategic settings for case management. Each of these will be addressed in the following subsections.

Identification of Patients for Case Management

One approach to identifying patients for case management is embodied in the following statement: "All patients need their care managed; not every patient needs a case manager."[3] Case management as a process focuses on patients whose cases are considered highly complex, generally less than 20 percent of the total patient population. It is important to distinguish between complexity and acuity. As a rule, case management is directed toward patients whose care, although complex, is not necessarily of high acuity or severity. Complexity of care needs is influenced by the interaction of various factors including a patient's health, social, emotional, and economic status. The greater the need for multiple services and disciplines to interact with the patient/family, the higher the complexity of care. Within this framework of complexity, patient populations who usually need case management services can be identified. Case management has been found to be beneficial when one or more of these factors are present:[4]

1. Patients for whom high care costs are anticipated or costly services have already been provided
2. Patients with repeated inpatient admissions or emergency department visits or those with disproportionately high usage of outpatient (physician office or clinic) services
3. Patients in high-risk socioeconomic groups (defined by lack of adequate social support or financial resources to procure needed treatments or services in a timely manner)
4. Patients who encounter significant variances from the interventions or from expected outcomes associated with a clinical path
5. Patients whose cases involve multiple physicians or multiple disciplines
6. Patients for whom patterns of illness and/or treatment are not immediately discernible
7. Patients who have been identified as strategic case management priorities for the organization, such as those whose treatments fall into key product lines

This approach to identifying patient populations for case management applies the principle of 20/80; that is, that case management be focused on the 20 percent of patient population who utilize or who are at risk for utilizing a high percentage of the organization's resources. Case management programs that cover the entire patient population within an organization tend to be very expensive and unnecessary. Case management is a resource and as such should be applied in those situations where it will most influence quality and cost outcomes.

In situations where clinical paths or other tools and systems are in place for organizing and sequencing care, the majority of patients can be managed effectively when clinical staff use these tools. Those patients who are inappropriate for clinical path management (either initially or over time) may be referred to case management.

Case Manager's Roles and Responsibilities

Patients meeting established criteria are referred to case managers to be screened for admission into their caseloads. Prospective case management patients may be identified beforehand through preadmission testing or screening systems. Alternatively, they may be identified upon admission by clinical staff during initial patient assessment. Referrals to a case manager may also be initiated when trigger points are reached — for example, when a patient experiences significant variances from a clinical path or is identified in other ways as not following the anticipated treatment pattern. Patients for case management should be identified as early as possible in the episode of care.

Once a patient is selected for case management, case managers work closely with the patient, their families and friends, health care team members, payers, and others to ensure that the patient will receive the care needed, when and where needed, and at the lowest cost possible. They do this first by assessing the patient's situation thoroughly, building on the database begun by the direct care clinicians. Based on the case manager's assessment, patient care goals are developed in conjunction with the patient and/or family and other health care team members and a plan to reach those goals is outlined. Once this collective effort is completed, the plan is implemented with close monitoring and evaluation by the case manager. The case manager often needs to negotiate for and procure services in a timely manner and anticipate patient care needs. If the plan appears to be ineffective, it is revised. Once goals have been met or when patients no longer need the services, they are discharged from case management. The case management process may extend over days, weeks, months, or even years.

The process just described is not unique to case management. What makes case management different from the usual patient care activities of the health care team, however, is the intense focus on patients whose condition is so complex as to demand extraordinary efforts of coordination. In designing a case management program within an organization, it is important to avoid duplication of functions. Not only is duplication costly, it may lead to conflicts that can negatively affect the smooth coordination of patient care and ultimately compromise outcomes.

Case Manager Networks

As implied in the preceding section, case managers do not function in isolation but orchestrate and enhance the contributions of all members of the health care team who relate to the patient and family. Therefore, the process of case management relies on the development and use of networks made up of services, disciplines, resources, and providers. Within internal systems of case management, the authority base of the case manager is usually a negotiated one requiring constant attention. Successful case managers seek to form productive partnerships and look for ways to strengthen those relationships to better serve patients, families, organizations, payers, and other providers.

Two examples of case management networks are depicted in figures 2-1 and 2-2. Figure 2-1 represents the network created within a community-based nurse case management model. Figure 2-2 illustrates the network within which an orthopedic case manager functions in a medical center.

Physicians are integral members of the network. They are primary coordinators of the medical components of the patient's care plan, especially in situations involving more than one physician. Oftentimes, physicians find partnership with a case manager to be supportive both of patients *and* physicians — especially in cases where multiple services must be negotiated for complex patient conditions. In this respect, case management provides a partner to facilitate the physician's efforts to coordinate the treatment plan effectively and efficiently as well as to respond to other patient-related issues. In their partner/networker capacity, case managers can provide physicians with specific information such as the patient's response to the planned course of treatment, an invaluable service to physicians.

Figure 2-1. The Nursing Network

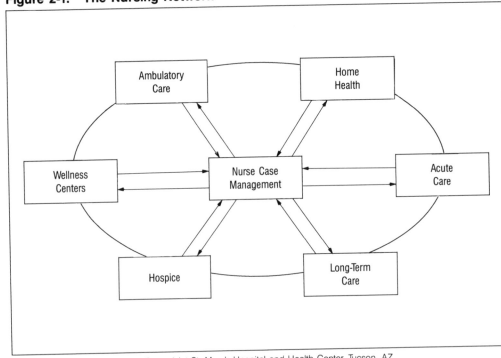

Reprinted, with permission, from Carondelet St. Mary's Hospital and Health Center, Tucson, AZ.

Figure 2-2. Orthopedic Case Manager Network

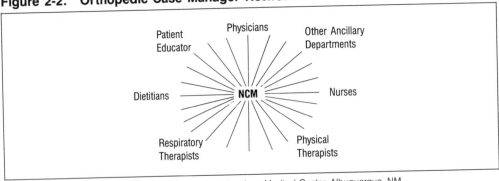

Reprinted, with permission, from Sophia Chu Rodgers, Lovelace Medical Center, Albuquerque, NM.

Case Manager Disciplines

Although not an exclusive arrangement, most patient care case managers come from the disciplines of nursing and social work. Case managers from either discipline often find that their primary partner represents the other discipline. Because patient care needs can be multidimensional, it may be useful to model the case management network on a nurse–social worker formal partnership. The partners then call on other members of the health care team as needed for specific patients or patient populations.

Case Manager's Primary Base

Strategically speaking, case managers are located so as to maximize the effectiveness of their interventions. Their sphere of influence and activity may encompass pre-admission care through acute care to posthospital care. For example, case managers may be based primarily within acute care facilities; alternatively, a community-based approach to case management may be designed. Selection of a base of operations for case managers depends on the needs and characteristics of the patient population as well as the goals established for case management.

The arena in which care is provided is also a factor, specifically as it relates to the financial reimbursement system in place. For example, with capitated payment systems, it is imperative that patients be well managed at the appropriate level of care. Circumventing hospitalization and expensive acute care services such as emergency care becomes crucial. In this scenario it becomes increasingly important to coordinate the patient's care throughout the continuum, from community to hospital and back to community, with the goal of reducing admissions.

Relationship between Case Management and Clinical Paths

Case managers may or may not use clinical paths as tools to guide patient care interventions and outcomes. Frequently, the patients referred to case managers are those for whom paths are difficult to construct or those who have deviated significantly from their paths. When the patient can be managed appropriately with a clinical path, case managers use it in conjunction with direct care providers. Ideally, direct care providers should have the primary responsibility for coordinating patient care using a clinical path, with the case manager becoming actively involved only when variances and/or complexity makes it difficult for the patient to be managed solely via staff interventions. Approached in this way, case management arouses fewer turf and competition issues. This approach also extends the number of clinicians actively involved in *managing* patient care, without additional staff.

In environments where paths are used, case managers may participate in writing the content for diagnosis-specific paths. However, to maximize utilization and acceptance of paths by all health care team members, case managers *should not* write paths single-handedly; clinical paths are most effective when they are written and used by multidisciplinary team members.

Case managers may also be involved in analyzing and addressing aggregate variances. They may participate in identifying significant patterns and trends in the aggregate variance data, in prioritizing those issues that require further action, and in developing and enacting action plans. In this capacity, case managers play a key role in the organization's quality improvement activities. It must be emphasized, however, that case managers *should not* be the only participants in the variance management process. All clinical disciplines involved in caring for the clinical path patient population must participate in the analysis and action components of variance management.

Case Management–Clinical Path Correlation

The correlation between case management and clinical paths is multidimensional, as shown in table 2-1. Each approach has certain elements in common, as summarized in the figure and as discussed in the following.

The foundation of case management is twofold: role (the case manager) and process (a set of activities and an approach to patient care issues). Clinical paths, on the other hand, are tools and systems. The *tool* reflects only part of the case management process, notably the plan. Ideally, the plan outlined on the path includes patient care interventions and outcomes. As tools, paths are used to organize and sequence specific elements of patient care to promote movement of the patient toward desired outcomes within an effective time frame. The *system* within which paths operate includes variance management (individual and aggregate), quality improvement, and use of clinical paths as the communication focus for all members of the health care team. Clinical

Table 2-1. Correlation between Critical Paths and Case Management

Element	Critical Paths	Case Management
Patient population	60% High volume Relatively patternable	20% or less High cost Complex, often difficult to pattern
Coordination/continuity provided	Plan	Provider
Core elements	Tool and system	Role and process
Time span	Often unit/area based	Continuum or episode based

paths cannot function in a vacuum; a role is necessary to manage the patient within the context of the path. Although that role can be assumed by the case manager, it is more efficient to consider incorporating the use of paths into clinical staff functions.

Correlation between the tool-and-system character of clinical paths and the role-and-process character of case management is also evident in the coordination and continuity provided by each strategy. Following paths supports continuity and coordination of the *plan* of care. Case management strengthens continuity among *providers*, which, it is hoped, also leads to coordination and continuity of the plan.

Another element of comparison between path-based care and case management involves patient populations appropriate to each strategy. Paths function well for 60 to 80 percent of the patient population (or one to two standard deviations within a bell-shaped distribution curve). These patients reflect high-volume cases whose care is relatively patternable. Conversely, case management is focused on 20 percent or less of the total patient population—those patients representing high costs and/or highly variable patterns of care.

Another point of comparison involves the use of case management versus path-based care. Although they should be written for an entire episode of care, clinical paths often focus only on components of the episode (the hospitalization component, for example). Case management should span the entire continuum of care, regardless of where the services are provided.

The relationship between the path framework and case management is further demonstrated in figure 2-3, which suggests that three elements are required for effective patient care management. Two elements, case management and the tools and systems for care coordination (clinical paths), already have been discussed. The third element, outlined in figure 2-3, is unit/department/discipline-based care coordination, which addresses the effectiveness of patient care provided within a discipline or department. For example:

- When multiple physicians are involved in one case, is one physician in charge of the medical plan of care, or do all physicians provide input and write orders without any central coordination?
- Is the nursing care for patients coordinated over the entire period of time that the patient receives care in a given area or are multiple nurses involved with no overall coordination?

When care coordination is ineffective at the unit/department/discipline level, more case management services may be needed. Each of the three elements—unit/department/discipline-based care coordination, case management, and clinical paths—are essential to the effective management of patient care.

Figure 2-3.   Relationship between Case Management, CareMap®, and Care Delivery Systems

Unit/Department/Discipline-Based Care Coordination (100%)	(Case Management) Continuum-Based Care Coordination (<20%)

(60–80%)
Tools and Systems for
Care Coordination

CareMap® System
Variance Management
Refocused Communication

Selection of a Clinical Path and/or Case Management Strategy

In designing a system for managing patient care, clinical paths and case management are obvious options. However, because they are separate and distinct, strategically speaking, health care organizations have several different options to choose from in achieving their objectives:[5]

- Clinical paths only
- Case management only
- Both clinical paths and case management
- Neither clinical paths nor case management (other approaches are chosen)

Organizations must select the strategy that best fits their objectives and goals and operates within their financial and staffing parameters. Neither paths nor case management is a panacea; neither approach solves all issues and problems related to patient management. The organization's goals for efficient coordination of patient care must remain at the core of system design. In this context, clinical path-based care and case management can each have a role and can be positioned for maximally effective use.

Conclusion

The goals of case management are fourfold: coordination of the care continuum, optimal clinical outcomes, effective management of hospital length of stay and resources, and cohesion among multiple disciplines. Case managers must screen their patient population to identify appropriate candidates for case management, help develop care goals and a plan for attaining them, and monitor the plan.

Case managers may help write critical paths but should not undertake writing them single-handedly. They also may assist in tracking trends that lead to variances from a particular path.

The clinical path is a tool (the plan of care) used to move a patient through a system (an organized, coordinated sequence of events) toward a predetermined outcome within a predetermined time line. Case management and clinical paths, although discrete entities, are related.

In designing a plan-of-care strategy, providers have at least four options from which to choose. They can use clinical paths only, case management only, both, or neither (devising another approach).

Notes

1. The Center for Case Management, South Natick, MA. Unpublished handouts and materials.
2. The Center for Case Management.
3. The Center for Case Management.
4. The Center for Case Management.
5. The Center for Case Management.

CHAPTER THREE

Clinical Paths and Patient Care Documentation

Janet S. Richards, Mary Jo Kocan, Hilary Monaghan, Susan Wintermeyer-Pingel, and Edward B. Goldman, JD

Before implementing clinical pathways, documentation strategies must be designed to answer *at least* the following questions: Which approach best meets documentation requirements? What factors weigh on the efficiency and effectiveness of the path? What action steps should be included in the documentation system? Which legal issues should guide documentation protocol?

This chapter gives practitioners and project coordinators recommendations on how to address documentation issues that arise with the use of clinical pathways. The chapter discusses benefits of multidisciplinary charting, approaches to reconciling path documentation with current charting methods, and the importance of making documentation accessible to all providers—inpatient and outpatient—who will use the system. The function of path documentation in minimizing risk liability also is addressed. There are many ways to document patient information when using clinical pathways, and strategies can differ from one organization to another. The chapter closes with pointers for implementing a documentation system.

General Documentation Requirements

Due to the current scrutiny of health care practices, it is essential that providers document patient care precisely and efficiently to show that the care delivered was appropriate for the patient's diagnosis. To meet this challenge, the documentation system must be accessible and easy to use, have a multidisciplinary format, avoid duplication, and work in tandem with established care paths.

Current methods of recording include problem-oriented charting that focuses the documentation of the care of the patient's specific nursing or medical problems; narrative charting, which in paragraph form, summarizes the events of a particular time period; and charting by exception, a relatively new method of documentation that presumes standards are met when there is no notation to the contrary. Many systems incorporate a combination of some of these. The essential elements of an effective documentation system are discussed in the following subsections.

Accessibility and Ease of Use

Unless it is accessible and comprehensible, no documentation system can reflect patient care adequately. A number of patient records are maintained away from the bedside, which makes locating them a time-consuming and frustrating task. In addition, caregivers may be required to record information on several different forms scattered throughout the chart. For example, a nurse's note might mention a patient problem by number, and yet the problem list containing the corresponding diagnosis may be elsewhere in the chart. This can obscure the goal recorded in the nurse's note, thereby confusing other team members. One way to avoid such confusion is to place pathway documentation at the patient's bedside so that it is readily available to all members of the team.

Multidisciplinary Format

Under pressure to shorten hospital stays and limit costs, providers must ensure that all disciplines involved in the patient's care work toward the same goals. An inherent risk in separate methods of patient care documentation is that the primary nursing goal may relate to one patient problem or body system, whereas the physician's medical goal may relate to another. Working at cross-purposes can set up a domino effect, spreading to other caregivers such as physical therapists and dietitians who may focus their patient care efforts in still other directions. Therefore, a multidisciplinary approach to setting patient goals—and recording progress—must be reinforced by a uniform and coordinated format.

The pathway documentation strategy should foster development of a multidisciplinary format. Such a team approach enhances collaborative goal setting among individual members of the health care team. For example, a patient is unable to ambulate because of medical instability such as arrhythmia. This would be documented on the multidisciplinary record, which might look like a clinical pathway. The therapist notes this and revises the physical therapy goals, incorporating them into the daily plan of care.

Nonduplication

Because patient care can become complex, in today's health care environment it is more important than ever to *thoroughly* document the care delivered, the patient's responses to therapy, the plan of care, and its outcomes. Traditionally, this has been done separately by each discipline and filed in different locations throughout the patient's chart. For example, the nurse may record the administration of pain medication on the medication chart, the patient's response to the drug on the flowsheet, and the recommendation to change the dosage (based on the patient's response) in a nurse's narrative note. The physician may then change the dosage and write a separate note in the physician's narrative summary. A physical therapist who subsequently attempts a treatment only to find that the patient cannot participate because of poor pain control documents this fact in yet another section of the medical record. So far in this scenario, five documentation episodes have occurred. Not only are these actions repetitious, they demonstrate lack of communication, coordination, and uniform format among team members.

A better system, which might include a multidisciplinary CareMap™ kept at the bedside, would have all disciplines charting in one place. This way, duplication is eliminated or minimized, the caregiver's time is used more efficiently, and the quality of patient care is enhanced.

Established Plans

It is important that care plans be developed for each patient type or diagnosis so that the anticipated course of treatment can be determined upon admission. Having predetermined plans in place that include multidisciplinary expectations of care eliminates repetition of routine nursing processes and medical protocols throughout the medical record. Thus, only exceptions (or variances) to preestablished paths would require documentation. Such a system would promote a concise format that includes all elements of patient information. Although a standard plan is developed by patient type or diagnosis, the format should be broad enough to allow for individualization among patients. Planned flexibility contributes to the overall success of the documentation system.

Documentation Requirements for Clinical Path Strategies

With the advent of clinical paths and a multidisciplinary team approach to patient care, a nontraditional system of documentation that allows for nonrepetitive charting in one place — preferably near the patient's bedside — is essential. Even though documentation procedures and requirements vary among institutions, certain elements are common to all systems. In addition to the requirements of the Joint Commission on Accreditation of Healthcare Organizations (JCAHO) and the Medicare Conditions of Participation, certain discipline-specific requirements should be met. For example, nursing documentation must meet American Nurses' Association standards, as well as those of nursing specialty organizations. When pathways are being used, documentation should be coordinated with standards in a manner that can be understood by those involved in the continuum of care.

Appropriate documentation of nursing care includes nursing intervention prescriptions, evaluation of patient's response, and/or outcomes resulting from care provided. The medical staff is required to maintain documentation that clearly and accurately reflects the diagnosis, therapeutic results of care rendered, and patient's progress during hospitalization and at discharge.[1] Clinical pathways can be valuable tools for meeting these requirements. The collaborative use of pathways directs health care professionals to follow established treatment plans designed to attain desired patient outcomes.

Clinical Pathways in Daily Practice

Paths can be incorporated into daily practice in several ways. Problem-oriented charting can include references to the pathway (if it is a permanent part of the chart) without repeating pathway information. References on bedside flowsheets to pertinent data on the pathway further pull together information when professionals monitor the progress of care delivered. A review of pathways on patient care rounds by physicians, nurses, and representatives from other disciplines allows for daily interdisciplinary monitoring. Clinical pathways should be accessible during these rounds and can be kept at the patient's bedside and/or in the chart, depending on the needs of the care providers.

Variance Collection Considerations

Collecting data about pathway variances is an essential activity of care quality management, action plan development, and care delivery evaluation. Variances should be tracked and documented in a manner that facilitates simple and focused occurrence trending. Special considerations should be given to those variances that affect patient length of stay or overall outcomes.

When a variance occurs between expected and actual treatment plan of care, documentation should identify the variance, its type (patient, clinician, or system), and its effect on outcomes achievement. This should be followed by a review of aggregate data about multiple patients and the long-term outcomes achieved.[2] Only patient variances should be addressed in the patient record. For legal reasons, clinician and system variances are tracked and recorded separately as part of a more confidential quality assurance document.

Variance data collection routinely has been labor-intensive, especially when the information is collected in narrative form. When variances are collected outside the patient record they should be recorded in a quantitative format that is user-friendly and clear, allowing clinicians to use the data to identify trends requiring timely action plans. The data collection tools should be as concise as possible while capturing the data needed to arrive at appropriate conclusions. However, tools must be flexible enough to accommodate patients who deviate from the pathway. For example, when a patient "falls off the path," as in an unexpected transfer to an intensive care unit (ICU) because of a change in condition, progress and events should be tracked. Depending on how long the patient is off the path, tracking may include data from resource utilization, patient variances (what took the patient off the path), and length of ICU stay. Once transferred back to the home unit, the patient can start anew on the pathway at a time determined by the health care team.

Initiation of a Clinical Pathway

Agreement on a process for integrating clinical pathways into daily operations ensures consistency of implementation as well as completion of related documentation. An example of such a process for the inpatient portion of a care episode is outlined below:[3]

1. Pathway coordinator is notified of admission.
2. Head nurse/designee assigns appropriate bed on unit.
3. Pathway coordinator initiates patient on pathway by:
   - Documenting in unit log (handwritten or computer database)
   - Entering dates on preprinted orders
   - Entering dates on pathway
   - Placing completed pathways in plastic folder on bedside chart and in main chart
4. Pathway coordinator talks with admitting physician to clarify any questions related to caring for this patient while looking at clinical pathway and preprinted orders.
5. Pathway coordinator talks with the nurse providing care for this patient to clarify any questions.
6. Variance documentation takes place throughout the admission and upon discharge; pathway coordinator completes the variance record and the unit log.
7. Ongoing communication between outpatient and inpatient care providers facilitates smooth transition of patient care through the continuum.

When routines of care within a pathway (such as those used prior to administering chemotherapy) are determined to be appropriate for the majority of patients, using preprinted orders can reduce the total time required of the physician to write orders. However, it should be emphasized that these are only guidelines; physicians must review the orders and consider individual patient differences before implementing them. Preprinted orders require the physician's signature (standing orders do not require a physician's signature and are implemented as a matter of routine) and can save time by predicting typical orders for the "average" case.

A case manager or another member of the health care team should track all pathway patients. A running log, one method of providing an overview of pertinent data, can include the patient's name, hospital identification number, pathway name, admission date, discharge date, expected length of stay, actual length of stay, and any comments related to that episode of care. (See figure 3-1.)

Figure 3-1. Example of a Running Log to Track Patients on Clinical Pathways

Patient Name	Reg #	Pathway	Date Admitted	Expected LOS	Date Discharged	Actual LOS	Pathway Coordinator	Comments

Clinical Path Documentation Considerations

Several factors can influence the development of an efficient pathway documentation system. The following list contains some issues to consider:

- Whether to include the pathway as a permanent part of the medical record
- Whether one documentation system should be used for all patients, regardless of whether they are on a pathway
- Where to keep the pathway during the episode of care
- How to coordinate outpatient and inpatient information
- Whether the system will be manual or computerized

Permanent Document?

Clinical paths contain many details of nursing interventions and planned activities considered essential elements in documenting a patient's progress during hospitalization. When they are made part of the permanent record, pathways can reduce the time needed for nursing documentation of routine care practices and, unless a variance occurs, may even eliminate the need for progress notes.[4] A similar efficiency of time can be realized when other disciplines also use the pathway to document their interventions. Unless incorporated into the medical record, path documentation is a duplication of information charted elsewhere.[5]

Including paths in the permanent record can also be disadvantageous. As working documents, the paths must accommodate the changes needed to individualize a patient care protocol, and unless such changes are made legibly and coherently, the overall value of the medical record may be compromised. Furthermore, without timely documentation of the rationale for each variance from the predetermined plan for a particular patient type or diagnosis, the clinical path and the medical record – and thus the appropriateness of care – may come under suspicion.

One Documentation System or Two?

As mentioned in chapter 1, when clinical pathways are developed, part of the planning effort should go toward examining how the clinical paths fit into the current charting system. Superimposing paths on an existing documentation system will promote redundancies in charting. For example, the interventions commonly found in nursing care plans are contained in clinical paths. To avoid duplicating this information, the documentation system can be designed so that the care plan merely *refers to the intervention*, which is recorded on the path.

Another consideration is how to manage patients for whose diagnoses there are no paths and patients whose conditions are such that an established path no longer is appropriate. The question, then, becomes whether to have two separate documentation systems or one system that allows integration of all patient types or diagnoses. An integrated system would consist of specific pathways for various diagnoses and surgical procedures and blank or generic pathways for patient populations for whom no pathways have been developed. It also would accommodate patients who have been removed from an identified pathway due to major variations in the care they require.

Maintaining two systems is an appealing option, especially in the early stages of implementation, when few pathways have been developed. However, unless the criteria for using each system are well defined, dual systems can lead to confusion and frustration for staff members.

Bedside or Chart Location?

As noted earlier in the chapter, to be most useful, paths must be accessible to all disciplines involved in the patient's care. Furthermore, paths must be updated frequently to reflect positive or negative progress. Having multiple copies in various locations (for example, on the patient's chart, at the patient's bedside, and in a nursing Kardex™) is impractical and it is a waste of effort to keep them all updated.

Another consideration related to accessibility is whether to share pathways with patients and families. Although doing so can increase their involvement, some providers feel that sharing this information may add to the patient's and/or the family's anxiety if care does not follow the established pattern.[6] If pathways are made accessible, then staff must be prepared to reassure all concerned in the event of variances.

At the University of Michigan Medical Center, keeping pathways at the patient's bedside has proved useful for several reasons:

- Nursing staff can refer to them throughout the shift, update the patient's progress, and document variances.
- Pathways are available for physician's rounds.
- Pathways are available for case manager's rounds.
- Pathways are accessible to all other disciplines (for example, dietitian or speech pathologist) involved in the patient's care.

One disadvantage to pathway placement at the bedside is that it is unavailable when the patient travels off the unit for therapies or diagnostic studies (physical therapy, radiology) unless the bedside chart is routinely sent with the patient. Keeping the path within the main body of the chart during the patient's hospital stay ensures that the pathway travels with the patient. On the other hand, this practice can limit access, especially for nurses who might use the time the patient is off the unit to catch up on paperwork.

Scope of Information Coordination?

Few documentation systems encourage the sharing of information between hospital staff who care for inpatients and those who care for the same patients in the outpatient setting. Clinical pathways contain information that could be useful to providers during posthospitalization follow-up. For example:

- A detailed account of the course of treatment and expected outcomes
- Any variations from the planned course of treatment
- The patient's response to treatment
- A summary of patient education provided

Inpatient staff can also benefit from knowing events that occurred during outpatient contacts prior to the patient's admission. This communication can be expedited by including the names and phone numbers of outpatient resources on the appropriate pathways.

Pathways developed collaboratively to include a preadmission, in-hospital, and postdischarge approach to care can result in a smoother transition for patients along the entire continuum of service. Coordination of information between inpatient and outpatient settings ultimately serves to help team members meet expected outcomes as efficiently and cost-effectively as possible.

In this system, care providers in both inpatient and outpatient areas can streamline efforts and avoid duplication of services because there is a consistent written plan of care. Facts related to the patient's medical history and current illness, already gathered by staff in the outpatient area, can be used by the inpatient staff. Outpatient staff can begin to prepare the patient for the hospital experience based on the typical pattern of care outlined in the clinical pathway. Inpatient staff can continue this preparation without repeating steps already mastered. Having an identified contact person in the outpatient setting makes it easier to address any special issues or concerns related to a particular patient, promoting consistency and continuity. By reviewing patient variance information documented on the clinical pathway or in some other specified part of the medical record, outpatient staff can concentrate efforts on problematic areas. In this way, all members of the health care team present a consistent plan, work towards the same goals, and build upon each other's efforts.

Computerized or Manual Documentation?

Because of the volume of detail contained in clinical paths and because of the tailoring or "fine-tuning" required to meet individual patient needs, pathway documentation is better suited to computerized than to manual systems. In addition, a pathway lists many tasks that are documented routinely, and transcription of this list onto a medical record document via computer can make the documentation process faster, easier, and more complete.[7] Some benefits of a computerized pathway documentation system include:

- Improved capability to make pathway changes to account for preexisting patient conditions
- Ease in changing pathway content, course, and/or time frames based on patient's response to treatment, an action sometimes referred to as "detours" or "extensions"
- Improved pathway accessibility to all disciplines, even when the patient is off the unit
- Enhanced potential to share information between outpatient and inpatient settings
- Improved pathway legibility when individualized to meet patient needs
- Ease of variance documentation and data collection

A disadvantage of computerized clinical path documentation systems is the need for computer skills, which may require extensive staff training. In settings where paper systems are still in place, resistance to change, availability of financial and time resources, and projected outcomes improvement must be weighed against converting from a manual to a computerized system.

Risk and Liability Considerations

The primary function of the medical record is to chronicle those facts on which diagnosis and treatment are based. Detailed descriptions of a patient's condition and the clinician's response to recorded observations demonstrate the thought process (or rationale) behind the delivery of care. In addition, a well-documented record can help protect a facility against liability or, in the event of litigation or charges, help document the medical events in question. Because of the level of detail required in medical record documentation, however, it is often impractical for health care providers to document everything. Consequently, they record only what they remember (when charting at the end of a shift or a procedure, for instance) or what they judge to be important.

The medical record is also a vital tool used to communicate patient information among health care professionals. The goals, then, for incorporating clinical paths into the chart are to minimize recording time, to describe clearly and concisely the patient's condition, and to provide a complete picture of the patient's progress and care plan.

Hospital Case Management lists 10 key questions to ask when evaluating critical paths for legal and risk management purposes:[8]

1. Does the path meet patient record requirements as set by state law or other governmental or accrediting organizations?

2. Is there complete patient identification on each page?
3. Does the critical path serve as a documentation enhancement rather than as a substitute for care documentation?
4. Are entries, treatments, and observations as detailed on the critical path initialed, timed, and dated?
5. When stated intervention does not occur, has the reason been evaluated and the variance noted and explained?
6. Does the hospital have policies and procedures governing pathway use, including accurate and timely completion of critical paths and delineation of who may make entries?
7. Are the critical paths developed to ensure that standardized orders do not replace appropriate medical judgment?
8. Have attending and consulting physicians specifically given their approval for use of the pathways for each individual patient?
9. Has the hospital's risk manager and/or legal counsel reviewed the paths prior to use?
10. Do the critical pathways cover only standard diagnoses?

Potential liability concerns about path-based patient care need to be addressed during the initial orientation of those who will use the paths. This can be done through educational sessions attended by the medical staff and the hospital's legal representative. It should be emphasized that pathways do not represent standing orders and that medical judgment and decision making still must dictate what is appropriate for the individual patient. Pathways are descriptors of the accepted *standards* of practice and are the foundation for identifying desired outcomes. *They do not replace critical and informed thinking.* Based on a patient's medical condition, changes may be made in pathways as deemed appropriate by caregivers.

In a litigious health care climate, physicians' concerns regarding incorporating clinical paths into the permanent record center on the following theme: "If the pathway says I should do *X,* and *X* doesn't get done, will I be sued if the outcome isn't to the patient's satisfaction?" It is important to understand that the pathway is an outline of steps, not the standard of care (in a court of law, the standard of care is established by expert testimony). The standard of care is what a *reasonably prudent* practitioner would do in the same or similar circumstances.

A specific pathway should reflect the profession's best thinking, but guidelines do not set the standard. Litigation poses a threat only if the standard of care is violated and patient injury (including death) is the result. Again, the health care profession, not the pathway, sets the standard of care; whether the standard is violated is a matter of professional opinion. Any care that departs from the pathway should do so for a reason based on the patient's condition—a reason that should be documented clearly in the record. Because pathways outline the important elements of care, omissions are less likely and, therefore, patient care should be enhanced and the likelihood of litigation minimized.

To avoid the possibility that a pathway might be used by a plaintiff's attorney against the facility, care should be taken to create paths that can be met realistically. It is important for practitioners to identify the patient care that they believe to be appropriate at the time and that they have the ability and capacity to deliver. Pathways are not wish lists for enhanced resources; they must be achievable with existing resources.

The ability to identify the pathway that existed in a given time period is critical: An organization's ability to identify the pathway in effect *during a specific time frame* affects its liability. Because standards of patient care may change over time, pathways are subject to revision. A coding system should be developed to identify the period during which a particular pathway was in use. One such system uses a code that includes the DRG, the unique number assigned to that pathway, and a third number to designate the current revision. (See figure 3-2.) This code is printed on the pathway.

It cannot be overemphasized that the use of clinical pathways does not eliminate the need for practitioners to apply critical thinking or skilled decision making. Pathways should make the documentation of care a more precise process and guide practitioners to a more careful description of the care provided.

Documentation Action Strategy

Providing a complete description of care delivered and patient responses is required of all health care professionals. Meeting this mandate consumes a significant amount of time for all disciplines, regardless of whether they succeed in recording all appropriate information. A system that incorporates expected patient outcome into routine treatments, procedures, and interventions as outlined on a clinical path time line has the potential to reduce the documentation burden for all disciplines.

To create a documentation system that integrates pathways, it is important to get users involved in the planning phase. Step 1 in achieving this is to *form a steering committee* composed of representatives from all identified user groups. Users such as medical records and risk management personnel, as well as other nonclinical health care team members, should not be overlooked. The committee should get a comprehensive look at the facility's current documentation strategy so as to successfully enhance the quality and completeness of care documentation.

In step 2, members *identify the documentation requirements and preferences of their respective groups*. This examination should include the definition of goals for each discipline's documentation system and the attributes of an ideal system. For example, the documentation system for the nursing staff should accomplish the following goals:

- Demonstrate the relationship of care to patient outcomes
- Work efficiently
- Avoid interfering with the time needed for patient care activities
- Meet regulatory standards review
- Provide for easy and prompt retrieval of data

The factors cited at the beginning of this chapter (accessibility, a multidisciplinary format, absence of duplication, predetermined plans) should also be addressed in committee deliberations.

Once the desired system components have been agreed upon, a *draft of the suggested documentation format* should be made (step 3). The steering committee should review this draft with their colleagues and incorporate their feedback into a final plan. Because changing a familiar documentation system can generate feelings of discomfort and mistrust, future users must be convinced of the potential benefits a new system can offer. Consensus by all users should be arrived at prior to implementation.

Step 4 involves *pilot testing the documentation system* in several areas with different patient populations to ensure that the system applies to all patient types. Step 5 is to *evaluate the pilot system* to ensure compliance and to identify strong and weak points. A time study should be performed before and after the pilot system is introduced.

In step 6, *making corrections and revisions*, changes are made as needed to adhere to requirements and regulations and to capitalize on any progress made during the pilot test. All involved staff should give input to this step.

Finally, in step 7, *user training and orientation* should be initiated. This ensures that users appreciate the productivity improvements possible with clinical pathways.

Figure 3-2. Clinical Path Codes

Thoracic (4C/TICU)

Pathway	Code	Dates in use	Code	Dates in use	Code	Dates in use	Code	Dates in use	Code	Dates in use	Code	Dates in use
DRG 107 Coronary Artery Bypass Graft												
Uncomplicated Coronary Artery Bypass Graft	107.1.1	1/16/91 →2/18/91	107.1.2	2/18/91 →7/15/91	107.1.3	7/15/91 →1/1/92	107.1.4	1/1/92 →present				
DRG 105 Heart Valve Surgery Procedures												
Mitral valve replacement (prosthetic)/or repair	105.1.1	8/5/91 →2/1/92	105.1.2	2/1/92 →present								
DRG 105												
AICD generator with leads and patches	105.3.1	4/1/91 →8/5/91	105.3.2	8/5/91 →present								
DRG 155												
Esophagectomy with gastric pull-through	155.1.1	4/1/91 →10/30/92	155.1.2	10/30/92 →5/1/93	155.1.3	5/1/93 →present						
Repair of hiatal hernia	155.4.1	4/1/91 →10/30/92	155.4.2	10/30/92 →present								
DRG 075												
Lobectomy	075.1.1	4/1/91 →2/1/92	075.1.2	2/1/92 →10/30/92	075.1.3	10/30/92 →present						
Lung bx	075.3.1	2/1/92 →10/30/92	075.3.2	10/30/92 →present								
Lung wedge resection	075.2.1	4/1/91 →2/1/92	075.2.2	2/1/92 →10/30/92	075.2.3	10/30/92 →present						

Representatives from all disciplines that will use the pathways should be apprised of the system's benefits and of the findings of the efficiency study performed during pilot testing. In addition to generating enthusiasm for the new system, effective end-user education increases the likelihood that path-based treatment will positively enhance the patient care experience. These seven steps are listed in figure 3-3.

Conclusion

Efficient management of health care information has the potential to improve patient outcomes. By eliminating duplicative documentation and enhancing communication among all disciplines, the health care team can concentrate on patient outcomes or on planning alternative strategies for individual problems or needs.

The issues discussed in this chapter can influence the success or failure of the clinical path documentation system. Problems can be avoided, or at least minimized, if consideration is given to these issues early in the pathway planning phase so that an efficient and effective system is in place when paths are introduced.

Figure 3-3. Seven-Step Plan for Documentation Strategy Evaluation

Step 1.	Form steering committee.
Step 2.	Identify documentation requirements and preferences.
Step 3.	Draft documentation format.
Step 4.	Pilot test documentation system.
Step 5.	Evaluate pilot.
Step 6.	Correct problems and make revisions.
Step 7.	Educate users.

References

1. Joint Commission on Accreditation of Healthcare Organizations. *1993 Accreditation Manual for Hospitals.* Vols. I and II. Oakbrook Terrace, IL: JCAHO, 1992.

2. Wood, R. G., Bailey, N. O., and Tilkemeier, D. Managed care: the missing link in quality improvement. *Journal of Nursing Care Quality* 6(4):55–65, 1992.

3. University of Michigan Medical Center, 8B Coordinated Care Committee. Ann Arbor, Feb. 1993.

4. Zander, K. Quantifying, managing, and improving quality. Part II: the collaborative management of quality care. *The New Definition* 7(4):1–2, 1992.

5. Coffey, R. J., Richards, J. S., Remmert, C. S., LeRoy, S. S., Schoville, R. R., and Baldwin, P. J. An introduction to critical paths. *Quality Management in Health Care* 1:45–54, 1992.

6. Mosher, C., Cronk, P., Kidd, A., McCormick, P., Stockton, S., and Sulla, C. Upgrading practice with critical pathways. *American Journal of Nursing* 92(1):41–44, 1992.

7. Ashworth, G. B., and Aubrey, C. Collaborative care documentation by exception system. *Proceedings of the Annual Symposium on Computer Applications in Medical Care,* pp. 109–13, 1992.

8. American Health Consultants. Critical paths as legal documentation: the dangerous waters of charting by exception. *Hospital Case Management* 1(3):58–60, 1993.

CHAPTER FOUR

The Interface of Clinical Paths and Practice Parameters

John T. Kelly, MD, PhD

As private and public efforts to reform health care delivery continue to accelerate, strategies to evaluate and improve quality and utilization have become increasingly important.[1] Widespread support for quality improvement and effective utilization management has escalated the use of tools such as clinical paths and practice parameters to assist clinical decision making.[2-4] *Practice parameters,* strategies for patient management developed to assist in clinical decision making, are also called *practice guidelines* and *clinical policies.* Practice parameters is the term used throughout this chapter.

The American Medical Association (AMA) and the American Hospital Association (AHA) have promoted the use of practice parameters.[5,6] The Joint Commission on Accreditation of Healthcare Organizations (JCAHO) encourages accredited institutions to use practice parameters as part of their quality improvement efforts.[7] The federal Agency for Health Care Policy and Research (AHCPR) has facilitated the development, dissemination, and implementation of practice parameters.[8] The Health Care Financing Administration (HCFA) uses practice parameters as a central component of its Health Care Quality Improvement Initiative.[9] State legislation and many federal and state legislative proposals promote the use of practice parameters. Numerous managed care organizations, health maintenance organizations, and other delivery systems also use practice parameters.[10,11]

This chapter discusses the use of practice parameters in quality improvement and utilization management strategies, including the development of clinical paths, and addresses issues related to the development and implementation of practice parameters and clinical paths. This discussion emphasizes that scientifically sound and clinically relevant practice parameters provide a useful foundation for the development of clinical paths.

Incorporation of Practice Parameters into Clinical Path Development

Effective quality improvement and utilization management are complex activities that require expert clinical knowledge regarding the appropriate management of specific conditions. Practice parameters, developed by respected organizations and based on reliable scientific information and expert clinical judgment, are valuable tools to assist clinical decision making.[12] By incorporating practice parameters into quality improvement strategies, including the design of clinical paths, physicians and other health care professionals can enhance their performance and improve care delivery.[13] The AMA, whose policy position is that medical care should be based on accepted principles of medical service and the skillful and appropriate use of health professionals and technology, also promotes the following principles:[14]

- The criteria for assessing quality of care should be developed and agreed on by the professionals whose performance will be reviewed.
- Practitioners should be assisted in improving their knowledge and in modifying their practice patterns where indicated.

In keeping with these principles, the AMA has provided guidance in using practice parameters in quality assessment, quality assurance, and quality improvement programs.[15] These strategies have application in the development of clinical paths and play an increasingly important role in the quality programs of many health care organizations. The eight steps listed below, originally proposed by the AMA for incorporating practice parameters into quality programs, are relevant to the integration of practice parameters into the design of clinical paths:

1. Issue identification
2. Issue refinement
3. Identification of relevant practice parameters
4. Evaluation of practice parameters
5. Modification of practice parameters
6. Dissemination/implementation of practice parameters
7. Evaluation and feedback
8. Periodic review of practice parameter recommendations

When appropriate, quality programs may establish working groups or small task forces of physicians and other health professionals to examine specific topic areas. To illustrate the interrelationships between practice parameters and clinical paths and the implications of each of the eight steps, the activities of a typical cardiology task force (comprised of physicians involved in managing cardiac patients and also nurses, pharmacists, and other health professionals) are described in the following sections.

Step 1: Issue Identification

The first step in implementing practice parameters in quality-related activities, including the design of clinical paths, involves the identification of specific clinical areas of interest. These clinical issues may emerge from the concerns of physicians or other health care professionals. Prioritization of clinical areas for quality assessment and quality improvement may be based on many different factors, such as:

- Availability of relevant and high-quality practice parameters
- Publication of new or updated practice parameters
- Improvements in the methods of diagnosis and treatment that are expected to benefit a significant number of individuals
- Significant and unexplained variances in current practice patterns
- Concerns over quality, utilization, or risk management issues
- Utilized services involving relatively substantial expenditures
- Activities and requirements of regulatory, accrediting, payer, and other oversight organizations

- Legislative issues and requirements
- Professional liability considerations

The task force is aware of a wide variety of potential cardiac care issues that may be addressed through the activities of their quality program. Task force members consider whether they should examine the indications for specific services or procedures, service delivery processes, or patient outcomes information.

Step 2: Issue Refinement

To refine the specific clinical issues to be addressed and identify those that best meet the quality program's objectives, the cardiology task force prioritizes their quality efforts to ensure that specific cardiovascular services and procedures are being provided appropriately, effectively, and efficiently. Members of the task force review the cardiovascular services provided in their institution; these services include acute myocardial infarction (AMI) management, cardiac pacemaker implantation, cardiac catheterization, percutaneous transluminal coronary angioplasty (PTCA), and coronary artery bypass graft (CABG).

Step 3: Identification of Relevant Practice Parameters

In carrying out step 3, the task force relies on its familiarity with the AMA's *Directory of Practice Parameters*,[16] which lists approximately 1,600 parameters developed by national physicians' organizations and other bodies such as the AHCPR and the National Institutes of Health. Members also consult the AMA's *Practice Parameters Update*,[17] which lists recently completed practice parameters. By examining these publications the cardiology task force identifies in excess of 100 cardiovascular practice parameters sponsored by over a dozen different organizations. A broad array of issues, ranging from prevention of coronary artery disease to recommendations for specific procedures (such as PTCA and CABG) are included in these practice parameters. Several practice parameters, developed by the American College of Cardiology and the American Heart Association (ACC/AHA), focus on specific cardiovascular services and procedures. (See figure 4-1.)

The cardiovascular topics addressed by existing practice parameters are reviewed by the task force to see whether they suggest clinical issues that might be addressed. The group also considers newly published practice parameters, because these may suggest a need for further study of specific cardiology services and practices in their institution.

After thorough deliberation, the cardiology task force agrees to focus their quality improvement efforts on the management of acute myocardial infarction and to develop clinical paths for this patient population. Of the more than 100 cardiovascular practice parameters identified in the *Directory of Practice Parameters* and

Figure 4-1. Examples of Cardiovascular Practice Parameters

- Guidelines for the early management of patients with acute myocardial infarction
- In-hospital cardiac monitoring of adults for detection of arrhythmia
- Interventional catheterization procedures and cardiothoracic surgical consultation
- Guidelines for implantation of cardiac pacemakers and antiarrhythmia devices
- Guidelines for coronary angiography

Reprinted, with permission, from M. C. Toepp and N. Kuznets, editors. *Directory of Practice Parameters: Titles, Sources, and Updates.* Chicago: American Medical Association, 1993.

Practice Parameters Update, the task force identifies six practice parameters that address the management of acute myocardial infarction. (See figure 4-2.)

Step 4: Evaluation of Practice Parameters

Once the practice parameters that refer to the clinical area of interest are identified, they are collected and evaluated. The task force compares the six practice parameters on acute myocardial infarction and, after close scrutiny, selects those most relevant to the issues they wish to address. At this point, the identified practice parameters are disseminated to, and reviewed by, the physicians and other health care professionals who will use the practice parameters. This process provides important opportunities for input to the cardiology task force.

Step 5: Selection and Modification of Practice Parameters

The selected practice parameters are used to develop clinical paths for acute myocardial infarction. Recommendations in the selected practice parameters may be suitable for inclusion without change in the clinical path. Alternatively, the recommendations may need to be modified to accommodate relevant scientific or clinical information or to address factors specific to their institution. Examples of such information are recently published scientific articles or the clinical experiences of the physicians and other health care professionals who will use the clinical path to guide their care of patients. Practice parameters endorsed by respected local physicians are more likely to gain acceptance among physicians and other health care professionals.[18] Modifications in the practice parameters may be necessary to form a consensus on appropriate medical practice.

Although the management of acute myocardial infarction is the main topic of the six practice parameters selected, many issues within that subject are addressed by these practice parameters. For example, the ACC/AHA practice parameter on the early management of patients with acute myocardial infarction addresses:[19]

- Use of analgesia, atropine, anticoagulants and platelet inhibitory agents, beta blockers, calcium channel blockers, countershock, lidocaine, nitroglycerin, oxygen, pacemakers, and thrombolytic therapy
- Detection and quantification of acute myocardial infarction
- Follow-up therapy after thrombolysis

Figure 4-2. Practice Parameters on Acute Myocardial Infarction

Practice Parameter	Sponsoring Organization
Early care for the acute coronary suspect	American College of Cardiology
Emergency department: rapid identification and treatment of patients with acute myocardial infarction	National Institutes of Health/ National Heart, Lung, and Blood Institute
Evaluation of patients after recent acute myocardial infarction	American College of Physicians
Guidelines for early management of patients with acute myocardial infarction	American College of Cardiology/ American Heart Association
Serum enzyme assays in the diagnosis of acute myocardial infarction, recommendations based on a quantitative analysis	American College of Physicians
Thrombolysis for evolving myocardial infarction	American College of Physicians

Reprinted, with permission, from M. C. Toepp and N. Kuznets, editors. *Directory of Practice Parameters: Titles, Sources, and Updates.* Chicago: American Medical Association, 1993.

- Indications for monitoring, percutaneous transluminal coronary angioplasty, and surgical intervention
- Management of pump failure and shock
- Predischarge evaluation
- Transportation

All of these issues are important in managing patients with acute myocardial infarctions and, at some level of detail, will be incorporated into their clinical path; however, the task force chooses to address the appropriate use of thrombolytics in greater detail. This leads to their evaluation of the indications and contraindications for thrombolytic therapy listed in the ACC/AHA practice parameter as a basic framework from which to establish recommendations. The task force is especially interested in the ACC/AHA's list of absolute and relative contraindications to thrombolytic therapy. (See figure 4-3.) Upon reviewing the ACC/AHA practice parameter, the task force accepts the recommendations. The task force also endorsed the National Institutes of Health's and the National Heart, Lung, and Blood Institute's (NIH's/NHLBI's) recommendation that eligible patients receive thrombolytic therapy within 30 to 60 minutes of arrival at the emergency department.[20] The task force carefully reviewed the NIH/NHLBI analysis of common causes of delay in treatment and suggested protocols for management of the AMI patient in the emergency department.

Step 6: Dissemination/Implementation of Practice Parameters and Clinical Paths

To be incorporated effectively into patient management practices, the recommendations of specific practice parameters, as modified by local physicians and other health care professionals, must be disseminated appropriately. Strategies such as educational programs, correspondence (memos, bulletins), and dissemination of articles from peer reviewed journals can be effective. The recommendations in the practice parameters can be used to develop algorithms to assist in clinical decision making.[21] Clinical paths

Figure 4-3. ACC/AHA Contraindications to Thrombolytic Therapy

Absolute Contraindications:

1. Acute internal bleeding
2. Suspected aortic dissection
3. Prolonged or traumatic cardiopulmonary resuscitation
4. Recent head trauma or known intracranial neoplasm
5. Diabetic hemorrhagic retinopathy or other hemorrhagic ophthalmic condition
6. Pregnancy
7. Previous allergic reaction to the thrombolytic agent
8. Recorded blood pressure greater than 200/120 mm Hg
9. History of cerebrovascular accident known to be hemorrhagic

Relative Contraindications:

1. Recent trauma or surgery more than 2 weeks earlier (trauma or surgery more recent than 2 weeks, which could be a source of rebleeding, is an absolute contraindication)
2. History of chronic severe hypertension with or without drug therapy
3. Active peptic ulcer
4. History of cerebrovascular accident
5. Known bleeding diathesis or current use of anticoagulants
6. Significant liver dysfunction
7. Prior exposure to streptokinase or APSAC

Reprinted, with permission, from the American College of Cardiology and the American Heart Association (ACC/AHA). Guidelines for the early management of patients with acute myocardial infarction. *Journal of the American College of Cardiology* 16:249–92, 1990.

can be based on practice parameter recommendations. Incorporation of practice parameters into the design of clinical paths provides an effective mechanism to disseminate recommendations and facilitate their implementation. The cardiology task force chooses to disseminate the ACC/AHA and NIH/NHLBI practice parameter recommendations relevant to use of thrombolytics by developing a clinical path designed for patients with acute myocardial infarction.

Clinical paths may address all recommendations included in relevant practice parameters, or they may focus only on selected recommendations. Clinical paths may outline the general strategy for patient management; specify particular diagnostic and therapeutic interventions; identify the specific sequence or timing (for example, day, shift, hour) for certain diagnostic and therapeutic services; or address issues such as physician and nursing responsibilities, roles of other health professionals, transfer and discharge criteria, and documentation. As emphasized throughout this book, physicians, nurses, and others who will be guided by the clinical paths should be involved in their development prior to implementation.

In developing the clinical path for myocardial infarction, the cardiology task force supplements the ACC/AHA and NIH/NHLBI practice parameter recommendations, because the practice parameters do not address clinical path issues that are institution specific. For example, the ACC/AHA practice parameter does not address the optimal sequence and timing of specific diagnostic tests (such as electrocardiogram, cardiac enzymes, and chest X ray); where certain services should be provided (such as emergency department or coronary care unit); the roles and responsibilities of various personnel (such as emergency physician, admitting physician, consulting physicians, emergency department and coronary care unit nurses, pharmacist, and ancillary personnel); the use of standardized orders and protocols; or documentation requirements. To assist in defining these institution-specific issues, the task force reviews recommendations developed by allied groups such as the American Nurses' Association, the American Society of Hospital Pharmacists, the Emergency Nurses Association, and the Society of Critical Care Medicine. The cardiology task force also reviews clinical paths developed by other organizations and identifies approaches to patient management that can be adapted for use at their institution.

The clinical path for patients admitted for management of myocardial infarction ultimately contains a combination of practice parameter recommendations and facility-specific recommendations. (See figure 4-4.) Because the cardiology task force chose to focus on thrombolytic therapy, the clinical path includes detailed criteria for appropriate use of this intervention. Other elements of care in the clinical path are outlined with less specificity.

Step 7: Evaluation and Feedback

After dissemination and implementation of the clinical path, a data-collection system is established to provide information on past, current, and evolving practice patterns for managing patients with acute myocardial infarction. The cardiology task group provides input to the design of the data-collection system, ensuring that the data items to be gathered are relevant to clinical practice. The data-collection system helps clinicians evaluate their performance in relation to the practice parameter recommendations incorporated into the clinical path. Data collection may focus on variance reporting performed concurrently during each patient's hospitalization. Data collection and analysis may also focus on retrospective evaluation of the consistency between aggregate practice patterns and the recommendations in the clinical path. By identifying the frequency of specific variances from the clinical path recommendations that relate to thrombolysis, the task force can assess actual practice within their institution and develop strategies to modify practice as needed.

Figure 4-4. Sample Myocardial Infarction Clinical Path (first two days)

	Emergency Room	Coronary Care Unit Day One	Coronary Care Unit Day Two
Tests	Electrocardiogram Initial CPK with isoenzymes Initiate laboratory studies on standing orders PTT SaO_2 Portable chest X ray	CPK q 8 hr × 2, isoenzymes if CPK > 100 Electrocardiogram with chest pain Consider echocardiogram	Electrocardiogram Consider stress electrocardiogram Consider cardiac catheterization SaO_2 (room air)
Treatments	O_2 2–4 liters per minute Cardiac monitor	O_2 2–4 liters per minute Cardiac monitor	Cardiac monitor O_2 PRN if pain free and no signs of congestive heart failure and SaO_2 > 92 Consider nicotine patch if patient is smoker
Medications	Sublingual nitroglycerin Intravenous morphine sulfate (prn) 1 enteric coated aspirin IV nitroglycerin drip (if pain not controlled)	Intravenous morphine sulfate (prn) B-blocker Antianxiety agent (prn) IV Heparin SQ/IV ASA 1 per day IV nitroglycerin drip (if pain not controlled) or nitropatch if pain free	Morphine sulfate (prn) B-blocker Antianxiety agent (prn) Heparin SQ/IV ASA 1 per day IV nitroglycerin drip (if pain not controlled) or nitropatch if pain free Hep lock
Treatment with Thrombolytic	Administer Streptokinase/TPA within 30–60 minutes according to protocol if no contraindications*		
Consults			Social Services Cardiac Rehabilitation
Nutritional Care		4 gm low sodium, low cholesterol, low-fat diet as tolerated	4 gm low sodium, low cholesterol, low-fat diet as tolerated
Teaching	Teach patient to report *any* chest pain	Orient to CCU Reinforce reporting of any chest pain	Reinforce reporting of any chest pain Begin cardiac teaching protocol Show cardiac cath video to patients who may be candidates for catheterization
Documentation	Document indications for and contraindications for thrombolysis in progress notes		

* Contraindications listed on thrombolytic administration protocol form.

(Presented as a sample clinical path; not endorsed by the AMA or intended for use without review, modification, and acceptance.)

In analyzing variances from the practice parameters embodied in the clinical path for patients with myocardial infarction, the cardiology task force discovers that thrombolytic therapy often diverges from the recommendations in the ACC/AHA and NIH/NHLBI practice parameters and that physician-specific and institution-specific factors cause these variations. For example, many patients for whom thrombolytics are indicated do not have timely physician orders for such therapy; other patients for whom thrombolytics are ordered do not receive treatment in a timely manner owing to faulty internal processes (for example, inadequate coordination among the emergency department, coronary care unit, laboratory, and pharmacy). The task force also discovers that physicians' documentation of indications and contraindications for the use of thrombolytics are not recorded in patients' medical records in a consistent fashion. The task force shares these findings (along with the recommendations in the ACC/AHA and NIH/NHLBI practice parameters and the clinical path) with relevant physicians and other health care personnel to improve compliance with the ACC/AHA and NIH/NHLBI practice parameters and the clinical path.

More specifically, in the management of acute myocardial infarction patients, the task force evaluated data on the time intervals from arrival at the emergency department to the initial ECG, from the ECG to the decision to treat with thrombolytic therapy, and from the decision to treat with thrombolytic therapy to the start of drug infusion, and shared these data with key health care professionals. Then the task force used the following questions proposed by the NIH/NHLBI practice parameter to evaluate the care of acute myocardial infarction patients in the emergency department:[22]

- How does a patient who the prehospital care provider or triage nurse suspects may be having an AMI come to the attention of the treating physician?
- What is the process and how swift is the process for getting the ECG and/or its interpretation to the treating physician?
- Who has the authority to order thrombolytic therapy for an emergency department patient having an ST-segment-evaluation AMI?
- Is thrombolytic therapy routinely administered in the emergency department or deferred to the coronary care unit?

Next, the task force developed specific recommendations regarding the roles and responsibilities of the medical, nursing, technical support, and pharmacy staffs. The task force made recommendations on the resources and support needed from the hospital administration. Then the task force developed clinical paths, protocols, and standing orders to facilitate implementation of its recommendation to reduce delays in the timing of administration of thrombolytics. The task force subsequently monitored the impact of the clinical path and related efforts on management of acute myocardial infarction patients, and used these data to improve the clinical paths. The task force also collected and disseminated data on the performance of individual physicians and other health care professionals, and distributed data on the performance of other institutions which had instituted similar clinical paths related to the management of acute myocardial infarction patients.

Using other clinical path variance data, and with input from physicians and other caregivers, the task force identifies additional opportunities for improvement in clinical decision making and patient management. With the objective of improving the quality, utilization, and efficiency of services provided to patients with acute myocardial infarction, the task force implements specific strategies and proposals to make other changes needed to enhance compliance with other suggestions in the clinical path, improve clinical outcomes, decrease unnecessary resource consumption, and improve patient satisfaction.

Step 8: Periodic Review of Practice Parameters

The cardiology task force does not disband after initial development and implementation of the clinical path. Practice parameter recommendations included in the clinical path, as well as other suggested clinical and service issues, should be reviewed periodically and modified as needed to maintain their relevance to current practice. Modifications to the clinical path may be made whenever one or more of the following conditions occurs:

- Medical knowledge advances
- New practice parameters are developed
- Local conditions change to create opportunities for more effective and efficient patient management strategies
- Improved clinical paths are identified

Physicians and other health care professionals who will use the practice parameters and clinical paths should be actively involved in their review and modification.[23] The cardiology task force and other interested professionals periodically review variance data and continually improve the processes of care for patients admitted with acute myocardial infarction.

Benefits and Caveats

Two key benefits emerge from activities related to the development and implementation of practice parameters and clinical paths: identification of key clinical decision points along the management continuum for specific patient types and valuable information regarding the sequence and timing of specific services and processes. Compilation and analysis of such information provide an essential foundation for strategies to improve clinical decision making and clinical processes. As illustrated in the following examples, physicians, other health care professionals, and patients derive benefit from the development and implementation of practice parameters, which result in the following improvements:

- Performance of fewer cesarean sections, which results in a decrease in C-section rates with no increase in fetal or maternal morbidity or mortality[24]
- Proper timing of prophylactic antibiotic administration, which correlates with a 50 percent decline in incidence of deep postoperative wound infections[25]
- Appropriate patient monitoring during general anesthesia, which results in a marked reduction in the incidence of hypoxic injuries[26]
- Proper use of cardiac pacemakers, which results in a significant decline in pacemaker utilization rates[27]
- Appropriate and efficient patient transfer from coronary care units and intensive care units, which shows improved utilization of these special care areas[28-30]

Similar benefits have been identified with the use of clinical paths, many of which are detailed in subsequent chapters. Such successes have encouraged the widespread use of practice parameters and clinical paths.[31]

The availability and utility of practice parameters for the development of clinical paths vary with the specific clinical areas of interest. More than 1,600 practice parameters are currently available from national organizations, and hundreds more practice parameters are developed annually. Many other practice parameters can be obtained from regional and local organizations. However, there are many clinical areas for which practice parameters have yet to be developed.

Considerable variation exists among practice parameters in the level of detail they contain. Some offer highly specific clinical recommendations, whereas others present broad strategies with limited attention to the step-by-step details of individual patient management. Consequently, practice parameters may be either unavailable or too broad to assist physicians and other clinicians in the development of clinical paths, which ordinarily focus on highly specific clinical and service aspects of patient management.

Some health care professionals may be concerned that practice parameters and clinical paths will increase their exposure to professional liability or malpractice claims. Physicians in particular share concern that they will be automatically liable if, for legitimate medical reasons, they choose to digress from relevant practice parameters or clinical paths and subsequently an undesirable outcome occurs. Comprehensive analysis of the legal implications of practice parameters indicates that these concerns are unfounded.[32] Practice parameters and clinical paths do not create new liabilities for physicians; instead, they may serve to help physicians control their liability risks.

The fact that medical practice varies from a practice parameter or clinical path does not, by itself, establish physician (or other health care professional) failure to meet the required standard of care. Generally, relevant practice parameters and clinical paths will serve only as evidence of the standard of care, not as an absolute or inflexible mandate that must be followed in all circumstances. Most practice parameters and clinical paths are unlikely to become absolute standards because the judicial system does not apply predetermined standards of care in medical malpractice litigation. Standards are determined on a case-by-case basis pursuant to competing evidence introduced by each litigant as to what the applicable standard of care should be.[33]

Because practice parameters and the clinical paths based on them may become the focal point in a professional liability or malpractice proceeding, physicians must appropriately document their reasons for variances in a particular case. A timely statement of reasons noted in the patient's medical record can provide persuasive evidence that any deviation from the practice parameter or clinical path was consistent with the exercise of due care that prevailed at the time. A medical record notation explaining why a particular practice parameter or clinical path was followed is also helpful in explaining retrospectively how a patient was managed.

Practice parameters and clinical paths often address the roles and responsibilities of various health care professionals, including physicians, nurses, laboratory personnel, and others.[34] Clinical path development strategies that include adequate input from those caregivers who will be affected by the recommendations are more likely to meet with acceptance and achieve success than development strategies without similar input. Physicians and other clinicians are less likely to endorse practice parameters and clinical paths if they have not been involved in their development or review, do not accept their recommendations, or do not believe their use will improve patient care.

Given that there often may be more than one way to manage individual patients or a specific clinical issue, practice parameters and clinical paths, as indicated earlier, must allow adequate flexibility for physicians, other health care professionals, and patients. Practice parameters and clinical paths should be an aid to, not a replacement for, responsible decision making concerning optimal ways to meet the needs of individual patients.

Strategies to increase effectiveness or efficiency in managing patients might justify certain limitations of choice in the recommendations in practice parameters or clinical paths. However, arbitrary elimination of reasonable clinical options may not be acceptable to physicians, other health care professionals, or patients. Patients with similar clinical problems often differ significantly from each other due to the presence of other clinical issues. "One-size-fits-all" approaches or highly prescriptive strategies, which rigidly delineate the exact order and time of specific interventions, may not be as effective as practice parameters and clinical paths, which allow for—and even promote—appropriate flexibility. Physicians and other health care professionals should also be informed if resource use and other financial considerations were used in the development of specific recommendations for patient management and how such issues influenced specific aspects of the practice parameters or clinical paths.

Conclusion

Successful strategies to improve the quality and utilization of health care services must take into account relevant scientific information and clinical experience, identify optimal ways to manage individual patients, and achieve acceptance by physicians, other health care professionals, and patients. Properly developed practice parameters and clinical paths, modified as necessary to meet institution-specific and patient-specific needs, are important mechanisms to facilitate these goals.[35,36] Practice parameters provide a valuable scientific foundation for the development of clinical paths. Moreover, clinical paths provide an effective mechanism to facilitate dissemination and implementation of the recommendations in practice parameters and to improve patient management. Numerous challenges remain in the development of practice parameters and clinical paths, the adaptation of practice parameters and clinical paths to individualized patient management, and the maintenance of appropriate clinical flexibility. Nevertheless, practice parameters and clinical paths are promising approaches in the design of effective methods to improve the quality and utilization of health care services.

References

1. Chassin, M. R. The missing ingredient in health reform: quality of care. *JAMA* 270:377–78, 1993.

2. Woolf, S. H. Practice guidelines: a new reality in medicine; I: recent developments. *Archives of Internal Medicine* 150:1811–18, 1990.

3. Woolf, S. H. Practice guidelines: a new reality in medicine; II: methods of developing guidelines. *Archives of Internal Medicine* 152:946, 1992.

4. Woolf, S. H. Practice guidelines: a new reality in medicine; III: impact on patient care. *Archives of Internal Medicine* 153:2646, 1993.

5. Kelly, J. T., and Toepp, M. C. Practice parameters: development, evaluation, dissemination and implementation. *Quality Review Bulletin* 18:405–9, 1992.

6. American Hospital Association. *CPG Strategies: Putting Guidelines into Practice.* Chicago: AHA, 1992.

7. Joint Commission on Accreditation of Healthcare Organizations. *1994 Accreditation Manual for Hospitals.* Oakbrook Terrace, IL: JCAHO, 1993.

8. Van Amringe, M., and Shannon, T. E. Awareness, assimilation, and adoption: the challenge of effective dissemination and the first AHCPR-sponsored guidelines. *Quality Review Bulletin* 18:397–404, 1992.

9. Jencks, S. F., and Wilensky, G. R. The health care quality improvement initiative: a new approach to quality assurance in Medicare. *JAMA* 268:900–903, 1992.

10. Gottlieb, L. K., Margolis, C. Z., and Schoenbaum, S. C. Clinical practice guidelines at an HMO: development and implementation in a quality improvement model. *Quality Review Bulletin* 16:80–86, 1990.

11. Coleman, R. J. Promoting quality through managed care. *American Journal of Medical Quality* 7:100–105, 1992.

12. Institute of Medicine, Committee on Clinical Practice Guidelines. *Guidelines for Clinical Practice: From Development to Use.* M. J. Field and K. N. Lohr, editors. Washington, DC: National Academy Press, 1992.

13. American Medical Association. *Using Practice Parameters in Quality Assessment, Quality Assurance, and Quality Improvement Programs.* Chicago: AMA, 1992.

14. American Medical Association. *Policy Compendium.* Chicago: AMA, 1993.

15. Toepp, M. C., and Kuznets, N., editors. *Directory of Practice Parameters: Titles, Sources, and Updates.* Chicago: American Medical Association, 1993.

16. Toepp and Kuznets.

17. American Medical Association. *Practice Parameters Update.* Chicago: AMA, 1993.

18. Lomas, J., Enkin, M., Anderson, G. M., and others. Opinion leaders vs. audit and feedback to implement practice guidelines. *JAMA* 265:2202-7, 1991.

19. American College of Cardiology and American Heart Association. Guidelines for early management of patients with acute myocardial infarction. *Journal of the American College of Cardiology* 16:249-92, 1990.

20. National Institutes of Health and National Heart, Lung, and Blood Institute (NIH/NHLBI). *Emergency Department: Rapid Identification and Treatment of Patients with Acute Myocardial Infarction.* Bethesda: NIH, 1993.

21. Hadorn, D. C., McCormick, K., and Diokno, A. An annotated algorithm approach to clinical guideline development. *JAMA* 267:3311-14, 1992.

22. NIH/NHLBI.

23. American Medical Association. *Implementing Practice Parameters on the Local, State, and Regional Level.* Chicago: AMA, 1993.

24. Myers, S. A., and Gleicher, N. A successful program to lower cesarean section rates. *New England Journal of Medicine* 319:1511-16, 1988.

25. Larsen, R. A., Evans, R. S., Burke, J. P., and others. Improved perioperative antibiotic use and reduced surgical wound infection through use of computer decision analysis. *Infection Control and Hospital Epidemiology* 10:316-20, 1989.

26. Pierce, E. C. The development of anesthesia guidelines and standards. *Quality Review Bulletin* 16:61-64, 1990.

27. Kelly, J. T., and Kellie, S. E. Appropriateness of medical care. *Archives of Pathology and Laboratory Medicine* 114:1119-21, 1125, 1990.

28. Weingarten, S., Ermann, B., Bolus, R., and others. Early "step-down" transfer of low-risk patients with chest pain: a controlled interventional trial. *Annals of Internal Medicine* 113:283-89, 1990.

29. Weingarten, S. R., Riedinger, M. S., Shinbane, J., and others. Triage practice guideline for patients hospitalized with congestive heart failure: improving the effectiveness of the coronary care unit. *American Journal of Medicine* 94:483-90, 1993.

30. Eagle, K. A., Mulley, A. G., Skates, S. J., and others. *JAMA* 264:992-97, 1990.

31. Lumdson, K., and Hagland, M. Mapping care. *Hospitals and Health Networks* 67(18):34-40, Sept. 20, 1993.

32. Johnson, K. B., Hirshfield, E. N., Ile, M. L., and others. *Legal Implications of Practice Parameters.* Chicago: American Medical Association, 1990.

33. Hirshfield, E. B. Should practice parameters be the standard of care in malpractice litigation? *JAMA* 266:2886-91, 1991.

34. Hoffman, P. A. Critical path method: an important tool for coordinating clinical care. *Quality Review Bulletin* 19:235-46, 1993.

35. American Medical Association. *Attributes to Guide the Development of Practice Parameters.* Chicago: AMA, 1990.

36. Spath, P. *Succeeding with Critical Paths.* Forest Grove, OR: Brown-Spath & Associates, 1993.

CHAPTER FIVE

The Interface of Clinical Paths and Continuous Quality Improvement

Robert J. Marder, MD

The interaction between development of clinical pathways and implementation of continuous quality improvement (CQI) methods is similar to the principles of wave mechanics. As two waves are about to cross paths, one of three things can happen, depending on the phase of each wave: If they cross at their peaks, they augment each other and make a doubly powerful wave; if they cross at their troughs, again they add to each other and make a doubly deep trough; however, if they cross during opposing phases—one at its peak and the other at its trough—they neutralize one another.

The catalyst for developing quality improvement (QI) programs and for formulating clinical pathways often comes from different driving factors. Quality improvement is driven by a long-term goal toward process improvement, a better understanding of systems, and better overall control of those systems.[1] Clinical path development is usually driven by a more immediate need for control of specific resources.[2] If these programs are viewed as separate and distinct, they can be like two waves meeting at their troughs, doubly draining institutional resources, or like waves in opposite phases, where little forward motion is achieved despite the presence of two powerful forces. If thought is put into coordinating and integrating these activities by identifying and building on the common goals of each, a doubly powerful force will develop that can move the organization forward toward the shore or, in this case, toward the objective(s).

This chapter discusses three issues: the commonalities of QI and clinical paths from both theoretical and practical standpoints; how that relationship fits with the performance improvement standards of the Joint Commission on Accreditation of Healthcare Organizations (JCAHO); and the physician's role in programs for clinical pathways and QI. Discussions show how QI and clinical paths are linked by the four principles of process selection, description, measurement, and reengineering. Each principle bears on the systems changes that underlie continuous quality improvement and continuous clinical path improvement.

Principles of Quality Improvement and Its Application to Clinical Paths

Quality improvement is built on the principle of understanding and controlling process variation through systems thinking.[3] Because QI originated in the manufacturing environment, many health care professionals initially did not see its relationship to patient care. The notions that all providers work within systems and that individual efforts are strongly affected by those systems is somewhat difficult for health care professionals, who are taught the importance of individual authority and responsibility. Traditionally, care providers have viewed the processes of patient care as being highly individualized.[4] Now they are learning that health care performance is improved through systems interaction, as represented by the following equation:

$$X \quad + \quad Y \quad + \quad XY \quad = \quad P$$

(individual)   (systems)   (interaction between   (performance)
individual and systems)

As QI principles were explored in the health care environment, it became increasingly clear that viewing how patients are cared for as a series of steps or processes does not diminish the patient–caregiver interactions in providing care.[5,6] It simply implies that some things are done routinely in the process of caring for patients. Seeking a better understanding of those routine aspects of patient care is another way of saying that caregivers will engage in *process analysis*.

QI Principles of Process Analysis

The QI component most strongly related to clinical pathways is process analysis. Four key principles of process analysis underlie most QI approaches: process selection, process description, process measurement, and process reengineering. These principles, discussed in the following sections, are summarized in figure 5-1.

Process Selection

The first step in analyzing processes, a step that may appear obvious, is to select the right processes for change. Principles of QI support the concept that the processes selected for improvement should be those that are *most important to the task(s) performed*, rather than those that are easily analyzed but less key to performance. For example, the main business of a copier manufacturing firm is to design and build copying equipment. Therefore, the firm would select key processes that relate to copier design, sales, and marketing as the first area in which to apply QI techniques. Although QI principles certainly also apply to other areas (such as how the personnel department operates), it clearly is not the area that would have the biggest impact on the company. Similarly, if the main business of health care is the care of patients, then

Figure 5-1. Four Key Principles of Process Analysis

Principle	Key Focus
1. Process selection	Picking the right processes to work on by focusing on processes most important to your mission, incorporating customer–supplier needs and expectations, and communicating shared vision
2. Process description	Understanding the process by describing its sequence, participants, and relationship to other processes
3. Process measurement	Applying measurement to the key outcomes and critical steps to determine the causes of variation
4. Process reengineering	Using the understanding of systematic causes of process error, inefficiency, and duplication to design better ways of doing things

it would appear that the key processes to select for improvement are those that have the most impact on patients.

An aspect inherent to key process selection is the understanding that limited resources preclude analyzing or "fixing" processes in all areas. Although it would be nice to understand and control every process, the reality is that doing so would create a diminishing return for the amount of time invested. Similarly, health care providers cannot develop a pathway for every disease or patient condition. Therefore, it is essential to prioritize the most important processes that would have the greatest impact on the organization.

Another aspect in key process selection is an understanding of customer–supplier relationships. The word *customer* is unpopular among many health care providers because they feel it diminishes the patient–provider relationship. Although QI does not require that parties in a relationship be referred to as "customers," it does require understanding that in a process there are two roles: receiver of goods or services (the customer) and provider of goods or services (the supplier). Knowing who the receivers/customers are and who the providers/suppliers are is critical in many aspects of process analysis, but it is particularly important in the initial key process selection. Obtaining input from those who receive the results of the process – the customers – is critical to knowing which processes are most important to them. In health care, customers primarily are thought to be patients, but they also include physicians, nurses, technologists, pharmacists, and others who receive information or materials from someone else in the organization in order to do their jobs. Obtaining input from those who perform the process is critical to understanding which processes stand to benefit most from improvement. This customer–supplier orientation is essential to viewing a job task as part of a system and identifying those processes that most influence the system.

A third aspect that drives process selection is *shared vision*,[7] which is defined by the question, "Who picks the key processes?" Upper management often determines the key processes without the benefit of detailed knowledge of how those processes affect their customers. That information is vested with those who interact with the customers on a daily basis. In other situations, either middle or lower managers might decide from their limited perspective to work on what is most bothersome *to them*, not necessarily what is of highest significance to the organization. This problem is evident in hospitals where departments and disciplines frequently select quality measurements independent of consultation with the hospital's medical, nursing, and administrative leaders. A shared and well-coordinated approach to process selection is essential to appropriate process selection.

Shared vision implies that team members at all levels of the organization understand the organization's central goals and mission, so that when they go about identifying or selecting key processes, they will use the same criteria of relative importance throughout the organization. Arriving at a shared vision is a challenge that requires the concise translation of the organization's mission statement into the specific tasks or processes that are performed on a day-to-day basis. It is true that this may be done to some extent on a broad scale, but it is very difficult to look at every aspect of the organization and relate it to a single mission. That is why an oversight leadership group should be involved in determining the key processes to ensure that the choices align with the organization's mission, values, and vision.

Process Description

Quality improvement methods include a toolbox of various techniques useful for describing and understanding processes.[8,9] These tools, many of which come from other disciplines, have been assigned certain roles by QI and are applied on a routine basis.[10] Some of the tools (such as Ishikawa, or fishbone, diagrams) involve brainstorming techniques, whereas others (such as flowcharts and control charts) are more structured.

Once selected for analysis, a process can be understood only if it can be described adequately. Again it may seem easy enough to describe in detail a task performed routinely and to assume it to be a key process. Yet it is through these rigorous methods of process description and analysis that inefficiency, duplication, and error are identified.

Articulation of the tasks involved in a health care process can be tedious and, in some cases, threatening. Frequently there is concern among caregivers that such detailed process description will eliminate the exercise of professional judgment. In truth, process description simply points out activities that occur routinely and where decisions are made along the care continuum; it does not eliminate decision making.

A fundamental principle underlying process description is that those directly involved in the process are best suited to describe it. It is dangerous to assume complete understanding of what others do or why they do it—erroneous assumptions lead to erroneous process descriptions. It is through the interaction of all disciplines involved in the process that it becomes clarified as part of a larger system rather than a set of isolated tasks.

Maintaining a systems focus is essential to process description. Too often job tasks are compartmentalized due to a focus on the immediate activity at hand, without realization of how the tasks fit in with what others do. This narrow view is common among health care workers. For example, ambulatory care providers tend to focus on the outpatient component, and hospital providers focus on inpatient activities. This occurs without consideration on the part of either group as to the relative importance of these two delivery sites. Clearly, however, the patient's condition upon admission and throughout hospitalization is influenced by prehospital ambulatory care processes. Similarly, postdischarge support systems provided to the patient will affect the long-run efficacy of care received in the hospital setting. Understanding where individual processes fit into the larger system is critical to process analysis, and providers must maintain a systems focus when describing and assessing the effect of their respective processes on the larger health care system.

Process Measurement

Once a process is described, the next step is to assess its performance by measuring some part of the process or its outcome. This measurement focus, often called *statistical quality control,* guides caregivers in their search for key process elements that have the most impact on outcomes. One tool that graphically displays process measurement data is a control chart. (See figure 5-2.) There are several types of control charts, but a discussion of which type to use for specific kinds of data is beyond the scope of this chapter.

A process that simply varies up and down randomly within a set of statistically determined limits of variation is influenced by *common cause variation,* meaning that the process is operating routinely. If the objective is to improve outcomes—that is, to reduce the amount of variation or change the mean variation—the process itself must be changed. When process variation fluctuates as a result of situations not inherent in the process, statistical control principles suggest that something extraordinary has affected routine practices. This deviation is called *special cause variation;* to determine its cause, the process must be analyzed so that a process improvement strategy can be designed.[11,12] The control chart patterns in figure 5-2 illustrate how statistical process control helps in identifying out-of-control processes.

Statistical quality control helps disclose how much variation is occurring in a particular process and in turn determines whether the process is in the state of statistical control. This state describes a process whose variations are attributed to random or common cause variation, not to special causes.[13] Once this control state is reached, the question then becomes whether the extent of process variation is desirable. If not, an investigation of process activities is undertaken to reduce the variation. A summation of action steps taken in statistical control methods is shown in figure 5-3.[14]

Figure 5-2.   Examples of Common Control Chart Patterns

1. Pattern of a process in control
   All data points are within upper and lower control limits and no special cause patterns are evident. Variation is attributed to common cause.

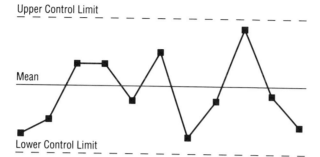

2. Patterns of processes out of control (special causes)
   a. One or more data points outside of control limits

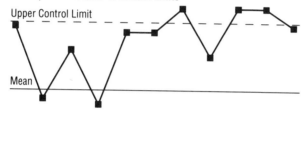

   b. All data points within control limits, but multiple consecutive (8-10) points or below the mean.

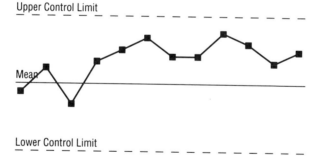

   c. All data points within control limits but wide variation of points around the mean (zigzag pattern)

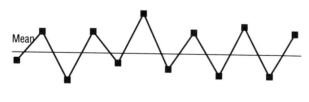

Figure 5-3. Taking Action on Process Variation

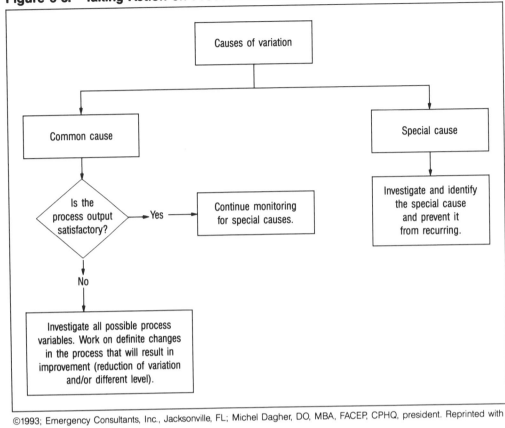

Understanding process variation is critical to process management and analysis. The fact that outcomes and each task performance in a process do not always correlate should come as no surprise to providers. For example, variations in patient outcomes despite similarity of treatment protocols is a common occurrence, one routinely attributed to patient physiology or disease severity. Furthermore, no task or set of tasks is performed in exactly the same manner each time. Health care professionals accept that variation is inherent in service delivery outcomes as well as in its processes. Statistical control methods help document measure variation so that caregivers (especially process managers) can understand it and, as a result, know how much difference between outcomes and processes is due to random chance and how much is due to special causes.

One example is the hospital infection control department, which for several years has used rudimentary principles of statistical control. Nosocomial infections occur at an expected rate per month, although the average varies from month to month. The range of variation that will probably occur over a period of time can be calculated. If the rate exceeds this predicted range, investigation must determine what caused the unexpected rate. Analysis may reveal any number of causes, for example, a carrier of a particular organism in the operating room, failure to follow policy on precautions against infection, or the transfer of an epidemic from the community to inpatients by newly admitted patients. This analysis is similar to special cause variation analysis, because the reaction stems from an unusual rise in nosocomial infection rates. Even when the average rate is fairly consistent, however, medical and administrative leaders may insist that the average rate can be reduced even further. To achieve that objective, an in-depth analysis of the current infection prevention systems can be done and current processes changed with the overall goal of reducing the average number of infections per month. This improvement project would be the result of desire to reduce common cause variation by changing the process. Although traditionally the infection control department has not applied the pure scientific principles of statistical control, it has used similar concepts.

In health care quality assurance, providers are accustomed to setting thresholds for many processes at 100 percent because doing so appears to replicate professional standards. The control limits set in statistical quality control are not the same as standards but serve to help management or the owner of the process (that is, those charged with responsibility for it) to assess accurately whether the process is in a state of control. Once this state is achieved, statistical quality control techniques help in the investigation of process improvement choices and help in the determination of the degree to which improvements actually reduced undesirable variation.

Standards, on the other hand, are intended to define the ultimate expectations of the ideal process. Control limits are merely guides used to determine the extent to which each process is considered to be in control and, if out of control, what special causes might be responsible. Standards are the *limits* of process variation that are acceptable to medical staff and/or administrative leadership. By continually refining the process and measuring the success of those refinements using statistical control techniques, leaders can determine whether process variation consistently remains within desirable limits, in which case another key process can be selected for improvement investigation or reengineering.

Process Reengineering

The fourth aspect of process analysis, process reengineering, is the most creative and most rewarding—another way of saying "Let's find a better way." It is best done, however, using the principles of process selection, description, and control. This means several things; for example:

- Using a customer–supplier focus so that when a task is performed differently it is sure to benefit those affected by the process
- Using process description so that when steps are selected for reengineering, those so chosen are sure to fit into steps that already work well
- Maintaining a systems focus that highlights the impact that a process change has on surrounding processes
- Using measurement tools that treat the newly designed process as a hypothesis of improvement rather than as a certainty

Too often, a change is made hastily, without knowledge of whether the change really makes a difference. Reengineering without measurement can be rewarding on the personal level but disastrous on the organizational level. If the four principles described are applied thoughtfully, process reengineering becomes a continuous quality improvement approach rather than a "done deed." Success is defined by the limits of process variation, which is deemed to be desirable—using objective data obtained from statistical quality control. If success is not achieved, the approach must be redesigned to reach that goal.

Relationship of Process Analysis to Clinical Pathways

What implications do these principles of QI impart in the development of clinical pathways? Clinical pathways are simply a means for describing processes, and in their best form they serve two purposes: They help care team members understand and improve the important functions that guide patient management pertaining to a particular illness or procedure, and they enhance the team's ability to coordinate those functions among members. At a minimum, they standardize already-existing routine services and achieve some efficiency in those services. Given that pathways are process descriptions, it follows that the principles of quality improvement should be applied with ease to process analysis throughout a clinical pathway development program. Correlation between QI and paths is summarized in figure 5-4.

Recalling the first QI principle of process analysis—process selection—leaders must identify a target process for change that is worth the time and effort of those who will work on it. Because clinical pathways take the time and effort of people involved in direct patient care (often voluntarily), the pathway should deal with an important patient population. In this context *important* can be defined by any number of criteria (for example, volume, resource consumption, organizational strategic plans, poor outcomes, internal or external complaints, or patient satisfaction surveys). Volume, resource consumption, strategic plans, and internal complaints identify a supplier focus toward selecting target processes. For purposes of this discussion, then, poor outcomes, external complaints, and patient satisfaction surveys constitute the customers' viewpoint about what is important. Although some customer-oriented criteria can be biased, both perspectives (supplier and customer) are important. Unfortunately, health care leaders historically have given more weight to the former than the latter.

Once consensus concerning what is important in process selection has been achieved, process improvement efforts must be coordinated to ensure the optimum benefit to the organization. Again, shared vision and an oversight structure are key elements here. Typically, in hospitals each department decides what it thinks is important, but crucial to the success of a pathway program is departmental interaction with hospital leadership to prioritize time and efforts so that pathways are developed where they are most applicable. As will be discussed in the last section of this chapter, leadership style, particularly the physician component, bears strongly on successful pathway selection.[15,16]

Given that clinical paths are descriptions of processes, it follows that in the development program the second QI principle of process analysis—process description—is assumed to be essential. A number of tools can be used to describe health care

Figure 5-4. Application of QI Principles to Clinical Pathways

QI Principles of Process Analysis	Clinical Pathways
1. Process selection	• Pick something important to patient care for your organization. • Obtain broad leadership input into pathway selection.
2. Process description	• Allow format flexibility. • Involve all participants. • Discuss customer–supplier expectations.
3. Process measurement	• Treat pathways as hypotheses of best care, not standards. • Measure both cost and quality outcomes. • Measure only critical steps or outcomes. • Use control charts to link process variance to outcome impact. • Integrate measurement into documentation.
4. Process reengineering	• Consider the need or basis for current orders or test sequences. • Develop consensus on current practice. • Incorporate practice guidelines. • Consider outpatient impact on inpatient care.

processes. Pathways use a matrix format (see figure 5-5), which lends itself more readily to standardization of routine (thus predictable) daily practices. Surgical procedures in particular tend to be more amenable to this type of format. Medical areas may be more suitably presented in an algorithmic format (see figure 5-6, p. 70) that outlines decision options the clinician can take at various points along the patient care continuum, based on a patient's response to therapy. As long as both formats are viewed as process descriptions, one can be converted to the other for specific users (such as nurses, physicians, or patients).

In general, form should match function. Insisting on a "one-size-fits-all" format overlooks the advantage of engaging multiple disciplines in process improvement. Even the matrix form can be modified to show the function–activities relationship. For example, the orthopedic pathway model at Rush-Presbyterian-St. Luke's Medical Center in Chicago started with the critical functions (wound management, pain control) and then defined the tasks related to those functions (assessment, tests, medications). This clarified the purpose and the outcomes of each task and was more readily acceptable to physicians and clinical staff.

In pathway development all participants should engage in a dialogue of their expectations and needs. Matrix format pathways clearly delineate which tasks are the responsibility of nurses, physicians, or other caregivers—in other words, process participants. However, this format does not always flesh out the role of customers and suppliers in each step of the process (for example, what the nurse does depends on the physical therapist, and vice versa). Pathway design will be enhanced to the extent that its development brings all disciplines to the table so that they can better understand the needs and expectations of everyone involved. Similarly, to the extent that there is a sharing of information as the pathway is utilized, a customer–supplier dialogue of expectations and needs will naturally ensue. To set the foundation for this dialogue, it is necessary to invest time in engaging *all* disciplines at the start of pathway development. Allowing one discipline to monopolize pathway design and development only to share a nearly finished product with others for review just prior to implementation compromises team ownership of clinical pathways.

The third principle—process measurement—links QI to clinical pathways on a value-added basis. Because a common building block for many pathways is the immediate need to reduce resource consumption (translated here as length of stay), it is tempting to implement pathways with minimal or no measurement plans just to "get things going." However, with a little more foresight, pathways can be an effective tool for managing both quality and cost. In selecting outcomes measurements, if both cost and quality issues are considered in outcomes assessment, the measurements ultimately will aid in establishing the value of a pathway. For example, a pathway that reduces length of stay but further complicates a patient's condition is of little value. Unless complications are considered as a pathway measurement component and their data assessed along with length-of-stay data, from the physician's standpoint there is little or no value in a pathway that cannot ensure that the quality of patient care will not be sacrificed for the sake of cost control.

Another aspect of measurement that applies to pathways is *how much to measure*. Some pathways are developed on the assumption that because everything *can* be measured, everything *must* be measured. It is important to stress not only key processes but their key outcomes. That is, it may suffice simply to measure outcomes (cost and quality); so long as desired outcomes are achieved, it may not be necessary to measure whether each step of the process occurred. Assume, for example, that an orthopedic total hip pathway requires five dressing changes and that the outcomes monitored are wound infections and length of stay. Whereas it might be important to document when dressing changes *did not occur* (a variance), it might be less important to monitor changes closely and spend effort educating the staff about a variance that has no impact on wound infections or length of stay. One opportunity provided

Figure 5-5. Matrix Format for Primary Total Hip Replacement Pathway

PRIMARY TOTAL HIP PATHWAY MATRIX

Patient Name_____ Age_____ Sex_____
MR # _____

Function	Activity	Pre-Op/ ___/___	OR Day/ ___/___	Post-Op #1/ ___/___
Hemostasis/ Thromboembolic Prophalaxis	Tests	Protime/PTT (Coumadin Pts.) CBC T & C 1 unit for hips (10cc clot) U/A and C&S on admission	Protime/PTT @ 4 PM (Coumadin Pts) Heme Panel*	Protime/PTT @ 4 PM (Coumadin Pts) Heme Panel
*Note: Heme panel = Hgb/Hct & Total WBC w/o diff CBC = Hgb/Hct, RBC indices, Total WBC w/ dif & Quant. platelets	Assessement	Assess for transfusion Assess for Sequential Compression Device if cannot anti-coagulate	Assess for transfusion Criteria < 11 Anticipated blood loss with antologous unit expiration < 10 - active bleeding - anticipated mod/massive bldg. -marginal cardiac reserve/02 capacity < 9 - above criteria -suspected bone marrow suppresion < 8 - MD discretion	Assess for transfusion See criteria
	Medications	No NSAIDS 10-14 days pre-op	If Coumadin -first dose 1 hr pre-op -level maintained at 50%. If Enoxaparin 30 mg subQ bid No NSAIDs	If Coumadin adjust to ProT If Enoxaparin 30 mg subQ bid No NSAIDs
	Treatments	Measure for thigh high TEDS and tape TEDS to chart	Apply TEDS	Apply TEDS
	Education	Anticoagulant instructions		Instruct on anticougulants
	Clinical Outcomes			No DVT/PE, Stable Hgb, Hct No Hemmoragic Complications
Pain Management	Assessement		Pain assessment q 4 hr. when awake	Pain assessment q 4 hr. when awake
	Medications		If motor deficit, contact anesthesia to DC epidural If inadequate pain relief, contact anesthesia to adjust dose -PCA (if no epidural)	If motor deficit, contact anesthesia to DC Epidural If inadequate pain relief, contact anesthesia to adjust dose -PCA (if no epidural)
	Clinical Outcomes		Adequate pain relief (Pain Scale Score _____)	Adequate pain relief (Self report scale)
Wound Management	Assessment			Wound Drainage
	Treatment		- Service to D/C drain & collection devices when clotted or <50cc in 8hr. for 2 shifts	Change OR drsg if excessive drainage - Surgical Service - Service to D/C drain & collection devices when clotted or <50 cc for 2 shifts
	Medications	Order Ancef (if allergic vancomycin)	Ancef started in OR (Vancomyacin if Penicillin allergic)1 hr prior to incision; 1 gram load dose/1 gram q8x3	Ancef q8h (Vancomycin q12h if Pen. allergic)
	Clinical Outcomes		No hematoma/dehiscence/infection	No hematoma/dehiscence/infection
General	Tests	Chest x-ray EKG if greater than 40yr SMA 18 Hepatitis B profile if no autologous blood donation		
	Consults	Medical consult	Case Manager (Discharge Planner) to consult for discharge services	
	Medications		Colace q A.M. Compazine or Tigan for nausea PRN	Colace q A.M. Compazine or Tigan for nausea PRN
	Assessments		Skin Assessment I & O q 8 hr. VS q 4 hr. Circulation and Neuro q 2h x8h; q4h x 4h	Skin Assessment I & O q 8 hr. VS q 4 hr. Circulation and Neuro q4h
	Treatments		Introduce inspiratory spirometer	Inspiratory spirometer q 4 hr.
	Diet	NPO	IV orders Clear liquid as tol.	IV -> Heplock Advance diet
	Elimination		Order stool softeners Order raised toilet seat if 5'4" or taller Foley with epidural	Prune juice PRN
	Education	Pre-op standards of care	Reinforce precautions	
	Clinical Outcomes		Braden Score >17 No IV restarts needed	Braden Score >17
	Discharge Planning		Nursing to notify utilization mgmt. NCRC	NCRC to review case

Disease/DX_____ Patient Name_____ Age_____ Sex_____ Disease/DX_____
Procedure_____DATE_____ MR #_____ Procedure_____DATE_____

Post-Op #2/ ___/___	Post-Op #3/ ___/___	Post-Op #4/ ___/___	Post-Op #5/ ___/___
Protime/PTT @ 4 PM (Coumadin Pts) Heme Panel	Protime/PTT @ 4 PM (Coumandin Pts) Heme Panel	Protime/PTT @ 4 PM (Coumadin Pts) Heme Panel	Protime/PTT @ 4 PM (Coumadin Pts) Heme Panel
Assess for transfusion See criteria	Assess for transfusion See criteria	Assess for transfusion See criteria	Assess for transfusion See criteria
If Coumadin adjust to ProT If Enoxaparin 30 mg subQ bid No NSAIDs Iron supplement when PO intake is adequate Apply TEDS	If Coumadin adjust to ProT If Enoxaparin 30 mg subQ bid No NSAIDs Iron supplement when PO intake is adequate Apply TEDS	If Coumadin adjust to ProT If Enoxaparin 30 mg subQ bid No NSAIDs Iron supplement when PO intake is adequate Apply TEDS	If Coumadin adjust to ProT If Enoxaparin 30 mg subQ bid No NSAIDs Iron supplement when PO intake is adequate Apply TEDS
No DVT/PE, Stable Hgb, Hct No Hemmoragic Complications	No DVT/PE, Stable Hgb, Hct No Hemmoragic Complications	No DVT/PE, Stable Hgb, Hct No Hemmoragic Complications	No DVT/PE, Stable Hgb, Hct No Hemmoragic Complications
Pain assessment q 4 hr. when awake	Pain assessment q 4 hr. when awake	Pain assessment q 4 hr. when awake	Pain assessment q 4 hr. when awake
D/C Epidural Start oral meds PRN: (offer prior to therapy) Darvacet N 100, Vicodan ES Tylenol, Tylenol -PCA (if no epidural)	D/C PCA Start oral meds PRN: (offer prior to therapy) Darvacet N 100, Vicodin ES Tylenol, Tylenol	Oral meds PRN: (offer prior to therapy) Darvacet N 100, Vicodan ES Tylenol, Tylenol	Oral meds PRN: (offer prior to therapy) Darvacet N 100, Vicodan ES Tylenol, Tylenol
Adequate pain relief (Self report scale)	Adequate pain relief (Self report scale)	Adequate pain relief (Self report scale)	Adequate pain relief (Self report scale)
Wound Drainage	Wound Drainage	Wound Drainage	Wound Drainage
Surgical Service-Change drsg with ABDs use paper tape, non-occlusive, optional tubular drsg to hold (PRN if excessive drainage) - Service to D/C drain & collection devices	Surgical Service - Change dressing (PRN if excessive drainage)	Surgical Service - Change dressing (PRN if excessive drainage)	Surgical Service - Change dressing (PRN if excessive drainage)
Ancef 1 dose in A.M. (Vancomycin if Penicillin allergic)			
No hematoma/dehiscence/infection	No hematoma/dehiscence /infection	Wound dry & intact	-afebrile (temp <100 for 24 hours)
Colace q A.M. Compazine or Tigan for nausea PRN	Colace q A.M. Compazine or Tigan for nausea PRN	Colace q A.M. Compazine or Tigan for nausea PRN	Colace q A.M. Compazine or Tigan for nausea PRN
Skin Assessment I & O q 8 hr. VS q 8 hr. Circulation and Neuro q 8h Inspiratory spirometer q 4 hr.	Skin Assessment D/C I & O VS q 8 hr. Circulation and Neuro q 8h Inspiratory spirometer q 4 hr.	Skin Assessment VS q 8 hr. Circulation and Neuro q 8h Inspiratory spirometer q 4 hr.	Skin Assessment VS q 8 hr. Circulation and Neuro q 8h Inspiratory spirometer q 4 hr.
D/C Heplock General diet Prune juice PRN Fleets Enema PRN D/C Foley when D/C Epidural	General diet Prune juice PRN Fleets Enema PRN	General diet Prune juice PRN Fleets Enema PRN	General diet Prune juice PRN Fleets Enema PRN
Braden Score >17	Chest clear to auscultation Tolerate general diet Void freely Braden Score >17	Braden Score >17	Braden Score >17
			Discharge day 5 1) NCRC arranges for protime/physical therapy at home and other services pm 2) NCRC arranges delivery of additional equipment PRN for home use 3) Transfer to outside rehabiliation facility or ECF on selected patients

(Continued on next page)

Figure 5-5. (Continued)

PRIMARY TOTAL HIP PATHWAY MATRIX

Patient Name_____ Age_____Sex_____

MR # _____

Function	Activity	Pre-Op/ ___/___	OR Day/ ___/___	Post-Op #1/ ___/___

Rehabilitation	Consults	Pre-op Home Visit (optional)
		
		PT Presurgery evaluation (optional)
			Write PT consult for hips & knees
			Write OT consult for hips only
				PT evaluates pt/ OT evaluates pt
				PM & R consult on selected pts
				Criteria
				1) Co-morbidities
				  COPD; Asthma; Cardiac limitations
				  Obesity; Neurologic Process
				  Hemiparesis from new or remote CVA
				  Pre-exisiting weakness from
				  disease (polio, diabetic neuropathy,
				  Parkinson's diesase, etc.)
				  Arthritis in other joints
				  Myopathy (i.e. steroid-induced)
				  Pain (non surgical); Neurologic Process;
				  Previous poor function, prior to surgery
				2) Post-Op Complications
				  Increased pain; DVT; Acute Stroke
				3) Social Issues
				  Living alone; Multiple stairs;
				  Poor family support systems

	Assessment	ROM, Muscle Strength, Balance, Endurance, Level of Mobility, Gait Equip Needed (Elev. Toilet Seat, Chair) Environmental Limitations, Caregiver availability for support with post Op program. Need for Rehab or other consult		Pain Assessment pre- PT

	Treatments		THR
			  Regular pillow for abduction
			  Eggcrate
			  Hip flexion not to exceed
			  90 degrees
			  No adduction of operated leg
			  No internal rotation of operated leg
				THR
				  Regular pillow for abduction
				  Eggcrate
				  Hip flexion not to exceed
				  90 degrees
				  No adduction of operated leg
				  No internal rotation of operated leg
				
				PT (Daily frequency determined by PT evaluation of patient's progress)
				Treatment Number ____

	Activity		Trapeze	Bathroom, chair, & ambulation when approved by PT
				1) Cemented or Hybrid THR or TKR
				  -WBAT
				  -crutches or walker
				2) Cementless THR or TKR
				  -touchdown weightbearing
				  -crutches or walker
				THR
				1) Trochanter slide or osteomy
				  -touchdown weightbearing
				2) -active/passive abduction per
				  surgical protocol

	Education	Positioning Tran. Train. Rev of Amb. Protocol, Post-op Exer and Rationale
		  -Ankle Exercise
		  -Quad and Gluteal Sets.
		  -Arm strength
		  -ROM-No Active Add.
		  -Flexion Limited to 90 Deg.
			Reinforce post-op teaching with patient and family	

	Clinical Outcomes			Pain Control adequate to participate in PT
		THR - no hip dislocation	THR - no hip dislocation	THR - no hip dislocation

Disease/DX _____ Patient Name _____ Age _____ Sex _____   Disease/DX _____

Procedure _____ DATE _____ MR # _____   Procedure _____ DATE _____

Post-Op #2/ ___/___	Post-Op #3/ ___/___	Post-Op #4/ ___/___	Post-Op #5/ ___/___

PM&R Consult if
Post-Op Complications
  Increased Pain; DVT; Acute Stroke
	PM&R Consult if
	1) Post-Op Complications
	   Increased pain; DVT;
	   Acute Stroke; Increasing
	   Wound Drainage/erythema
	
	2) PT outcomes not met
		PM&R Consult if
		1) Post-Op Complications
		   Increased pain; DVT;
		   Acute Stroke; Increasing
		   Wound Drainage/erythema
		
		2) PT outcomes not met
			PM&R Consult if
			1) Post-Op Complications
			   Increased pain; DVT;
			   Acute Stroke; Increasing
			   Wound Drainage/erythema
			
			2) PT outcomes not met

Pain Assessment pre- PT	Pain Assessment pre- PT	Pain Assessment pre- PT	Pain Assessment pre- PT

THR
  Regular pillow for abduction
  Eggcrate
  Hip flexion not to exceed
   90 degrees
  No adduction of operated leg
  No internal rotation of operated leg
 	
PT (Daily frequency determined by
PT evaluation of patient's progress)
Treatment Number ____
Bathroom, chair, & ambulation
when approved by PT
	THR
	  Regular pillow for abduction
	  Eggcrate
	  Hip flexion not to exceed
	   90 degrees
	  No adduction of operated leg
	  No internal rotation
	   of operated leg
	PT (Daily frequency determined by
	PT evaluation of patient's progress)
	Treatment Number ____
	Bathroom, chair, & ambulation
	when approved by PT
		THR
		  Regular pillow for abduction
		  Eggcrate
		  Hip flexion not to exceed
		   90 degrees
		  No adduction of operated leg
		  No internal rotation
		   of operated leg
		PT (Daily frequency determined by
		PT evaluation of patient's progress)
		Treatment Number ____
		Bathroom, chair, & ambulation
		when approved by PT
			THR
			  Regular pillow for abduction
			  Eggcrate
			  Hip flexion not to exceed
			   90 degrees
			  No adduction of operated leg
			  No internal rotation
			   of operated leg
			PT (Daily frequency determined by
			PT evaluation of patient's progress)
			Treatment Number ____
			Bathroom, chair, & ambulation
			when approved by PT

Instruct on body mechanics, transfer techniques		Home exercise program from PT	Instruct on anticoagulants

Pain Control adequate to
participate in PT
Isometrics - independent
 	
THR - no hip dislocation
	Pain Control adequate to
	participate in PT
	THR, modified bridging
	   -independent
	
	THR - no hip dislocation
		Pain Control adequate to
		participate in PT
		Independent Transfers-
		   sup-sit, sit-stand, wheel-bed
		
		THR - no hip dislocation
			Pain Control adequate to
			participate in PT
			THR
			Independent ADL (OT)
			Independent ambulation
			on level surface & stairs with
			assistive device
			THR - no hip dislocation

Figure 5-6. Algorithm Format for Medical Clinical Path

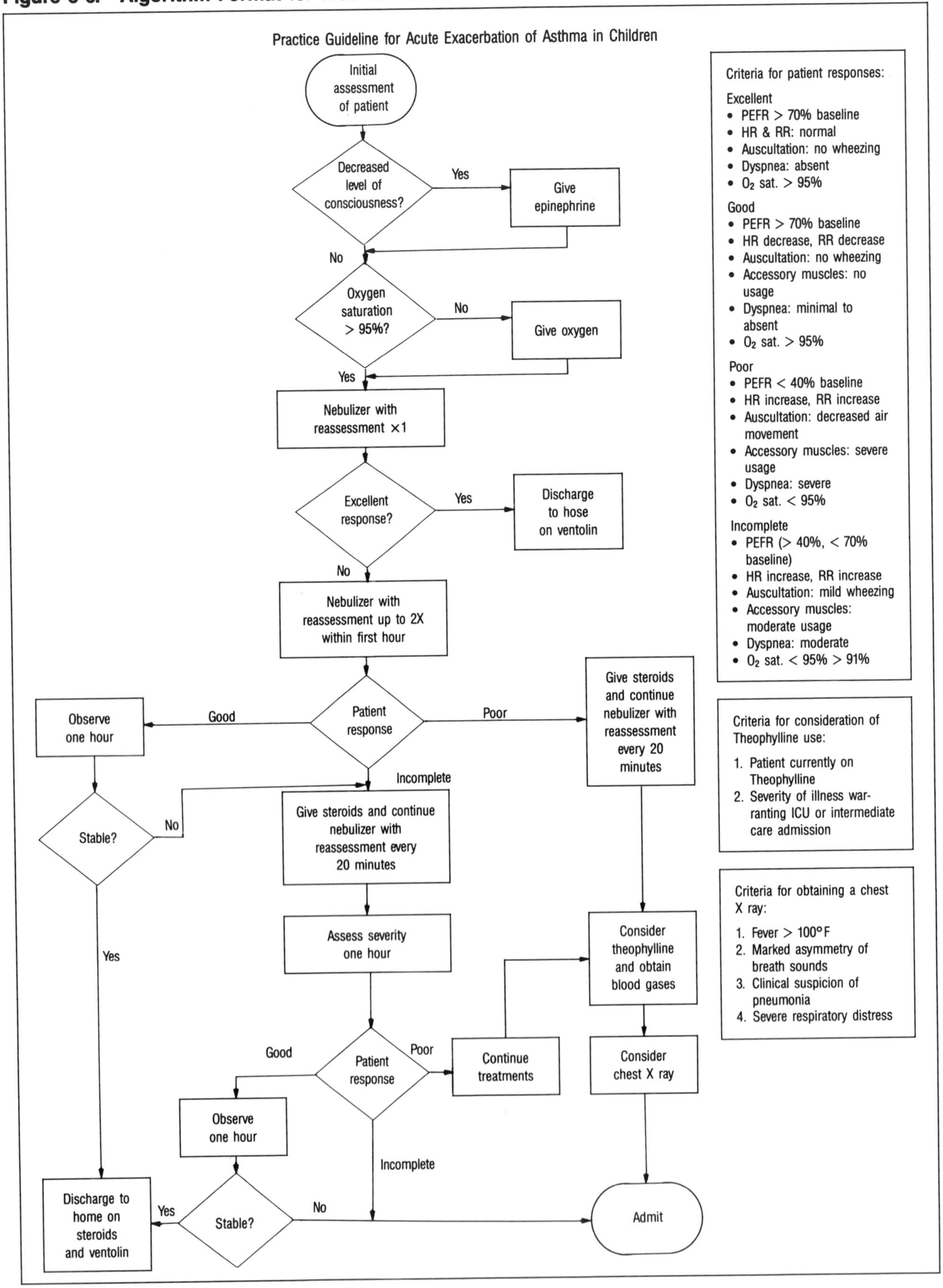

Practice Guideline for Acute Exacerbation of Asthma in Children

by pathways is to determine what is really critical to a process and what steps are desirable but not necessarily critical. In the initial stage of pathway pilot testing, a number of pathway steps might be measured to determine which ones pose the biggest problems and which ones seem to be operating well. On an ongoing basis, however, it may be important to measure only those critical outcomes the pathway was designed to achieve and those key steps initially found to cause problems or to affect outcomes.

An efficient tool for identifying these critical processes and outcomes is the control chart described earlier in this chapter. (See figure 5-2, p. 61.) Charts can help clinicians determine whether outcomes or processes are exhibiting special or common cause variation. Armed with this information, they can better design the changes needed to improve performance.

By measuring the processes that occur (or do not occur) as well as the outcome objectives, pathway users learn which processes are important. The outcomes measurement approach to analyzing pathway variance promotes path-based patient care as a dynamic rather than a static process. This is important because a number of physicians fear that pathways will lead to "cookbook medicine" whereby they are bound to follow predetermined but outdated protocols simply because they are in writing.[17] Continued pathway analysis, which in turn fosters continued quality improvement, should go far to allay such fears. With practice, pathway programs can be viewed as commitments to scientific hypothesis testing rather than recipes handed down through generations.[18]

Once it is shown to have sufficient value and to be outcomes focused, the measurement component of pathway development must be integrated into the pathway process itself. Finding ways to incorporate pathways into the medical record and into routine documentation systems is essential to pathway success. As stressed in chapter 3, pathways should avoid duplicative documentation for the caregiver and provide the best information for analysis without the need for closed chart review.

The fourth QI principle – process reengineering – guides pathway development by providing opportunity for caregivers to examine whether doing things differently might result in better patient care. Reengineering can be the most time-consuming component of pathway development, but it also can be the most beneficial to users. After all, if pathways simply catalog current standard orders without considering the sequencing of those orders, the only accomplishment might well be no more than standardization of inefficiencies. If pathways focus narrowly on isolated tasks and are viewed as finished products rather than as opportunities for continuous improvement, then today's pathway based on current practices and standards will become tomorrow's outdated cookbook recipe.

It is in the area of process reengineering that clinical practice guidelines can have the most potential impact on pathways and thus on quality management. Practice guidelines should be incorporated into initial pathway design, but as new guidelines are developed, pathway format should allow for a means to compare current institutional practice to that proposed in the new guideline. Part of the problem with practice guideline assessment in most health care facilities is difficulty in determining the degree of conformity to a guideline because institutional consensus on current practice has not been articulated. Until leaders provide a forum in which to assess current practice, such as process reengineering, integrating new guidelines rapidly into patient care will remain a problem.

Relationship of Clinical Pathways to JCAHO Performance Improvement Standards

To understand how clinical pathways fit into the JCAHO performance improvement standards, a brief review of the characteristics of these new standards is needed.[19-21] The first characteristic is that JCAHO standards are *process and function focused*, rather than indicator focused. In the past, departments were told to pick quality indicators of important aspects of care and then, if indicator results deviated from predetermined thresholds, to assess the reason for this difference. The JCAHO's 10-step monitoring and evaluation (M&E) model underlying this approach is similar in essence to the process improvement models currently advocated. However, because initially JCAHO surveyors tended to emphasize measuring something rather than how to pick what to measure, indicators were often selected without understanding which processes, if any, they were related to and whether the chosen measurements would lead to opportunities for improvement. As a result, many hospitals found that their measurement resources failed to yield satisfactory return on improvements.

Therefore, the new standards are best viewed as an evolution in emphasis, not in substance. Their process focus emphasizes spending more time in the initial phase of identifying key processes and describing them well before arriving at the measurement component. Indicators (or measures) are just as important today, only more clearly identified as the tools that help caregivers understand processes rather than as the primary focus of activity.

A second characteristic of the new standards, according to the JCAHO, is that they are *patient focused*, not department focused. The performance improvement standards ask, from a patient's perspective, "What have you done as an organization of related disciplines to improve the processes of patient care?" These standards suggest that because most care processes involve caregivers from various disciplines working together, the improvements may be most efficiently designed by individuals working as an interdisciplinary team rather than as separate entities. In other words, although the standards do not require interdisciplinary teams, they do advise that process improvement activities include all individuals, professions, and departments directly involved in the process chosen for improvement.

The third characteristic of the new standards is their emphasis on *data use* (to improve care) rather than just data collection. The underlying assumption here is that when identifying a target process for improvement, having data on hand about that process before and after any intervention will facilitate understanding as to whether the intervention achieved its goals. As a result of this emphasis, data-collection resources can be focused on areas where active intervention is occurring, rather than on areas monitored routinely, which may only help maintain the status quo. This does not mean that no data should be collected on critical areas that appear to be operating well; doing so helps maintain control. However, collecting data about aspects of care that routinely show 100 percent compliance should not be the major focus of a performance improvement program.

How do these three characteristics relate to clinical pathways? Clinical pathways can position an organization to comply with JCAHO quality (performance improvement) standards while addressing critical resource issues necessary for its survival (as summarized in figure 5-7). By being process focused, clinical pathways describe both the process tasks and the relationship of the disciplines within the process, thereby

Figure 5-7. Comparison of 1994 JCAHO Performance Improvement Standards Intent with Clinical Pathways

JCAHO Standards	Clinical Pathways
1. Process focused	Describe patient care processes.
2. Patient focused	Describe care of a patient with a specific disease and the services provided by all caregivers.
3. Data use to improve organizational performance	Measure process and outcome data to improve patient cost and quality outcomes.

outlining which departments or disciplines can get recognition from the JCAHO for their pathway activity. By being patient focused, pathways describe the process for managing a specific patient population or procedure throughout the entire hospital episode and beyond. They also allow for reengineering processes around patient expectations if those expectations are obtained by use of appropriate survey tools. Third, clinical pathways use data to improve care by creating interventions whose effects can be quantified. Even though the driving factor for many pathways will be efficient resource use (length of stay, number of tests ordered, sequence of tests, and the like), the delineation of pathway outcomes relative to cost and quality issues allows them to demonstrate improvement in cost without loss of quality, improvement in both cost and quality, or improvement in quality without increase in cost. Any one of these results constitutes improved organizational performance.

Organization of QI Programs around Clinical Pathways

Because the characteristics of clinical pathways seem to be in tandem with JCAHO characteristics of performance improvement standards, there is tremendous opportunity to organize QI programs around clinical pathways rather than developing pathway programs in a vacuum separate from resources devoted to quality enhancement. Pathways require measurement and, given current staffing levels in hospitals today, measurement resources are scarce. In the same vein, QI activities require measurement. By integrating these two activities, when they meet as two waves at their peak, they will be in phase and double their impact. Pursued separately, they will produce a doubly deep trough of resource consumption.

Another scarce resource is caregivers' time and ability to contribute to creative efforts. In the past, quality assurance activities were viewed as voluntary or add-on activities for both the medical staff and other caregivers. If multiple programs require these same types of contributions, scarce resources will be spread even more thinly. Consequently, close attention must be given to whether a clinical path program can help replace some of the QI program's standard components without sacrificing compliance with JCAHO standards. The remainder of this section explores several ways in which this can be accomplished.

Multidisciplinary Teams

By designing a quality structure based on functional units or teams rather than departments, the structure will promote development of multidisciplinary quality improvement teams whose primary focus can be the design of clinical paths. This approach will ensure that time spent in quality activities is focused toward process improvement (for example, pathways) rather than simply on monitoring. It also minimizes duplication of activities among physicians, nurses, and other clinicians looking at the same issue independently and furthers interdisciplinarity with regard to the use of data-collection resources.

Multidisciplinary Oversight and Analysis

Multidisciplinary oversight of critical pathway development for functional areas, coupled with analysis of other key processes amenable to improvement, engages all caregivers involved in patient management. Such a structure fulfills JCAHO standards of active organizationwide participation in performance improvement rather than only uncoordinated and independent departmental-level participation. A multidisciplinary oversight and analysis structure also provides opportunity for equitable discussion and debate about organizational prioritization of improvement strategies. A sample structure is shown in figure 5-8.

Figure 5-8. Example of Leadership Oversight Structure for Clinical Path Program

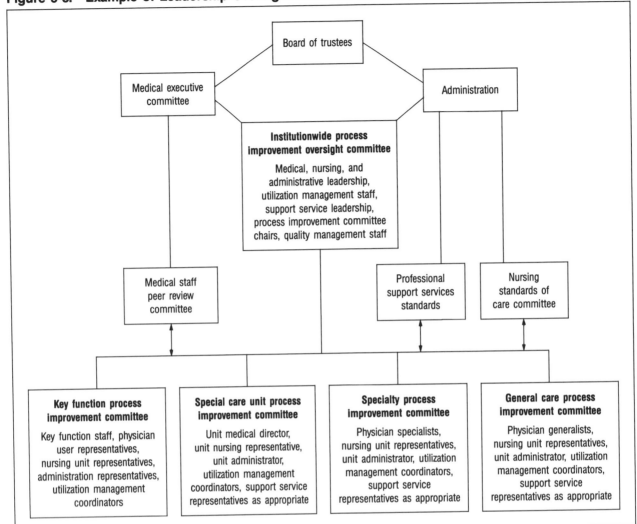

Integration of Data-Collection Efforts

As indicated earlier in the chapter, integrating pathways into the quality improvement program streamlines data-collection activities or at least facilitates gathering of more data without need for additional resources. If quality improvement data-collection systems can be integrated into the pathway variance and outcomes reporting systems, valuable information can be obtained during the patient's episode of care. In turn, the need for retrospective review of closed records is reduced.

Personnel Ownership

Organizing the quality improvement program around pathways results in clinical personnel working on areas of improvement closest to their interests rather than monitoring performance just because they are required to measure it. The major satisfaction gained from this approach is the opportunity for caregivers "in the trenches" to improve systems they work with on a daily basis. Through personnel—and personal—ownership in the program, not only is individual fulfillment enhanced, physicians and clinical staff are motivated to develop more pathways.

Key Patient Care Functions

Pathways follow a series of patient functions for a given disease. Therefore, it is likely that they will span some or all of the key patient care functions defined by the JCAHO:[22]

1. Rights of patients and organizational ethics
2. Assessment of patients
3. Entry to setting or service
4. Nutritional care
5. Treatment of patients
   - Medication use
   - Blood and blood products use
6. Operative and other invasive procedures
7. Education of patients and family
8. Coordination of care

As pathway programs develop and proliferate throughout hospital departments and services, assessment of these key functions can be decentralized to the various multidisciplinary teams that oversee pathway projects. Ultimately, this will eliminate the need for central resources devoted to making independent assessments of these activities.

An aspect of the JCAHO quality standards that a pathway program will not necessarily fulfill is the peer review requirement for the medical staff. If quality issues identified during pathway variance reporting are used to identify cases requiring peer review, this needs to be done in a traditional peer review structure, not in a multidisciplinary team setting. Thus, there is still a need for the medical staff to retain department- or discipline-specific committees for peer review functions.

Role of the Physician in Clinical Pathways

Many pathway programs are initiated with the fervent hope on the part of nursing and/or administrative personnel that patient care processes will be controlled more effectively. Unfortunately, it may only be *after* paths are developed that physicians "buy in" or their involvement is elicited. Some hospitals seek physician involvement early on in the pathway implementation stages, only to be met with lukewarm response or, even worse, frank opposition to the initiative expressed. There is no magical formula for gaining physician involvement, given the impact that the environmental dynamics and cultural climate of individual organizations have on this issue. Certain strategies, however, can increase the likelihood of physician participation in clinical pathway development.

Educate the Medical Staff

Prior to developing pathways, it is essential to articulate the facility's philosophy of pathway use. As mentioned earlier in the chapter, many physicians are skeptical about the use of pathways because they fear that the pathways may hamper their ability to provide individualized patient care. This belief stems from a misunderstanding that pathways predetermine care for *all* patients. In a climate of increasing external restrictions on patient management, physicians are often reluctant to impose what they view as additional restrictions on themselves. Open and honest dialogue and consensus among physician leaders and medical staff as to how pathways will be used are essential components of effective physician participation. At Rush-Presbyterian-St. Luke's

Medical Center, caregivers found that a discussion of the principles of clinical pathways development (figure 5-9) was helpful in guiding and directing the pathway development program with physicians.

Include Physicians on the Leadership Team

Physicians should be a part of the leadership team in selecting pathways.[23,24] They should be involved in the oversight structure that determines which pathways will be developed first. Physicians who feel that the pathways selected for development represent low-priority patient groupings will have little regard for the project and will be less willing to participate.

Involve Physicians in Pathway Design

Physicians must be viewed as critical customers and suppliers in the process.[25] They should be engaged in designing pathways and in achieving consensus in those areas where pathways will affect them. This investment can be achieved more readily if physicians agree on pathway use at the beginning of the project.

Figure 5-9. Principles for Clinical Pathway Development

Pathways represent the consensus of the most effective and efficient means of care for the *typical* patient (that is, the majority of patients) with a given disease or condition. Pathway development is not useful to define care for the ideal patient (too few to be worth the effort) or for every patient (too complex to be manageable).

A key goal of pathways is to optimize patient care resources with patient care outcomes. The achievement of this goal is through the following principles:

1. Development
   a. Pathway development is physician directed with input from the various health care professionals and support personnel involved with the given disease or condition.
   b. When the current care process for the typical patient with a given disease or condition is defined, the resources used in patient care and the timing of the required services will come under appropriate professional scrutiny.
   c. When interdisciplinary dialogue on the ideal process for efficient and effective care is stimulated, innovations in the delivery of patient services can be achieved.

2. Implementation
   a. For attending physicians, pathways do not restrict physician decisions or choices in the care of individual patients. For those physicians choosing to use the pathway at the time of admission, the pathway represents an efficient means of directing the patient's care given that the patient's condition remains within the boundaries of anticipated outcomes. The physician may choose to vary from the pathway at any time during the patient's course.
   b. For nursing and other professionals, the pathways provide a means of anticipating routine patient care services to achieve more efficient care; the defined outcomes provide a means for assessing the effectiveness of those services. Pathways will not place non-physicians in a "gatekeeper" role to modify physician choices in the care of individual patients.
   c. For resident physicians, pathways provide an educational tool for the management of the typical patient including the pre- and post-hospitalization phases. Participation in pathway development and implementation will also prepare the residents in the appropriate use of pathways when they practice in other settings.

3. Evaluation
   a. When the expected outcomes from the use of the pathway are determined, data will become available to relate system problems and practice patterns to the processes of care.
   b. Pathways will achieve increased compliance by physicians through the analysis of aggregate data on physician practice relative to patient outcomes. Use of aggregate data to modify physician performance will be through peer review mechanisms of the Departmental and Medical Staff structures.

Solicit Physician Input in Process Improvement Activities

Physicians must be viewed as an essential component of the process evaluation and improvement effort.[26,27] With traditional quality assurance approaches, physicians were asked to review individual cases and determine whether the clinicians involved were "good" or "bad." However, no provisions were made for promoting physician involvement in improving those systems within which they were bound to work. Fear of physician suggestions for organizational or administrative improvements should pose no obstacle to their involvement so long as improvements are tested and supported by current data. Generally speaking, because of their medical training, physicians tend naturally toward analytic or systems thinking.[28] Even those who may not have the larger organizational management perspective have enough office practice experience to provide valid input.

Because they may be responsible for the full continuity of patient care, physicians can bring to the team a broader perspective than the hospital staff on factors outside the hospital that affect inpatient care. This perspective can add a creative dimension to process reengineering. To further ensure the success of individual pathways, it is essential to promote the pathway as the health care team's best approximation of what team members believe is the best way to manage patients.

Clarify Philosophy and Goals

If pathways are introduced as hypotheses rather than as certainties, the program will be seen as one that supports pathways that are capable of being measured, tested, and modified.[29] This philosophy recognizes that variation in the process is acceptable, even expected. The real question asked by the pathway program is not whether the process varied but whether the variance made a difference in outcome.

Two common pathway goals are to identify a variance and its relation to outcome and to intervene with case management once a variance is identified. The first goal requires the gathering of sufficient aggregate data to look for patterns and trends; the second requires active and concurrent intervention to ensure that patient care flows appropriately and that adjustments are made when needed. If case management is used to assist patient flow rather than to serve a gatekeeper function, then physicians will find pathways not only acceptable but helpful for their patients. However, if the pathways are viewed as unmodifiable on a case-by-case basis and nurses or other case managers are placed in the position of gatekeepers, the pathways will contribute only conflict and tension.

Clearly then, the best use of pathway variance data for modification of practice patterns is through aggregate data analysis rather than case-by-case review.[30] This philosophy promotes a systems viewpoint, which suggests that there are many reasons why variance occurs, and physician practice patterns are only one. This attitude differs markedly from the traditional quality assurance view, which suggested that whenever a variance occurred it was a physician's fault.

Conclusion

The development of clinical pathway programs and the development of quality improvement programs have much in common. Both strategies are based on the same principles of process selection, description, measurement, and reengineering. Pathway implementation offers the health care organization the opportunity to integrate quality improvement around specific clinical functions rather than administrative processes. Physician participation in the pathway development process can be obtained successfully if the organization understands the physicians' leadership role in the process.

Clarifying pathway use as a hypothesis, instead of a standard of care, will secure better acceptance of path-based patient care by physicians and other care team members. Pathways are not an end unto themselves but a means of achieving a better understanding of the systems and processes used to help sick people get well.

References

1. Berwick, D. M. Continuous quality improvement as an ideal in health care. *New England Journal of Medicine* 320:53–56, 1989.

2. Coffey, R. J., Richards, J. S., Remmert, C. S., LeRoy, S. S., Schoville, R. R., and Baldwin, P. J. An introduction to critical paths. *Quality Management in Health Care* 1:45–54, 1992.

3. Senge, P. M. *The Fifth Discipline: The Art and Practice of the Learning Organization.* New York City: Doubleday/Currency, 1990.

4. Berwick, D. M. The clinical process and the quality process. *Quality Management in Health Care* 1:1–8, 1992.

5. Berwick, 1989.

6. Joint Commission on Accreditation of Healthcare Organizations. *Striving toward Improvement: Six Hospitals in Search of Quality.* Oakbrook Terrace, IL: JCAHO, 1992.

7. JCAHO, 1992.

8. Melum, M. M, and Sinioris, M. E. *Total Quality Management: The Health Care Pioneers.* Chicago: American Hospital Publishing, 1992.

9. Walton, M. *The Deming Management Method.* New York City: Putnam Publishing Group, 1986.

10. Melum and Sinioris.

11. Walton.

12. Brassard, M. *The Memory Jogger Plus+.* Methuen, MA: GOAL/QPC, 1989.

13. Stratton, B. The quality glossary. *Quality Progress* 26(2):20–29, 1992.

14. Dagher, M. In Search of Quality: Using Statistical Process Control to Measure and Improve Healthcare Performance. Material from workshop sponsored by the Quality Assurance Section of the American Health Information Management Association, Atlanta, Oct. 15, 1993.

15. Berwick, 1992.

16. Lewis, A. Reinvigorating stalled CQI efforts through physician involvement. *Physician Executive* 19(2):32–36, 1993.

17. James, B. C. TQM and clinical medicine. *Frontiers of Health Service Management* 7(4):42–46, 1991.

18. Berwick, 1992.

19. Joint Commission on Accreditation of Healthcare Organizations. *1994 Accreditation Manual for Hospitals.* Oakbrook Terrace, IL: JCAHO, 1993.

20. New AMH format highlights patient care functions. *Joint Commission Perspectives,* Special Issue on 1994 AMH:1–2, 1993.

21. Quality assessment and improvement standards continue to evolve. *Joint Commission Perspectives,* Special Issue on 1994 AMH:1–2, 1993.

22. New AMH format highlights patient care functions. *Joint Commission Perspectives,* Special Issue on 1994 AMH:1–2, 1993.

23. Berwick, 1992.

24. Lewis.

25. James.

26. Berwick, 1992.

27. James.

28. Snyder, D. A. TQM: A paradigm for physicians. *Physician Executive* 19(4):39–41, 1993.

29. Berwick, 1992.

30. James.

PART TWO

Case Studies: Experiences from Eight Institutions

CHAPTER SIX

Clinical Paths at Rhode Island Hospital

Susan E. Simundson and Diane Lavoie

Rhode Island Hospital (RIH) is a 719-bed tertiary medical center located in Providence. The hospital has 26 patient care units and a nursing staff of 1,200 registered nurses. It is the primary teaching hospital for the Brown University School of Medicine, with training programs in most specialties. The medical staff is a mix of full-time faculty and voluntary physicians. Because of its inner-city location and designation as the Level I Trauma Center for southeastern New England, it serves a large indigent population. There is no publicly supported city or county hospital in Providence. In fiscal year 1992, RIH served 30,500 inpatients and provided 94,500 emergency department visits and 76,000 outpatient visits.

This chapter describes a number of initiatives, begun in 1984, that led to the implementation of clinical paths in 1990. A formal plan and process was not initiated until late 1990, when a change in leadership and a financial imperative caused the hospital to move forward.

Historical Background

In 1984 physicians in the division of general internal medicine conducted research on the use of clinical path protocols (referred to as critical paths at RIH) to influence physician practice patterns. The study compared patients of a group of 12 physicians prior to and subsequent to implementation of protocols for specific diagnoses. Study results showed that the use of protocols was a significant factor in altering physician behavior; specifically, a 15 percent reduction in total average charges due to a decline in utilization of electrocardiograms, X rays, laboratory tests, and drugs was noted.[1] Hospitalwide implementation of critical paths did not occur at this time, however, but their use remained a research topic. Meanwhile, no operational changes were made. Authors of this study were instrumental in the later development of clinical paths, convinced by their research that cost savings can be achieved with changes in physician practice patterns.

In early 1988, hospital nursing management invited Karen Zander, considered the leading figure in nursing case management and clinical path development, to address the nursing staff. A group of nurses who cared for coronary artery bypass graft (CABG) patients was eager to develop a clinical path and was instrumental in sparking the interest of the cardiovascular thoracic (CVT) surgeon. Working together, these caregivers developed the first clinical path for Rhode Island Hospital and implemented it on the CVT nursing unit. There was no fanfare and little administrative support.

Case management, as defined by Zander, is a patient care delivery system that focuses on outcomes that occur within specified time frames while utilizing appropriate resources. This model designates the nurse caregiver as the case manager, accountable for the patient during the whole episode of illness, regardless of which unit the patient is on at any given time. This model has been adapted over time due to the nursing shortage in the mid-1980s, controversy over whether to expand the staff nurse's role or designate case managers, and the diminishing role of clinical specialists. Many different models are now in use.

Case management continues to be viewed as the vehicle of collaboration among nurses, physicians, and other health care providers to establish clinical paths (or guidelines) for planning treatment courses for specific diagnoses. Clinical paths are case management tools that are expected to ensure appropriate quality of care while minimizing length of stay and controlling resource utilization. Paths are the basis on which nursing is to establish an individualized plan of care for each patient.

In 1989 the vice-president for patient services initiated an educational program in case management for the nursing department. Physicians, nurses, and other health care providers met to develop clinical paths for diagnoses in their areas of expertise. However, no organizational plan was in place for using case managers; at the time, the hospital used agency nurses to address staff shortages and did not believe current hospital staff could support a case manager model. The added expense of case manager salaries and the lack of consensus as to what level of education and experience was required for case managers were further deterrents.

In fiscal year 1990, the hospital faced a $14 million operating loss and was forced to change fundamentally the way care was delivered. Part of the overall strategy was to focus more strongly on physician practice patterns, particularly length of stay and resource utilization. The department of clinical management was established in July 1990 as a central clearinghouse for these analyses and efforts.

Hospital leadership changed in October 1990 with the recruitment of a new president, whose past experience had been in a hospital system that used clinical paths to control length of stay and ancillary services utilization. Upon his arrival, he urged RIH management to consider the same strategy, thus accelerating the hospital's development of clinical paths.

Clinical Management Steering Committee

In reaction to the hospital's financial situation and in response to recommendations by its new president, the chief operating officer began to examine RIH's ongoing efforts related to clinical paths, length-of-stay reduction, and analysis of physician practice patterns. The clinical management steering committee was established in the fall of 1990 to merge these efforts and develop a more aggressive focus. The committee's goal was to develop strategies and mechanisms to streamline the care of inpatients in the medical service, with the objective of improved financial performance and quality of care. Paths would be used to promote collaboration and empower nurses to implement a plan of care. The group was to meet monthly to review data and develop an implementation plan for path use. The committee also would monitor postimplementation progress by reviewing variances and changes in length of stay on an ongoing basis.

The original committee was made up of 10 members: the chief operating officer, vice-president of medical business affairs, vice-president of patient services, chief of medicine, attending medical staff (three members), director of continuing care/utilization review, nursing coordinator, and director of clinical management (who has overall administrative responsibility for the function and chairs the monthly meetings). As a result of organizational restructuring, the senior vice-president for service quality and the director of medical nursing were added to the committee.

Clinical Path Development Process

The committee agreed to develop paths for the top 20 high-volume medical diagnoses whose length of stay exceeded national averages. Although hospital staff did develop one surgical path, the major thrust was in medicine, where length-of-stay problems were the greatest. Drafts of paths developed by staff nurses as part of the case management educational effort were used as a baseline for some diagnoses, and division directors wrote the first draft if none had been completed by nursing. Multidisciplinary work groups (consisting of full-time physician faculty, voluntary physicians, the chief medical resident, nurses, and dietary and other therapists) edited and revised the drafts. Division directors reviewed all guidelines for their specialties, with the chief of service granting final approval prior to path implementation.

Because the goal was to develop paths that represented the standard of care unique to Rhode Island Hospital, paths were not based on a review of the literature. However, an attempt was made to align length of stay with the Health Care Financing Administration (HCFA) mean, although the committee deferred to what the physicians believed was appropriate from a clinical point of view. In most cases, the expected length of stay outlined by the physicians was consistent with the HCFA mean, although much lower than actual practice at the hospital.

In January 1991 the steering group began meeting biweekly, with a goal to implement 20 paths by March 1991. Later in the process, meetings were held weekly to meet the deadline. The original goal of 20 paths was not achieved because protocols for several high-volume diagnoses could not be standardized, treatment plans depended on etiology, and there were no predictable plans of care. On March 1, 1991, the hospital began using 13 medical paths and 1 surgical path. As of mid-1993, 25 medical paths and 50 surgical paths were in place. These diagnoses cover roughly 60 percent of medical patients and 30 percent of surgical patients, regardless of attending physician. Figure 6-1 lists the diagnoses for which clinical paths are being used at RIH.

All members of the health care team participated in nursing unit in-services for path use, which were repeated as necessary in an attempt to reach all unit employees. Presentations were given at house officer conferences, medical staff meetings, and faculty staff meetings to ensure physician awareness of the process and use of clinical paths. In addition, copies of the paths were mailed to all house officers and physicians, a monumental communication effort due to the size of the institution and the number of physicians on staff (approximately 700 admitting physicians – 300 in the department of medicine alone).

Clinical Path Design

The format used for clinical paths was adopted from the first model used at New England Medical Center, with activities listed down the left-hand column and time increments progressing from left to right. The path covers inpatient care only, although on some of the surgical diagnoses the path is started when the patient arrives for preadmission testing. (Figure 6-2 shows an example of this format for cholecystectomy.) Time increments for the path are selected depending on typical progress of patients, for example, acute care by day (as in figure 6-2, p. 85); intensive care in blocks of hours (as in the CABG path shown in figure 6-3, p. 86); in weeks (as in the rehabilitation protocol shown in figure 6-4, p. 87); or in emergency department 15- to 30-minute blocks, depending on the diagnosis.

Figure 6-1. Clinical Paths in Use at Rhode Island Hospital

Approved Medical Critical Paths (in use)

Acute leukemia induction
Acute pancreatitis
Angina, unstable
Asthma
Atrial fibrillation, new onset
Cardiac cath, elective
Cellulitis
Chest pain, rule out myocardial infarction
Congestive heart failure
Chemotherapy
Chronic obstructive pulmonary disease
Cerebrovascular accident
Diverticulitis
Diabetic foot ulcer with cellulitis
Diabetic ketoacidosis
Fever of unknown origin secondary to neutropenia
Myocardial infarction
Pneumonia
PTCA, elective
Pyelonephritis
Seizure, first occurrence
Seizure, recurring
Septicemia
Syncope
Upper GI bleeding

Approved Surgical Critical Paths (in use)

Cardiovascular/Thoracic
AICD
CABG (coronary artery bypass graft)
Cardiac valve replacement
Lobectomy

General Surgery
Appendectomy
Bowel resection—large
Bowel resection—small
Cholecystectomy—laparoscopic
Cholecystectomy—nonlaparoscopic
Colostomy
Esophagogastrectomy (intensive care stay only)
Hernia, inguinal and femoral
Mastectomy/node dissection
Parathyroidectomy for tumor and/or
   hyperparathyroidism
Thyroidectomy for graves
Thyroidectomy, subtotal for tumor
Thyroidectomy, total
Thyroid lymph node dissection

Neurosurgery
Anterior cervical discectomy and fusion
Craniotomy for epidural hematoma
Craniotomy for meningioma
Gamma knife with arteriogram
Gamma knife without arteriogram
Laminectomy—single level (discectomy)
Laminectomy—multilevel (discectomy)
Myelogram
Transphenoidal hypophysectomy
VP shunt for hydrocephalus

Ophthalmology
Endophthalmitis: instillation of antibiotics
Scleral buckling/retinal detachment
Vitreous operations

Orthopedics
ACL (anterior cruciate ligament) repair
Fractured hip
Lumbar laminectomy/discectomy
Myelogram
Total hip (lateral)
Total hip (posterior)
Total knee replacement

Otolaryngology
Laryngectomy
Tonsillectomy and adenoidectomy

Plastic Surgery
Free muscle flap transfer
Breast reconstruction
Rhinoplasty

Urology
Cystectomy/ileal loop
Nephrectomy (nonneoplastic)
Prostatectomy, radical retropubic
Radical retroperitoneal lymph node dissection
Suprapubic prostatectomy
Transperitoneal radical nephrectomy
TURBT (transurethral resection of bladder tumor)
TURP (transurethral resection of prostate)

Vascular Surgery
AAA (abdominal aortic aneurysm)

Approved Psychiatry Critical Paths (in use)

Electroconvulsive therapy

Approved Rehabilitation Critical Paths (in use)

Cerebrovascular accident
Lower extremity amputation

Figure 6-2. Clinical Path for Cholecystectomy (Nonlaparoscopic)

Rhode Island Hospital
Dept. of Surgery
© 1992 All Rights Reserved
Resident_____

TITLE: CHOLECYSTECTOMY (non-laparoscopic)
DRG: 198
EXPECTED LOS: 4 DAYS

ADMISSION DATE:_____
DISCHARGE DATE:_____
ACTUAL LOS:_____

	DAY 1 SDA	OR	DAY 2 POD 1	DAY 3 POD 2	DAY 4 POD 3 Discharge
CONSULTS	OR Permit Anesthesia			Dietary prn	
TESTS	PATs: lab 1 wk prior EKG prn + req for males >45 females >50 Chest x-ray prn		CBC Lytes		
TREATMENTS	Weight Teds prn--------- VS------- IV fluids--------	q1h x 2, q2h x 3, then q4h Check abd dressing----- CDB with VS-----	------>q8h.. D/C or chg to INT-----	------>D/C INT Check incision-----	-------->D/C -------->D/C -------->D/C
MEDICATIONS	Analgesics IM--------	--------	--------	Analgesic PO-----	-------->D/C
ACTIVITY	OOB with assist	Bedrest/chair with assist Assist w/care	Ambulate hall w/assist Assist w/care	Ambulate independently Self care prn-----	-------->D/C -------->D/C
NUTRITION	NPO	NPO	Clear liq - Advance as tolerated	Advance as tolerated------	-------->D/C
ELIMINATION			Check for bowel sounds	Check BM Supp prn	If no BM before discharge supp/fleet enema prn
EDUCATION	Pre/post-op teaching Low fat diet teaching prn----- (physician preference)	--------	--------	Low fat diet teaching prn (physician preference)	Review discharge meds, instructions and follow-up appointments
PSYCHOSOCIAL	Patient/family support-----	--------	--------	-------->D/C	
DISCHARGE PLAN	Admit Assessment Continuing care prn		VNA referral prn	Review discharge instructions (physician preference)	
PROGRESS FOLLOWED	Yes No	Yes No	Yes No	Yes No	Yes No
CRITICAL PATH Rev. 8/92	RN SIGNATURE	RN SIGNATURE	RN SIGNATURE	RN SIGNATURE	RN SIGNATURE

Figure 6-3. Clinical Path for Coronary Artery Bypass Graft

Rhode Island Hospital
Division of CVT Surgery
RIH Surgical Foundation, Inc.
© 1992 All Rights Reserved
Resident _____

TITLE: **CABG-SICW**
DRG: **106/107**
EXPECTED LOS: **24 HOURS**

ADMISSION DATE: _____ TIME: _____
DISCHARGE DATE: _____ TIME: _____
ACTUAL LOS: _____

	0-1 HOUR ADMIT TIME	1-4 HOURS TIME	4-8 HOURS TIME	8-12 HOURS TIME	12-16 HOURS TIME	16-20 HOURS TIME	20-24 HOURS TRANSFER
CONSULTS	CVT resident Resp. therapist	Social services					
TESTS	Admission lab EKG Chest x-ray	ABGs K	ABGs K H&H	ABGs K H&H	ABGs K	CBC/Lytes/BUN Cr/ABGs EKG Chest x-ray	K
TREATMENTS	IV access Monitor: EKG/zero cal SG A Line, LAP Alarms on, cuff pressure Tape chest tubes 20 cm suction Check pacer/demand on Ventilator Complete systems assessment	Initial CO / CI SVR / PCW HR / rhythm q 1 h Autotransfuse prn Chest tube output q 1 h Check pacer cables + wires Suction/ambu @ 100 O Dec FiO2 Systems assessment	CO/ CI/ SVR/ PCW q4h Date dsgs Cuff pressure Document rhythm Change to IMV Decrease FiO2 to 40% Systems assessment	Monitor pressure/ zero / cal Dec IMV to 8 Systems assessment	Cuff pressure Chest tube output q 2 h Document rhythm Decrease IMV to 4 / PFTs Extubate to FM / 40% OZ Systems assessment	2 IVs-cordis/perip D/C SG & LAP Zero/cal monitor Inc spirometry q 1 h Systems assessment	D/C A line Cuff pressure Change AV Pacer to V Pacer ——> Systems assessment
MEDICATIONS	IV drips Antibiotic q8h	Analgesic IV q 4 h prn Begin digitalization	Wean IV drips Antibiotic 8 hr I & O		SC / IM Analgesics Alternate agents Antibiotic 8 hr I & O	D/C Lasix prn Completed digitalization	Antibiotic 24 hr I & O
ACTIVITY	Bedrest	Turn s to s x1 HOB to 30	Turn q2h		HOB to 45-60	OOB X 1	Transfer to JA-2 via stretcher w monitor +O2
NUTRITION	NPO NGT	Intermit suction Irrigate NG Tube q 2-3 h				D/C	Start sips/advance as tolerated
ELIMINATION	Foley catheter q 1 h output	q 1 h output	S+A / sp gr / heme	S+A / sp gr/heme	S+A / sp gr/heme	q 2 h output	
EDUCATION	Orient family/ICU Continuous ICU Orient / patient					Reinforce preop teaching	Orient to transfer
PSYCHOSOCIAL	Family Support						Notify family of patient transfer
DISCHARGE PLAN						Transfer summary sheet to JA-2 Transfer Orders	Notify N2 to coordinate transfer time
PROGRESS FOLLOWED	Yes No	Yes No	Yes No	Yes No	Yes No	Yes No	Yes No
CRITICAL PATH Rev 3/93	RN SIGNATURE	RN SIGNATURE	RN SIGNATURE	RN SIGNATURE	RN SIGNATURE	RN SIGNATURE	RN SIGNATURE

Figure 6-4. Clinical Path for Rehabilitation after Cerebrovascular Accident

Rhode Island Hospital
Dept. of Physical Medicine
© 1992 All Rights Reserved
M.D. (Attending)
M.D. (Rehab)

TITLE: REHAB CVA
DRG:
EXPECTED LOS: 4 WEEKS

DATE ADMIT TO REHAB:
DATE DISCH FROM REHAB:
ACTUAL REHAB LOS:
TOTAL RIH LOS:

	WEEK 1 — DAY 1-2 Admit	WEEK 1 — DAYS 3-7	WEEK 2	WEEK 3	WEEK 4	(extended stay)
CONSULTS	Social service; OT; PT	Dietary prn; Rehab counselor prn; Speech prn (7); Psych prn (10); Brace shop prn (11)				This column is for patients with extended stay
TESTS	PTA daily (1); Stool OB (2); Other (3)	PVR, UA, C+S prn (12)	PTA Mon, Wed, Fri or prn (1)	> >	Review PTA schedule; D/C	
TREATMENTS	VS BID and prm; I+O; Splint application at HS and prm (4); Teds (5)	VS BID and prm; I+O ...D/C prn; Splint at HS and prm; Speech (6) (M-F days); PT, OT (M-F days); Teds	Splint at HS prn; Speech (M-F days) prm; PT, OT Mon-Fri (days); Teds prn	VS; Splint at HS prn; Speech (M-F days) prm; PT, OT (M-F days); Teds D/C prn	D/C; Review schedule for home therapies	
MEDICATIONS	ASA/ Coumadin/ Heparin prn (Non-hemorrhagic CVA only)(1); Stool softener and/or laxative prn; Other (6)				Review meds for home	
ACTIVITY	OOB with assist; Assist w/bed + wheelchair mobility; ADL's with patient; Elevate affected extremity on pillow when in bed, lap tray or w/c trough when OOB if non functional--->	OOB with assist; Progressive ambulation with adaptive device (hemi-walker, cane, or quad cane) + decreasing level of assistance	OOB with assist	OOB with assist	Activity to continue after discharge per MD/PT --->	
NUTRITION	Supervise/advance to puree diet/thick fluids prn (7); or; Diet as tolerated				Review nutritional needs	
ELIMINATION	Monitor stool/urine output; Bowel program (8); Bladder program (9)	Monitor stool/urine output; Bowel program; Bladder program	Monitor stool/urine output; Bowel program; Bladder program	Monitor stool/urine output; Bowel program; Bladder program	Review bowel and bladder program prn	
EDUCATION	Orientation to rehab unit and routines w/patient and/or family; Fall precautions prn w/patient and/or family; Safety Education prn w/patient and/or family--->	Meds, nutrition, bowel and bladder program, skin assessment and care, etc; Disease process teaching	Reinforce education-family involved with OT, PT, nsg etc w patient/family return demonstration; Functional-transfers, amb, ADLs with family	Review diet information	Review discharge instructions; Safety; Skin; Follow-up appointments	
PSYCHOSOCIAL	Rehab information shared with patient and/or family; Assessment by psych-team --->					
DISCHARGE PLAN	Admission assessment	Bi-weekly team meeting for goal setting and home care; Home Care Coordinator		Home visit with PT, OT, and patient prn (13); Bi-weekly team meeting for goal setting and home care; Equipment Needs; Family meeting prn	VNA form prn; Physician and therapy follow-up appointments; Prescriptions written	
PROGRESS FOLLOWED Critical Path	RN SIGNATURE	RN SIGNATURE	RN SIGNATURE	RN SIGNATURE	RN SIGNATURE	RN SIGNATURE

Clinical Path Documentation System

The unit secretary is responsible for selecting the appropriate path, in consultation with the nursing caregiver, on the basis of the patient's admitting diagnosis. Information documented on the path by the unit secretary includes the name of the attending physician; whether the patient is being treated by a resident; the name of the nurse practitioner, physician assistant, or resident (if applicable); patient demographics from the addressograph stamp; and admission and discharge dates. One copy is maintained in the patient's chart for the physician to review as orders are written, and one copy is kept in the Kardex™ file for nursing documentation and review. No documentation by physicians is required. The copy of the path in the patient's chart is discarded after discharge. The secretary removes the path from the Kardex™ file and stores it for later review by clinical management staff.

Nurses using the path are instructed to review the day's activities. If the patient is progressing as outlined on the path, progress can be noted by circling "yes" next to "progress followed critical path" at the bottom of the column for that time increment. Spaces are provided for all three shifts to sign off on a patient's progress, which ensures that all staff share this responsibility. Any activity or test not performed is circled on the front of the path, documented as a variance on the back, and dated. The staff nurse caring for the patient is charged with documenting in the space provided comorbid conditions and other reasons why a patient is not progressing as planned. During the change of shift, the nurse giving the report is then able to explain what has not been done and why. This variance reporting increases continuity of care and helps keep the patient on path.

The documentation system was designed around the clinical path as the nursing plan of care. Individual patient problems are identified and addressed in the newly developed Kardex™ files. The path is not used to document any other patient activities.

At present, clinical paths at RIH are not part of the permanent record. As a result, staff nurses question their value, particularly the relevance of duplicate documentation. If paths were incorporated into the permanent record, charting by exception would be possible and nurse documentation time would be reduced. However, physicians are reluctant to make this change because of perceived medical and legal risk implications. Specifically, they fear being required to follow paths strictly and being held accountable if they do not.

The position of the hospital's risk management department is that no legal liability is incurred in using critical paths so long as individual variances are documented adequately. Even without a path in the record, in event of a lawsuit or liability charge, an expert witness would testify to a community standard of care (which in all likelihood would be similar to the path). Ultimately, evidence indicating that the physician followed the path supports the contention that he or she provided acceptable care.

Clinical Paths Used As Indicators

Clinical paths for pneumonia, chronic obstructive pulmonary disease (COPD), and pyelonephritis are being used to collect data on physician-identified clinical indicators for quality assurance purposes. A key element of care on the path is identified as a clinical indicator so that when reviewing the path, staff nurses easily can document whether the indicator was met. For example, the department of medicine tracked whether a sputum culture was obtained for all pneumonia patients on day one.

The pharmacy department, in conjunction with a multidisciplinary work group, has developed detailed guidelines to parallel clinical paths that recommend specific medications and dosages, with lower cost formulary medications being noted. The pharmacy guidelines are not printed on the paths used on the patient care unit but are included in a house officer's manual. The departments of clinical management and medicine designed a pocket-size manual containing all medical paths and other relevant information for house officers.

Variance Analysis

As explained in chapter 1, a variance occurs any time a patient's progress deviates from the path, including a length of stay that was longer than expected. These deviations are categorized as clinician, system, or patient variances. For example, if a physician orders something not on the path or neglects to order something included on it, a clinician variance occurs. A delay in scheduling tests is a system variance (the expectation being that a test can be scheduled within 24 hours). Variances that occur because of the patient's condition, comorbidities, or failure to progress are patient variances. Analyzing variances keeps caregivers focused on the patient's plan of care while at the same time disclosing trends in patient management that affect outcomes.

Using Variance Analysis for Patient Management

Patients who vary significantly from paths are taken "off path," and in such cases the path no longer is used as a case management tool. For example, the diagnosis "chest pain/rule out [r/o] MI" allows the nurse to switch to an unstable angina path or an MI path after the end of day two. (See figures 6-5, 6-6, and 6-7, pp. 90–92.) A more experienced nurse who feels comfortable with the process may use two or more paths when the patient has multiple diagnoses, following the guidelines for both.

Staff nurses are expected to respond to variances concurrently by talking to the attending physician, intervening in scheduling of tests, or modifying the patient's plan of care. As mentioned previously, these variances are discussed during shift report.

On one unit at Rhode Island Hospital, pilot testing is currently under way for the use of a nurse case manager, the primary goal being better resolution of patient variances. The case manager will focus on off-path patients in an attempt to get them back on path. To meet overall responsibility for coordinating and facilitating the management of patient care (including its clinical, financial, and social aspects), the case manager collaborates with all members of the health care team from preadmission to postdischarge. The second goal of the pilot is improved variance documentation.

After discharge, the path is removed from the Kardex™ file and sent to the office of clinical management, whose staff review each path to determine whether patients "followed path." Depending on the adequacy of documentation by staff nurses, variance information typically is not validated by chart review. All variance data are analyzed manually, in spreadsheet format, and reports by diagnosis are generated monthly. Reports describe the number of patients on path, expected length of stay, actual average length of stay, number of patients who followed path, number who did not, and reasons for extended length of stay. Surgical departments receive specific patient information.

Patient and clinician variances are shared with clinical managers, who in turn share them with staff nurses and with chiefs of service. In the department of medicine, the clinical management committee of nurses, physicians, and administrators reviews this information for trends in specific variances. The chief of medicine delegates issues for follow-up to a working group of physicians.

Each surgical chief has his or her own method of communicating variance information to staff physicians. For example, in the urology department all variant cases are discussed at monthly faculty meetings. Hospital system delays are shared with relevant department managers, who receive patient-specific information and dates of service so that they can resolve problems internally.

Figure 6-5. Clinical Path for Chest Pain, Rule Out Myocardial Infarction

Rhode Island Hospital
RIH Medical Foundation, Inc.
© 1992 All Rights Reserved
TEACHING_____ RESIDENT_____
ATTENDING_____
NURSE PRACTITIONER_____

TITLE: CHEST PAIN, R/O MI (1)
DRG: 143
EXPECTED LOS: 1 DAY

( ) MD To Initial to Verify Working Diagnosis

Admission Date:_____
Discharge Date:_____
Actual LOS_____

	Day 1	Day 2 Discharge after MI R/O	
CONSULTS	Cardiology prn	Cardiac diet class prn	
TESTS	CBC CPK w/Fract. Q8 X3 (2) Glucose EKG Chest X-Ray	Book stress test as outpatient prn and/or consider outpatient w/u for etiology of pain EKG	**ON DAY 2** If NEGATIVE for M.I. and FREE OF CHEST PAIN but not discharged, indicate as variance on back.
TREATMENTS	O2 Cardiac Monitor-------- IV/INT-------- I&O--------	O2 prn --------D/C prn INT--------D/C prn --------D/C prn	
MEDICATIONS	Heparin SC/IV prn-------- ASA-------- Analgesic-IV prn-------- Anxiolytic meds prn-------- Nitrates if indicated Beta Blocker unless contra indicated prn Calcium channel blockers prn	--Continue if started--------> Switch to PO-------->	**ON DAY 2** If NEGATIVE M.I. but CHEST PAIN continues (unstable angina), proceed to Day 2 of Unstable Angina path.
ACTIVITY	Bedrest/commode	Ad lib if enzymes negative	
NUTRITION	3 gm Na Low Cholesterol No stimulants	-------------->	
ELIMINATION	Check for daily BM.......... Test stools for home if on heparin		
EDUCATION	Cardiac Teaching: risk factors, exercise- include family Smoking Cessation program prn Review of meds	Review discharge instructions, dietary instructions, review of meds and follow-up appointments	**ON DAY 2** If POSITIVE for M.I., proceed for Day 2 of M.I. path.
PSYCHOSOCIAL	Patient/family support.......... ORM assessment (Advance Directives)	-------------->	
DISCHARGE PLAN	Admission assessment Continuing care assessment		
PROGRESS FOLLOWED CRITICAL PATH	Yes _____ No _____ RN SIGNATURE D _____ E _____ N _____	Yes _____ No _____ RN SIGNATURE D _____ E _____ N _____	

Rev. 4/94

Figure 6-6. Clinical Path for Angina, Unstable

TEACHING _____ RESIDENT _____
ATTENDING _____
NURSE PRACTITIONER _____

TITLE: ANGINA, UNSTABLE (1)
DRG: 140
EXPECTED LOS: 3 DAYS

( ) MD To Initial To Verify Working Diagnosis

ADMISSION DATE: _____
DISCHARGE DATE: _____
ACTUAL LOS: _____

	DAY 1	DAY 2	DAY 3	DAY 4 Transfer to OR if CABG scheduled or DISCHARGE prn
CONSULTS	Cardiology prn	Cardiac diet class prn	CVT prn of PTCA indicated CABG day 4 if indicated (see CABG path)(3)	
TESTS	CPK, w fract q8h x 3 (2) Lytes, BUN, Creat prn CBC, Glucose EKG Chest X-ray prn Book Cardiac Cath prn	EKG	EKG prn Cardiac Cath prn (See Cardiac Cath path) (4)	
TREATMENTS	O2 Telemetry/Monitor---- IV/INT----	O2 prn Telemetry prn IV/INT prn	O2 prn Telemetry prn IV/INT prn PTCA prn (See PTCA path) (5)	
MEDICATIONS	Heparin IV prn Nitrates if indicated ASA Analgesic prn Anxiolytic meds prn Ca Blockers prn Beta Blockers prn	Heparin IV Nitrates prn ASA Analgesic prn Anxiolytic meds prn Ca Blockers prn Beta Blockers prn	Heparin IV Nitrates prn ASA Analgesic prn Anxiolytic meds prn Ca Blockers prn Beta Blockers prn	
ACTIVITY	Bedrest/Commode	OOB---> chair BRP	Ad lib or as ordered Post Cath/PTCA bedrest prn	Ad lib
NUTRITION	3 gm Na Lo cholesterol No stimulants			
ELIMINATION	I & O Monitor BM's Test stools for heme if on Heparin	I & O Monitor BM	I & O prn Monitor BM	
EDUCATION	Med review Cardiac risk factors Smoking Cessation program	Cardiac Cath teaching---- Angina teaching---- Group Cardiac classes----	------>Continue prn ------>Continue prn ------>Continue prn	
PSYCHOSOCIAL	Pt/family support---- ORM assessment (Advance Directives)	----------------------	----------------------	---------------------->
DISCHARGE PLAN	Admission assessment Continuing care assessment Outpatient rehab referral prn	VNA referral prn	Discharge prn	
PROGRESS FOLLOWED	Yes No RN SIGNATURE D ___ E ___ N ___	Yes No RN SIGNATURE D ___ E ___ N ___	Yes No RN SIGNATURE D ___ E ___ N ___	Yes No RN SIGNATURE D ___ E ___ N ___

CRITICAL PATH Rev. 4/94

Figure 6-7. Clinical Path for Myocardial Infarction

Rhode Island Hospital
RIH Medical Foundation, Inc.
TEACHING _____ RESIDENT _____
ATTENDING _____
NURSE PRACTITIONER _____

TITLE: MI (1)
DRG: 122/121
EXPECTED LOS: 5 DAYS

(   ) MD TO INITIAL TO VERIFY
WORKING DIAGNOSIS

ADMISSION DATE: _____
DISCHARGE DATE: _____
ACTUAL LOS: _____

	DAY 1 CCU	DAY 2 TRANSFER	DAY 3	DAY 4	DAY 5	DAY 6 DISCHARGE BY 9:00 AM
CONSULTS	Cardiology prn to consider Thrombolytic therapy	Cardiac Diet Class prn; Psych. Liaison Nurse prn				
TESTS	CBC; CPK w/Fract. Q8 X3 (2); Glucose,Lytes; BUN, Creat; Labs as per thrombolytic protocol; EKG; Chest X-ray	Book non-invasive tests LLST, ECHO) day 5 or 6 prn; PT (6); EKG	PT (6); EKG	PT (6)	Low level stress test (recom.); PT (6); EKG prior to discharge	PT (6)
TREATMENTS	Oxygen; Cardiac Monitor; IV-KVO; I & O	O2 prn; INT; Weight	D/C Oxygen; -----> D/C; -----> D/C		-----> D/C; -----> D/C	
MEDICATIONS	Heparin (3); ASA; Analgesic-IV prn; Anxiolytic meds prn; Nitrates if indicated; IV Beta Blocker unless contra indicated; Channel blocker prn; Lidocaine IV prn; Thrombolytic therapy (4) or cardiac cath lab as indicated	Switch to; Consider Coumadin day 2-3(6); Consider Cath if not considered on day 1; Ace Inhibitor prn	-----> D/C		-----> D/C; -----> D/C; Review discharge meds; -----> D/C; -----> D/C; -----> D/C	
ACTIVITY	Bedrest/Commode	Bed/Chair; BRP	Ambulate Ad Lib in Room	Ambulate in hall	Ambulate prn/stairs prn	
NUTRITION	3 gm Na Low cholesterol; No stimulants				-----> D/C	
ELIMINATION	Check for daily BM; Test stools for OB if on Heparin				-----> D/C	
EDUCATION	Cardiac Teaching (5) include family: risk factors, exercise, Smoking cessation program prn; Review of meds	Begin step down unit-rehab program; Booklet: Heart Attack What's Ahead	Group Class: anatomy, risk factors, nutrition, emotional support, stress, disch. prep.	Group class; Stress test teaching; Reinforse Smoking cessation program prn	-----> D/C	Review of cardiac topics with patient; Coumadin book prn; Nitro review prn; Med schedule
PSYCHOSOCIAL	Pt/Family support; ORM assessment (Advance Directives)					
DISCHARGE PLAN	Admit assessment; Continuing care assessment; Outpatient Rehab Referral prn		VNA Referral prn; Review 9 am discharge		Obtain d/c diet, obtain d/c order and prescriptions; Review with patient; Schedule post-hospitalization cardiac rehab prn	
PROGRESS FOLLOWED CRITICAL PATH Rev. 3/94	Yes___ No___; RN SIGNATURE; D___ E___ N___	Yes___ No___; RN SIGNATURE; D___ E___ N___	Yes___ No___; RN SIGNATURE; D___ E___ N___	Yes___ No___; RN SIGNATURE; D___ E___ N___	Yes___ No___; RN SIGNATURE; D___ E___ N___	Yes___ No___; RN SIGNATURE; D___ E___ N___

Using Variance Analysis for CQI

As a result of clinical path variance analysis, some paths at RIH have been revised. For example, many patients who started on the path for chest pain/rule out myocardial infarction were ruled out for an MI but were not ready for discharge on day two. It was recognized that the condition of unstable angina also required a path and one was created (figures 6-5 and 6-6, pp. 90 and 91). Expected lengths of stay have been adjusted for various diagnoses. Changes in technology and medical practice have also resulted in alterations to paths.

Since implementation of clinical paths, ancillary areas have been much more responsive to scheduling requests and for the most part have met the expectation of a 24-hour turnaround. Some areas have added new equipment, such as a densitometer to run cardiac enzymes, and have expanded hours of operation to accommodate patient needs. These departments welcome real data on delays in their areas, rather than anecdotal complaints that are difficult to address.

Sharing paths with patients and families has received a positive response at RIH and is seen as a means to improve patient satisfaction, which in turn bears on the quality of care. For this reason, nurses on the CVT unit are developing a version of the CABG path that is patient-friendly. These paths, written in nontechnical and easy-to-understand language, will be incorporated into the general teaching program for all CABG patients the day before surgery. If patient-friendly paths are successful for this group of patients, it is likely that they will be developed for other diagnoses across the hospital.

Facing Obstacles to Variance Analysis

The biggest block to variance analysis is the sheer *volume of data*. The paths of approximately 800 patients per month must be reviewed, and there are no automated systems to support the process. It is the hospital's intention to computerize clinical path review during the next phase of upgrading the patient information system (anticipated to occur between 1994 and 1996). In the interim, the clinical management department is examining better ways to manage the data collected.

A second obstacle is *incomplete documentation by staff nurses*. For example, it is not always possible to ascertain from documentation on the clinical path the real reasons for extended length of stay or variation in physician practice patterns. Because the path is not part of the medical record and staff nurses must document in more than one place, the importance of the path is sometimes minimized and documentation may be neglected. If paths become part of the permanent record and charting is done by exception, it is expected that variance documentation will improve. Furthermore, if physicians and nurses communicate more effectively about the patient's plan, nurses can better understand reasons for path deviations and in turn be better equipped to document them. The case manager pilot now under way is expected to facilitate these needs.

A third obstacle to variance analysis is a *lack of physician interest and involvement*. It has been difficult to engage physicians in the data-review process because their interest lies more with clinical issues related to their own patients or with hospital-wide system problems that, if solved, could facilitate their practice. Management needs to show physicians how they can benefit from participating in variance analysis. For example, physicians have reacted positively to the opportunity to discuss the variation in their practice as compared to their peers and the clinical path. Meetings are held with 6 to 10 physicians who treat patients with a given diagnosis and are non-threatening and educational in nature. The physicians are able to share knowledge on treatment protocols and new technologies. The focus of these discussions is how to improve the quality of patient care, a goal which all physicians share. Results of the discussion may be changes in clinical practice as well as identification of hospital operational problems.

Interfacing with Other Departments

There is no formal interface among departments of clinical management, utilization review, quality assurance, and service/quality, although lines of communication are open and there is some integration of data collected. For example, clinical management reports system delays to the utilization review committee. As the hospital's service/quality initiative becomes more integrated into daily operations, clinical paths can become benchmarks, and variance data can be used by process improvement teams. Another interface occurs through the hospital's senior vice-president for service/quality, who is a member of the clinical management committee and supports its endeavors.

Three medical paths are being used to collect information on clinical indicators for quality assurance (chest pain, unstable angina, and myocardial infarction). In addition, the director of clinical management is a member of the quality assurance committee, which facilitates collaboration between the two departments. Any major quality issues discovered as part of the variance documentation process can be brought to this committee.

Results and Benefits of Clinical Path Implementation

Certain areas have been shown to benefit (or remain stable) due to implementation of clinical paths at RIH. These areas are length of stay, health care team interaction, and resource allocation.

Impact on Length of Stay

The hospital went from a $14 million loss in 1990 to a $4 million positive net income from operations in 1992. A major factor in achieving this financial turnaround was reduction in the average length of stay. The average length of stay for adult patients declined from 8.91 days in fiscal year 1990 to 7.05 days in fiscal year 1993, a 21 percent decrease. During this same period, the average length of stay for clinical path DRGs declined by 23 percent. (Table 6-1 shows changes in length of stay for selected clinical path DRGs.) The consensus among leaders at RIH is that the use of paths, although only one of several strategies aimed at reducing LOS, has helped heighten overall awareness of the need to reduce length of stay, thus enhancing efforts already under way by utilization review, continuing care, and ancillary services to achieve a quicker turnaround on test results.

Direct variable cost savings related to length-of-stay reduction from fiscal year 1990 to fiscal year 1993 is in the range of $3 million. Average cost per discharge remained relatively stable during this period, with increases lower than the rate of inflation. In addition, increased bed capacity due to fewer patient days enabled the hospital to accommodate increased admissions.

Impact on Interactive Patient Management

The implementation of clinical paths has been the impetus to bring different caregivers together to solve common problems related to patient care. An example is the care of patients with diabetic ketoacidosis. The path recommended that the patient be admitted to the medical intensive care unit (MICU), be transferred to a routine unit on day two, and be discharged on day three. The staff endocrinologists said that many of these patients would not need to be admitted to the MICU if they could receive

Table 6-1. Average Length of Stay (ALOS) for Selected Clinical Path DRGs

DRG	Diagnosis	FY90 ALOS	FY91 ALOS	FY92 ALOS	FY93 ALOS
001	Craniotomy	9.28	8.44	7.73	7.53
024	Seizure and headache	9.24	8.80	5.96	4.73
088	COPD	7.15	8.39	7.38	6.56
089	Pneumonia	10.06	10.32	8.09	7.98
112	Vascular procedure	6.53	6.00	5.68	4.93
121	MI	13.01	11.60	11.04	10.82
138	Atrial fibrillation	8.20	5.62	5.35	4.79
140	Angina	4.33	4.27	3.97	4.06
148	Bowel procedure	18.88	17.15	16.04	14.18
175	GI bleed	4.07	3.40	3.22	2.77
209	Joint procedure	12.68	11.59	11.45	10.12
210	Hip and femur	19.57	15.65	14.31	10.98
258	Mastectomy	5.58	4.29	3.57	2.79
320	Kidney and UTI	11.04	9.95	7.79	7.22
336	TURP	7.90	7.00	6.42	4.11
416	Septicemia	16.27	12.37	11.75	10.56
All clinical path DRGs		8.54	7.38	6.92	6.56
All adult patients		8.91	7.93	7.33	7.05

an insulin drip on a routine unit and have immediate blood sugar results with use of a bedside glucometer. These physicians worked together with nursing, pathology, and administration to provide education and support for these services so that patients could avoid a costly stay in intensive care. The group continues to evaluate the use of bedside glucose testing.

Impact on Resource Allocation

The only administrative and analytical staff dedicated full time to the clinical path program are the director of clinical management (who has a master's degree in hospital administration), the nursing coordinator (who has a master's degree in nursing), and a secretary. Direct costs for this staff and supplies are approximately $125,000 per year. Staff nurses, physicians, and administrators have contributed their time in developing paths and monitoring variances. There have been no new expenses related to their efforts.

The use of clinical paths has had a minor impact on staff nurses' time. The majority of staff nurses surveyed reported spending an average of 15 minutes per day on paths, which, they believe, is an appropriate amount of time. They feel, however, that using paths creates more paperwork. Management is working to include the path in the permanent medical record and to computerize the clinical path process.

Clinical Path Success Factors at RIH

The experience at RIH demonstrates that certain factors are essential to developing and implementing a clinical path program successfully. Among them are networking among similar institutions, educational programs for path users, a pilot unit, strong physician and nurse leadership, and incorporation of paths into existing multidisciplinary systems.

Networking with Other Institutions

There is a wealth of information in the literature about implementing a clinical path process. Hospitals should research what has been successful at similar institutions. A review of the literature may be followed by phone calls or site visits when possible; most authors are happy to share their knowledge and success stories. Hospital managers should develop a tentative structure and process for their own institution and establish a steering committee to carry out the plan.

Educational Programs

A hospital needs support from key physician and nursing leaders from the start. One of the first tasks of the steering committee is to put together an educational program for these individuals on the concept of clinical paths and the benefits of using them. This education can be provided through a variety of vehicles—physician staff meetings, grand rounds, RN staff meetings, one-on-one sessions, newsletters, bulletin boards, and so on. Each person who becomes a supporter of the clinical path process can help to communicate to the rest of the organization.

Pilot Unit

Once the foundation has been laid, a working group can start by designing a path for one diagnosis on a pilot unit. A unit that already operates well and has strong nursing leadership is the best candidate for a pilot program. By incorporating paths into existing forms, everyone benefits from reduced documentation and paperwork requirements. To do this, the critical path must be part of the permanent medical record. This strategy also prepares the institution to move from a manual to an automated system.

Communicating the success achieved on the pilot unit before expanding to other diagnoses on other units will make it much easier to gain acceptance of smaller physician groups and nurse groups, who can in turn bring their peers on board. A pilot also provides an opportunity for potential problems to surface in the process before they spread across the hospital.

Strong Physician Leadership

As already noted, strong physician leadership is crucial to the successful implementation of clinical paths. The physician at the forefront of this effort should be an active clinician, a risk taker respected by peers, able to manage conflict, and willing to "sell" the concept of clinical paths to other physicians. This responsibility should be well defined and the physician adequately compensated for his or her time. Expectations and responsibilities of chiefs of service in support of this process should be stated clearly in their job descriptions.

Multidisciplinary Approach

All members of the health care team, not only staff nurses, should develop and use the paths as a standard of care. Attending physicians, house staff, therapists for given diagnoses, discharge planners, utilization review nurses, pharmacists, and others should be represented on the steering committee. Because different disciplines use different frameworks, it is necessary to arrive at common terminology (for example, *clinical paths* versus *practice guidelines*) beforehand.

Future Directions

Rhode Island Hospital has been successful in its effort to implement clinical paths for a wide variety of diagnoses. Many benefits, particularly length-of-stay reduction and a renewed focus on patient care, have been realized. A strong program is in place, but continued challenges and improvements are anticipated. One goal for the near future is to include clinical paths in the permanent medical record to reduce physician and nurse documentation time and formally incorporate paths into the delivery of care. The hospital faces obstacles in achieving physician support but believes that the obstacles will be overcome.

Another goal is to automate the clinical path process as part of the hospital's patient information improvement system. A path would automatically be assigned to a patient on the basis of admitting diagnosis. Each day on the path would be stored in the information system as a standard set of orders. Physicians could then simply order the whole set or adjust them as needed for an individual patient. Nursing documentation would be simplified by allowing charting by exception, noting only when the patient *did not* follow the appropriate path. These exceptions automatically would be stored as variances and used in later analysis.

The hospital is in the process of evaluating the current organizational structure for utilization review/discharge planning, quality assurance, and clinical management. These separate departments work independently, and yet their responsibilities overlap in many areas. Communication among departments is adequate, but leaders recognize that there should be a more formal interface.

There is still a need to improve physician interest and involvement in the process. Physicians have been surveyed regarding their use of clinical paths and have provided insight into how to increase their participation. They want more information on the results of using paths, particularly what the effect was on their own patients, and they want improvement in hospital systems. Hospital leaders are working to meet these expectations.

Finally, RIH believes that clinical paths will be a necessary tool for success in the changing health care environment. Although Rhode Island has a low rate of managed care penetration relative to other parts of the country, it is expected to increase. The hospital views clinical paths as a necessary tool to be able to compete in terms of cost and quality. A growing demand for outcomes measurement is anticipated, and the modification of paths to include expected outcomes will be one of the institution's future activities.

Conclusion

Rhode Island Hospital has found clinical paths to be a successful way to manage patient care. It has proved that financial goals can be achieved at the same time a high level of quality care is maintained. Hospital leaders anticipate that the process will evolve over time as the hospital faces new challenges, but they believe that the basic concept of standards of care management will continue to be a central focus in the provision of health care.

Reference

1. Wachtel, T., Moulton, A., Pezzullo, J., and Halolsky, M. Inpatient management protocols to reduce health care costs. *Medical Decision Making* 6:101–9, 1986.

Clinical Paths at Douglas Community Hospital

Cynthia Pringle, Stephen Baker, Darlene Martch, Sonja Bray, and Mike Holbert

Douglas Community Hospital (DCH) is a 118-bed Health Trust Hospital located in southwestern Oregon in a community with two other hospitals (another community hospital and a Veterans Administration hospital). Competition for market share is very high. However, the more demanding challenge for DCH is to continually develop ways to better manage patient care. Additionally, because of payer emphasis on managed care, the hospital must prove itself to be a cost-efficient, high-quality provider to compete for contracts.

In 1991 the administrative staff, with input from the utilization management staff, agreed that one way to maintain high quality and cost efficiency was through the development and use of clinical paths, or as they are called at DCH, *care tracks*. The use of clinical paths at DCH is a way to ensure that each patient receives the same high-quality standard of care in the most cost-effective manner.

The medical staff identified several areas where clinical paths can influence patient care. Because the care of Medicare patients is already being reviewed by the Health Care Financing Administration (HCFA), the physicians felt it important to align DCH's clinical paths along similar guidelines to promote consistency. As national clinical practice guidelines are developed, they can be integrated into the paths. Additionally, by analyzing the cause of variances, optimal patient care practices can be identified and the paths updated to reflect improvements.

The other major focus of clinical paths concerns the alignment of hospital services. Physician-generated paths help to focus hospital care on the most important components of patient care that will yield the best outcomes. Collaboration among physicians and hospital staff is seen as the best way to achieve optimal patient outcomes. Review of variances, along with other total quality management tools, will determine whether recommended standards of care are being practiced by all members of the health care team.

Clinical Path Development

To develop clinical paths at Douglas Community Hospital, a multidisciplinary task force was formed with representatives from utilization management, pharmacy, respiratory care, nursing, and the medical staff. Physician team members, as well as other key staff, received extensive education in the use of clinical paths and case management as well as information on how these patient care management methods correlate with continuous quality improvement. Once educated, team members served as a training resource for all physicians and hospital staff. It was agreed that education of all members of the health care team would be a key success factor in DCH path-based strategy.

Total Hip and Knee Replacement

Armed with knowledge in the use of path-based patient care, the team identified the target populations for whom the first paths would be designed. Financial and length-of-stay information covering the hospital's highest-volume diagnosis-related groups (DRGs) was analyzed. The first clinical path was designed for patients undergoing total hip and total knee replacements (DRG 209), the category demonstrating highest volume and longest length of stay. In addition, the task group perceived that a surgical care path (rather than a medical one) would be easier to design because it required consideration of fewer patient-related variables.

The records of patients who had undergone total hip and knee replacement during the previous year were reviewed, and the common elements of care for each day of hospitalization were identified. The task group also found that after the second postoperative day, these patients did not seem to require acute care services. By the third postoperative day, most patients were only receiving physical and occupational therapy, neither of which need be provided in an acute setting. Therefore, the task group agreed that patients could be transferred to a level of skilled care on the third day postop. The hospital had recently acquired swing-bed (skilled care) approval from Medicare, and patient transfer to swing-bed status could easily be made a part of the clinical path for DRG 209.

The task group presented the completed path to all orthopedic physicians and explained in detail how the elements of care had been identified and why transfer to skilled care was being recommended on the third postop day. The physicians agreed that the clinical path represented their practice pattern but expressed concerns about the accountability/liability involved with maintaining the path as a permanent record in the patient's chart. Therefore, it was used only as a guideline, not as a means to document care, and it was not kept in the patient's record.

During the next year, the utilization management staff concurrently reviewed the charts of patients undergoing total hip and knee replacements. Path guidelines were compared with actual practices, and extended stays (beyond three days postop) were attributed to three factors: patients not being placed in swing-bed status on the third day, nursing staff not being proactive and requesting swing-bed status for patients, and physicians not transferring the patient to swing-bed status because of documentation issues. To address the length-of-stay variances, a three-step action plan was developed as follows:

1. Throughout the year, utilization management representatives would attend nursing staff meetings to provide education regarding the benefits of using swing beds.
2. Bedside nurses would rotate through the utilization management department, spending eight hours observing the hospital experience as seen through the eyes of utilization managers.
3. Administrative representatives would attend orthopedic physician meetings to present data that compared financial and length-of-stay information before and after development of the total hip and knee replacement path.

Figures 7-1 and 7-2, respectively, illustrate the clinical pathway's impact on length of stay and financial resources at DCH. Currently, the orthopedic department physicians

Figure 7-1. Impact on Length of Stay of Clinical Path for Total Hip and Knee Replacement

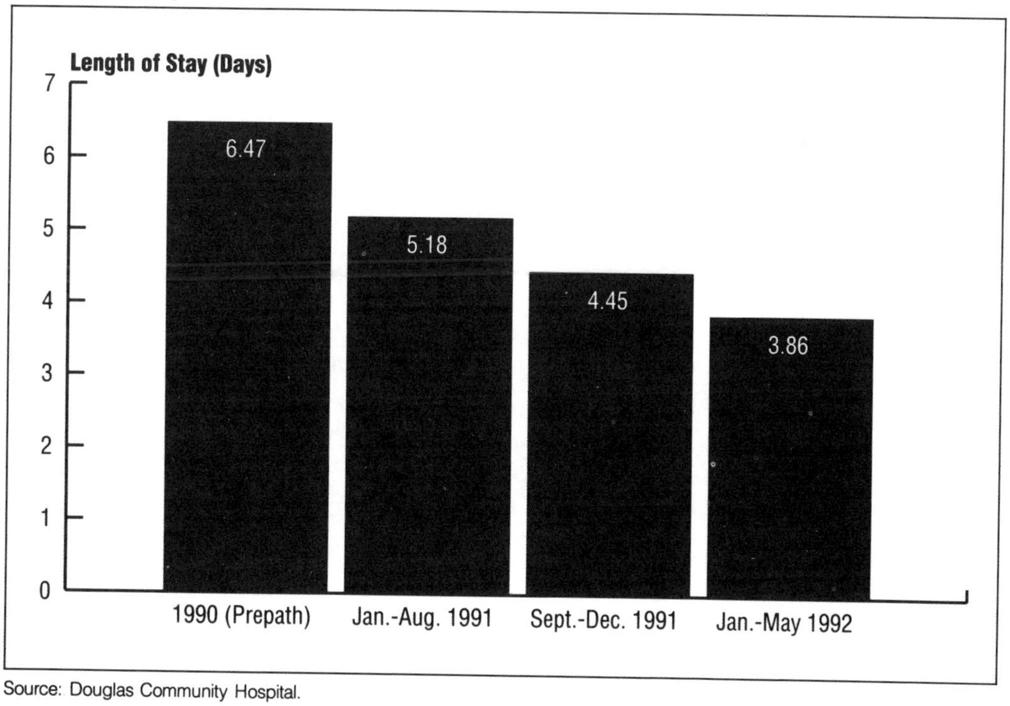

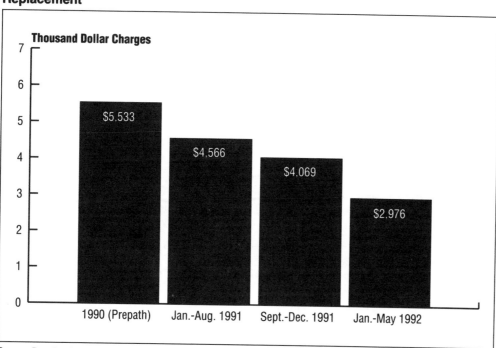

Source: Douglas Community Hospital.

Figure 7-2. Financial Impact of Clinical Path for Total Hip and Knee Replacement

Source: Douglas Community Hospital.

are reviewing the use of this path to decide whether it can be placed in the patient's medical record.

Myocardial Infarction and Simple Pneumonia

Although medical admissions usually have more patient care variances than do surgical admissions, the task group chose next to develop clinical paths for patients with myocardial infarctions (MIs) and simple pneumonia. These diagnoses were chosen because they represent a high number of admissions at DCH. Each of these medical DRGs also showed evidence of varied lengths of stay and charges.

All records for patients admitted with an uncomplicated MI and simple pneumonia for the preceding 12 months were reviewed by the task group. The team met for one hour each week, over a three-month period, to evaluate the care given to these patient groups and to formulate a preliminary clinical path for medical staff approval. To ensure that current guidelines for patient care were integrated into the paths, task group members researched the literature to identify up-to-date recommended practices. For example, the respiratory care representative helped to define the use of updraft treatments and oximetry for the simple pneumonia path.

Clinical Path Format

Decisions about the format for DCH's paths required discussion and input from all disciplines. From the physicians' viewpoint, paths should not promote "cookbook medicine" but be a tool both for physicians and hospital staff to use in monitoring and improving patient care and outcome. Physicians, nurses, and other staff also wanted a format that would help them comply with the documentation standards of the Joint Commission on Accreditation of Healthcare Organizations (JCAHO) and the requirements of other external review groups, such as the state peer review organization. By combining the requirements of all external groups into one path format, the task force hoped to minimize duplication and facilitate compliance. Therefore, criteria used by physicians in their peer review activities were incorporated with those of the peer review organization and with nursing standards of practice into one form, as shown in figure 7-3, a clinical path for pneumonia.

Variance Reporting

Initially, the clinical paths were used as a reference guide for physicians and other clinicians during the process of care, but no formal mechanism for collecting variance data was incorporated into the path strategy. Informally, some departments began to use the path framework to gather quality measurement data. For example, the pathway for total hip and knee replacement patients has medication-related care elements, such as *preoperative antibiotic given preinduction of anesthesia* and *intravenous medications changed to oral route when patient is tolerating oral intake*. Each day a clinical pharmacist reviews the care elements in the medication function of the paths to determine when and why deviations are occurring. By reviewing compliance with the pharmaceutical care elements, the clinical pharmacist can intervene while the patient is in the hospital as well as collect data for the quality measurement activities of the pharmacy and therapeutics committee.

The plan for more formal variance reporting included addition to the chart of a variance tracking sheet (see figure 7-4) for documenting the existence of a variance, its cause(s), and the intervention undertaken upon its discovery. For example, if the path suggests that the patient's intravenous (IV) line be discontinued on the third

Figure 7-3. Pneumonia Clinical Path

PNEUMONIA (DRG 89) Care Track

	DAY 1 / ADMIT	DAY 2	DAY 3	DAY 4 - 5
TESTS	CBC, profile, sputum specimen with gram stain prior to antibiotic treatment, PA and lateral chest x-ray; oximetry on admission, then q shift PRN; blood culture		Chest x-ray, CBC	
DIET	Diet as tolerated			
ACTIVITY	BRP, OOB in chair 1 x shift, bath with assistance	Ambulate in hall 1 x shift		Full activity as tolerated.
TREATMENT	O2 at 2L based on assessed need per oximetry (Sats <88%); updrafts or metered dose inhalers q 4 hrs PRN if evidence of bronchospasm; VS q 4 hrs; I&O-push fluids or IV hydration.		Evaluate use of updraft treatment and possibility of changing to medi-dose inhalers; if on O2, evaluate per oximetry findings.	
MEDICATION	Antibiotics that would cover community-acquired pneumonias (i.e. H. Flu, resistant Strep) or aspiration, change as culture/gm stain indicates; Tylenol 10 grains PRN temp; heparin IV lock/IV as ordered.		Change IV antibiotics to PO if afebrile	
KEY NURSING ACTIVITY/FUNCTION	Assess chest sounds/ respiratory status q 2 hrs; orient to unit/equipment; universal precautions as appropriate; ambulate per order; incentive spirometer (initiated by RT and RT teaching on use of inhalers)/CDB teaching.		Documentation of clinical findings relating to pathogen is documented on the progress notes for coding of diagnosis.	Home medications/instructions given to patient/familySO.
DISCHARGE PLANNING	Assess patient for home needs/disposition status.		Plan for discharge is in place with referrals made.	
ADMISSION/DISCHARGE ACTIVITIES	Patient rights: Code status addressed on admission if >65 or if RN requests; patient directive to physician addressed.			Discharge if afebrile.

Figure 7-4. Variance Tracking Report

Care track: _____

Date	Unit	Care track day	Variance/cause	Action	Signature

hospital day and the physician has written no orders to this effect, the nurse calls the physician. Should the physician choose to continue the patient on IV therapy, he or she is asked to document the rationale and any significant clinical variation in the progress notes. Variance reporting is the responsibility of all members of the health care team; however, utilization management staff conduct a concurrent review as part of the variance analysis process. If the physician's rationale for the variance is not documented in the chart or if the variance is thought to be inappropriate, the case is reviewed retrospectively by the utilization management committee. The variance form is then removed from the patient's chart after discharge and stored in the utilization management office to serve as a source document for variance data collection.

Physicians have expressed anxiety about reporting variances, specifically about their cases being reviewed if variances occurred but no rationale was provided. To overcome this resistance, the task group stresses that variances are expected and that by documenting both variance and rationale in the record, physicians further protect themselves against liability should they deviate from practice guidelines or known standards of care. Furthermore it is emphasized that variance information is used primarily to revise/improve the pathway, not to censure the physician.

Overcoming Barriers to Success

Physicians and administrators at DCH have encountered several barriers to clinical pathway development and implementation. Two key pitfalls discussed here are physician resistance to change and overregimentation of path guidelines.

Physician Resistance to Change

Because physician acceptance was imperative to the program's success, very early on in the implementation phase it was a given that relying solely on nonphysician utilization management staff could not overcome physician resistance. For example, the utilization management staff initially presented the pneumonia clinical path to the family practice division, only to be met with refusal by the division to participate in the design and implementation of paths. Reasons ranged from "fear of losing control" to "no one is going to tell us how to practice medicine." As expected, the division as a group expressed its frustration and anxiety regarding the future direction of health care reform. However, individual physicians privately expressed their acceptance of paths but were unwilling to voice their opinions openly.

To overcome this resistance, the task force stepped back and planned an implementation strategy that would better address the physicians' concerns up front through one-on-one peer education. The three physician advisers for the utilization management program at DCH received extensive education and training in the benefits of path-based patient care, thus becoming "champions for the cause." They regularly attend medical staff division meetings and help with educating *all* physicians in utilization management and quality improvement issues. In response to the concerns expressed by the family practice division, two advisers attended a division meeting and presented information regarding the use of clinical paths. As partners equally vested in the health care system, the advisers were able to address their peers' concerns in a nonthreatening manner. Upon seeing the advisers' support, the family practice physicians were more open to change and, as a result, the division decided to explore use of the clinical path for pneumonia.

Having observed that information was the key to physician acceptance, administrators furthered their information-sharing effort. This led to shedding light on physician practice patterns while gaining their acceptance of path-based patient care.

Once administrators began sharing information about the financial impact of physician practice patterns by comparing individual practice patterns with outcomes, it became clear which physicians had better outcomes (patients with shorter lengths of stay and lower costs). This strategy allowed physicians to see not only the effects of their individual practice patterns but also how their practices compared with those of their peers.

The DRG-specific comparative reports contain data about average patient charges per physician (each of whom is listed by his or her hospital-assigned number) and the department average. At the division meeting, where the financial reports are shared, each physician is given his or her number in a sealed envelope. Sharing this information at one DCH division of internal medicine meeting generated vigorous discussions about utilization and quality improvement activities. The utilization management physician advisers were present at the meeting and interpreted the financial information to show how path-based treatment could promote more consistent management and outcomes among patients. Once the medical staff better understood the data and how the data represented actual practice variations, they became more supportive of the path strategy.

The utilization management physician advisers candidly answered concerns about variances, again stressing that timely documentation of a variance and rationale for it should be part of the physician's progress notes. This way, advisers explained, in the event of postdischarge insurance inquiries, questions on appropriateness of care, court action, or pending legal action, physicians will be well served. Advisers also pointed out that a test should not be ordered if it would not affect the treatment plan or clinical course. For example, an inpatient being treated for pneumonia does not need a CT scan of the sinuses to determine presence of a sinus infection if the treatment would not change.

As a result of the extensive discussion surrounding paths and of the financial information provided to physicians, their acceptance was further secured and practice patterns looked at more closely. The division of internal medicine approved placing the clinical path for simple pneumonia on the patient chart.

Overregimentation of Paths

In designing the initial path for pneumonia, the team specified which antibiotics were appropriate for different types of pneumonia as well as which ones cost the least. The physician advisers felt that a less stringent and more generic approach, such as listing *antibiotic therapy* rather than specific antibiotics, was initially more appropriate. Once the physicians became more comfortable with the use of clinical paths in patient management, the utilization management committee could begin encouraging more detailed recommendations.

As part of the overall utilization management process, the hospital already has in place a pharmacy education program that addresses the appropriate and cost-effective use of medications. The program provides for the pharmacist to leave a pharmacy educational sheet on the patient chart for the ordering physician to review. This program may eventually be incorporated into DCH's path strategy.

Clinical Paths and the Organization's Quality Goals

The development and implementation of clinical paths at Douglas Community Hospital has helped physicians and hospital staff focus on the aspects of patient care that have the most impact on outcomes. Paths serve as multidisciplinary patient care plans used by physicians, nurses, and other health care team members to help them comply with guidelines or remember to document their rationale for deviating from guidelines.

The quality improvement value of clinical paths has already been verified with improved patient satisfaction, better communication, and enhanced patient outcomes. For example, by using path variance data, the hospital identified that patients undergoing total hip and knee replacements were staying in the hospital longer to receive physical therapy and occupational therapy aimed at regaining their prehospitalization functional status. Discussions with physicians and staff resulted in earlier transfer of these patients to skilled beds, where they could continue their therapy treatments in a less costly environment.

Although it was known that ambulating patients is a key to preventing deconditioning and longer hospital stays, data from variance analysis showed that patient ambulation was not receiving the attention it should from the nursing staff. For example, if a physician ordered "ambulate the patient ad lib," nurses assumed that the patient would ambulate on his or her own — an assumption that proved to be wrong. This situation was felt to be both a quality and a utilization management problem. Quality was affected because patient outcomes were not what they could be, and extended hospital stays exposed patients to other risks (such as falls and nosocomial infections). The situation was a utilization management concern because longer lengths of stay meant the unnecessary use of health care resources. To encourage regular ambulation, at the beginning of each shift a health care team member is assigned to ambulate specific patients. Subsequent monitoring of path variances in the area of ambulation showed a significant decrease in this problem. Therefore, the use of clinical paths that address components such as ambulation is an effective quality improvement tool.

Future Plans

The next step for Douglas Community Hospital is to develop patient-friendly versions of clinical paths, the rationale being that the patient and family who know what to expect during the hospital episode will be oriented toward the same goals as the health care team. Patient versions will be written in easy-to-read lay language, with a disclaimer emphasizing the possibility of path treatment variances if in the physician's opinion they become necessary to help attain desired outcomes.

The hospital also plans to broaden paths to include prehospitalization and posthospitalization care elements. Surgical care tracks will include the preadmission expectations. For example, total hip replacement patients will be provided preoperative training by physical therapists. Another goal is to have both the surgical and medical paths include posthospitalization care plans that address such services as outpatient rehabilitation and home health follow-up.

Conclusion

The clinical path project at Douglas Community Hospital will continue to expand as more paths are added to the patient care regimen and as their use is shown to improve quality and resource efficiency. Activities thus far have been admirable, although limited. As experience is gained in using the care track tool, it will prove to be DCH's most effective resource for achieving the organization's long-term provision of cost-effective patient care that is of the highest quality available in the community.

CHAPTER EIGHT

Clinical Paths at Columbia/HCA Chippenham Medical Center

Kathleen B. Jarrell

Chippenham Medical Center (CMC) is a 470-bed general hospital located on the southern edge of Richmond, Virginia, serving a densely populated suburban area. It is a 20-year-old community hospital owned by Columbia/HCA Healthcare Corporation and has an active family practice residency program and a newborn intensive care unit. Annually the hospital provides for 2,200 births and 450 cardiac surgery procedures; it has the busiest private emergency room service in the state with separate pediatric and critical care emergency centers. Recent improvements include renovation of a women's medical center, a radiation oncology center, and a sports medicine and outpatient orthopedic complex.

Initial Case Management and Clinical Path Activities

The administration at Chippenham Medical Center has maintained a long-term vision of health care excellence for the population served by the hospital. In trying to match resources, cost, and quality of care to best serve patient health care needs, hospital leaders came to recognize case management as a strategy for the future. They further realized that tighter controls on length of stay and cost reimbursement requirements led to the care of hospitalized patients strongly influenced by insurance companies and the government. The hospital leaders perceive case management as a channel for patient advocacy as well as a means of ensuring an edge in negotiating for financial reimbursement, thereby retaining control of health care dollars. The purpose of case management, which is essential to CMC's vision of in-hospital care for the 1990s and beyond, is to achieve positive patient outcomes within a specified time frame (or length of stay [LOS]) by utilizing appropriate resources.

Chippenham Medical Center's initial impetus for developing clinical paths (which were originally referred to as critical paths) as a case management tool arose from its desire to contain costs, promote continuity of care, shorten length of stay, analyze variances, improve physician and patient satisfaction, and establish a nursing standard of care.[1] When patient populations for clinical path development were chosen, high volume cases were examined because a predictable hospital course was perceived as amenable to path development. In addition, it was important to evaluate the patient's route from admission to discharge so as to assess whether that route also would be suitable for path development. Route assessment may be more important at the outset of path development; as the development team learns more about how clinical paths are used to direct patient care, this element may become less significant. Other considerations in initiating path development include standardization of resources needed to achieve desired outcomes and the resultant multidisciplinary collaboration to effect those outcomes.[2]

Early Efforts at Clinical Path Integration

The integration of clinical paths into CMC's case management system began in 1988 with the creation of an orthopedic clinical coordinator position for the purpose of initiating case management for patients undergoing total joint replacement.

Orthopedic Surgery Case Management

Groundwork for CMC's first effort at clinical path development began with the recognition of the extended length of stay of the total joint population (an average of 14 days compared with the Health Care Financing Administration [HCFA] average of 11 days) and its other characteristics of high volume, high cost. An additional consideration was that all total joint replacement patients were cared for on one nursing unit with a stable staff. The orthopedic clinical coordinator was encouraged to develop a multidisciplinary clinical path to coordinate the care of this diagnostic category.

A clinical path development team, headed by the orthopedic clinical coordinator, was made up of representatives from nursing, physical therapy, occupational therapy, social work, and dietary. The team targeted several opportunities for improvement, including physical therapy methods, ambulation guidelines, and pain management. Over the next several months, two total joint replacement clinical paths (total hip replacement and total knee replacement) were written by the orthopedic clinical coordinator, the orthopedic nurse manager, staff nurses, and physical therapists, with input from physicians and other members of the health care team. Subsequent to chart reviews and multidisciplinary meetings, a 10-day path was written and eventually approved by the orthopedic physician group. Physicians were given the opportunity to participate in the development process; their input primarily entailed review of the various rough drafts of the path and suggestions based on their individual practice patterns.

The orthopedic physicians worried that their practices would be ruled by "cookbook medicine" and were concerned that the paths would not be adaptable to changing patient conditions and individualization of orders to accommodate varying patient needs. The orthopedic clinical coordinator was pivotal in gaining physicians' acceptance of the path by listening individually to their concerns and addressing each issue to their satisfaction. He also was key in coordinating staff education by collaborating with the education department to develop in-services and to present a nursing grand rounds that focused on orthopedic case management and clinical paths.

Cardiac Surgery Case Management

In 1989 a clinical path was developed for patients undergoing coronary artery bypass graft (CABG). The catalyst for initiating this path was a marketing concern identified by a critical care nurse managers' focus group. It was reported that postdischarge satisfaction surveys of cardiac surgery patients noted patients' displeasure with apparent fragmentation of care. Specifically, care traversed three or four units: a medical/surgical telemetry unit on admission, the surgical intensive care unit (SICU), the progressive care unit (PCU), and a second (nonemergent) medical/surgical telemetry unit. A CABG clinical path was seen as a way of providing more cohesive care as well as improving patient satisfaction levels. The CABG patient population also met the criteria of high volume, high cost, and a structured hospital course, resulting in a relatively straightforward clinical course to map.[3] Length of stay was not identified as a major issue at the time because many patients were being discharged within the HCFA guidelines (11 days for DRG 107). However, prior to path implementation (1989), Medicare average LOS at CMC was 15 days; in 1993, LOS had dropped to 10 days. With the implementation of a 6-day postop path in April 1994, and plans under way for a revision to a 5-day postop path, further reduction in average LOS is expected by late 1994.

In 1989 the cardiac surgery task force was comprised of the nurse managers of the SICU, PCU, the two medical/surgical telemetry units, the director of cardiac rehabilitation, a nurse educator, and the critical care clinical nurse specialist. The cardiac surgeons were represented by their clinical nurse specialist initially. Respiratory therapy was consulted about the respiratory interventions on the path. An 8-day postop path was written over approximately six months.

When the clinical path concept was initially presented to the cardiac surgeons, length of stay was not emphasized as much as examining quality of care from a *nursing* viewpoint and increasing patient satisfaction. (There are many reasons for initiating case management, and decreasing length of stay need not be the primary impetus.) However, after being apprised of the advantages to the nursing staff and to patients, for the first few years physicians focused on the clinical path as a nursing path, to guide nursing care, to orient nurses to cardiac surgery, and to analyze variances from a nursing perspective. Over time, the emphasis on clinical paths and on length of stay resulted in the modification of physician practice patterns. Currently, more than 50 percent of CMC's coronary artery bypass patients are discharged by postop day six.

Concurrent with cardiac surgery path implementation, educational activities were initiated for staff, physicians, and other members of the health care team. As with orientation for the total joint replacement clinical path, in-services were utilized but a clinical coordinator role was not in place at that time. The nurse managers on the individual units coordinated the implementation of the cardiac surgery clinical path.

Early Efforts in Path Documentation and Variance Analysis

Clinical paths were printed on bright pink paper to ensure easy identification by the staff and to facilitate removal from the medical record once the patient was discharged. Variances were noted on the form by the nursing staff and, upon patient discharge, completed paths were sent to the nursing quality assurance department. Data was not tabulated from the paths, and data collection and variance analysis were identified as weak links in the clinical path program. The critical care nurse managers recognized the importance of tracking variances to determine whether the clinical path interventions needed revision.

Because the clinical path was not a permanent part of the chart, nurses were expected to "double document." This problem contributed to inadequate nursing documentation on both the total joint replacement and cardiac surgery clinical paths. Cardiac surgery documentation has improved since the cardiac clinical coordinator began tracking patients' daily progress and discussing variances with the staff. Initially, the paths were adequately completed for about 45 percent of the patients seen. The average now is about 80 percent, with improvement gradually increasing.

Improved total joint replacement documentation is expected with implementation of bedside computer terminals in the orthopedic center by fall, 1994. In addition, fold-down desks outside patient rooms are being trialed on one unit to provide all disciplines easy access to the clinical path and other pertinent patient information.

By May 1992, the task of tabulating and analyzing path variances for cardiac surgery was formally delegated to the new position of cardiac case manager. Results of a retrospective study on use of the cardiac surgery path and chart reviews prompted a revision of the CABG path. Subsequent in-services and an educational campaign to reacquaint staff nurses with their clinical path responsibilities were launched. Also, two new paths were developed: percutaneous transluminal coronary angioplasty (PTCA) and cardiac catheterization. In addition to duties associated with early discharge planning, multidisciplinary collaboration, and family assessments, the cardiac case manager position also embraced the responsibilities of data collection and variance analysis.[4]

Efforts to Recruit Nurse Case Managers

Efforts to recruit staff nurses to case manage critical path patients by following the New England Medical Center model[5] were unsuccessful. Chippenham Medical Center nurse managers and clinical coordinators identified the following obstacles to this approach:

- Lack of buy-in among the staff nurses
- Perception by staff nurses that managing patients with clinical paths constitutes job enlargement rather than job enrichment
- High use of a "flexi-pool" (backup personnel, unassigned to any specific unit, but sent where the need for additional staff is most acute), which requires ongoing education on clinical paths

The unsuccessful attempts to involve staff also may have been influenced by unit demographics, given that each unit has a discrete patient mix. The patients undergoing cardiac surgery or total joint replacement were singled out for case management activities over other patients.

Plans to expand the case management program and initiate other cardiac clinical paths were curbed by physicians' resistance to what they envisioned as cookbook medicine, to having their patient charts (and in essence their practice patterns) scrutinized by someone else, and to their perceived loss of control over patient care. At this time, terminology was changed from *critical path* to *clinical path* (as suggested by physicians); the title *cardiac case manager* was also changed to *cardiac clinical coordinator*. For approximately the next year, case management did not expand beyond the cardiac surgery and total joint replacement patients. Although five pediatric clinical paths were developed for fractures, a case manager was not assigned to follow that patient population due to relatively low volume of those diagnoses. However, as physicians began reading and hearing about cost containment, reduced length of stay, and case management at medical conferences and in medical literature, the barriers to clinical paths began to diminish. At the end of 1993, the executive committee of the medical staff mandated the development of two clinical paths per service over the following two months. Chippenham Medical Center's vision of case management was becoming a reality through physician support.

Barriers to Early Clinical Path-Based Case Management

Aside from resistance among physicians and lack of buy-in from staff nurses, other barriers impeded CMC's original clinical path development and case management strategy. One barrier was risk liability. When the total joint replacement and cardiac surgery paths were first approved by the critical care committee and the board of directors, concern was expressed about risk liability if a patient's treatment did not mirror the prescribed path. The hospital's legal counsel substantiated this concern and recommended that the clinical path be excluded as a permanent part of the medical record. This stance paved the way for better physician acceptance of paths but diminished the paths' importance in the eyes of the nursing staff. This in turn created another barrier to success, the problem of double documentation, which discourages staff cooperation due to the extra paperwork involved. Another obstacle was the physicians' failure to follow the paths despite their agreement to do so. For example, when patients met criteria for transfer or discharge but no order was written, a path variance was reported. Physicians attributed these variances to unique patient needs and complained that the path failed to allow for individual variations. Also, physicians often quoted a longer length of stay to their patients than the path stated, making it difficult for nursing staff to prepare patients for discharge at postop day 10, for example, when the patients expected to be discharged on postop day 12 or 14.

Current Case Management and Clinical Path Activities

Having identified strengths, weaknesses, and barriers to successful program implementation, the hospital now has a more effective foundation for path-based care. Like other organizations that initiated case management and clinical paths while unable to secure the level of commitment needed, the hospital draws on its early experiences to move toward the next generation of coordinated patient care.

With strong physician support that has developed over the last year, the model of case management is being redesigned at Chippenham Medical Center. The hospital legal counsel now recommends the inclusion of the clinical path as a permanent part of the medical record. Approximately 20 paths are in the process of being developed, with implementation scheduled for the summer of 1994. Chippenham Medical Center is excited about the commitment from the physicians, and the staff is very positive about learning how to use clinical paths to improve patient care. The barriers to clinical path implementation are diminishing.

CMC's Format for Clinical Paths

For the most part, the original path format has remained intact, with only slight modifications as needed. Nine areas (or activities) related to patient care are included in each path:

1. Functional level/activity
2. Consults
3. Diet
4. Diagnostic tests
5. Nursing treatments
6. Medications
7. Education
8. Discharge planning
9. Patient outcomes

Patient outcomes are the expected response to a specific treatment regimen. Given that case management is based on preestablished clinical outcomes, adding patient outcomes to the path seemed a logical inclusion.[6] By reviewing the expected patient outcomes, a general overview of the patient's progress is obtained. Furthermore, patient outcomes are the focus around which the entire continuum of care is organized across all disciplines.

Time frames are formatted so as to organize the hospital experience along a time continuum. Such characteristics of the patient population as age, HCFA guidelines, insurance carriers, and CMC average LOS for the specific diagnosis are taken into consideration when deciding on the time frame.

Time frames can be modified as necessary. For example, the cardiac catheterization path added a one-hour recovery room visit, defining the expected outcomes of the hour-long episode. The purpose was to identify patient transport problems with the goal of an hour recovery-and-return-to-unit time frame. Although dividing a patient's stay into hours rather than days is not the most commonly used unit in acute care clinical paths, other time frames (weeks, even months) have been used for home health and rehabilitation clinical paths.

In developing clinical paths at CMC, it has been beneficial to have designed a recommended format. Some variation of this format is acceptable (for example, physical therapy as a separate activity on the total joint replacement clinical paths). Modifications to the path format presently under discussion include changing "nursing treatments" to "nursing process" and adding a separate activity for respiratory therapy when appropriate. However, the basic nine areas are included in every path. This results in easier utilization by all disciplines, as well as ensuring inclusion of basic aspects of care for each patient population, such as education and discharge planning.

CMC's Patient Group Focus for Path Development

Patient population has been the central focus in determining which diagnoses are amenable to clinical path development. Shared characteristics among patient groups have helped guide this development: high risk, high volume, high cost, and extended hospital stays.[7] Another factor, considered initially in selecting patient groups, was predictability. Predictability is the relative ease with which care (and therefore the hospital experience) can be mapped for certain diagnoses. Surgical diagnoses in particular follow a more structured course. In contrast, medical diagnoses (for example, chronic obstructive pulmonary disease [COPD] or cerebrovascular accident [CVA]) do not adapt as readily to a path format. However, with careful chart review and a multidisciplinary planning approach, care teams have met with success in mapping the hospital experience of the majority of patients with common diagnoses.

Improving quality of care as a selection factor also has yielded good results at Chippenham Medical Center. For example, the need to standardize care for pediatric fracture patients was identified, resulting in development of pediatric fracture clinical paths. The paths have ensured that appropriate physical therapy is provided and the necessary home equipment is ordered. (See figures 8-1 and 8-2.)

By evaluating quality rather than focusing strictly on cost concerns, multidisciplinary teams have identified challenges to coordinating care for another patient group: those admitted with CVAs. Development of the CVA path allows for patient evaluations by physical therapy, speech therapy, occupational therapy, and social service. This collaborative effort is expected to improve coordination of services, which will have a positive impact on quality of care and patient satisfaction.[8]

A clinical path facilitates problem resolution (or identification of potential problems) in care delivery to specific patient populations. A path also can help patient management teams delineate specific responsibilities or add a new dimension of care to enhance outcomes as well as patient and physician satisfaction. In terms of delineating responsibilities, for example, the pediatric fracture paths stated the expected patient outcomes related to crutch walking (see figure 8-1, p. 115), an area regarded as both a nursing and physical therapy responsibility. Occasional failure to expedite this care step had been identified as a problem area, especially on weekends, when no therapist is available. Including crutch walking in a goal statement on the clinical path is intended to prompt the nursing staff to ensure that the patient received instruction in crutch walking prior to discharge. In addition, a brief explanation of cardiac rehabilitation levels was added to the revised cardiac surgery clinical path. This has been helpful to educate all members of the health care team about the patient's expected activity level. It is also used to guide nursing care and patient education on weekends when cardiac rehab is not available.

Another example of how clinical paths improve quality of care is demonstrated in the cardiac surgery clinical path. Early interventions to prevent pulmonary

Figure 8-1. Chippenham Medical Center Nursing Department Pediatric Clinical Path (Lower Extremity Fracture)

CHIPPENHAM MEDICAL CENTER
NURSING DEPARTMENT
PEDIATRIC CLINICAL PATH

LOWER EXTREMITY FRACTURE - CLOSED REDUCTION IN THE EMERGENCY ROOM

DATE   / /   / /

Evaluation	Admission/ER	Admission to Peds	1st Day After Admission - Peds
Activity	Bedrest	Bedrest	Up with crutches.
Diet	NPO	Advance as tolerated.	Regular
Consults	Orthopedics	Child Life Specialist	PT-NWB Crutch walking or wheelchair (per doctor's order/age appropriate).
Diagnostic	X-ray of affected limb. CBC, SMA6, UA		
Nursing Treatments	VS on admission. Neurovascular checks Q1H. Pain Management IV (if ordered) Ice, elevate extremity on two pillows. Cast care after closed reduction.	Routine VS Neurovascular checks Q2H. Observe for compartment syndrome (see Acute Compartment Syndrome Reference Sheet). → Elevate foot of bed. Cast care (see Cast Care/Spica Care Sheet).	→ → → → → Neurovascular checks with VS. → → → → → D/C IV → → → → → → → → → →
Meds	Analgesic (IM, IV) Sedation for closed reduction.	Analgesic (IM/PO)	PO Analgesic
Education	Prepare patient/family member for procedure.	Orient to unit, activity, pain med., cast care, neuro-vascular checks, etc. Review appropriate cast care teaching and reinforce with handout.	a. Discharge instructions. b. Crutch walking NWB/wheelchair (age appropriate). c. Cast care, ice, elevate extremity. d. Discharge pain med. e. Activity. f. Home equipment education. g. When to notify MD. h. RTC _____
Discharge Planning		Assess need for SS eval., home equipment, educational needs.	→ → → → →
Outcomes	1. Pain controlled by IM/IV analgesic. 2. Neurovascular checks stable.		a. Pain controlled by oral analgesic. b. Cast D&I - no bleeding, drainage, or foul odor. c. Afebrile, WBC WNL. d. Neurovascular checks, VS WNL. e. Crutch walking NWB/wheelchair transfer. f. Patient/family demonstrates use of equipment/supplies, knowledge of discharge meds., cast care, when to notify MD, etc.

Initials:
  7a-3p/7a-7p:
  3p-11p/7p-7a:
  11p-7a:
	_____
	_____
	_____
		_____
		_____
		_____
			_____
			_____
			_____

LE-ER-FX.CP

115

Figure 8-2. Chippenham Medical Center Nursing Department Pediatric Clinical Path (Upper Extremity Fracture)

CHIPPENHAM MEDICAL CENTER
NURSING DEPARTMENT
PEDIATRIC CLINICAL PATH

UPPER EXTREMITY FRACTURE - CLOSED REDUCTION

DATE   /   /   /   /

EVALUATION	ADMISSION/ER	PEDS AFTER PROCEDURE	D/C DAY
Activity	Bedrest	BRP with assistance.	Up ad lib with sling.
Diet	NPO	DAT	DAT
Consults	Orthopedics		
Diagnostic	X-ray of affected limb.		
Nursing Treatments	VS on admission. Ice, elevate extremity. Cast Care (see Cast Care Standard). Neurovascular check Q1H. IV (if ordered). Pain management.	Routine VS → → → → → → → → → → → → → → → → → → Neurovascular check Q2H. Observe for compartment syndrome (see Acute Compartment Syndrome Reference Sheet). → → → → → → → → → → → → → → → → → →	→ → → → → → → → → → → → → → → Neurovascular check with VS. D/C IV → → → → →
Meds	Meds for sedation during closed reduction. Analgesic (IM, IV)	Analgesic (IM, IV, PO).	Analgesic (PO)
Education	Prepare patient/ family member for procedure.	Orient to unit, activity, pain med., cast care, neurovascular checks, etc. Sling application. Review appropriate cast care teaching and reinforce with handout.	Discharge Instructions Sling Application, Ice, Elevate Extremity Cast Care When to Notify MD Discharge Med RTC _____
Discharge Planning		Assess need for SS evaluation, home equipment, hygiene, educational needs.	→ → → → →
Outcomes	1. Pain controlled by IM/IV analgesic. 2. Neurovascular checks stable.		a. Pain relieved by oral analgesic. b. Cast D&I. c. Afebrile, WBC WNL. d. Neurovascular checks, VS WNL. e. Patient/family demonstrates understanding of cast care, use of sling, activity, discharge med., when to notify MD.
Initials 7a-3p/7a-7p: 3p-11p/7p-7a: 11p-71:	_____ _____ _____	_____ _____ _____	_____ _____ _____

UE-FX-CR.CP

complications are emphasized. This path was recently revised and the patient's pulmonary status is being addressed more aggressively, an opportunity for improvement identified through variance analysis. Patients are now transferred out of the intensive care unit on the first postop day and are out of bed for meals; pulmonary toilet has been increased in frequency to every one to two hours throughout the postop stay and is a focus of the case manager's daily assessment of the patient.

Another purpose for selecting a patient group for clinical path development is to educate nurses and other health care team members on the standard of care for a specific diagnosis. The diagnosis may be one in which increased volume is anticipated or one for which "flexi-pool staff" or orientees require additional help to determine where nursing responsibilities lie or what patient outcomes are desired. For example, flexi-pool staff may be unfamiliar with outcome goals for patients diagnosed for radiation oncology. The cardiac surgery and total joint replacement paths are used as educational tools during nursing orientation. In particular, the total joint path has been invaluable in assisting critical care nurses with management of complicated total joint replacement patients.

CMC's Process for Writing Clinical Paths

At present, the physicians, service groups, the executive committee of the medical staff, nursing administration, and ancillary departments can recommend the development of a clinical path. The recommendation is discussed with the appropriate service chiefs, and the feasibility of developing a successful clinical path is determined. When the general consensus is in favor of further pursuing the specific path development, a team is appointed with input from the service chief(s) and nursing administration. The team is composed initially of three or four physicians from the particular service, including the service chief(s), the case manager coordinator and/or the clinical nurse specialist (coordinator of the task force), appropriate nurse managers, the director of health information systems, a representative from nursing administration, and any other health care team members appropriate to the diagnosis. The first meeting entails review of LOS data, comparing Chippenham with HCFA/DRG recommendations and community norms. The purpose of developing the clinical path is discussed, along with decisions regarding length of path (or LOS), defining the patient population (for example, unstable angina admitted to critical care), and improving quality of care (early implementation of therapies, discharge planning on admission, and others). Team members are encouraged to express their concerns about developing and implementing the path. When possible, plans are described to address each concern.

Once the diagnosis has been identified for path development, the process then includes four major steps. These steps—data research and compilation, chart review, identification of benchmarks and desired outcomes, and draft writing—are described in the following subsections.

Data Research and Compilation

Data gathering and compilation are derived from both external and internal sources. Regarding *external sources,* current literature is reviewed for changes in the standard of practice or new patient management methods. The community standard of practice is also researched. When differences are identified between CMC practice and community practice, these discrepancies are evaluated in terms of the effect on quality patient care. Another external source is examples of current clinical paths from other hospitals. These paths are published in the literature or can be purchased from various sources. Commercial paths, specific to the diagnosis being examined for path development, assist in reviewing practice patterns from other hospitals and other physicians. *Internal sources* for path development would include input from all disciplines who are involved in the care of the patient. Patient discharge surveys and CMC physician practice patterns are also examined. As stated in the previous section, research also serves to identify regional norms for length of stay and compare them with average LOS at CMC.

External and internal sources are culled further to identify and evaluate differences regarding length of stay in critical care units, use of ancillary services, frequency of laboratory tests, use of prophylactic medications, and other treatment components.

Chart Review

Chart review is performed concurrently with research and data compilation. Careful retrospective case review of CMC patients is essential in understanding the patient route of care throughout the hospitalization episode, the hospital's norm for the patient category under review, and differences in practice patterns among physicians. Usually an average of 10 to 20 charts per diagnosis are reviewed. This number is dependent on how many physicians admit patients with this diagnosis, the degree of correlation in their practice patterns, and variations in length of stay. For example, the hospital's two cardiac surgeons who perform most of the adult cardiac procedures engage in virtually the same practice patterns for patients whose conditions are uncomplicated. Therefore, 5 to 10 charts per physician were reviewed to describe the practices of the cardiac surgery physicians.

On the other hand, a greater number of physicians admit pediatric patients for bronchiolitis and asthma diagnoses. The length of stay varies significantly among the various physicians. Approximately 10 charts per physician were reviewed in order to trend the practice patterns of physicians treating these diagnoses at CMC. Thus fewer than 20 charts were reviewed for cardiac surgery path development, but more than 60 for the pediatric respiratory diagnoses.

In writing clinical paths at CMC, it has also proved beneficial to review patient charts that represent both average and extended lengths of stay. Each path is written to encompass 75 percent of the patient population for whom the path will apply. An advantage of reviewing charts of patients with an extended length of stay is that the most frequently occurring complications can be disclosed. Thus, paths can be written to include early interventions to prevent some of these complications. For example, pulmonary complications were addressed in the cardiac surgery population in the initial clinical path by including all the respiratory treatments, as well as patient education by the respiratory therapy department and nursing about the importance of coughing and deep breathing, and the use of the incentive spirometer. In the total joint replacement population, a physical therapy component was stressed because patient outcomes rely on an active therapy program. Extended LOS was frequently the result of lack of compliance with the treatment regime.

Identification of Desired Outcomes

Clinical paths that do not state the interim (short-term) and ultimate (long-term or discharge) patient outcomes desired may be ineffective. Whether daily, unit-specific (interim), or discharge (ultimate) outcomes are described, clear criteria by which to assess patient progress and path appropriateness are essential.[9] In writing the outcomes segment, it is helpful to ask the following questions: What does the patient need to gain from the hospital experience before he or she can be discharged? Before transfer to another unit? On a daily basis? As path development progresses, interventions are included to promote the patient outcomes established. Examples of interim outcomes used in CMC clinical paths include:

- Tolerating p.o. fluids without vomiting
- Showing chest tube drainage < 100 cc in the last 8 hours

- Maintaining stable cardiac rhythm
- Demonstrating ability to ambulate 150 feet with assistance
- Maintaining stable vital signs and temperature < 100.5°F

Ultimate discharge outcomes have been described as follows:

- Taking 75 percent of diet
- Ambulating 300 feet without assistance
- Demonstrating knowledge of wound care procedure
- Verbalizing medication schedule and dosage
- Wounds healing without redness or drainage
- Demonstrating no EKG changes for 24 hours

Once an adequate number of charts have been reviewed, drafts can be compiled.

Draft Writing

At present the case manager coordinator and/or the designated clinical nurse specialist coordinates the team meetings, assigns/performs chart reviews and data collection, incorporates data analysis into the path, assists in writing the path, edits the path, and distributes the various drafts as they are completed. At CMC, the physicians are presently driving the path development. Nursing and medicine are the key players. Once editing is completed, all members of the health care team involved in the care of the patient are given the opportunity to review the path. Their input and suggestions are weighed and modifications to the path are made. This cycle of review and revision continues until the final draft has been written. The final draft is then presented at the service meeting, where approval is sought from the physicians who will be using the clinical path.

CMC's Process for Projecting Length of Stay

Once charts have been reviewed and interim and discharge outcomes have been established, a decision about the targeted length of stay is made. First, CMC compares its average LOS with the HCFA length of stay for the same patient category. If HCFA is not applicable (non-Medicare age group), the DRG LOS is used. The total joint replacement path originally was written for 10 days (a reduction of four days). Then the path was shortened to five days with the addition of a detailed discharge plan. However, because of variances from the five-day path (due primarily to a shortage of posthospital skilled and rehabilitation beds) a revised eight-day path was developed. Currently under scrutiny is posthospital care alternatives for patients undergoing total joint replacement, with a view toward reinstating the five-day path.

In comparing HCFA length of stay for CABG patients with CMC Medicare length of stay, CMC found a different scenario. The HCFA length of stay for patients in the DRG 107 category (cardiac bypass patients) was 11.4 days. The majority of the hospital's cardiac surgery patients were discharged at postop day eight or nine, but the Medicare population had an average LOS of 15 days. An eight-day LOS was authorized for the original path, but since that time patients have been discharged more frequently at postop day five or six. The Medicare population has seen a significant drop in LOS to 10 days. The path has been revised to a six-day path to reflect the change in physician practice patterns. Plans are underway to further reduce the postop LOS to a five-day path.

Decreasing patient length of stay is not the only goal of clinical paths and case management. Occasionally a longer stay might result from improved quality of care. Two examples are COPD and CVA, which are presently being developed at CMC.

Improved resource use may yield better patient outcomes, and this may translate into a longer hospital stay – at least initially. Once the path is in place, review and revision of target lengths of stay are recommended within three to six months. An appropriate decrease in length of stay may then be incorporated into the path.

CMC's Methods for Achieving Buy-In among Clinical Path Users

Formal as well as informal educational sessions have been built into the implementation time frame to facilitate path acceptance among prospective users. At CMC, educational tools include posters for physicians and staff, brief inservices, a video presentation, a key managers' presentation, and pertinent information in the monthly hospital newsletter. Articles are featured regularly in the CMC nursing newsletter, the *Stethoscoop*, that explain the goals of case management. Issues of both newsletters also present interesting case studies.

One of the goals of case management at Chippenham Medical Center is to provide maximum quality of care in a concise time frame. The facility recognizes that various disciplines are important allies in providing high-quality care during the patient's hospitalization. This orientation has advanced the commitment to multidisciplinary collaboration.[10] Patient care outcomes are the responsibility of *all* health care team members across *all* involved disciplines. Even so, the nursing staff is ultimately responsible for comparing recommended path interventions with actual care practices on each shift. Thus, they must document variances adequately, a case management compliance challenge being resolved at CMC. At other hospitals, the availability of bedside computers has proved to benefit the case management process by making daily clinical path documentation easier and more accessible. A pilot program centered on bedside computer terminals is being investigated.

One effort to promote improved documentation at CMC was to locate the path within the nurses' notes. This strategy significantly increased staff awareness of the path and in turn upgraded charting compliance. The problem, however, is that this method removes the path from the chart, which hampers direct access to the path for disciplines other than nursing.

As previously mentioned, the accessibility of clinical paths to all disciplines has been addressed in one area of the hospital through the recent addition of fold-down desks outside each patient room. Nurses' notes, graphic sheets, and the clinical path are kept in these desks, and are thus available to any staff member working with the patient. The appropriate sample clinical path is kept on the chart at the nurses' station as a reference for physicians.

CMC's Case Managers

At CMC, the role of the case manager is exemplified by the responsibilities of the cardiac case manager. The cardiac case manager, whose official title is cardiac clinical coordinator, assesses patients whose progress after cardiac surgery follows the course outlined by the clinical path. With an average daily caseload of 15 to 20 patients, the case manager obtains patient background information by reading charts and discussing each patient's progress daily with the nursing staff. When a variance is identified, or when the patient is in danger of falling off the path, either the nursing staff or the case manager notes this fact on the path variance record (figure 8-3). The case manager discusses intervention options with the staff and with other members of the health care team, including the physician. If the patient is already off the path, this is noted on the clinical path, and interventions are identified to attempt to position the patient back on track and towards recovery.[11] For example, when a patient's impeded mobility from age-related changes affects his or her progress, the case manager discusses the need for a physical therapy consult with the attending physician. Other

Figure 8-3. Variance Record

VARIANCE RECORD

DATE	ITEM NOT ACCOMPLISHED	CAUSE/CODE*	WHAT WAS DONE

*CODE: A: PATIENT
B: CAREGIVER
C: SYSTEM

interventions include range-of-motion exercises, out-of-bed for all meals, and family and nurse-assisted ambulation to increase endurance. In addition, the case manager assesses the patient's nutritional status, and ensures that the appropriate dietary interventions are implemented, that is, nutritional supplements, dietary consult for food preferences, and possibly a pharmacy consultation to evaluate medication-induced anorexia. An occupational therapist may also be consulted to increase the patient's participation in activities of daily living. All of these interventions are coordinated by the case manager. Other responsibilities of the case manager include presenting patient care conferences, early discharge planning, and multidisciplinary rounds.

Patient Care Conferences

When a patient currently is off the path or is expected to fall off the path for an extended period, the case manager coordinates a patient care conference with the nursing staff and appropriate members of the health care team to determine what measures should be instituted. Occasionally, such conferences reveal that the patient is responding appropriately to the current interventions, and is positioned for recovery. A patient recently discharged mirrored this situation; his arthritis was slowing his progress and he was running a low-grade fever. In this instance, the care conference focused on supporting the patient and family emotionally, encouraging compliance with the aggressive pulmonary toileting, supporting and sharing the goals of the physical therapist, ensuring the patient was not nutritionally depleted, and educating the patient and family in interventions to increase endurance.

At other times, the patient's outcome may be uncertain, or it is clear that the patient may be off the path and recovery is significantly delayed (that is, reintubation, sternal wound infection, or life-threatening arrhythmias). The case manager assists the nursing staff in determining what interventions are needed to progress the patient toward discharge. Consultations are frequently a result of patient care conferences. Other common outcomes of the conferences include a daily schedule for the patient which promotes balancing rest with activity, planned patient/family education, and discharge planning.[12]

Early Discharge Planning

Early discharge planning is a major emphasis of CMC's cardiac case management strategy.[13,14] Discharge care plans are completed on every patient within 24 hours of admission and reassessed as the patient progresses through the care continuum. The cardiac case manager addresses discharge concerns with the patient and family as early as possible in the hospitalization. Besides assessing the home situation, the case manager ensures that adequate discharge instructions are provided to the patient and family. Throughout the hospitalization, patients and families are educated about how to care for the patient at home, what his/her limitations are and for what period of time, and how their significant other will need help (for example, assisting with meal preparation, laundry, grocery shopping). Discharge plans are always addressed whenever a patient care conference is convened. Goals are formulated to move the patient toward the optimal discharge plan, with input from the family, physician, therapists, nurses, and social worker. Occasionally the family is invited to attend a patient care conference.[15]

Weekly Multidisciplinary Rounds

The case manager coordinates weekly multidisciplinary rounds on two nursing units, the surgical intensive care unit and the progressive care unit. Presently at CMC, the nurse manager (or a designee), social worker, dietitian, respiratory therapist, pharmacist, physical therapist, chaplain, cardiac rehabilitation nurse, home health coordinator, occupational therapist, and—when scheduling permits—the physician attend the weekly multidisciplinary rounds. Discharge planning and the patient's progress toward discharge are again emphasized. During these multidisciplinary rounds any patients placed on a path are assessed as to whether they are following the path and how well they are progressing.

Multidisciplinary rounds provide a quick overview of patient progress, assist in detecting potential problems, and promote early intervention.[16] Furthermore, with all team members present, timely action occurs. The goals and interventions formulated at the patient care conferences and multidisciplinary rounds are documented on the progress notes so as to promote communication among all disciplines and to provide a record of the discussions. The cardiac case manager coordinates the multidisciplinary rounds, drawing on a background of expert clinician skills and familiarity with the patient's present hospital experience. The educational requirements recommended to fulfill this role are discussed in the following section.

Educational Requirements

At a minimum, case managers should hold a BSN and demonstrate expert clinical skills.[17] A master's degree is strongly preferred. At CMC, both case managers are masters' prepared. The roles of a case manager mirror those of the advanced practice nurse as defined by Hamric and Sprouse: educator, administrator, researcher, clinical expert, and consultant.[18] The case management process clearly encompasses all of these roles. The advanced practice nurse has the global perspective to effectively administer the case management role. This person incorporates the five roles of the advanced practice model in working with the staff nurses, patients and families to effect positive clinical outcomes, cost containment, and decreased length of stay, all of which form the basis of case management.[19]

CMC's Process for Variance Data Collection and Analysis

The case manager assists the staff in identifying variances from the clinical path. A variance occurs when a patient no longer follows the clinical path. A positive variance occurs when the patient is progressing more rapidly than the path states. A negative variance occurs when a patient is progressing slower than the path, and usually results in an extended length of stay. The three most common sources of variance are the patient, the caregiver, and the system(s).[20] An example of a *patient variance* is problematic blood sugar management of a patient with diabetes, resulting in an extended length of stay. A *caregiver variance* arises from extra tests ordered by the physician, failure to implement a necessary order, or failure to discharge the patient once discharge criteria have been met. Examples of *system variances* are inability of the hospital to perform tests within a certain established time frame, resulting in treatment delays, or a lack of bed availability, causing a transfer delay.[21] Once a clinical path is implemented at CMC, every variance is documented, and those occurring most frequently are analyzed. Over time, it has become clear that certain variances are more significant than others. For example, on the cardiac surgery path, whether the patient's temporary pacing wires are discontinued on postop day three or five had no influence on length of stay. However, what caused the delay is important: Does the patient have atrial fibrillation? A prolonged prothrombin time? Or was it overlooked by the physician or physician's assistant? Conversely, if a patient is unable to ambulate in the hallway with minimal assistance by postop day four, an extended length of stay is likely, and a plan to correct the impending variance is developed.

A form for manual tracking of cardiac surgery patients is used to collect data such as length-of-stay information, variance details, and discharge planning activities. The case manager completes the form as he or she follows a patient throughout the hospital stay, noting when the patient experiences an extended length of stay in any area. The incident is coded as a patient, caregiver, or system variance, and basic information is noted as the cause of the variance and whether the variance was justified. For patients who are off path, more detailed information is tracked, such as medications, laboratory data, and interventions implemented to correct the variance. Consults are recorded and discharge planning needs are tracked.

The variance data are input into a computerized spreadsheet program (Lotus™), but because this program is not relational, manual analysis of the variance data is performed. Over the next 6 to 12 months, the hospital plans to use a relational database for capturing and reporting variance data.

Effective Use of Variance Data

Through retrospective variance data analysis, the most common variances to the cardiac surgery path have been identified as respiratory complications, arrhythmias, wound infections and related symptoms (fever, red wounds, draining wounds), and slow patient progress. Respiratory variances are being addressed by involving respiratory therapists in a more active role, increasing use of incentive spirometry and deep coughing, mobilizing patients earlier, and decreasing use of sedation during the first 24 hours postop.

To facilitate patient progress, assessment is made of preop nutritional status (for high-risk patient groups) and postop status as their recovery progresses, which requires a more active role for the dietitian. Specifically, use of supplemental "milk shakes" composed of skim milk and a flavored instant breakfast powder has been a popular addition to the cardiac surgery patient meals, when appropriate. Sugar-free "shakes" are also available for the diabetic population. Loss of appetite has been a common complaint of postoperative cardiac surgery patients. In addition to supplements, a transitional diet has been developed for postop day two, when a regular diet approved by the American Heart Association is ordered. The transitional diet includes foods that are associated with the pediatric BRAT diet (bananas, rice, applesauce, toast, canned fruits, custard, creamed soups), all tailored to a low-fat diet. An emphasis on maintaining adequate nutrition intake postoperatively is designed to reduce the slow-to-progress variance and to promote wound healing.

The staff is becoming more knowledgeable about identifying variances for patients on the cardiac surgery path and initiating interventions during hospitalization. For example, when a patient consumes less than 50 percent of his or her meals, this variance alerts the nurse to examine daily intake more closely. One of the patient outcomes is that the patient will consume 50 percent or more of the diet. For patients unable to meet this outcome, the nurse would intervene by notifying the case manager or the dietitian, or by discussing supplement options with the patient and relaying the preferences to the dietitian. The benefits of concurrent interventions are emphasized with the staff by the cardiac case manager during daily rounds.

The Future of Case Management at CMC

Implementation of case management and clinical paths at CMC is continually evolving, given the hospital's ongoing response to changes required in its patient management strategy. With the mandate by the executive committee of the medical staff to begin development and implementation of clinical paths by service, administration is tying the program together with the continuous quality improvement (CQI) initiative. Utilizing flow charting to examine the process of path development, from initial decision-making to the three-month path evaluation, has been helpful in streamlining the operation. Histograms, Ishikawa diagrams, and flow charts are being used for problem solving and data assessment. By identifying the specific purpose(s) for developing each clinical path, the basis for ongoing evaluation of the path is established. If reducing length of stay is the purpose of a specific path, the evaluation will assess whether reduction occurred and to what extent. If another purpose is to cue nurses to cardiac rehab instructions on weekends, whether this occurs on weekends will need to be evaluated. Improving patient care and patient satisfaction are major concerns of the program. The institution has targeted several areas for improvement. The remainder of this chapter highlights a few areas in which these changes are beginning to occur.

Patients and Families

A patient-friendly version of the clinical path is being developed for the cardiac surgery patients. At present, the plan is to focus on goals for the postop days, emphasizing mobility, ambulation, selfcare, discharge planning, and respiratory interventions. This approach would allow both patient and family to participate actively in the patient care process while emphasizing the importance of compliance with the prescribed treatment regimen. The "patient path guidelines" would be reviewed with the patient preoperatively by the case manager.

CMC is also developing a patient satisfaction tool to evaluate patient and family satisfaction postdischarge as related to the clinical pathways. One of the purposes of this assessment is to evaluate the effectiveness of the case management program from the patient's perspective, and to provide information for the CQI program.

Physicians

To respond to physicians' concerns about case management, several educational processes have been developed, including a video, poster sessions, educational information shared at service meetings, a monthly newsletter highlighting clinical paths, the availability of literature supporting clinical pathways, a physician handbook on the clinical pathway program, and information from the hospital attorney. A presentation which would provide continuing medical education (CME) credit for physicians is being investigated. In addition, active involvement in the development and revision of clinical paths is occurring as influenced by the executive committee decision. Educating family practice residents about clinical paths will be an asset to the program in years to come when they become members of the active medical staff.

Computerization

CMC is rapidly moving towards adoption of the clinical path as a permanent part of the medical record. With the possible installation of bedside computers, the clinical path would be readily available for review and documentation by all members of the health care team, would facilitate capture of path variance data, and would automatically generate monthly reports for analysis.

Program Expansion

The case management program at CMC is being expanded to include path development for patients admitted with CVA, myocardial infarction, pneumonia, carotid endarterectomy, and other high-volume, high-cost diagnoses.

Conclusion

The administrators, physicians, and case managers have a vision for the future of patient care at Chippenham Medical Center. Their goals include improving quality of care in the environment of change, containing costs so as to enter the 21st century as a strong competitor in the health care market, and improving the satisfaction of the patient, physician, and staff. We are committed to the philosophy of case management and the utilization of clinical paths as the tools to meet these goals, as is evidenced by the name of the case management program here at Chippenham, "Pathways to Quality." Our hospital's mission statement encompasses this vision, emphasizing "comprehensive services . . . to make Chippenham the first choice of our patients, a leader in the delivery of quality healthcare services."

References

1. Giuliano, K. K., and Poirier, C. E. Nursing case management: critical pathways to desirable outcomes. *Nursing Management* 22(3):52–55, 1991.

2. Del Togno-Armanasco, V., Olivas, G., and Harter, S. Developing an integrated nursing case management model. *Nursing Management* 20(10):26–29, 1989.

3. McKenzie, C. B., Torkelson, N. G., and Holt, M. A. Care and cost: nursing case management improves both. *Nursing Management* 20(10):30–34, 1989.

4. Strong, A. G. Case management of a patient with multisystem failure. *Critical Care Nurse* 11(6):10–18, 1991.

5. Zander, K. Nursing case management: resolving the DRG paradox. *Nursing Clinics of North America* 23(3):503–20, 1988.

6. Bower, K. A. Managed care: controlling costs, guaranteeing outcomes. *Definition* 3(3):14–16, 1988.

7. Giuliano and Poirier.

8. Olivas, G. S., Del Togno-Armanasco, V., Erickson, J. R., and Harter, S. Case management: bottom line care delivery model. Part II: adaptation of the model. *JONA* 19(12):12–17, 1989.

9. Zander.

10. Del Togno-Armanasco, Olivas, and Harter.

11. Ritter, J., Fralic, M. F., Tonges, M. D., and McCormac, M. Redesigned nursing practice: a case management model for critical care. *Nursing Clinics of North America* 27(1):119–28, 1992.

12. Strong.

13. Strong.

14. Combs, J. A., and Rusch, S. C. Creating a healing environment. *Health Progress,* May 1990, pp. 38–41.

15. Strong.

16. Del Togno-Armanasco, Olivas, and Harter.

17. Ritter, Fralic, Tonges, and McCormac.

18. Hamric, A. B., and Spross, J. A. *The Clinical Nurse Specialist in Theory and Practice.* 2nd edition. Philadelphia: W. B. Saunders, 1989.

19. Hanneman, S. G., Bines, A. S., Sajtar, W. S. The indirect patient care effect of a unit-based clinical nurse specialist on preventable pulmonary complications. *American Journal of Critical Care* 2(4):331–38, 1993.

20. Bower.

21. Bower.

CHAPTER NINE

Clinical Paths at Norton Psychiatric Clinic

Connie Anton and David A. Casey, MD

Norton Psychiatric Clinic, located in Louisville, Kentucky, is an affiliate of Alliant® Health System. In 1988 the clinic expanded its inpatient psychiatric services to include a geropsychiatry unit devoted to the care of patients age 65 and older. A highly dedicated multidisciplinary team carefully designed the unit and planned the program to accommodate the special requirements for treatment of this patient population. The physical layout of the unit and safety features allow the debilitated elderly patient maximum independence and participation. The geriatric psychiatry activity program is paced to match the need for a stimulating environment that takes into consideration the declining physical abilities of its inpatients. Prospective staff are screened for their desire to work with geriatric patients and given a one-week classroom orientation. Staff education is emphasized with mandatory in-services held several times a year. Even under ideal circumstances, it is a challenge to serve this population and, in particular, to meet the needs of elderly psychiatric patients within imposed time constraints. Although DRG exempt, the unit receives a fixed Medicare reimbursement for the majority of its patients. The hospital assumes a significant financial risk in the complicated treatment of geriatric psychiatry patients.

A Quality Improvement Approach in Psychiatry

In 1989 Alliant Health System took an aggressive approach to controlling health care costs by instituting a total quality management (TQM) philosophy throughout the organization. Alliant's commitment to providing a cost-effective delivery system included implementation of what it referred to as critical path (hereafter termed clinical path) processes in patient care. In the psychiatry department, a quality improvement team was formed to utilize a quality management approach to map out patient care processes. The goal was to improve inpatient psychiatric treatment while conforming to the corporation's managed care goals: to assure quality, provide a cost-effective system, provide services specified in the health care policy, and maintain consumer satisfaction.

Historically, quality improvement teams at Alliant had not dealt with direct patient care issues and were skeptical about applying industry-based quality management methods in the clinical setting. Additionally, many concerns were expressed about defining psychiatric care by diagnosis, a fundamental aspect of clinical paths. In fact, no psychiatry clinical paths were found in the literature to support the project. The team, comprised of seven registered nurses and one physician consultant, followed an industrial standard of a quality improvement process. At Norton Psychiatric Clinic this process was translated into a focus on three areas: data collection and analysis (from which an opportunity for improvement is identified), clinical path design (influencing factors), and path implementation.

Data Collection and Analysis

The team gathered data on the current admission, discharge, and care practices. Admission and discharge records from the preceding 12 months were scrutinized to determine the most frequent diagnoses and average length of stay. Checksheets were devised for chart reviews for the purpose of examining patterns of care for elderly psychiatric patients. Data collection included diagnostic tests, presenting symptoms, medications, disposition, and patient's age. Because all team members were from the same department, more than the usual barriers were encountered — inadequate time for meetings, lack of support from staff who were not involved, and the added demands of data collection. All of these difficulties were eased to some degree by asking staff on the late-night shift to assist in data collection while patients slept. Through use of the checklist, one chart could be reviewed in an average of 20 minutes. Once this shift became involved, others volunteered. Before long, staff members on all shifts were participating in data collection; and with increased involvement, support and enthusiasm for the project grew.

Data collection revealed that major depression and dementia accounted for 75 percent of patient diagnoses on the geriatric psychiatry unit. Eventually, patient profiles, such as the one shown in figure 9-1, emerged from the data gathered.

The team's work focused on solving problems that were revealed by systematic collection of data, as opposed to relying on decisions based on "gut" feelings. The team became acutely aware that each patient activity had at least three interpretations:

1. Staff perception of how the activity occurs
2. How the activity actually occurs
3. How staff would like the activity to occur

This lesson was learned repeatedly during data analysis. For instance, it was staff's perception that electroconvulsive therapy (ECT) was part of the treatment for a large percentage of the psychiatry patients. Actual data reported that less than 10 percent of patients underwent ECT in 1989.

Figure 9-1. Sample Patient Profile (Dementia)

Average patient age	80
Percent of patients with:	
Sleep disturbance	82%
Appetite disturbance	60%
Sleep *and* appetite disturbance	53%
Incontinence	46%
Falls	29%
Percent discharged home	50%
Percent discharged to nursing home	47%
Percent discharged on:	
Antidepressant medication	34%
Neuroleptic, antianxiety medication	68%

From the beginning there was a perception that length of stay for geriatric psychiatry patients could be reduced. As the team progressed, reducing length of stay as a focus was replaced by a focus on improving processes (that is, each step of patient care delivery) in order to meet length-of-stay goals. Chart review helped identify at what point in a process delays were likely to occur. For example, an agitated, demented patient's level of cooperation could interfere with laboratory specimens being drawn, with diagnostic examinations being completed, or with patient history being obtained. Improved understanding of the processes of care as revealed by data analysis helped the team plan in advance how to deal with these problems, thus minimizing delays and ensuring a better quality of care for the patient. The team reaffirmed that early diagnosis means beginning a medication regimen sooner, thereby shortening a patient's stay in an unfamiliar environment. Furthermore, providing patient and family education early on in the hospitalization experience can help expedite treatment and patient disposition decisions.

Analysis of hard clinical data guided the team in identifying opportunities for improvement. Although each patient was unique, certain steps were routine and could be anticipated for all patients with the same diagnosis. Once identified, these steps could be planned for in advance by the treatment team. Clinical paths for geriatric psychiatry focused on the "typical" symptoms suffered by a hospitalized geriatric patient diagnosed with dementia or depression. Typical presenting symptoms included sleep and appetite disturbances, incontinence, and agitation.

Issues Affecting Clinical Path Design

The first problems addressed were those clinical issues most often dealt with – safety, nutrition, sleep, patient education, and discharge planning. Components of the existing program were incorporated into clinical paths mapped out to achieve realistic clinical outcomes in these areas. Previously the program consisted of a geriatric protocol of events without regard to patient diagnosis or length-of-stay goals. The clinical paths were designed to be patient centered with a fiscally responsible length of stay. Key patient activities were sequenced within usual time frames based on the expert knowledge of clinicians working the unit. These time frames became interim goals to be met in an effort to maximize each day, thereby meeting length-of-stay targets.

Problem solving often involved consultation with other disciplines, as is the case with collaboration between dietary and rehabilitation services. For example, patient falls are the number-one safety issue on the geriatric psychiatry unit, where the risk rate is higher than for any other patient group. Several factors increase this risk, two being the side effects of medications and the mental disorders that compromise awareness of environmental hazards.[1] Even with a well-defined falls protocol, patient falls continued to be a significant quality of care issue at Norton Psychiatric Clinic, where data indicated that patient falls may be associated with toileting inadequacy. Therefore, the dementia clinical path emphasized assessment and management of patient incontinence, especially urinary incontinence. Chart data analysis led to additional fall prevention interventions being incorporated into the path as shown in the following.

Treatment Process – Dementia

Key events	Outcomes
Day 1: Mini mental status exam Falls protocol Continence care Evaluation	Free from injury
Day 2: Ambulation assistance Guidelines	
Day 3: Physical therapy Evaluation	

Rehabilitation services staff agreed to provide patient-specific ambulation assistance guidelines for the nursing staff by morning of day two. These guidelines briefly describe the patient's abilities and needs regarding ambulation and are placed on the front of the chart.

Chart data showed nutrition also to be a frequent problem and that often a patient lost anywhere from two to five pounds within the first few days following admission. Dementia patients appeared particularly at risk for nutrition deficits. Prepath protocol called for weighing the patient twice a week and for a dietary consultation. A more aggressive approach was outlined on the clinical path:

Treatment Process — Dementia

Key events	Outcomes
Day 1:	D/C weight = or > admission weight
• Weigh on admission and then ×2/week	
• Calorie count ×3/day	
• Intake and output ×3/day	
Day 2: Dietary evaluation	
Day 4: Nutrition/hydration assessment	

In addition to the problem areas noted at the beginning of this section, examination of chart data raised questions about the completion of diagnostic exams. Once ordered, within what time frame should tests be completed? Without a specific goal, tests often were delayed from shift to shift. The team set test-completion goals but from a patient's perspective, that is, guided primarily by consideration for the patient's diagnosis. For example, a CT head scan is a frequent part of the evaluation for an elderly psychiatric patient and could have implications for the diagnosis, medications, or consultations with other physicians. Thus, to ensure test results as soon as possible, it was concluded that elderly persons presenting with symptoms of depression should have their CT scan performed by day three of admission; those with indications of dementia (frequently symptomized by agitation) should have the test performed by day four. The extra day allowed dementia patients more time to adjust to the clinic environment, staff, and routines, which would enhance the likelihood of their cooperation with staff. The dementia clinical path in current use at Norton Psychiatric Clinic is shown in figure 9-2.

Clinical Path Implementation

Once the paths were mapped out, the entire team experience was reported to the psychiatric medical staff. The team utilized histograms, pie charts, and bar charts as visual aids. (See the sample bar chart in figure 9-3, p. 133.) Each step recommended on the paths had supportive data from chart reviews, and each path had a proposed length of stay that was based on current data and process improvements. Physicians had a number of questions regarding data collection and the clinical path process, and the fact-based approach employed by the team helped address their concerns and secure their approval of the paths.

Clinical paths were implemented in the geriatric psychiatry unit in February 1990. Nurses on the quality improvement team conducted mandatory staff education sessions that focused on proper path usage, with strong emphasis on the communication aspects. Paths are initiated by the nurse upon patient admission and serve as communication tools for all disciplines. Nursing utilizes the paths for shift report and to update physicians and other disciplines in the morning staff meeting. Social work,

Figure 9-2. Dementia Critical Path

DEMENTIA CRITICAL PATH
NORTON HOSPITAL
DRG 429 PATH # N0024

Patient label:

Admit date: _____ Disch. date: _____
Expected LOS: __14__ Actual LOS: _____
Treatment date: _____

Suicide attempts #
Psychotic features
Patient falls #
Readmits within 31 days
Readmits within 1 year
Transfer to _____ /from _____
a medical/surgical unit
Treatment of concurrent medical problems/
Dx: _____

	DAY 1 (admit)	DAY 2	DAY 3	DAY 4	DAY 5	DAYS 6 - 10	DAYS 11 - 14
ASSESSMENTS/ EVALUATIONS	H&P, MMSE, nrsg assess, VS, lifestyle questionnaire, continent care evaluation, elimination pattern evaluation	SW contact with family, dietary evaluation	audiology appt scheduled, PT evaluation, continent care re-evaluation, elimination pattern re-evaluation	Reevaluate privilege level	SW evaluation, psych testing, OT evaluation, Tolerates Meds, Free from falls	SW contact with family, continent care re-evaluation, elimination pattern re-evaluation, Leisure Assessment	stabilization of meds, SW family conference, continent care re-evaluation
TESTS	EKG	routine labs, CXR	BDI	CT scan, EEG	PPD	BDI - day 9	BDI - day
CONSULTS		MD consults notified				MD consults complete	
DIET/FLUID BALANCE	calorie count, I&O, weigh (2x/wk - Tues. & Fri.)			nutrition/hydration assessment		nutrition/hydration stable	
ACTIVITY/ SAFETY	unit priviledge, falls protocol	ambulation asst guidelines, AM exercise	sleep disturbance assessment, AM exercise	AM exercise, OT Group, Therapy Group	AM exercise, Restraints utilized -passive -posy vest -leather waist -wheelchair	sleep pattern stable, AM exercise daily	AM exercise daily
EDUCATION				Tuesday Nite family Nite referral		"The 36-Hour Day" given, educational film shown, ADRDA referral, Family Nite	d/c instructions given

NO024.XLS 2/6/92 ngv

1 of 2

©1991 Alliant Health System

(Continued on next page)

Figure 9-2. (Continued)

Treatment date:

	DAY 1 (admit)	DAY 2	DAY 3	DAY 4	DAY 5	DAYS 6 - 10	DAYS 11 - 14
	N M U	N M U	N M U	N M U	N M U	N M U	N M U
TREATMENT TEAM PLANNING/ DISCHARGE PLANNING						multi-disciplinary team mtg D/C plans complete	multi-disciplinary team mtg O.P. f/u scheduled living arrangements finalized transfer form
VARIANCE ANALYSIS							
FACTS RE: VARIANCE							
STEPS TO CORRECT VARIANCE							

Figure 9-3. Sample Bar Chart

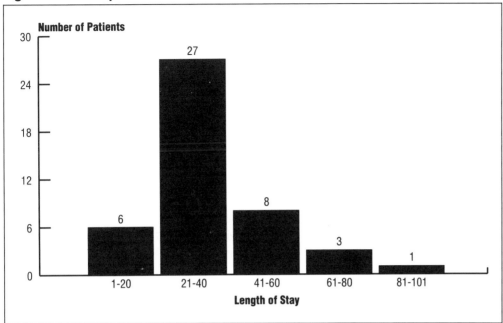

psychology, and activities staff document patient progress on the path. It is the one paper on the unit that can communicate multidisciplinary progress. A staff member can see at a glance whether a family meeting has occurred, psychological testing is completed, or a patient is fully integrated into the activities program.

Once the paths were implemented, it was recognized that a combination of factors within the unit could contribute to variation in the process. Some of these include the number of admissions and discharges occurring on a shift, patient mix, staff–patient ratio, and the overall functional status of the patient group. Any one or combination of these could influence the completion of tasks that move patients along the path.

Implementation of clinical paths not only helps define the intensity of patient care, it clarifies unit staffing requirements through review of each patient's path. For example, if 7 out of 10 inpatients are diagnosed with dementia, then maximum staffing is required to provide the care defined. Establishing a sense of ownership among staff for those issues within the team's control led to dialogue and negotiation among shifts. If a shift was unable to complete all inpatient chest X rays, for example, shift turnover reports might disclose that the same shift always has this responsibility, whereas another shift routinely is charged mostly with patient baths. In such a case, two shifts might negotiate to split the two tasks so that patient chest X ray completion *and* baths can be achieved in a timely manner. This way, resources are used more efficiently as well.

The collaboration between shifts for patient care delivery was facilitated by the goal oriented structure of the paths. As the team discussed details of patient care, they began to focus on the care being delivered, instead of the staff involved. Team members became adept at redistributing shift workloads. Furthermore, there was more emphasis on what was right *for the patient*. This patient-centered attitude resulted in innovative restructuring of activities to accommodate patient needs. Now, for example, not only do day and evening shifts administer patient baths, but the night shift routinely administers baths to those who typically awaken very early. Clinical paths, therefore, help reinforce the concept that care should be planned and delivered based on the patient's needs.

Multidisciplinary Participation

As a tool, a clinical path gives an overview of how each discipline fits into the overall picture of patient care. Furthermore, each discipline has responsibility for documentation of the patient's progress along the recommended path. With the path used as a baseline, progress is discussed and updated daily at morning team meetings. Six elements are included in the morning shift report:

1. Patient's name and age
2. Diagnosis, anticipated length of stay
3. Brief medical history
4. Patient's day number
5. Patient's present condition and critical activities of that day
6. Evaluation of progress (compliance or lack of compliance with clinical path)

The communication that occurs during this concurrent review keeps the multidisciplinary team focused on patient treatment goals. It also emphasizes the interdependence of team efforts. For instance, a social worker often cannot make recommendations on disposition until the occupational therapist and psychologists have completed their evaluations. Often nursing staff will have suggestions on how these other disciplines can obtain patient cooperation for these activities. Information about a patient's most functional time of day, behavioral approaches, or a patient's ability to tolerate an activity can clarify or modify treatment goals. Ultimately, teamwork and communication are enhanced by the clinical path program.

Benefits of Clinical Paths

Since the inception of clinical paths at Norton Psychiatric Clinic, benefits have been documented in three areas: length of stay, falls, and quality indicators. Overall length of stay in geriatric psychiatry decreased from 27 days in 1989 to 14 days in 1992. The incidence of patient falls dropped from 49 to 19 over the same period. These improvements are attributable to two things: standardization of routine steps, which contributes to care being delivered more efficiently; and early identification of patients with potential discharge problems or safety risks, coupled with timely interventions, which minimizes treatment delays.

The use of clinical paths also helps support the facilitywide quality improvement plan by providing a source document for quality indicator data. The following data elements are documented on the paths:

- Number of suicide attempts
- Number of patient falls
- Evidence of readmission within 31 days
- Evidence of readmission within one year
- Incidence of transfer to or from a medical or surgical unit
- Treatment of concurrent medical problems and type of problems

This data has been helpful in explaining variation in length of stay on the geriatric psychiatry unit and in analyzing the impact of reducing length of stay with the implementation of clinical paths.

Information from path variance reports and quality indicators have resulted in several path modifications that further ensure continuous quality improvement. Analysis of information obtained from path-based care processes generates questions from caregivers: Is this the best way to meet patient needs? Was there something else we should have done? Such questions prompt further discussion, process analysis, and improvement opportunities, all of which perpetuate the ongoing cycle of quality improvement.

Physician Perspective

Traditionally, physicians resist measures that they perceive to interfere with their autonomy in delivering patient care. For this reason they are unlikely to support clinical path development and implementation unless their inclusion in these processes is ensured. Physicians' acceptance of the facility's geriatric psychiatry clinical path program reflects their level of participation.

Clinical paths provide for tracking of crucial steps of patient care so as to prevent bottlenecks and unnecessary delays. Physician authority to admit, order individualized treatments, and discharge is not altered by the clinical path process; nor is physician accountability for the patient's quality of care. From the physician's point of view, however, some variables that can affect length of stay are out of his or her control — for example, the type of patients admitted, the severity of illness, the patient mix, and the patient's physiological response to medications. Although these factors can influence length of stay, they do not compromise the quality of care delivered.

Physicians, like staff and administrators, are faced with a multitude of bureaucratic and clinical concerns and may be reluctant to invest their time in clinical path development unless the benefits can be demonstrated. For this reason, research is essential to evaluate the suitability of clinical paths for broader application in psychiatry.

Conclusion

The clinical path has proved to be a successful patient care management system for geriatric psychiatry at Norton Psychiatric Clinic. Its incorporation into daily care delivery has educated caregivers to the realities of limited resources and mandates for improved management in the struggle to provide the best possible patient care. Defining clinical paths by diagnosis helps the care team identify and address functional status issues for elderly psychiatric patients. By anticipating the basic elements of care, the team can sequence problem-specific interventions and execute them consistently, thus enhancing the patient's potential to meet desired outcomes within designated time frames.

Once positioned to envision the care to be delivered, practitioners can reorganize activities and resources around the patient's requirements. The clinical paths themselves, as well as the process by which they are developed, serve to heighten physician and staff awareness of cost-effective health care delivery. A new mind-set emphasizes efficiency as well as quality of care delivery. Physicians and staff feel more empowered and responsible to scrutinize the process as well as outcomes of hospitalization. Teamwork and communication are crucial to team efforts.

Reference

1. Poster, E. C., Pelletier, L. R., and Kay, K. A retrospective cohort study of falls in a psychiatric inpatient setting. *Hospital and Community Psychiatry* 42(7):714–20, July 1991.

Bibliography

Anton, C., Atkins, R., and Metcalf, E. Incorporating total quality management into daily care delivery. *The Quality Letter for Healthcare Leaders* 3(4), May 1991.

Berwick, D. M., Godfrey, A. B., and Roessner, J. *Curing Healthcare.* San Francisco: Jossey-Bass Publishers, 1990.

Clinical Paths at Mercy and Unity Hospitals

Sharon A. Henry

Mercy Hospital and Unity Hospital, divisions of Healthspan Corporation (Healthspan), are located in Coon Rapids and Fridley, Minnesota, respectively. Mercy Hospital has 271 patient beds, and Unity Hospital has 275. The case management and clinical path programs at both facilities have become the cornerstone for the cardiovascular program's continuous quality improvement process.

The facility-specific name for preestablished patient management protocols is *anticipated recovery pathways* (or *ARPs*), but for consistency the term used in this chapter is *clinical pathways* (or *paths*). The impetus for this strategy began in 1989, when development of a coronary artery bypass graft (CABG) clinical path was initiated. Both development and implementation comprised a grass-roots, nursing-focused effort to enhance the quality of care in selected patient groups. Since that time, path-based patient care has evolved into a comprehensive and ambitious, multidisciplinary quality improvement process. By discovering how path-based patient care and case management can influence cost and quality, developers helped advance the clinical pathway model from its small hospital beginnings to become a key organizationwide strategy. Specifically, pathways have:

- Provided an infrastructure for program assessment and development
- Stimulated multidisciplinary communication and cooperation
- Led to tangible improvement in patient care and outcomes
- Provided important data that link the processes of care with patient outcomes
- Enhanced physician peer review activities

As a result of these initiatives, Healthspan's case management and clinical path strategies have grown into a collaborative and coordinated process of patient care delivery. To appreciate the philosophy behind this evolution, it is essential to understand the origin and progression of the process. The examples used throughout this chapter are specific to cardiovascular medicine, although similar strategies are being applied in other disciplines.

Historical Perspective

In 1989 Healthspan was expanding its open-heart surgical program to a new hospital setting and searching for ways to compete in the highly competitive cost and quality environment of the Minneapolis/St. Paul marketplace. Having learned about managed care and case management models at various conferences, hospital leaders decided to try out these patient care methodologies.

The initial decision to "trial" clinical pathways in cardiology was made by a small but key group of individuals. This task group (team) included the following:

- Nursing vice-president
- Nursing directors
- Cardiology vice-president
- Cardiologists
- Cardiovascular surgeons
- Internists
- Cardiovascular program director
- Medical director for cardiovascular program
- Intensivists
- Key clinicians:
  - ICU/CCU nursing
  - Telemetry nursing
  - Cardiology department leadership
  - Cardiovascular nurse clinicians
  - Cardiac rehabilitation

Four patient groups were the first selected for clinical path development:

1. CABG (DRGs 106, 107)
2. Valve surgery (DRGs 104, 105)
3. PTCA (DRG 112)
4. Cardiac angiogram (DRGs 124, 125)

These groups were selected because of their high volume, potential for increased cost, variability of practice patterns, interest of clinicians, and ease with which they lent themselves to pathway design due to a procedure-specific focus. Another advantage to starting with cardiovascular patients is that the number of physicians involved in their care is small, making it easier to secure physician approval and, therefore, easier to initiate pathways.

Barriers to the Cardiac Clinical Path Prototype

The CABG and cardiac valve surgery clinical pathways were pilot tested and revised over a six-month period before other paths were introduced. The first paths were deliberately general in nature, making room for patient care options so as to gain endorsement from *all* physicians whose patients were path candidates. During the first year of implementation, several barriers were identified:

- Paths not developed for all patient populations (result: parallel systems in use cause confusion for caregivers)
- Lack of widespread physician involvement in development and implementation (result: physician resistance due to lack of knowledge)
- Inconsistent leadership among first-line managers in development, implementation, and evaluation/analysis phases (result: inconsistent case manager practices)
- Lack of consistent knowledge and education regarding model (result: lack of widespread enthusiasm from hospital administration)
- Unclear "rules" of implementation (result: inconsistent pathway use throughout hospital or program)

- Inadequate resources for path model (result: inability to monitor variances, implement changes, and attain desired outcomes)

In addition, complaints about double documentation led to noncompliance with variance charting procedures. A tendency to focus on process minutiae overshadowed recognition of greater goals. Inconsistent use of the model throughout all patient populations resulted in two patient care management systems and confusion on the part of caregivers. The medical staff voiced concerns about their practices being restricted by practice parameters and cookbook medicine and about legal liability in using a path-based model to direct patient care. All of these barriers were ascribed to a lack of education and understanding of path-based patient care and case management on the part of both the hospital staff and physicians.

Steps to Overcome Barriers

To overcome these impediments, three strategies were integrated into the case management/clinical path process:

1. Identify physician champions for each program service or unit and elicit their support in educating other physicians on the benefits of clinical paths and case management.
2. Incorporate the clinical path model into existing documentation systems.
3. Integrate the pathway model with the organization's overall utilization and quality management programs.

The global tactics used to accomplish these strategies are outlined below. The particulars of each tactic are included in the detailed discussions found elsewhere in this chapter.

Identify Physician Champions

Hospital administration identified physician leaders who were respected by their clinician peers and personally credible and who endorsed the same goals and vision as those stated in the organization's case management philosophy. The logical place to begin the search was with the medical director or chief of service. To evaluate the candidates' "champion potential," hospital leaders met with each physician to discuss key issues of the path development process, six of which are sketched below:

1. *Reimbursement:* How informed is each physician about state, federal, and marketplace health care reform, and what are their associated concerns?
2. *Hospital attitudes:* Do they have concerns about hospital operations? For example:
    - Systems
    - Nursing care
    - Services
    - Ancillary services
    - Care delivery processes
    - Administration
    - Patient satisfaction
    - Finances
3. *Vision:* What is their projection for the future with regard to:
    - Their practice
    - The hospital
    - Their department's clinical path program

- How paths fit into larger systems
- Physician hospital organizations (PHOs)
- Integrated service networks (ISNs)

4. *Personal motivation:* What are their financial and professional incentives? For example, are they providers for managed care systems? Are they gatekeepers?

5. *Definitions:* How do they define "quality"? Do they understand continuous quality improvement principles? How do they define "outcomes"? How do they determine length of stay for their patients?

6. *Commitment:* What is their level of commitment to the organization and to its continuous quality improvement program? How would they apply their vision and continuous quality improvement strategies to enhance clinical services and involve physician peers?

Using this screening process, leaders recognized physicians who shared the hospital's singular vision and purpose for its case management/clinical path strategy. They also identified physician champions who eventually played a critical role in advancing this effort.

A professional, trusting relationship must be established among all leadership team members. For example, when cardiology physician leaders were first approached, the pathway model was described fully and examples provided. It was important to explain the advantages of path-managed patient care in terms of outcomes and process improvements and clearly articulate the expectations for physician involvement.

These tactics yielded several physician champions, first and foremost, the cardiovascular program medical director, who strongly supported the program from the very beginning. In addition, physician leadership has been identified in the departments of internal medicine, oncology, medical affairs, emergency medicine, cardiovascular surgery, general surgery, anesthesiology, orthopedics, obstetrics/gynecology, pediatrics, and pulmonary medicine. Each of these leaders is a proactive advocate of path-based patient care and case management. All are committed to the principles of continuous quality improvement and can articulate the process to physician groups (or others) as requested. It has been Healthspan's experience that medical staff acceptance of the path model hinges on the ability of physician champions to address practice questions (such as, Is this cookbook medicine? What do you mean by "best practice" and how do we get there? What's wrong with practice variation?) and other concerns of importance to their peers.

Incorporate Clinical Path Model into Current Documentation Systems

To overcome documentation barriers, the cardiac clinical pathway model has gradually evolved to encompass many different aspects of patient care. The current prototype combines several types of documentation into one master road map with the following components:

- *Kardex*™: At Unity Hospital the ARP includes the traditional Kardex format and information at the top of the document.
- *Care plan:* Includes a collaborative problem list and focus areas and expected outcomes of care and goals for each phase of care. Initial, intermediate, and discharge outcomes are tracked as met or not met for CQI purposes.
- *Standard of care:* Includes the identification of what is done for each case type and when it is done.
- *Standards of practice:* Includes *how* we care for case types and can refer to more lengthy standards found elsewhere.
- *Important aspects of care documentation:* Includes *key events* that are documented as met or not met and are trended. These are tracked for CQI purposes.

- *Quality management tools:* Includes tracking and trending of outcomes and key events.
- *Documentation tools* (in certain cases): When "charting by exception" is employed the only additional notes that need to be recorded are variances or exceptions to the stated standard of care in the body of the path and the "unmet" outcomes in the plan portion.

A discussion of how the case management/clinical path model is used for these purposes is included in the development and design section of this chapter.

Integrate Pathway Model with Utilization and Quality Management Programs

As use of the cardiac clinical path model progressed, it became apparent that blending the process into the organization's overall utilization and quality management strategies was imperative. To promote this integration, Mercy Hospital and Unity Hospital formed a case management steering committee. The committee's purpose is to guide development and implementation of managed care and case management at the two hospitals. This function includes coordinating the process with utilization and quality management systems (for example, outcomes research and medical staff peer review), as well as other related activities.

In 1991 the case management steering committee established several global goals for achieving the degree of integration desired at Mercy and Unity. These include the following:

- Promote collaborative practice, coordination of care, and continuity of care.
- Direct the contributions of all care providers toward the achievement of optimal patient outcomes.
- Facilitate the achievement of expected and/or standardized patient outcomes.
- Facilitate timely discharge and/or discharge within an appropriate length of stay.
- Promote professional development and satisfaction of hospital-based registered nurses and other interdisciplinary groups.
- Promote efficient and effective management of resource utilization.

As a first step in integrating the two initiatives, the original task group that developed the cardiovascular clinical path prototype in 1989 expanded to include representatives from a number of other areas. The new development task group was called the cardiovascular quality improvement team (figure 10-1).

Figure 10-1. Cardiovascular Quality Improvement Team

- Physicians
  - —Internists
  - —Intensivists
  - —Cardiologists—chairperson—leader
  - —Pulmonologist
  - —Anesthesiologist
  - —Thoracic surgeons
  - —Nurse clinicians
- Nursing
  (Line and direct nursing supervisors)
  - —Operating room
  - —Intensive care unit—case managers
  - —Post coronary care unit—case managers
  - —Cardiovascular case managers
  - —Cardiology
- Department representatives
  - —Laboratory
  - —Pharmacy
  - —Respiratory therapy
  - —Cardiac rehab
  - —Home care
  - —Quality management/Medical records
  - —Pastoral care/Social service
  - —Case management
  - —Management information systems
  - —Financial services
- Clinical registered dietitian
- Administrative vice-president
- Cardiac program director/facilitator

The role of the team is to oversee the many diverse activities related to the cardiovascular program (for example, variance analysis and quality indicator data analysis). It is at the quality improvement team level that case management principles and product line management reach the desired level of integration with the organization's continuous quality improvement efforts. (See figure 10-2.) The group meets monthly with the following agenda rotation:

- Business meeting every three months
- Quality improvement (QI) meetings every three months

The cardiovascular QI team is represented on the case management steering committee by the cardiovascular program director. Similar QI teams are being formed in other departments and units.

Clinical Pathway Development and Design

The clinical pathway model developed in 1989 looked quite different from the ones in use today for the same case types. Current design is much more sophisticated and incorporates expected patient outcomes, key events, and objective indicators for outcomes measurement and task completion.

Both the tool and the development process have evolved, and much has been learned along the way. One thing that has remained constant, however, is the multidisciplinary approach to generating a pathway, as discussed in the following section.

Multidisciplinary Team Approach

The cardiovascular quality improvement team represents a cross-section of disciplines. Among the members are nursing leaders and staff from telemetry and ICU units; cardiac rehabilitation therapists and registered nurses; cardiac program registered

Figure 10-2. Quality Management Integrated Approach

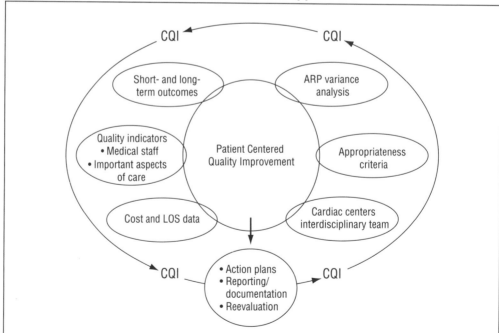

nurses; nursing directors, pastoral care/social service staff, registered dietitians, and nurse clinicians.

Concurrent with pathway development and design was a communication and input-gathering process that included key physician stakeholders, namely, administrative vice-presidents responsible for the relevant patient population areas, quality management departments, and ancillary departments. The goal was to integrate their input into the recommended path protocol once a draft and proposed implementation process had been prepared.

The cardiovascular QI team reviewed approximately 15 records (charts) of patients undergoing CABG procedures (DRG 107) to begin mapping out a standard of practice. The team then added to this description all of the standing orders used by physician groups caring for this patient case type. Orders included cardiovascular surgery, anesthesiology, cardiology, and routine CCU or telemetry if applicable.

The team listed the tasks (tests, assessments, treatments, and other activities) on the vertical axis of the pathway and the expected length of stay (eight days) on the horizontal axis. This model path included *only* postop care and combined ICU and step-down unit care on the same map. Development of this first clinical pathway took place over several weeks, progressing according to the following schedule:

- *First meeting:* Two hours in length, tasks and content delegated to members
- *Second meeting:* Two hours in length, content merged, draft tool completed
- *Third meeting:* Five weeks from start of project, details completed, refinement of draft, final-version draft and implementation discussed
- Shared draft with constituencies (physician champions, medical staff, administration, relevant departments, and caregivers)
- *Fourth meeting:* Designed learning packets for staff and provided short presentations at staff meetings to the *few* units that would trial the ARPs for patient care
- *Fifth meeting:* Developed a program-specific manual for using the clinical path and a process for collecting paths and variance sheets

Due to time constraints, only one path was developed, but its design was flexible enough to allow for a range of treatment options to accommodate a variety of the clinicians' preferences. This format helped ensure endorsement among prospective users. Approximately one year after implementation and variance and patient outcomes analysis, physician practice patterns have become more focused. A "best practice" approach that describes recommended daily tasks and practices was integrated into the design. This approach is applied in developing all clinical paths. The order in which the next paths were developed was:

- Inpatient cardiac rehabilitation, phase I
- PTCA (DRG 112)
- Coronary angiogram (DRGs 124, 125)
- Acute myocardial infarction (AMI, DRGs 121, 122)
- Angina (DRG 140)
- Chest pain (DRG 143)
- Thrombolytic therapy
- Arrhythmia (DRGs 138, 139)
- Outpatient cardiac rehabilitation, phases II and III
- Preop CABG (all phases)
- Abdominal aortic aneurysm (AAA, DRG 110)
- Congestive heart failure (CHF, DRG 127) and continuing care pathway after discharge from acute care
- Myocardial infarction with other diagnosis

- Home care CABG and valve surgery
- Cardiac cath lab procedures

Scope of Clinical Pathways

The first pathways focused only on inpatient care, but the teams quickly learned that prehospital functions and postdischarge management were also critical components. By looking at the entire episode of care, the health care team became better able to provide comprehensive patient management.

Nonhospital providers were included on the cardiovascular QI team very early in the development process. For example, nurse clinicians from the cardiologist's and cardiovascular surgeon's offices were team members from the beginning and now have equal voice along with hospital and physician team members. They always participate in development, design, implementation, and evaluation and analysis functions. Also, home care providers were invited to participate on the team approximately one year after the first path was implemented.

After analyzing variance data, the team began to appreciate the need for expanding the paths to include the entire episode of illness. Current cardiovascular pathways cover the entire experience for CABG patients: catheterization (cath) laboratory procedures (figure 10-3, p. 146), preop testing and education (figure 10-4, p. 148), postop experience (figure 10-5, p. 152), outpatient rehabilitation (figures 10-6 and 10-7, pp. 156–159), and home care.

The team is currently working on a perioperative path to cover the time frame for CABG and valve procedures. The next project is to expand all cardiovascular path time frames to cover preop and postdischarge experiences. Clinical pathways for congestive heart failure, cardiovascular surgery, and acute myocardial infarction currently are being developed using the CABG model.

Upon being contacted for satisfaction and functional status information, patients voiced a desire to participate in their care and have their own daily reference document. As a result of this feedback, a patient and family version of the CABG clinical protocol was developed (figure 10-8, p. 160). These patient-friendly pathways have become excellent educational tools.

Clinical Path Sequencing

Mercy and Unity have progressed from one path for the total CABG experience sequenced in *days* (days 1 through 8) to more than a dozen protocols that *flow carefully* from one to the other based on different time increments according to case manager and patient care team preference and experience. For example, the emergency department pathway is sequenced in *minutes* and *hours,* as is the path used by the cardiac cath lab. The operating room plans to sequence its CABG clinical path by *phases* of care (for example, preinduction, induction, intraoperation, and transfer).

The ICU staff uses a pathway arranged in *time blocks* such as the first 24 hours after admission, then up to 36 hours. The next blocks are in shorter segments spread out from the time a patient first reaches the ICU (when care is the most intense), to gradually expanding blocks until transfer to the telemetry unit, where once again traditional day sequencing is used for that part of the pathway. Cardiac rehabilitation and home care use increments based on *visits.*

Clinical Path Deployment

The clinical path is considered the case management tool of choice at the hospitals and is a permanent part of each patient's medical record (a concern voiced regarding the original model). Bedside nurses and other clinicians use it to guide care and document task completion and outcomes achievement.

The admitting nurse, responsible for determining which path is appropriate for the patient, completes the admissions information (admission date, case type, start date, and preexisting condition details) on the path. The nurse is also responsible for reviewing the protocol with the patient and/or the family and obtaining their signatures on the path where indicated. The path is maintained on the nursing unit in a plastic protector or on a clipboard in the chart rack.

As a communication tool (discussed later in the chapter) the pathway is updated regularly to ensure that all members of the health care team know the patient's *current* status. The attending caregiver on each shift reviews the patient's critical activities and goals listed on the path. Completed activities are highlighted with a yellow marker and initialed. If an item does not apply, a black line is drawn through it and "NA" is written in next to the item. Caregivers are responsible for updating and individualizing the documentation. For example, a test completed as planned is crossed off. An intervention for which a stop order is issued (for example, "intravenous line discontinued") is crossed off and the stop date noted on the pathway. When interventions continue across days of care, the bedside nurse "arrows" the task to the next day, for example, "regular diet →". When the patient is moved to another unit, it is the transferring nurse's responsibility to update the path form to reflect the patient's current needs and orders.

The tool also is used by the social services, cardiac rehab, occupational therapy, physical therapy, dietary services, patient education, speech therapy, and respiratory care departments. Staff from these departments document their interventions by initialing next to the order.

Long-Term Clinical Paths

In response to staff feedback on the management of long-term patients, an alternative long-term path format has been designed. In this context, *long term* is defined as a hospital stay anticipated to exceed 15 days. The first page of the long-term path is the same as that of other pathways; so is the second page, except that it does not include the daily progression. This way, the second page can be used throughout the patient's entire stay, if space allows.

The long-term format is used on new admissions if the admitting nurse anticipates the patient will stay *at least* 15 days, based on the severity of illness. If during the hospital episode it becomes apparent that the length of stay will exceed 15 days, the second page of the long-term format can be added to the original first page.

The long-term clinical path is generic in design, meaning that it is not prewritten for any DRG or patient category. As is the case with other paths, the long-term form is a permanent part of the patient's medical record and must be kept current. Like the DRG-specific format, every item on the long-term document must be dated and discontinued items crossed out with stop date noted.

Special Circumstances

Certain situations may create the need for variations in the path-based processes of care. For example, nursing staff may determine that a patient's condition no longer is appropriate for path management. At Mercy Hospital and Unity Hospital this occurs when length of stay more than doubles expectations or when a patient experiences multisystem failure. The decision to take a patient off path must be documented on the form by noting the decision date and name of the decision maker. If it becomes appropriate to restart the path, the reactivate date and name of decision maker likewise are noted. All stop and restart decisions are shared with other involved disciplines.

Sharon A. Henry

Figure 10-3. Anticipated Recovery Plan for CABG Patients (Cath Laboratory Procedures)

ANTICIPATED RECOVERY PLAN

Profile: Time In _____ Time Out _____

Case Type CORONARY ANGIOGRAM / LV ANGIOGRAM   Ht ___ Wt ___ Allergies _____

DRGs ___ Expected LOS 60 minutes Old chart to cath lab   Family Whereabouts _____

Admit Date ___ DC Date ___   Physician _____ Date _____

Init	Signature	Init	Signature	Init	Signature

NRSG DIAG. AND COLLABORATIVE PROB.	PATIENT/FAMILY OUTCOMES
1) Anxiety related to perceived or actual threat to biologic integrity.	Patient will be more at ease which will increase understanding of procedure. ----> Chest pain absent. Peripheral pulses present.
2) Potential altered peripheral tissue perfusion related to bleeding or thrombic formation.	MD and cath lab staff will keep patient informed as procedure proceeds.
3) Potential decreased cardiac output related to myocardial ischemia or electrical factors.	Brief interpretation of results of study may be given to patient immediately post-procedure. - OR - Instruct patient that results of study will be given after MD has reviewed the views taken during the study. A plan of care will then be discussed with patient and family by MD.

Clinical Occurrence	1 - 15 MINUTES	15 - 30 MINUTES	30 MINUTES	45 MINUTES	60 MINUTES
NURSING ASSESSMENT	Check patient ID band for correct scheduled patient. Compile data & assess: HT, WT Heart rhythm VS Peripheral pulses - auscultated or palpated and marked (R)___ (L)___ LOC Document on Nurses notes. Pt admitted into computer. 6 Lead EKG done. Oximeter placed on patient.	Monitor pt. hemodynamics --- Note if developing any chest pain. --- Assess patient for need of sedation Monitor O2 saturations. --- Begin O2 at 2l/nc for O2 sat ≤ 92%.	---> Hemodynamic review. Site observance: CMS & developing hematoma. Peripheral pulses - auscultated or palpated and documented on Nurses' notes. LOC documented.	Document on Nurses' Notes	
NURSING ACTION/ TREATMENTS	Betadine scrub of bilateral groin sites/arm site. Drape pt for procedure. Record Heparin d/c time on floor.	Instillation of local anesthetic to groin/arm site by MD. Insertion of arterial sheaths Insertion of coronary catheter	Views taken of coronary vessels. Views taken of LV. Computer tracing obtained.	Sheath removed from catheter sites. Pressure applied to site x 10 minutes. Brachial site: straight arm board applied & √ pulse.	Betadine Ointment & Tegaderm dressing applied to groin site.
MEDICATIONS (See medication record)	Check IV sites for patency & note type of IV sol'n presently infusing & rate. Document on Nurses' notes.	Administer sedation meds as ordered by MD and monitor accordingly. Monitor infusing IV solutions. ---			Documentation completed of IV sol'ns presently infusing.

5/93   Page 1

146

Case Type CORONARY ANGIOGRAM (LV ANGIO)

ANTICIPATED RECOVERY PLAN (continued)

Clinical Occurrence	1 - 15 MINUTES	15 - 30 MINUTES	30 MINUTES	45 MINUTES	60 MINUTES
ACTIVITY/SAFETY	Instruct pt regarding surroundings: Narrow Exam table Several Monitors Close proximity of X-ray equipment.	Flat bedrest with legs extended.			Transfer pt to cart from exam table via slider board. Side-rails up on pt. cart. Flat bedrest with legs extended.
DIET	NPO--------->				
ELIMINATION	Bedpan------------>				
D/C PLAN			Update and document variances--------->		Review discharge plan with Cardiologist. Charting completed. Report called to assigned patient care unit regarding patient status. Discharge patient per protocol.
TEACHING/ PSYCHOSOCIAL SUPPORT	Provide support and reassurance to patient.----> Review with patient the flow of the procedure. Instruct patient to let staff know if he/she develops chest pain or other symptoms----->				Instruct patient of the need to remain flat - bedrest with legs extended Instruct patient in site care and complications. Plan of care will be interpreted and discussed by MD with patient and family - Activity level - Frequent V.S. - Checking site frequently - Checking CMS & pulse - Report chest discomfort.
RADIOLOGY/ OTHER *	Observe radiation precaution x-ray equipment in close proximity to patient. Ask about previous contrast dye allergy.				
LABORATORY *	12 Lead EKG in chart. Note lab results on ARP. Record any lab results during procedure on computer Nurses' notes.----> Creat Hgb PT K+ Plts				

5/93   Page 2   I am aware that my care is being managed by an ARP.
                                            Patient/Concerned Other Signature_____

Figure 10-4. Anticipated Recovery Plan for CABG Patients (Preop Testing and Education)

Mercy Hospital - ANTICIPATED RECOVERY PATH

Open Heart (Pre-Op)
DRG's:
Expected LOS: 2 days

Directions for use:
1) Utilize every shift, every day.
2) Collaborative problem areas/review outcomes & indicate date initially met.
3) Clinical occurrences.
   A. Circle unmet interventions/goals.
   B. When/if circled item is completed, write "done" date & initial.
   C. Cross out NOT APPLICABLE (NA) items.
   D. Check when information given, etc.
4) Individualize to each patient.

Collaborative Prob./Focus Areas	Initial	Intermediate	Date Initially Met
	PATIENT/FAMILY OUTCOMES		
1) Knowledge deficit R/T Pre and Post Open Heart surgery.	Patient is prepared for surgery which is scheduled for Date_____ Time_____	Patient will verbalize understanding of pre-op education, treatments and procedure.	

CLINICAL OCCURRENCES	Pre-Op Date_____	AM OR Date_____
Nursing Assessment/Action	Wt. on admission (use chair scale) & daily V.S. qid Notify surgeon of chest pain. ( ) H&P on chart ( ) Teds hose-measured for appropriate size ( ) Consent signed for scheduled operative procedure ( ) Hibiclens shower (#1) day before OR ( ) Old chart to floor ( ) Laxative as needed/ordered (MTA: magcitrate to be given A.M. of day prior; For OP's - Cardiac Centers will obtain Mag Cit from pharmacy & PCU nurse to administer to patient before 3 P.M.)	( ) AM wt._____ Kg/_____ # Ht._____ ( ) Wt/Ht tape to front of chart with masking tape ( ) AM V.S._____ ( ) Allergies_____ ( ) Allergy band on ( ) Blood Band on ( ) ID band on ( ) Clip (By OR) chin to ankles ( ) Hibiclens (#2) shower after clip Remove: ( ) Dentures ( ) pins ( ) contacts ( ) glasses ( ) Prothesis ( ) wigs ( ) jewelry ( ) MAR on chart ( ) Blue plate in chart ( ) Old chart to OR ( ) To OR via_____ at_____ ( ) TEDs sent with belongings to ICU ( ) Belongings sent to ICU ( ) Belongings sent home with family documented in nursing notes. ( ) Ht/wt and patient report called to ICU. ( ) Family whereabouts_____
Laboratory/Tests per M.D. order	Labs on chart ( ) Hepatitis B surface antigen ( ) CBC ( ) UA ( ) electrolytes ( ) lipid profile ( ) creat. ( ) ABG's on RA ( ) 2 units PRBC's - Type & Cross ( ) 8 pack Plt's on redos, valve replacement or if > 72 years old. If not done past 5 days ( ) SMA -12 ( ) PT ( ) PTT ( ) Plt count ( ) Bleeding time Call any significant abnormal labs to surgeon	
Radiology/Other	( ) CXR ( ) Spirometry done and report on chart ( ) EKG within 24° of surgery	

(Continued on next page)

Figure 10-4. (Continued)

CLINICAL OCCURRENCES	PRE-OP	AM OR
Medications	Tylenol PRN pain/headache MOM 30cc qd PRN ( ) Continue home meds except Coumadin aspirin, and Persantine if OK with cardiology. Chloral Hydrate qHS PRN sleep	( ) Pre-meds given_____ ( ) Pork heparin 5,000 units on call to OR (Dr. Gannon's patients only) ( ) Cefazolin 1gm IV for pre-op holding if not allergic. If allergic, IV vancomycin - (send with pt. to OR - tape to front of chart) (Zinacef 1.5 mg IV for Dr. Gannon's patient's only)
Diet	Low fat, low cholesterol diet. If diabetic, add home diet. ( ) NPO night before surgery	( ) NPO since_____
Elimination	I&O	( ) Void on call to OR
Activity/Safety	Up ad lib	( ) Bedrest with siderails up after pre meds given. Special needs: Visual_____ Hearing_____ Communication_____
Goal Setting	Cardiac Rehab to evaluate and assist in identifying short term and long range goals. STG_____ _____ LRG_____ _____	

CLINICAL OCCURRENCES	PRE-OP	AM OR
Teaching	( ) 1. Date of surgery _____ Time _____ Flexibility of OR explained. ( ) 2. Pt. knows diagnosis _____ and can state reason for procedure. ( ) 3. Name of Surgeon _____ Cardiologist _____ ( ) 4. Viewed Pre-op video "Heartbeat better". ( ) 5. Received pamphlet "You and Your Heart Surgery". American Heart Assn. "CABG surgery" or Heart Valve surgery. 6. Seen by other department. ( ) RT ( ) Cardiac Rehab ( ) MDA Pre-op protocol (to evaluate) 7. PCU pre-op teaching ( ) Rational for TEDs/acces ( ) Pre-anesthesia ( ) Need Heplock/IV ( ) OR ( ) NPO ( ) Monitor ( ) Need to inform nurse of chest pain ( ) Frequent V.S. ( ) Instructed/demonstrated use of heart pillow ( ) Use side muscles to move upper part of body to protect incision and sternum. ( ) Don't pull on siderails to get in and out of bed ( ) Ambulation progression ( ) Need to inform post-op of pain, discomfort, location/relief measures.	
Psychosocial Support	( ) Seen by chaplaincy/social service	
Discharge Planning	( ) Assess home situation at family support systems. Include family/S.O. in pre-op teaching.	
	Ancillary Staff	Ancillary Staff

61-45577 1/20/94

Figure 10-5. Anticipated Recovery Plan (Postop Experience)

Mercy Hospital - ANTICIPATED RECOVERY PATH

OPEN HEART/PCU
DRG's: 107
Expected LOS: 5 da

Directions for use: 1) Utilize every shift, every day.
2) Collaborative problem areas/review outcomes & indicate date initially met.
3) Clinical occurrences.
   A. Circle unmet interventions/goals.
   B. When/if circled item is completed, write "done" date & initial.
   C. Cross out NOT APPLICABLE (NA) items.
   D. Check when information given, etc.
4) Individualize to each patient.

Modifiable risk factors: ( ) Diabetes ( ) Hypertension ( ) Lack of exercise ( ) Obesity ( ) Hypercholesterolemia ( ) Stress ( ) Smoking

Collaborative Problems/Focus Areas	Initial/Stabilization	Intermediate	Date Initially Met	Discharge	Date Initially Met	Met at D/C Yes No
	PATIENT/FAMILY OUTCOMES			PATIENT/FAMILY OUTCOMES		
1. Alteration in comfort R/T surgical procedure.	Pain is absent or controlled with ordered meds—	-Actively participates in ADL's.		-Patient's rhythm has been stable for 24°		
2. Potential impaired gas exchange R/T atelectasis.	Assessments indicate adequate oxygenation	-Pt's O$_2$ saturation maintains 92% or > on room air.		-Patient's VS have been stable for 24°		
				-Incisions intact and healing without evidence of infection.		
3. Alteration in CO (decreased) R/T arrhythmias & decreased myocardial contractility	Arrhythmias are identified & treated. Maintains hemodynamic stability without IV drips.	-Pt verbalizes understanding of signs and symptoms of Wound complications ___ Chest pain ___ Impaired elimination		-Pt/family verbalizes understanding of home meds: • able to describe med name, dose, action, main side effects.		
	CV assessment indicates adequate tissue perfusion.	-Pt meeting estimated nutritional needs (consuming a minimum of 50% of meals)		-Pt/family verbalizes understanding of diet instructions: NAS, low chol, LSF, LF. (Dietitian)		
4. Knowledge deficit.	Pt/family express understanding of IS, thoracic splinting, activity progression.	-Pt/family verbalizes understanding of wound care instructions.		-Pt/family verbalizes understanding of activity/exercise instructions. (Cardiac Rehab)		
		-If diabetic, Pt home regime is established (home accu check schedule, insulin and/or oral hypoglycemics).		-Pt is able to ambulate 3-6 min. & climbs 3-12 stairs with minimal fatigue (Cardiac Rehab)		
		-Pt/family has an available, able and willing support system in place for post discharge.				
		-Pt verbalizes understanding of available community resources (Fri support gp, Cardiac Club, Smoking clinic) as appropriate.				

Clinical Occurrences	PO 1/Date_____	PO 2/Date_____	PO 3/Date_____	PO 4/Date_____	PO 5/Date_____
Nursing Assessments	DC foley. May straight cath x3 prn. (MWHL) If pt Diabetic, check with M.D. re: changing accuchecks to ac & hs. Remove sternal dsg, replace if oozing. Use minimal tape. Use stockinette instead of tape whenever possible.	Check inc q8° —→ Check sternal stability q8° —→ Women with large breasts to wear bra for support. —→ Secure P.W. to chest. —→ Change dsg QD while pt. has pacer wires. Cleanse with H₂O₂ around site. —→ Use of H₂O₂ to cleanse remove serous crusts from staples.	—→ —→ —→ —→ —→ —→	D.C. pacer wires by C.V. clinician. -Assess heart sounds b/4 D/C'ing -Bedrest x1 hr after pulled. -Assess heart sounds & for sx of tamponade. —→	—→ —→ —→ —→ —→
Lab/Tests	CXR q A.M. by 9:00 A.M. as long as pt. has chest tubes (MWHL). CXR POD 1/only (MTA).	CBC and SMA6		EKG, CBC, lytes, PA and L lateral CXR (MWHL). Valve pt: PT daily after Pacer wires d/c	
Medications	If valve pt., check QD PT & INR and call for Coumadin order. Document if Surgeon or Cardiologist is managing PT/anticoagulation therapy. Upon Tx to PCU: -D/C I.V. meds & antibiotic if CT out -D/C KCL prn supps, Lasix, Valium -Assess pain control. -Encourage IM Dem/MS POD 1 vs p.o. narc. If pt. nauseated, consider possible med causes...Persantine, narcs. Procan, Beta-blockers.	(Continue IV antibiotic while CTs in - MWHL) —→ Encourage pt. to take p.o. pain meds. Q 3-4 hrs. esp. before C. Rehab & H.S. or 2400. MOM @ H.S. Tylenol #3/Darvon	—→ —→ Duc. supp. if no BM Ask for reorder of SQ heparin after 10th dose if pt. not out of bed POD 3-4 (MWHL).	Provide MED-IN-FORM cards to pt. & family. POD 5 if dc POD 6 —→ If pt. Diabetic, check for home insulin or oral hypoglycemic meds. —→	—→ —→
Diet	Diet as tolerated. Family may bring favorite foods. CIB shakes if needed.	If Diabetic, check with M.D. re: Diab. features on diet.		Dietitian to instruct NAS & low cholesterol & low fat diet for home.	
Hemodynamic Monitoring	-MWHL: 24hr fluid limit of 2400cc x48 hrs. If IV required titrate IV & PO fluid intake to meet fluid limit. -MTA: Saline lock IV when po intake >1000cc. -Telemetry with arrhythmia protocol as written. -V.S. q4h W/A. -Saline Lock IV -Weight on transfer & daily in A.M.	—→ —→ —→ —→	—→ —→ —→ —→	D/C telemetry 3rd day after transfer if: 1) NSR x 24 hours 2) On no anti-arrhythmic meds (Beta blockers & lanoxin not considered anti-arrhythmics) 3) Pacer wires have been removed * If all conditions above not met confer with Cardiologist re: telemetry.	
	Patient experienced Atrial Fib? YES NO Intervention required? YES NO	Pt experienced A Fib? YES NO Intervention required? YES NO	Pt experienced A Fib? YES NO Intervention required? YES NO	Pt experienced A Fib? YES NO Intervention required? YES NO	Pt experienced A Fib? YES NO Intervention required? YES NO

(Continued on next page)

Figure 10-5. (Continued)

CLINICAL OCCURRENCES	POD 1/Date ___	POD 2/Date ___	POD 3/Date ___	POD 4/Date ___	POD 5/Date ___
Treatments/ Pulmonary	I.S. q1-2h W/A; increase to q30" if febrile or Respiratory compromise. Follow RT oxygen per RT/Post extubation protocol for O_2 weaning & D/Cing.	If on O_2 sats are ck'd BID (b/4 0930 & at 1600). If > 92% continue weaning protocol until O_2 disconnued.	DC O_2 if sats ≥ 92% on room air or determined by surgeon. Keep O_2 setup in room on standby x 24 hours.	Spot check O_2 sats BID. Maintains oxygenation without supplemental O_2	
Chest Tube Management	-Maintain 20cm water pressure in Atrium suction setup. -Drainage should be serous. -Milk tubing as necessary. (Do not strip) -DC C-tubes when draining <100cc/8 hrs. x2 (CV Nurse Clinician). -Chg. CT drsg qd (& prn) until CT DC'd.	When CT pulled, remove dressing -after 24 hrs for MWHL. -after 48 hrs for MTA. -Replace dressing with band aid.	Remove band aid if no drainage.		
Activity	-Chair TID for meals. -Thigh-High Ted stockings. -Elevate legs when sitting or in bed. -Encourage to flex and extend feet, legs, thighs q2hrs.——>	Enc. pt. to wear comfortable exercise clothing. ——> AMB 4 min with assist 4-6 times per day/coordinate with cardiac rehab.	——> AMB 4-6 min 4-6 times a day. Coordinate with cardiac rehab.	——> AMB 6-8 min 4-6 times a day. Coordinate with cardiac rehab.	——> AMB 8-10 min 4-6 times a day. Coordinate with cardiac rehab. Ck with C.V. clinic if pt. can shower.
Safety	-Complete Safety Assess on transfer. -ADL's and partial bath. -BRP's with assist.				
Cardiac Rehab	Individualize treatments. Begin bedside rehab. Encourage family participation P.M.: Bedside/clinic cals up to 2.1 mets Walk up to 3 minutes 3-6 times. Review bedside ARP include pt. & family in post op care.	Clinic BID: A.M. Rehab. Cals up to 2.3 mets (7 min) Walk up to 4 min. P.M. Rehab. Walk up to 5 min Climb 3 steps Bike 3 min (optional) Initiate education Review ARP	Clinic BID A.M. Rehab. Cals up to 2.6 mets (9 min) Walk up to 6 min. Climb 6 stairs P.M. Rehab. Walk 7 min. Climb 9 stairs Bike 4 min (optional) Encourage family participation Initiate home program Complete home program. Make arrangements for one patient's rehab.	Clinic BID A.M. Rehab. A.M. cals (optional) Walk 8 min. Climb 12 stairs Bike 5 min. (optional) P.M. Rehab. Walk 9-10 min Climb 15 stairs Bike 6 min (optional) Continue home program.	Clinic BID If patient still in hospital, continue to advance as tolerated.

CLINICAL OCCURRENCES	POD 1/Date ____	POD 2/Date ____	POD 3/Date ____	POD 4/Date ____	POD 5/Date ____
Teaching		Teaching discharge outcomes: Verbalize understanding of: () purpose of telemetry () proper splinting techniques () arm limitations () incentive spirometer usage schedule. Review bedside ARP with patient. () Verbalizes understanding of above instructions. (Reinf.)	() Pain management () Describes TEDs wearing schedule & care () S.O. demonstrates TEDs application. () Identifies anti-constipation measures. () Lists symptoms of infection. () Describes incisional care. () Plans for 10# lifting restriction. () Reads discharge instruction pamphlet. () Verbalizes understanding of above instructions. (Reinf.)	() Activity progression () Plans for daily weights. () Identifies possible emotional reactions. () Defines sexual considerations. () Describes support group availability. () View "Heart Changes" video. () View "Risk Factors" video. () View Coumadin video. () Read Coumadin packet. () Verbalizes understanding of above instructions. (Reinf.) Optional: () Grocery Store Tour video () Managing Your Stress Response () "Heart Mate" series as appropriate () Channel 10 cable programs as appropriate	() Demonstrates pulse taking. () Develop risk factor modification plan. () Review home medications using med information sheets. () Verbalizes understanding of above instructions. (Reinf.)
	Ancillary Staff	Ancillary Staff	Ancillary Staff	Ancillary Staff	Ancillary Staff
Psychosocial Support	Assess need & implement interventions.	Visit by Mended Hearts Representative———>	Social Serv. to assess Medicare pts and others in need of services. ———>	———>	———>
	Ancillary Staff	Ancillary Staff	Ancillary Staff	Ancillary Staff	Ancillary Staff

1/26/94

Figure 10-6. Anticipated Recovery Plan (Inpatient Rehabilitation for CABG Patients) Phase I

CARDIAC CENTERS
MERCY HOSPITAL
CARDIAC REHABILITATION
ANTICIPATED RECOVERY PLAN

Name_____ Room Number_____ Date_____

* INITIAL REFERRAL NEEDED TO BEGIN REHABILITATION. * ACTIVITY WILL BE INCREASED DAILY PER PATIENT TOLERANCE. * EXERCISE PROTOCOLS ARE INDIVIDUALIZED ACCORDING TO PATIENT NEEDS. * EDUCATION FOR PATIENT AND FAMILY WILL BE PROVIDED. * HOME EXERCISE PROGRAM WILL BE GIVEN BEFORE DISCHARGE. * REHABILITATION TREATMENT TWICE A DAY. * WARM UPS INCLUDE DEEP BREATHS AND NECK TURNS.	DIET CLASS PRIOR TO DISCHARGE. DIETITIAN - LOW CHOLESTEROL/NO ADDED SALT. COMPLETED_____ (DATE/INITIAL)

CARDIAC REHAB PROTOCOL		NURSING STATION ACTIVITY

ROOM
 	
POD 1
 	
ROOM/CLINIC
 	
COMPLETED DATE_____INITIAL_____
	A.M. UE/LE CALS 1-4 MIN(2.1 METS)
	    WALK 1-2 MIN.
	
	REVIEW PALPATION OF PULSE, FOOT EXERCISE AND EXERCISE BREATHING.
	
	P.M. UE/LE CALS 2-6 MIN (2.1 METS)
	    WALK 1-3 MIN.
		ADL'S = ACTIVITIES OF DAILY LIVING
		
		CHAIR 3 TIMES A DAY FOR MEALS
		
		BATHROOM PRIVILEGES WITH HELP.
		
		ADL'S = PARTIAL BATH WITH ASSISTANCE FOR LEGS AND BACK.
		
		WALK 1-3 MIN WITH ASSISTANCE.

CLINIC
 	
POD 2
 	
CLINIC
 	
COMPLETED DATE_____INITIAL_____
	A.M. UE/LE CALS 4-7 MIN 92.3 METS)
	    WALK/TREADMILL 2-4 MIN (.8-1.3 MPH)
	
	P.M. UE/LE CALS 4-7 MIN (2.3 METS)
	    OPTIONAL
	    WALK/TREADMILL 3-5 MIN (.8-1.3 MPH)
	    BIKE/ARM ERGOM 2-3 MIN (0 - .5 KP)
		CHAIR 3 TIMES A DAY FOR MEALS.
		
		WALK (3-5 MINUTES) WITH ASSISTANCE.
		
		UP AS TOLERATED.
		
		ADL'S = PARTIAL BATH WITH ASSISTANCE FOR LEGS AND BACK

CLINIC
 	
POD 3
 	
CLINIC
 	
COMPLETED DATE_____INITIAL_____
	A.M. TREADMILL/WALK 4-6 MIN (.8-1.3 MPH)
	    CLIMB 3-6 STEPS
	    BIKE/ARM ERGOM. 3-4 MIN (0-.5 KP)
	
	P.M. TREADMILL/WALK 5-7 MIN (.8-1.3 MPH)
	    CLIMB 6-9 STEPS
	    BIKE/ARM ERGOM 3-5 MINU (0-.5 KP)
		CHAIR 3 TIMES A DAY FOR MEALS.
		
		WALK (4-7 MINUTES) WITH ASSISTANCE AS NEEDED.
		
		UP AS TOLERATED.
		
		ADL'S = PARTIAL BATH WITH ASSISTANCE FOR LEGS AND BACK.

CLINIC
 	
POD 4
 	
CLINIC
 	
COMPLETED DATE_____INITIAL_____
	A.M. TREADMILL/WALK 6-8 MIN (.8-1.6 MPH)
	    CLIMB 9-12 STEPS
	    BIKE/ARM ERGOM 3-4 MIN (0-.5 KP)
	
	P.M. TREADMILL/WALK 7-9 MIN (.8-1.8 MPH)
	    CLIMB 9-15 STEPS
	    BIKE/ARM ERGOM 4-6 MIN (0 - .5 KP)
	
	* PROVIDE HOME PROGRAM AND ACTIVITY GUIDELINES. ARRANGE FOR OUTPATIENT CARDIAC REHAB.
		CHAIR 3 TIMES A DAY FOR MEALS.
		
		WALK (5-9 MIN) INDEPENDENTLY IN HALLWAYS.
		
		UP AS TOLERATED.
		
		ADL'S = ? INDEPENDENT BATHING.

CLINIC POD 5	IF PATIENT IS STILL IN HOSPITAL THEN CONTINUE TO ADVANCE REHAB AS TOLERATED	

Figure 10-7. Anticipated Recovery Plan (Outpatient Rehabilitation for CABG Patients) Phase II

PROFILE:
* As indicated by physician
Red check indicates MD order

ANTICIPATED RECOVERY PLAN

Case Type __Phase II Outpatients__

Physician _____ Phone: _____
Consults _____ Beeper: _____

DRG _____ Expected LOS _____ weeks
Secondary Diagnoses _____

RN/Therapist Initiated/Reviewed with pt/family

Admission Date _____

**PHASE II
OUTPATIENT CARDIAC
REHABILITATION**

Name _____ Age _____

Allergies (in Red)   Social History   Health History   Family/Emerg..Phone/Religion
Code
Status Special Needs::
        Visual _____
        Hearing _____
        Communication _____

STAFF ALERT: (use pencil)

MEDS: _____

Physician Referral _____

Target Heart Rate _____

BP seated   RA _____ LA _____

BP standing RA _____ LA _____

MURSE CLINICIAN: _____

Phone: _____

Beeper: _____

PROGRESS NOTE: _____

DISCHARGE SUMMARY: _____

NURSING DIAGNOSIS AND COLLABORATIVE PROGRAM	INITIAL PATIENT/FAMILY OUTCOMES	INTERMEDIATE PATIENT/FAMILY OUTCOMES	DISCHARGE PATIENT/FAMILY OUTCOMES
1). Anxiety related to perceived and/or actual threat to biologic integrity.	Patient will be more at ease and comfortable by demonstrating a gradual increase in level of activities at home and cardiac rehab-->	Patient will demonstrate an increase in exercise tolerance.
2). Knowledge deficit related to disease, meds, exercise and activity.	Patient/family will verbalize understanding of CAD, meds, exercise and activity.		Patient will verbalize understanding of the importance of continued exercise, meds and disease process.
3). An alteration of lifestyle relative to existing disease process or surgery.	Patient and family will verbalize fears & feelings about lifestyle changes.	Cardiac Rehab staff will keep patient informed of progress and reinforce home activity and alleviate fears.	Patient and family will verbalize understanding of lifestyle changes.

8/92 (Page 1 - front)

Health One Mercy Hospital

(Continued on next page)

Figure 10-7. (Continued)

Case Type: Phase II Outpatients
Nurse/Therapist Initiated: _____

ANTICIPATED RECOVERY PLAN (cont)

	INITIAL	INTERMEDIATE	DISCHARGE
ASSESSMENTS Initial assessment of patient to Phase II by Cardiac Rehab Staff	Initial assessment/orientation to Phase II by Cardiac Rehab staff to assess patient/families educational and psychosocial needs: Review: • Risk Factors ____ • Employment ____ • Diet ____ • Insurance ____ • Home exercise/activity ____ • Medications ____ • Physician appointments ____	• Encourage modifications of lifestyle changes to reduce risk of heart disease. • Reinforce healthier eating habits. • Cardiac rehab staff remind patient about insurance coverage. • Monitor home activity exercise records. • Document medication changes. • Review use of Nitroglycerin. • Cardiac rehab staff will send progress notes to physicians.	• Reinforce modification of risk factors. • Review activity level in regards to work. • Lowfat diet reviewed by dietitian. • Patient instructed to continue with home exercise and activity according to discharge level. • Review medications and reinforce use of NTG. • Send discharge summary to physicians including rhythm strips.
ORIENTATION To Phase II by Cardiac Rehab Staff	• Informed Consent ____ • Goals ____ • Schedule ____ • Weights ____ • Electrode Placement ____ • Palpation of Pulse ____ • Warning Signs ____ • Exercise Routine ____ • Perceived Exertion ____ • Support Groups ____ • Diet Class ____ • Educational Videos ____	• Remind patient of goals. • Continue schedule. • Monitor weights. • Check electrode placement. • Review warning signs. • Update and advance exercise when appropriate. • Encourage participation in support and diet sessions. • Review list of videos with patient & family.	• Review completed goals. • Discharge. • Review weight loss/maintenance gain with patient & family. • Instruct patient again on warning signs and what to do about them. • Review what patient has accomplished during Phase II and importance of continued exercise for 20 - 30 minutes, 3-5 times a week. • Encourage patient to attend Phase III for maintenance exercise. • Instruct patient to continue to use perceived exertion to monitor exercise and activity at home. • Instruct patient in discharge THR. • Give patient information on support groups and diet class. • Patient instructed about continued use of videos for education and support.
REHAB ACTION/ TREATMENTS	Weigh patient each session---------- Blood Pressure Seated RA____ LA____ Standing RA____ LA____ Record BP from highest arm. Mount resting rhythm strip and higher HR's during exercise. Monitor and record resting rhythm strip and HR on each piece of equipment----------	Blood pressure from R or L arm. Record before calisthenics, before exercise, 2 - 3 times during exercise, and after cool down walk. --------> -------->	Review weight guidelines with patient & family. Review resting, exercise and post exercise blood pressure with patient and family. Patient will be aware of arrhythmias. Documentation to physician and medical records.

8/92 (Page 1 - back)

Health One Mercy Hospital

Case Type __Phase II Outpatients__
Nurse/Therapist Initiated: _____

ANTICIPATED RECOVERY PLAN (cont)

	INITIAL	INTERMEDIATE	DISCHARGE
MEDS	NTG as needed----------------------->	Review use of NTG----------------------->	Reinforce use of NTG----------------------->
TARGET HEART RATE	Cardiac Rehab staff will use the target heart rate prescribed by the patient's physician.	Adjust and monitor target heart rate with approval of patient's physician.	Instruct patient in importance of monitoring target heart rate at home and reporting abnormalities to his/her physician.
ACTIVITY	Patient will start exercise and increase as tolerated.	Advance and adjust exercise as tolerated.	Review discharge exercise program with patient and family.
SAFETY	Monitor heart rate, blood pressure, weight, respiration, for signs and symptoms of distress.		
TEACHING	Review educational materials in "Take It to Heart".	--->	Reinforce continued use of educational tools presented to patient and family.
PSYCHOSOCIAL SUPPORT	Provide opportunity for patient and family feedback and questions.	Continue to follow needs and refer to appropriate source if needed.	Review needs of patient and family and instruct in continued use of support groups if needed.
DISCHARGE PLANNING	Assessment/Evaluation/Initiate outpatient rehab discharge planning.	Advance as tolerated.	Review program, progress, continued exercise and education with patient and family.
			Discharge summary to physician(s) and Medical Records.

Signature of Patient_____ Date_____

Signature of Nurse/Therapist_____ Date_____

8/92   (Page 2 - front)   Health One Mercy Hospital

Figure 10-8. Patient and Family Version of CABG Anticipated Recovery Plan

Patient: _____   Spouse: _____   Surgeon: _____   Cardiologist: _____

ANTICIPATED RECOVERY PATH

POD #2: ___	POD #3: ___	POD #4: ___	POD #5: ___	POD #6: ___
Sit in chair 3 X today	Sit in chair for all meals	Sit in chair for all meals	Sit in chair for all meals	Sit in chair for all meals
Bathroom privileges with help	Walk 2 minutes X 2 and as desired (with help) ( ) ( ) ( )	Walk 3-4 minutes X 2 and as desired ( ) ( ) ( )	Walk 4-5 minutes X 2 and as desired ( ) ( ) ( )	Walk 5-6 minutes X 2 and as desired ( ) ( ) ( )
Use incentive spirometer every hour ___ cc's	Use incentive spirometer every hour ___ cc's	Use incentive spirometer every hour ___ cc's	Use incentive spirometer every hour ___ cc's	Use incentive spirometer every hour ___ cc's
Eat regular diet. Family may bring favorite foods	Regular diet	Regular diet	Regular diet	Regular diet
	Prune juice and/or laxative if no bowel movement	Bowel function normal for you (suppository if needed)	Dietician consultation	Discharge after 1:00 PM, if approved by physician
Cardiac rehabilitation in room	Rest period and pain med prior to Cardiac Rehab (in clinic, AM and PM)	Rest period and pain med prior to Cardiac Rehab (in clinic, AM and PM)	Rest period and pain med prior to Cardiac Rehab (in clinic, AM and PM)	Cardiac Rehab in clinic (only in AM on day of discharge)
Begin discharge planning				

LEARNING PROGRAM

POD #2	POD #3	POD #4	POD #5	POD #6
Pulmonary care Incentive spirometer TCH	Pain differentiation TEDS and TEDS care Constipation	Lifting restriction Emotional reactions Sexual considerations	Pulse-taking demo	Review home meds
Telemetry	Progressive rest periods	Support groups	Develop plan for risk factor modification	*Read Med-In-form cards
Splinting	Infection symptoms Incisional care	*Read discharge instruction pamphlet	*View discharge video	Evaluate understanding of discharge instructions

Sometimes one path is discontinued in favor of another one. This special circumstance may be due to alteration(s) in diagnosis or in surgical procedure. When this occurs, the nursing staff must document the change and change the dates on both the discontinued path and the new one.

There are a few instances where secondary or supplemental clinical paths have been developed (for example, COPD). These supplements (and their interventions) are used concurrently with the primary diagnosis pathway. Time frames for expected outcomes may be less specific than those for primary diagnosis paths because supplements do not state the primary reason for a patient's hospitalization.

Clinical Paths as Communication Tools

The nursing staff uses the between-shift reporting process to plan the next steps in the patient's care based on pathway recommendations. The following information is exchanged during shift turnover:

- Patient's name, age, physician(s), diagnosis/surgical procedure/type of service delivery
- Patient's day number and anticipated length of stay
- Significant events that need to occur on this day per path protocol
- Evaluation of compliance with the path, source of variance (if any), documentation of corrective action ordered and taken, and by whom
- Questions regarding the need for case consultation on any patient for whom significant variances are identified

A typical shift turnover report using the clinical path as a guide might read as follows:

Patient is Mr. Kinney, age 52, in Room 1021. His physician is Dr. Jones. Diagnoses: recurrent chest pain. He is on an angina path, day two of a two-day LOS. Variances: bathroom privileges only, due to activity intolerance due to chest pain and shortness of breath on exertion. Cardiology has been consulted and will see tomorrow. Variances are documented.

Clinical Path Variance Documentation

At Mercy and Unity, a *variance* is defined as any deviation (or detour) from patient care activities outlined on the clinical pathway that can alter anticipated discharge date or expected outcomes. Negative variances are identified as those that contribute to prolonged length of stay or compromise anticipated outcomes.

Individual patient variances are identified by the caregivers during the course of care and documented in the chart. Once a corrective action plan is developed and initiated, it too is documented. Because variance reporting is done concurrently, it is often possible to reverse or avoid negative variance. Variances are monitored over time, and data eventually are collected within a case type for a number of patients. Aggregate information is analyzed by the case manager and the department QI team for patterns and trends.

Each clinical path is accompanied by a variance tracking sheet (figure 10-9). Throughout the patient's hospitalization each nursing staff shift notes variances (both positive and negative) on the variance sheet. An internal coding system for variance reporting aids in this documentation process (figure 10-10).

Figure 10-9.   Variance Tracking Sheet

UNITY VARIANCE TRACKING SHEET
Case Type_____DRG_____ICD9_____
ELOS_____ADMIT DATE_____D/C DATE_____
Unit_____Physician_____
Secondary Diagnoses/Surgeries_____
_____

BE SURE TO STAMP THIS SHEET, FILL IN ADMIT DATE, D/C DATE AND UNIT

DATE/ SHIFT	ARP DAY#	☑ ON PATH	VARIANCE (WHAT)	SOURCE (WHY)	ACTION Y / N	FURTHER EXPLANATION*	INITIAL/ DEPT

See codes listed on back

VARIANCE: Shows us how patients and clinicians differ from the norm, as well where an institution might improve it's service; ARP's are expected tasks and outcomes.   Variances are unexpected events.

Figure 10-10. Variance Tracking Departmental Codes

CAUSE/SOURCE CODES
5/93

DEPARTMENTAL CODES

22XX	Nursing	32XX	Surgery/Anesthesia	40XX	Dietary
23XX	Social Services	34XX	Pharmacy	41XX	Pastoral Care
24XX	Physical Therapy	35XX	Laboratory/Pathology	42XX	Patient Transport
25XX	Occupational Therapy	36XX	Radiology	43XX	Patient Registration
26XX	Respiratory Therapy	37XX	Cath Lab	44XX	Medical Records
27XX	Speech Therapy	38XX	Nuclear Medicine	45XX	Housekeeping
28XX	Cardiac Rehabilitation	39XX	Radiation Therapy	46XX	Stores
29XX	Dialysis			47XX	Central Supply
30XX	Enterstomal Therapy			48XX	Clinic
31XX	Chemical Dependency			49XX	Other

Match Department Codes with Appropriate Caregiver or System Variance

Example: **32XX** Surgery/Anesthesia with **XX33** Scheduling Conflict = 3233 for cause code column
35XX Laboratory/Path with **XX43** not available - 3543 Labs not available

PHYSICAL CONDITION

CARDIOVASCULAR
1330	Hematoma w/intervention
	* (specify)
1331	Other Rhythm Disturbances
	* (specify)
1333	Peripheral Pulse Variation
	* (specify)
1337	Chest Pain
1338	Bleeding After Lytics
1341	Hypotension
1342	Hypertension
1344	Acute CHF
1346	Digoxin Level Imbalance
	* (specify)
1349	Ventricular Tachycardia
1350	Atrial Fibrillation
1351	Asystole
1352	PVC's w/intervention
1353	Ventricular Fibrillation
1354	SVT
1355	Blocks * (specify)
1359	Low Cardiac Output/Cardiac Index
1389	Tele Cont./No arrhythmia

GI
1340	GI Bleeding
1381	Nausea/vomiting
1384	Diarrhea
1385	Nutritional Status * (specify)
1386	Constipation w/intervention
1388	Ileus

NEURO
1321	Vision Impairment
1322	Neurological change * (specify)
1323	Acute Mobility Prob. * (specify)
1314	Pre-existing mobility limitation
1324	Vertigo
1325	Mental Impairment * (specify)
1336	Swallowing Impairment

RESPIRATORY
1343	Low O$_2$ Saturations
1345	Pre-existing COPD
1347	Theophylline Level Imbalance
1356	Ventilator/Intubation Required
1361	Atelectasis/Effusion
1362	ARDS
1364	Pneumothorax
1365	Pulmonary Embolism
1366	Pulmonary Edema
1367	Failed Wean
1368	Respiratory Distress

RENAL
1371	Inadequate Urine Output
1373	Blood in Urine
1374	Incontinent
1375	Unable to void
1377	Clotted Access

MISCELLANEOUS
1310	Fever
1311	Infection * (specify source)
1312	Pain * (specify source)
1313	Bleeding * (specify source)
1319	Electrolyte Abnormality * (specify
1327	Diabetes Mellitus * (specify)
1339	Other Abnormal Lab * (specify)
1348	Other Drug Imbalance
1369	Venous Access Device * (specify)
1390	Anemia Requiring Tranfusion
1399	Patient Condition Other * (specify)
1401	Improved Progression/Ahead of Path
1403	Transfer to Another Hospital
1405	Pre-ARP Condition - * (specify)
1407	ARP (path D/C'd)
1498	Death

PATIENT/FAMILY
1210	Patient Not Available
1220	Patient Declines Treatment
1221	Pt. Declines OT 2° to Fatigue
1222	Pt. Declines PT 2° to Fatigue
1223	Patient Combative
1225	Communication Problem
1226	Coping Difficulties
1228	Difficulty learning
1229	Physical Inability to Perform Task
1230	Patient Uncooperative/Indecisive
1299	Other Patient Decision * (specify)
1510	Family/Sig. Other Not Available
1520	Family/Sig. Other Declines Treatment
1530	Family/Sig. Other Indecisive
1599	Family Other * (specify)

CAREGIVER

PHYSICIAN VARIANCES * SPECIFY PHYSICIAN
2111	Date or Time of Treatment Changed
2113	Added Orders
2116	MD Orders Not Available
2117	Lack of Continuity/Management
2118	Diagnosis Not Given Yet
2119	Needing Clarification of orders/ restrictions
2121	Physician Did Not Order
2122	No Rounding
2131	Late Rounding
2132	Untimely Callback
2133	Waiting for Consult from other MD
2199	Physician Other * (specify)

CAREGIVER VARIANCES
XX11	Delayed Treatment/Activity
XX13	Omitted Treatment or Item
XX15	Unscheduled Intervention for Another Patient
XX19	Other Decision * (specify)
XX22	Lack of Continuity
XX24	Order Not Transcribed/Transcribed Correctly
XX29	Other Omission * (specify)

INTERNAL SYSTEM VARIANCE

SCHEDULING ISSUES
XX31	Department Closed
XX32	Department Overbooked
XX33	Scheduling Conflict
XX34	Patient having Dialysis
XX35	Patient in Diagnostic Dept.
XX39	Other * (specify)

RESOURCE/INFO ISSUES
XX41	Staff Unavailable
XX42	Bed Unavailable
XX43	Diagnostic/Tx Results Not Available
XX44	Computer Unavail/Mal Function
XX45	Equipment Unavail/Mal Function
XX46	Supplies Unavailable
XX47	Education Materials Unavailable
XX48	Medical Records Unavailable
XX49	Other * (specify)

TRANSPORTATION DELAYS
XX51	Patient Transport Delay
XX52	Equipment Transport Delay
XX53	Supply Transport Delay

EXTERNAL SYSTEM VARIANCE
5511	Nrsg. Home Placement Problem
5512	Home Care Referral Problem
5513	Rehab Placement Problem
5515	Hospital Transfer Problem
5516	CD/MH Transfer Problem
5517	NH Delay Due to Co. Psych Assessment
5518	External Caregiver Unavail.
5521	Ambulance Delay
5522	Insurance Coverage Problem
5523	H & P Not Available
5524	Info Availability-External
5599	Other External Variance * (Specify)

During each shift a nurse determines whether the patient has detoured from the pathway. If no variance is identified, only the first three columns and the last column on the variance tracking sheet are completed (date/shift, path day #, " " in the third column to indicate that patient remains on path, and initials/department of staff recording the event). When a variance is identified, the remaining columns are completed. The variance is identified (for example, "diet not advanced due to ileus") and its cause (source) is coded along with whether actions were taken, additional pertinent comments, and initials/department of staff recording the event. Interventions taken as a result of the variance must be documented on the flow sheets or nursing notes contained in the patient's chart. The variance tracking sheet also is used to document a discontinued path, a patient transfer to another unit, or initiation of a new path.

The variance sheet *is not* a permanent part of the patient record. When the patient is discharged, the sheet is removed from the record by the medical records department staff and forwarded to the case manager for analysis.

Collaborative Variance Resolution

When a variance exists for more than 24 hours or when a case is particularly complicated, patient management may require development of a specific action plan. Action plans can be simple (such as "visit patient more frequently to encourage ambulation"), but sometimes they require a more collaborative effort through consultation. Several patient-focused conference options are available, four of which are described here: nursing case consultation, team meetings, family conferences, and interdisciplinary care conferences.

The *nursing case consultation*, requested by a staff nurse, usually is a 10- to 15-minute, nurse-to-nurse conference centered on problem solving for one or more specific patients. The goal is to arrive at treatment alternatives that will return the patient to the pathway. Sometimes other nurses, other disciplines involved with the patient over time, and case managers are included in the consultation. Meetings usually are scheduled around shift change and coordinated with the charge nurse. Consultation results are documented in the nursing notes.

Team meetings are regularly scheduled multidisciplinary conferences, generally held once or twice a week. All patients on the nursing unit are discussed, including those demonstrating path variances. Also, patients' length of stay to date, as well as the expected length of stay, is reviewed. Participants in team meetings may include representatives from nursing, social services, rehabilitation services, pastoral care, dietary services, utilization review, education department, case management, clinical nurse specialists, and insurance discharge planners.

When appropriate, social workers can arrange for *family conferences* to help facilitate communication among patient, family, and staff. Generally, the physician, social worker, and primary care nurse participate in these conferences, although ancillary staff involved in the patient's care are encouraged to attend. Family conferences usually include a review of the cause of the patient's hospitalization, current status, and plans for ongoing care and discharge.

For patients who present with very complex care issues, case management can arrange an *interdisciplinary care conference*. These conferences usually last 30 minutes and always include the patient's physician as well as nursing and ancillary staff. The patient's current condition, care management issues, establishment of interim hospitalization goals, and discharge planning are some of the topics discussed. Cases considered appropriate for interdisciplinary care conferences include those with complicated discharge planning issues, length of stay exceeding 20 days, three admissions in the past six months for which adequacy of previous discharge plans is suspect, and cases of multiple trauma.

Each collaborative effort reflects the Healthspan quality improvement team philosophy. Furthermore, each reinforces two key purposes of variance monitoring— optimal patient management through use of clinical paths and reduced length of stay.

Variance Analysis

Mercy Hospital and Unity Hospital currently have clinical paths for 196 case types, which produce mountains of variance sheets and reams of data. Gathering and reporting data manually required untold hours of caregiver and clinical manager time. Once computerized systems and customized software were installed, however, the process was streamlined.

Variance reports from each hospital are analyzed quarterly by the cardiovascular quality improvement team (figure 10-11). Graphic reports based on preliminary data analysis focus on areas of greatest concern and are prepared for discussion at the cardiovascular QI team meeting. Copies of all data also are distributed at the meeting.

Until 1993 the variance reporting and analysis process focused on tasks, systems, and patient conditions. Early that year the team took a different approach, identifying specific measurable outcomes for patients at discharge (discharge indicators), key events (tasks and some patient conditions), and expected patient outcomes for each time frame identified (for example, transfer from ICU postop day one). Staff is now in the process of collecting data from *unmet* outcomes and/or key indicators (variances). It is hoped that this change will reduce the volume of data collected while allowing for identification of the *most important* variances for quality of care improvement.

For each clinical path the team has identified specific key indicators and outcomes to be measured and which ones require caregivers to document as "met" or "unmet" on the clinical path. This change should make variance data more concise and focused; however, the cardiovascular QI team is concerned that, unless the right key indicators are identified for systems issues, the change may hamper its ability to identify certain system breakdowns. The variance reporting process will be closely monitored over the next year.

As the cornerstone of the quality improvement process at Mercy and Unity, variance analysis will likely replace traditional quality management activities and expand the scope of quality improvement throughout the episode of care. For example, variances experienced by cardiovascular patients after discharge (for example, inability to walk the prescribed two miles a day as identified at postop clinic visit) are reported to the QI team. This information becomes part of the data analyzed to develop work plans that enhance quality measurement activities. Examples of data sources include follow-up calls that are based on a standardized questionnaire to determine the patient's self-care status, an infection control program that includes a questionnaire answered by clinics on follow-up of all postop patients, a home care clinical path that allows for variances to be reported by home care team members, and readmission frequency reports.

These are some of the projected benefits of clinical paths. The following section describes advantages already realized at Mercy Hospital and Unity Hospital.

Benefits of Clinical Paths

The managed care/case management strategy is a patient-centered, outcomes-focused system that organizes and sequences the caregiving process for continuous improvement of cost and quality outcomes. The principles of managed care are followed for all patients to ensure that each receives the right care at the right time in an optimal setting from caregivers who apply clinical and management skills to maximum potential. The clinical path, coordinated through a collaborative effort by all disciplines involved in the patient's care, is the tool of choice for achieving these goals.

Figure 10-11. Cardiovascular Variance Report Excerpt (Mercy Hospital)

MAY, 1993
CARDIAC PROGRAM VARIANCE CODES FREQUENCY DISTRIBUTION REPORT
VARIANCES FROM: 01/01/93 THROUGH 03/31/93

VARIANCE DESCRIPTION	106	%	107	%	112	%	122	%	125	%	127	%	TOT	%
1407 OFF ARP/PATH	1	1%											2	0.3%
1315 GI			1	0%					1	1%			2	0.3%
1403 TRANSFER TO ANOTHER HOSPITAL			1	0%			1	1%					2	0.3%
1359 LOW CO-CI			2	1%									2	0.3%
1322 DRUG INTERACTION			2	1%									2	0.3%
1220 PT. DECLINES TREATMENT			2	1%									2	0.3%
2113 ADDED ORDER(S)											2	6%	2	0.3%
2111 DATE OR TIME OF TREATMENT									1	1%			1	0.2%
1320 URINARY PROBLEMS									1	1%			1	0.2%
3731 DEPARTMENT CLOSED									1	1%			1	0.2%
2119 PHYSICIAN DECISION							1	1%					1	0.2%
2811 DELAYED TREATMENT							1	1%					1	0.2%
1319 ELECTROLYTE ABNORMALITY	1	1%											1	0.2%
1649 ABNORMAL LAB	1	1%											1	0.2%
1210 PATIENT NOT AVAILABLE					1	1%							1	0.2%
4933 SCHEDULING CONFLICT					1	1%							1	0.2%
3233 SCHEDULING CONFLICT					1	1%							1	0.2%
2641 STAFF UNAVAILABLE			1	0%									1	0.2%
1383 NO BS			1	0%									1	0.2%
1316 HEMODYNAMIC			1	0%									1	0.2%
1332 PERIPHERAL PULSES ABSENT			1	0%									1	0.2%
1340 GI BLEEDING			1	0%									1	0.2%
1314 MOBILITY LIMITATIONS			1	0%									1	0.2%
TOTAL	87	100	220	100	134	100	85	100	84	100	31	100	641	100%

The clinical path is beneficial for the numerous patient care issues it addresses. For example, it stresses timeliness of care, case-specific problem identification, multidisciplinary involvement, and expected outcomes. Furthermore, it is nursing care oriented as well as medical care oriented, applying standards of care and routine orders that are specific to case type.

Benefits as a Tool

In daily practice the pathway has many applications as a tool. First and foremost, it is used as a *plan* for achieving desired outcomes, as an *outline* for managing and coordinating care, and as a *communication format* for collaboration among physicians, nurse clinicians, a multidisciplinary health care team, and patient and family.

As an *educational and orientation aid*, pathways delineate caregiver responsibility along each point of the care delivery spectrum. They also help guide patient and family education in terms of what can be expected from the prehospital, hospital, and posthospital experience.

Each pathway is a *documentation and evaluation tool*. Used properly, it guides and assesses care procedures and systems so as to identify where change is needed. It clarifies accountability, which in turn sharpens awareness of practice patterns and, ultimately, efficiency and effectiveness awareness. Both of these aid in controlling risk liability.

Finally, as a *communication medium*, clinical pathways facilitate input from all caregivers, patients, and families. All of these and other applications serve to make the patient management process more proactive and to empower all concerned.

Benefits as a "Best Practice" Strategy

Since development and use of clinical paths in cardiology, physicians have become more familiar and comfortable with their use—to the point that a number have written their own clinical practice guidelines and adopted path concepts in their practice patterns. With continued use of clinical pathways (approximately 95 percent of patients in DRG categories are placed on a path) and variance analysis, Mercy and Unity hospitals have experienced diminishing variation in practice patterns. Since 1989 these changes, coupled with improvements in the hospitals' health care delivery system, have resulted in significant service improvements; length of stay alone was reduced by 10 to 50 percent. (See figure 10-12.) Other outcome improvements include the following:

- Readmission rates dropped 10 percent.
- Costs decreased by 30 percent.
- Quality of service delivery improved as measured by quality management indicators.
- Patient satisfaction improved.
- Patient autonomy and postdischarge functional status improved.

In 1993 the medical and program directors for the cardiovascular program began meeting monthly with directors from the two other Healthspan metropolitan hospitals. The purpose of these meetings was to share experiences, outcomes, ideas, protocols, and care practices as reflected in the clinical pathways and to come to "best practice" decisions that can be shared at each institution.

Results of the Mercy and Unity quarterly cardiovascular QI team meetings are action plans that define the members' work for the next three months such as clinical path revision and expansion, process improvement, and practice changes. Examples of action plans to date include the following:

- Review patient selection criteria for CABG and valve surgery.
- Develop cost and length-of-stay data adjusted for severity of illness and age.
- Develop a home care clinical pathway.
- Review respiratory care management protocols and progressions.
- Review dysrhythmia/heart rhythm management protocols.
- Study pain management program.
- Implement outcomes follow-up measures.
- Streamline physician standing orders.
- Review arrhythmia management protocols.
- Design cardiorespiratory rehabilitation fast track.
- Examine postop nutrition.

Today, Mercy Hospital and Unity Hospital have a case management department and a quality management/utilization review department with interfaces and collaboration at many levels. Department directors have proposed a *complete* integration of the two departments that will result in one professional assigned to each program — cardiology, oncology, orthopedics, behavioral health, and so forth. This person will perform all support functions for quality, utilization review, and case management. From the cardiovascular teams' perspective, this plan is endorsed wholeheartedly because this change will further integrate product line management and case management.

Figure 10-12. Length-of-Stay Reduction over Four-Year Period (Open-Heart Surgery)

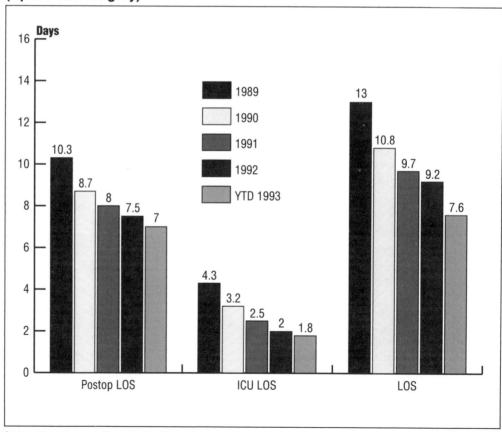

Source: Mercy Hospital, Coon Rapids, Minnesota.

Conclusion

The case management/clinical path model works best in a supportive environment—one in which caregivers feel comfortable sharing thoughts and ideas that will produce change. Committed leadership increases the chances for success with these endeavors. One of the most rewarding outcomes is improved collaboration among team members; while learning about one another's practices they arrive at "best practice" care delivery protocols. Physicians and other caregivers plan care *as a team* now. The biggest change occurred among registered nurse case managers, who, as a result of their involvement in the clinical path development process, have become much more visionary, accountable, motivated, creative, assertive, and self-actualized. Their practice continues to become less task oriented and more outcomes focused as they refine their nursing expertise.

The model used at Mercy and Unity Hospitals can be adapted for other hospitals and hospital systems. A clinical program/case management integration approach is recommended because the leadership for process outcomes change should come from those with common interests and levels of expertise. It should also be emphasized that a core group cannot implement a model without systemwide support that ensures top-down acceptance.

Clinical Paths at the University of Pittsburgh Medical Center

Sharon McCartney and Mary Beth Pais

Clinical paths are an integral part of a far-reaching work redesign process at the University of Pittsburgh Medical Center (UPMC) in Pittsburgh. To appreciate how clinical paths (originally called critical paths at the medical center) fit into comprehensive patient care strategy, they are discussed in the broader context of their multidisciplinary care management model for orthopedic patients. The model was first instituted on a 25-bed adult orthopedic unit. In the first year of the model 265 patients receiving total joint replacements (hip and/or knee) were admitted.

Historical Background of Patient Care Redesign Project

In November 1991 the executive vice-president of clinical services and the chairman of the department of orthopedic surgery discussed resource allocation and its implications for quality of patient care at UPMC. Their discussion, which focused on the rising cost of care for Medicare patients, led to the appointment of a multidisciplinary orthopedic resource utilization committee whose purpose was to achieve three goals:

1. To establish systems for effective and efficient utilization of resources
2. To achieve expected outcomes and minimize cost without compromising the quality of care
3. To promote collaborative practice patterns

The eight-member committee had the following makeup:

- Four physicians – three joint replacement surgeons (one chaired the committee, another was from the volunteer faculty) and one orthopedic trauma surgeon
- Two nurses – a clinical nurse manager (head nurse) of the orthopedic unit and an assistant clinical nursing administrator
- Two administrators – a staff assistant to the vice-president of clinical administration and an associate director of finance

At first the committee felt skeptical that these goals could be achieved easily and uncertain about its decision-making role. Members agreed from the outset, however, that today's acute care environment mandated a proactive multidisciplinary team approach to collaborative, effective, and efficient patient care. Committee consensus was that caregivers no longer can provide services in a loosely coordinated framework of daily physician orders on patient charts. Thus, team building was promoted through work analysis of daily responsibilities, which led to development of a case management model for total joint replacement patients.

Foundation for Case Management/Clinical Path Model

Patients receiving total joint replacement (hip and knee, DRG 209) comprised the patient population analyzed by the orthopedic resource utilization committee, because 80 percent of inpatients were admitted for this procedure. Furthermore, Medicare was the primary insurer for 85 percent of these inpatients. The problem identified by the committee was that actual cost of care for DRG 209 patients exceeded Medicare reimbursement limits. In addition, the Health Care Financing Administration (HCFA) changed the guidelines for physician reimbursement (which in itself fostered physician interest in the study). Another problem associated with this patient group was an increasing length of stay (over the 11 days recommended by HCFA) and increasing costs for technology, physical plant, and personnel.

Work analysis began with a review of detailed information provided by the fiscal operations department that delineated, among other items, gross charges per physician for each cost center. Physicians and nurses alike were defensive about their patient care plans as revealed by the data. It became evident that the committee's provider-specific approach to work analysis was an eye-opener for all committee members.

Given the two critical issues facing the committee—higher care costs for DRG 209 patients and changes in reimbursement parameters—rather than focus solely on the practice habits of individual caregivers, the committee explored all factors that affected cost and quality of care. These variables included:

- Patient population
- Provider practice variability
- Availability of support services such as:
  - Physical therapy
  - Occupational therapy
  - Nursing
  - Social services
  - Ancillary services
  - Operating room services
  - Prostheses charges
  - Anesthesia

After several months of work analysis, the committee recommended numerous improvement options that involved changes in the structure and coordination of patient care processes. These initiatives were the foundation for a multidisciplinary collaborative case management/clinical pathway model for total joint replacement:

- *Multidisciplinary assessment and education for preop total hip and knee replacement patients:* This activity, conducted by the patient care manager (discussed in the following section), provides for two, four-hour sessions each week, conducted by physical therapy, occupational therapy, social services, and nursing.

The assessment and education program prepares patients for every step of hospitalization, teaching them how to minimize complications and encouraging them to practice exercises and activities to achieve better functioning status. Prior to patients' admission for surgery, a foundation is laid for optimal discharge planning because, for example, a timely preop assessment can identify projected need for rehabilitation at an extended care facility upon discharge. Recent literature suggests that such programs alone decrease patient length of stay from one to three days.

- *Critical care processes:* These are identified for patients undergoing primary and revision total hip and knee replacements and for their caregivers.
- *Design and implementation of a critical path documentation tool:* The critical path (later renamed *clinical path*) is to be retained as a permanent part of the patient's medical record.
- *Preprinting of initial postop orders:* This strategy allows for anticipation of needs of primary and revision total hip and knee replacement patients and mirrors the critical path process.
- *Evaluation of prostheses costs:* This effort is intended to anticipate costs for standardized ("routine," or most frequently ordered) prosthetics.
- *Timely physical therapy treatments:* Identifying and positioning postop rehabilitation care is considered by the committee to be the single most important aspect of patient recovery.

The model based on these recommendations evolved naturally from the work begun by the committee in its efforts to study how the facility's resources were being used.

Multidisciplinary Patient Care Management Model

By evaluating the entire process of orthopedic care and blending diverse strategies aimed at improving that process, the University of Pittsburgh Medical Center successfully achieved the three goals set by the orthopedic resource utilization committee. Instead of being used as a stand-alone approach, the clinical pathway concept fit into the collaborative care management model as one of several actions designed to reengineer the process of orthopedic patient care. Key players in this process are the patient care manager and the primary clinical nurse.

Role of the Patient Care Manager

At UPMC, unit or department leadership for the collaborative care management process is provided by the clinical nurse manager, who is accountable 24 hours a day for the performance of high-quality care as well as administrative, fiscal, and supervisory functions. The unit *patient care manager* position was introduced to promote teamwork, coordination, and continuity of care throughout the unit or department, thus advancing accountability for patient care delivery strategies and outcomes.

Care managers function as clinical care experts and patient care coordinators. Under the direction of the clinical nurse manager they take on tasks related to unit-based staff development (for example, orientation and continuing education). Broader, systemwide staff development is centralized, accomplished on a consultative basis.

The patient care manager is the key communicator/coordinator for clinical problems that concern all patients on the unit, regardless of whether a formal clinical path is in place for that patient. In cases where a path has been activated, the care manager is responsible for monitoring achievement of expected outcomes within the specified time period, ensuring that *variances* (deviations from the path) are justified on the basis of a patient's individual needs and that all variances are well documented in a timely manner. Care managers are further charged with identifying and documenting the cause of variances—that is, whether they arise from patient and/or family, a facility system, or a clinician.

On the day of admission, the care manager reviews the clinical path with the physician, either during rounds or in a meeting called with appropriate clinicians. Care managers meet weekly with the multidisciplinary care team, made up of nurses, a physician (attending and/or resident), a physical therapist, an occupational therapist, a social service worker, a rehabilitation resident, a rehabilitation admissions coordinator, a home care coordinator, patient relations staff, and utilization review staff. The purpose of multidisciplinary care team meetings is threefold: to evaluate the needs of preop patients, to report patients' compliance or noncompliance with clinical path expectations, and to determine discharge planning activities for current patients.

Care managers also are responsible for directing and coordinating the unit's quality improvement plan. For example, they oversee the unit's patient call-back system (calling patients within three days of discharge and addressing any problems or concerns identified). Information gathered during the call-back process ties into the unit-based quality improvement program. (See the sample call-back form in figure 11-1.)

All patient care managers participate in a self-evaluation process as well as monitor the performance of staff members. Both roles enhance their ability to manage patient care because they retain some responsibility in managing those who provide the care. Even so, the clinical nurse manager is ultimately responsible for all unit personnel performance. Patient care managers meet at least weekly with the clinical nurse manager to review each patient's progress along the clinical path and to provide feedback on performance of assigned staff members. Although they assist in daily monitoring of patient care—indeed, 50 percent of their time is spent in direct care and role modeling—care managers are not counted in the unit's nursing staff allowance.

Managing change to promote a shared concern for the patient welfare is key to case management/clinical path success. Patient care managers are uniquely positioned to guide nursing practice while incorporating clinical expertise and a service-oriented philosophy in this patient-focused environment.

Roles of Nurse Caregivers

The *primary clinical nurse* (or *clinical nurse manager*) is responsible for preserving continuity of patient care delivery on his or her assigned shift. In conjunction with the patient care manager, the clinical nurse manager establishes a plan of care utilizing the clinical path as a guideline; the plan is updated throughout the patient's stay. The primary clinical nurse also is in charge of patient education.

Throughout a given shift the primary nurse confers with associate nurses every two hours for the purpose of assessing each patient in order to establish (or reestablish) priorities and delegate tasks as appropriate. Associate nurses generally are licensed practical nurses and patient service technicians.

Leaders at UPMC strongly favor limiting the number of caregivers at the bedside. With this in mind, leaders designed and implemented a new job classification called the *patient service technician* (PST). Trained to perform a variety of tasks previously completed by multiple departments, PSTs carry out direct patient care activities in conjunction with the primary and associate nurses. Specific PST duties include:

- Providing patient services related to activities of daily living (ADLs) such as personal hygiene and grooming
- Delivering and changing bed linen
- Delivering and setting up bedside meal service
- Stocking patient pantry
- Delivering water, recording intake and output

Figure 11-1. Patient Follow-Up Phone Call Protocol

University of Pittsburgh Medical Center
Montefiore University Hospital
Nursing Service Department, 11 North and 11 South

1. Do you feel that you and your family were adequately instructed or prepared for home care by the time of discharge?

   Yes _____ No _____

   Comments:

2. Any problems/complications since you were discharged?

   Yes _____ No _____

   Comments:

   Referral needed? (Example: home health, social services, physician)

3. While in the hospital:

   A. Did you feel your calls were answered promptly?

      Yes _____ No _____

   B. Do you feel they were answered within 15 minutes?

      Yes _____ No _____

   C. If not, were the reason(s) for delay explained to you?

      Yes _____ No _____

4. Is there any way in which we could have made your hospital stay better (other than what may have been mentioned above)?

   Yes _____ No _____

   Comments:

5. In the next few days you may be receiving a questionnaire in the mail about the care you received during your stay. We send out this survey to a random sample of patients and use the information we receive to help improve our services. We appreciate any feedback—positive or negative. So please, if you receive a survey, take a few minutes to complete it. It would really be of benefit to us.

Follow-up action: Diagnosis: _____

                                 Discharge date: _____

Explain below, if needed: Follow-up call due in 3 days: _____

                                 Date of call: _____

                                 By: _____

- Performing light housekeeping chores (tidying up bedside area, light dusting, removing trash)
- Providing limited respiratory care (O_2 delivery and setup, coughing and deep-breathing instruction, incentive spirometry instruction and reinforcement)
- Assisting physical therapist or occupational therapist with patient treatments administered on the unit as recommended by established protocols (for example, body mechanics, patient transfers, range-of-motion and strengthening exercises, and use of assistive devices)
- Assisting with phlebotomy (venipuncture for all routine and stat labs except blood cultures) (all staff have been cross-trained to acquire this skill)

Except for tasks associated with respiratory care, physical/occupational therapy, and phlebotomy, PST tasks are considered easily integrated, low-risk activities. Higher-risk tasks require more education and a supervised process of attaining competence.

The medical center expanded responsibilities for *licensed practical nurses* (LPNs) to conform with January 1991 revised rules and regulations governing the functions of LPNs in Pennsylvania. These enhancements, recommended to nursing administrators by UPMC clinical nurse managers and clinical coordinators whose units employ LPNs, include:

- Initial patient assessment with review of findings by registered nurse (RN)
- Preparation of discharge instructions subject to review and signature by RN
- Input to individualized patient plans of care and unit-based quality improvement activities
- Intravenous (IV) therapy including:
  - Hanging and discontinuing premixed and labeled minibags for peripheral and central access
  - Discontinuing IV fluid run into heparin locks and flushing with heparin
  - Discontinuing heparin locks
  - Monitoring and regulating IV fluid infusions continuously and changing IV bag as indicated
  - Turning off Imeds and PCA pumps at sound of machine alarm and notifying RN for any necessary intervention (*Note:* Machines are initially set up by RN for "allowed" medication)
  - Changing IV dressing according to procedure for peripheral and central lines

Because orthopedic patients require a high degree of hands-on assistance (including at discharge), virtually every patient needs assistance with ADLs. That is to say, the work is very labor intensive. Furthermore, ongoing innovations in orthopedic technology such as continuous passive motion machines, cryocuffs, and sequential compression devices are used by 10 to 20 inpatients on a daily basis, with a time investment anywhere from two and one-half to more than six hours per patient. For these reasons, and due to problems cited in the following subsection, maintaining low caregiver-to-patient ratios was imperative.

Problems Identified in the Care Process

During work analysis, the orthopedic resource utilization committee found that breakdowns in the systems of patient care services were related to a high number of off-unit patient trips. An audit of the unit's patient activity log over a two-week period in January 1992 (excluding Sundays, when physical and occupational therapy services are closed) disclosed a total of 341 off-unit trips, or 28.4 trips per day. Destinations are summarized for this 12-day period in table 11-1.

Table 11-1. Off-Unit Patient Trips (12-Day Audit)

Department (Destination)	Total Number of Trips	Average Number of Trips/Day
Physical therapy	288	24.0
Occupational therapy	21	1.7
Other (radiology, vascular lab, OR, etc.)	32	2.7

Off-unit trips contributed to other system breakdowns that resulted in time delays. For example, average escort time was calculated at 20 minutes per round trip. Thus, 24 trips per day to and from physical therapy represented 480 minutes, or 8 hours a day for escort services.

Patients frequently expressed concern about lengthy transport time; even when the time was reasonable, they *perceived* the time spent waiting for escorts to be excessive. They also complained about long waits for their therapy session to begin once they arrived in the department and about crowded department conditions. Additional delay was encountered whenever a patient had to go to the bathroom while waiting for an escort, transport, or a therapy session to begin.

Another problem identified in dialogue between physical therapists and unit staff was therapists' erratic workloads throughout a shift, which meant uneven utilization of resources. In addition, inadequate collaboration between therapists and nurses meant little or no time spent discussing individual patient needs. Thus, reinforcement of therapy protocols and expected outcomes was compromised – especially over the weekends because, as mentioned, neither physical nor occupational therapy was available on Sunday.

Additional problems related to coordinating physical therapy treatments included: failure to deliver referrals in a timely manner (which occurred most frequently when postop patients arrived from the postanesthesia recovery unit after the physical therapy department had closed for the day), failure to notify physical therapy staff of changes in a patient's status, scheduling conflicts, patient transport delays during peak times, and patient refusal of treatment. All of these system breakdowns diminished patient satisfaction, extended length of stay, and increased costs. A solution that resolved some of these problems is discussed below.

Unit-Based Physical Therapy as a Case Management Strategy

To resolve both cost and quality concerns with regard to orthopedic care, a unit-based physical therapy facility was implemented. This involved converting the department's patient lounge into a satellite gym for treatment sessions. This resolution is a prime example of multidisciplinary team collaboration to achieve optimal patient care management and outcomes. It is also a time-saving strategy because initial patient evaluation can be done either at the bedside or in the satellite gym. Therapists review the case manager's patient assessment and educational planning report with a view of visiting the patient immediately postop to arrange therapy sessions for the next day. The therapist remains available throughout the shift to provide feedback, assistance, and reinforcement of protocols both to the care team and the patient. The number of off-unit trips is reduced, as are some of the time and system delays cited earlier. Another positive outcome of this model is that as of January 1994 physical therapy is available to patients seven days a week.

The occupational therapy (OT) needs of patients will continue to be addressed. Because patients undergoing total hip replacement are the highest users of OT services, investigation of methods to incorporate these services into this care management model are under way.

The Clinical Path as a Tool for Collaborative Planning and Documentation

To facilitate the team approach to patient care and to minimize time spent documenting interventions, the multidisciplinary care management process included the development of clinical paths. The first step in developing clinical paths was to identify which components of care the path would cover. These key elements are called *standards of care/patient objectives*. Teaching/patient education and patient outcomes are inherent in each standard or patient objective. The standards of care/patient objectives include:

- Assessments/evaluations
  - Postoperative assessments and evaluations
  - Skin assessments
  - Cardiovascular assessments
  - Neurological assessments
  - Patient understanding of assessments
- Activity
  - Activities of daily living
  - Positioning/turning
  - Bed rest
  - Exercise/walking
  - Patient understanding of activity
- Treatments
  - Breathing (incentive spirometry)
  - Swan/central line
  - Wound care
  - Sequential compression device
  - Patient understanding of treatments
- Pain management
  - Pain scale
  - Sedation scale
  - Method of pain control
  - Patient understanding of pain management
- Medications
  - Drugs
  - IV therapy
  - Patient understanding of medications
- Tests
  - Blood work
  - X rays
  - Urinalysis
  - Patient understanding of tests
- Nutrition
  - Intake/output
  - Diet (liquids/solids)
  - Patient understanding of nutrition
- Elimination
  - Constipation prevention/remedy
  - Patient understanding of elimination
- Consults
  - Preop and postop
  - Cardiology, anesthesia, general medicine, and so on
  - Physical therapy
  - Occupational therapy
  - Patient understanding of consultations

- Discharge planning
  - Social service consult
  - Teaching (oral and written)
  - Review on expected length of stay
  - Patient and family needs
  - Patient understanding of discharge requirements
- Psychosocial factors
  - Family interactions
  - Relationships with others
  - Lifestyle
  - Spiritual needs
  - Anxiety status
- Patient outcomes
  - Infections
  - Return to operating room
  - Readmission
  - Morbidity

A clinical path "shell," or generic form, was designed so that as more paths were developed a consistent format would facilitate ease of documentation and communication among caregivers. (A sample outcomes pathway is shown in figure 11-2.) In addition to the clinical path as accepted by physicians, the documentation tool includes independent nursing actions and patient care needs (for example, pain management—patient can rate pain on a scale of 0 to 10). Clinical paths at UPMC also encompass patient–staff interactions and interventions, from preadmission through discharge. The shell and the total hip and knee replacement clinical path were fully implemented at UPMC in July 1992.

It is imperative that pathway content be developed with physician input. Most residents and nurses are aware of attending physician protocols for timely treatments and interventions. However, due to the volume of day-to-day patient unit activities, these routines sometimes are missed, a situation that contributes to an extended length of stay for the patient. Variations in practitioner practice patterns also needed to be addressed during path development.

In designing the total hip and knee replacement clinical path, the committee incorporated certain practitioner preferences into the path (for example, abduction pillow versus split Russell's traction after total hip replacement). The path was "built" by auditing 40 charts of patients who underwent total joint replacement. Postop orders were reviewed to identify the care protocols used by the orthopedic surgeons who performed the procedures. However, because each patient is unique, the paths were also designed to allow for individualization. Therefore, on the reverse side of each pathway, space is provided for documenting variances, as shown in figure 11-3 (p. 181). The clinician (physician or nurse) documents in longhand the variance or individual patient care needs, the intervention(s) undertaken to correct the variance, patient outcome, and the date on which the variance was resolved. The form is dated and signed by the appropriate caregiver. As a documentation tool, the path ensures a *personalized* plan of care throughout the patient's hospitalization. Charting by exception on the path also reinforces caregiver ownership, making documentation a more meaningful experience while decreasing the amount of time spent at it. Currently, only those variances defined as patient caused are documented directly on the path.

The patient care managers monitor the documentation tools daily. The primary clinical nurse or the patient care manager—or both—takes corrective action to modify or reverse the variance. The patient care managers summarize all variances (patient/family, system, provider, community) onto a monthly variance report tool. (See figure 11-4, p. 182.) The UPMC's legal department currently is examining total joint replacement clinical paths and variance reports to determine whether documentation of all variances should be included as a permanent part of the patient's medical record.

Figure 11-2. Sample Outcomes Pathway

UNIVERSITY OF PITTSBURGH MEDICAL CENTER
PATIENT FOCUSED OUTCOME PATHWAY

ADMISSION DATE: _____ DISCHARGE DATE: _____ EXPECTED LENGTH OF STAY(LOS): 7 (seven) Days ACTUAL LENGTH OF STAY: _____ Days

ASSIGNED CARE MANAGER: _____ R.N.

REFER TO THE FOLLOWING PATIENT FOCUSED OUTCOME PATHWAYS WHICH HAVE ALSO BEEN USED FOR THIS PATIENT: _____

STANDARDS OF CARE / NURSING OBJECTIVES	O.R. DAY DATE:	P.O. DAY #1 DATE:	P.O. DAY #2 DATE:	P.O. DAY #3 DATE:	P.O. DAY #4 DATE:	P.O. DAY #5 DATE:	P.O. DAY #6 DATE:	P.O. DAY #7 DATE:	STANDARDS OF PRACTICE / NURSING INTERVENTIONS P.O. DAY #8 DATE:	P.O. DAY #9 DATE:	P.O. DAY #10 DATE:	P.O. DAY #11 DATE:
ASSESSMENT/ EVALUATION	CHECK IF VARIANCE	CHECK IF VARIANCE	CHECK IF VARIANCE	CHECK IF VARIANCE	CHECK IF VARIANCE	CHECK IF VARIANCE	CHECK IF VARIANCE	CHECK IF VARIANCE	CHECK IF VARIANCE	CHECK IF VARIANCE	CHECK IF VARIANCE	CHECK IF VARIANCE
ACTIVITY	CHECK IF VARIANCE	CHECK IF VARIANCE	CHECK IF VARIANCE	CHECK IF VARIANCE	CHECK IF VARIANCE	CHECK IF VARIANCE	CHECK IF VARIANCE	CHECK IF VARIANCE	CHECK IF VARIANCE	CHECK IF VARIANCE	CHECK IF VARIANCE	CHECK IF VARIANCE
TREATMENTS	CHECK IF VARIANCE	CHECK IF VARIANCE	CHECK IF VARIANCE	CHECK IF VARIANCE	CHECK IF VARIANCE	CHECK IF VARIANCE	CHECK IF VARIANCE	CHECK IF VARIANCE	CHECK IF VARIANCE	CHECK IF VARIANCE	CHECK IF VARIANCE	CHECK IF VARIANCE
PAIN MANAGEMENT	CHECK IF VARIANCE	CHECK IF VARIANCE	CHECK IF VARIANCE	CHECK IF VARIANCE	CHECK IF VARIANCE	CHECK IF VARIANCE	CHECK IF VARIANCE	CHECK IF VARIANCE	CHECK IF VARIANCE	CHECK IF VARIANCE	CHECK IF VARIANCE	CHECK IF VARIANCE
MEDICATIONS	CHECK IF VARIANCE	CHECK IF VARIANCE	CHECK IF VARIANCE	CHECK IF VARIANCE	CHECK IF VARIANCE	CHECK IF VARIANCE	CHECK IF VARIANCE	CHECK IF VARIANCE	CHECK IF VARIANCE	CHECK IF VARIANCE	CHECK IF VARIANCE	CHECK IF VARIANCE
TESTS	CHECK IF VARIANCE	CHECK IF VARIANCE	CHECK IF VARIANCE	CHECK IF VARIANCE	CHECK IF VARIANCE	CHECK IF VARIANCE	CHECK IF VARIANCE	CHECK IF VARIANCE	CHECK IF VARIANCE	CHECK IF VARIANCE	CHECK IF VARIANCE	CHECK IF VARIANCE
NUTRITION	CHECK IF VARIANCE	CHECK IF VARIANCE	CHECK IF VARIANCE	CHECK IF VARIANCE	CHECK IF VARIANCE	CHECK IF VARIANCE	CHECK IF VARIANCE	CHECK IF VARIANCE	CHECK IF VARIANCE	CHECK IF VARIANCE	CHECK IF VARIANCE	CHECK IF VARIANCE
ELIMINATION	CHECK IF VARIANCE	CHECK IF VARIANCE	CHECK IF VARIANCE	CHECK IF VARIANCE	CHECK IF VARIANCE	CHECK IF VARIANCE	CHECK IF VARIANCE	CHECK IF VARIANCE	CHECK IF VARIANCE	CHECK IF VARIANCE	CHECK IF VARIANCE	CHECK IF VARIANCE
CONSULTS	CHECK IF VARIANCE	CHECK IF VARIANCE	CHECK IF VARIANCE	CHECK IF VARIANCE	CHECK IF VARIANCE	CHECK IF VARIANCE	CHECK IF VARIANCE	CHECK IF VARIANCE	CHECK IF VARIANCE	CHECK IF VARIANCE	CHECK IF VARIANCE	CHECK IF VARIANCE
DISCHARGE PLANNING	CHECK IF VARIANCE	CHECK IF VARIANCE	CHECK IF VARIANCE	CHECK IF VARIANCE	CHECK IF VARIANCE	CHECK IF VARIANCE	CHECK IF VARIANCE	CHECK IF VARIANCE	CHECK IF VARIANCE	CHECK IF VARIANCE	CHECK IF VARIANCE	CHECK IF VARIANCE
CAREGIVER INITIALS 7-3 / 7-7p 3-11 7P/11 - 7	Signature	Signature	Signature	Signature	Signature	Signature	Signature	Signature	Signature	Signature	Signature	Signature

Figure 11-3.   Variance Analysis Document

Individualized Care Needs (I C N)

The clinical pathway is a collaborative care plan and is not intended to be construed or to serve as a standard of medical care. Rather, it is intended to serve as a guideline to promote coordination and communication with respect to patient care, and may be modified to meet individualized care needs. Individualized care needs are to be noted on the appropriate portion of the form.

Imprint Patient Identification Plate Here

Date / Signature	Day of Path	Section/ Event	Individualized Care Needs	Interventions	Outcome	Resolved Date

Legend for " Resolved "   Column
Blank   =   Ongoing
N   =   Intervention   Not   Needed   Or
Intervention   No   Longer   Needed
R   =   Problem   Resolved

Figure 11-4. Monthly Variance Report

Patient	Physician	Date	VARIANCE: patient, system, provider, community	Intervention	Outcome

One patient care manager is designated to collect all patient variance data, which will be computer analyzed and eventually generated in a quarterly variance report (figure 11-5) prepared by the clinical nurse manager.

The quarterly report is sent to all committee members, orthopedic surgeons, and key members of the following departments: clinical administration, fiscal operations, quality assurance, utilization review, patient relations, social services, physical and occupational therapy, rehabilitation medicine, and home care. The report describes trends in specific areas, for example:

- Length of stay for patients attending the preop assessment and education program as compared to length of stay for patients who did not attend
- The volume of patients admitted by each physician and the percentage of each physician's patients who attended the preop assessment and education program
- The number and percentage of patients insured by Medicare/Medicaid and those insured by commercial carriers
- Patient satisfaction information (highlighting results from the patient follow-up phone calls, for example)
- A detailed analysis of length of stay and cost outliers, including more detailed information on most frequent outliers
- Projected and actual dollar savings in gross charges (patient room charges only)

This information provides an opportunity for input on continuous quality improvement efforts in the processes of orthopedic care. As a result, actions can be taken to correct or circumvent problems. Figure 11-6 illustrates comprehensive fiscal year-end data in specific areas of orthopedic care (length of stay, insurance providers, patient satisfaction indicators, physician admissions, outliers, and discharge statistics).

Educational Programs for the Health Care Team

Physician and staff orientation to a collaborative strategy for care delivery focused on the team approach promoted by the total joint replacement model. Their early involvement in the change process, coupled with open and clear lines of communication, went far to secure their acceptance. In time, the entire UPMC staff embraced the model—although not without some difficulty. Education and orientation were highly successful in overcoming some of the inevitable resistance to change. All members of the health care team took part in a general orientation program that included the following elements:

- Overview of the work redesign proposal (patient care manager's role, primary care nursing model, unit-based physical therapy and goals for occupational therapy, clinical paths as collaboration and documentation tools)
- Overview of the financial aspects of health care (DRG-based payment and utilization review)
- Change theory
- Team building
- Patient relations

Figure 11-5. Computerized Quarterly Variance Computer Report

CLINICAL PATHWAY VARIANCE REPORT
TOTAL JOINT PATIENTS PARTICIPATING IN PRE-OP PROGRAM

Patient Name	Physician	Diagnosis	Surgery Date	Class Date	Discharge Date	Complications	Length of stay	Discharged to:	Insurance	Variance

**Figure 11-6. Montefiore University Hospital Length of Stay Statistics—
Fiscal Year 1993**

MONTEFIORE UNIVERSITY HOSPITAL
LENGTH OF STAY STATISTICS - FISCAL YEAR 1993
Total Joint Replacement Patients
July 1, 1992 to June 30, 1993
265 Patients

AVERAGE LENGTH OF STAY
(*excluding outliers*)

With Preop
Program

Without Preop
Program

7.0 days *
(146 patients)

7.5 days **
(119 patients)

Average Length of Stay = 7.2 days
Note: Compares to 11 day length of stay for patients seen prior to January 1992)

* 41 outliers   ** 38 outliers

AVERAGE LENGTH OF STAY
(*including outliers*)

With Preop
Program

Without Preop
Program

7.8 days

8.2 days

Average Length of Stay for All Patients = 8 days
* *Excludes 3 patients with major complications; length of stays of 17, 38, and 55 days respectively*

LENGTH OF STAY COMPARISON
First Quarter to Fourth Quarter - Fiscal Year 1993

First Quarter (July, August, September 1992)		FOURTH QUARTER (April, May, June 1993)	
(*excluding outliers*)			
With Preop Program	Without Preop Program	With Preop Program	Without Preop Program
8.1 days *	8.5 days	7.0 days *	7.2 days **
(22 patients)	(18 patients)	(33 patients)	(23 patients)
Average Length of Stay = 8.3 days		Average Length of Stay = 7.1 days	
* 2 outliers		* 6 outliers	** 4 outliers
(*including outliers*)			
With Preop Program	Without Preop Program	With Preop Program	Without Preop Program
9.3 days	8.5 days	7.8 days	8.0 days
Average Length of Stay = 8.9 days		Average Length of Stay = 7.9 days	

(Continued on next page)

185

Figure 11-6. **(Continued)**

INSURANCE

Medicare/Medicaid	=	174 (66%)	patients
Commercial	=	91 (34%)	patients
TOTAL ADMISSIONS	=	265	patients

PATIENT FOLLOW-UP CALLS

Question (Quality Indicator)	Percentage of "Yes" Responses	
	Fiscal Year '92 Average	Fiscal Year '93 Average
Is there any way in which we could have made your hospital stay better?	13.75%	9.0%

NUMBER OF PATIENTS BY PHYSICIAN
July 1, 1992 through June 30, 1993

Physician	Total Knee	Total Hip	Attended Preop Class	Did Not Attend Preop Class	% Not Attending Preop Class *	Total # of Patients
A	72 (3 bilat.)	25 (1 bilat.)	69	28 (8 revisions)	20.6%	97
B	40	107	78	70 (22 revisions)	31%	148
C	2	2		4	100%	4
D	11	1	1	10	91.6%	11
E	3	1		4	100%	4
F		1		1	100%	1
TOTAL	**128**	**137**	**148**	**117**	**32.5%**	**265**

* Percentage does not include patients undergoing total joint revision.

SUMMARY OF OUTLIERS
TOTAL JOINT REPLACEMENT PATIENTS
July 1, 1992 through June 30, 1993

Outlier length of stay range = 9 - 17 days; Average length of stay = 10.9 days

Outlier Cause	Number of Patients
Wound drainage	19
No rehab beds: MUH	17
Greater Pittsburgh Rehab	2
Patient changed disposition/problems with disposition	11
Venous duplex dopler delay	10
I.C.U. stay during hospitalization	10
Hip or knee red/swollen	10
Poor knee flexion	5
Rheumatoid arthritis	4
Urological problems	4
Infection/possible infection	4
Hemophilia	2
Fractured trochanter - bedrest x 6 weeks	2
Blizzard '93	2
Patient refusing physical therapy	2
Pulmonary embolism	1
Deep vein thrombosis	1
CVA	1
Ogilvy's Syndrome	1
Parkinson's Disease	1
Swollen renal fistula	1

Note: There were 79 patients with an extended length of stay due to outliers, some patients had more than one outlier.

Figure 11-6. (Continued)

DETAILS ABOUT PATIENTS EXPERIENCING THE OUTLIER "DRAINAGE"
Total Number = 19; Average Length of Stay = 9.65 days

Physician	Total Hip Replacement Patients	Length of Stay
A 25 patients total	5 Patients with drainage = 20% 1 1 1 1 1	8.6 days 10 days 9 days 8 days 8 days 8 days
B 107 patients total	8 Patients with drainage = 7.4% 1 * 1 1 * 1 1 1 1 * 1	10.0 days 14 days 12 days 10 days 10 days 9 days 9 days 8 days 8 days
C 2 patients total	1 Patient with drainage = 50% 1	10.0 days 10 days

All physicians: 14 patients with drainage = 10.2%   9.53 days

Physician	Total Knee Replacement Patients	Length of Stay
A 72 patients total	2 Patients with drainage = 2.7% 1 1	9.8 days 11 days 9 days
B 40 patients total	3 Patients with drainage = 3.9% 1 1 1	9.6 days 12 days 9 days 8 days

All physicians: 5 patients with drainage = 3.9%   9.7 days

* Denotes patients who underwent total joint revision

PATIENTS DISCHARGED TO REHABILITATION FACILITY
43% of all patients were discharged to rehab

Quarter	Total Patients	To In-House Rehab Unit	To Another Facility
1	16	9	7
2	33	20	13
3	24	14	10
4	41	27	14
TOTAL	114	70 (61.4%)	44 (38.5%)

(Continued on next page)

Figure 11-6. (Continued)

PATIENTS DISCHARGED TO REHAB WHOSE LENGTH OF STAY WAS EXTENDED DUE TO
UNAVAILABILITY OF REHAB BED

# of Patients	Original Disposition	Actual Disposition	# Days of Extended Length of Stay
12	In House Rehab	In House Rehab	12 days
5	In House Rehab	Another facility	5 days
2	Another facility	Another facility	2 days
TOTAL = 19			19 days

PATIENTS DISCHARGED TO REHABILITATION FACILITY WHOSE LENGTH OF STAY WAS EXTENDED DUE
TO OTHER REASONS

# of Patients	Reason for Delay	# Days of Extended Length of Stay
16	Outliers	78 days
6	Patient changed disposition (from home to rehab)	9 days
1	Patient refused therapy initially	2 days
TOTAL = 23		110 days

PATIENTS WITH APPROPRIATE LENGTH OF STAY WHOSE STAY WAS EXTENDED

Actual Length of Stay	# of Days Extended	Reason Stay Extended
8	1	No MUH Rehab beds
8	1	No MUH Rehab beds
8	1	No MUH Rehab beds
8	1	No MUH Rehab beds
8	1	No MUH Rehab beds
7	1	No MUH Rehab beds
7	1	No MUH Rehab beds
6	1	No MUH Rehab beds
8	1	No outside rehab facility bed
8	1	Patient changed disposition
8	1	Patient changed disposition
8	1	Patient changed disposition
8	1	Patient changed disposition
8	1	Blizzard '93
8	1	Blizzard '93
7	1	Blizzard '93
8	1	Doppler delay
7	1	Doppler delay
8	1	Awaiting infectious disease consult for appropriate home antibiotics

Average actual length of stay = 7.7 days

Average number of days stay extended = 1 day

Specialty training was afforded to individuals more closely involved in different aspects of the care management process. The individuals and training included:

Care manager:

- Clinical path processes and development (multidisciplinary committee)
- Management issues and theory (leadership styles, delegation skills)
- Financial management (utilization review, chart auditing, fiscal accountability)
- Review/self-learning module for orthopedic orientation)

Primary nurse:

- Review/self-learning module for orthopedic orientation
- Delegation skills

Associate nurse (LPN):

- Review/self-learning module for orthopedic orientation
- IV therapy curriculum

Patient service technician:

- Housekeeping orientation
- Dietary orientation

UPMC staff concluded that clinical paths define and reinforce patient centered care. Instead of complaints about certain departments not performing their duties, there is now the question, "Where is the system breaking down for 'our' patients." This provides provider continuity.

Benefits of an Integrated Model

The comprehensive patient care delivery model implemented at University of Pittsburgh Medical Center concentrates on the entire episode of illness, from preadmission to postdischarge. This patient focus is augmented through proactive collaboration of all disciplines involved in patient care for a specific case type. To coordinate the care process, the nursing role has been restructured to interact with a patient care manager who works closely with other disciplines as well as the patient/family. This model further bridges the cost–quality dichotomy by standardizing resource use through identification and documentation of key care interventions. The medium that synthesizes these diverse aspects of care is the clinical path. The remainder of this chapter summarizes specific benefits realized from the work redesign project at UPMC.

Because clinical paths are based on practice patterns already proved efficient, a certain level of patient satisfaction can be expected. Early identification of problems or potential problems can expedite resolution and timely patient care.

Patients and families can be active participants in the caregiving process as a result of the patient assessment and education program. Once patients understand the desired outcomes of care, they work toward the same goals anticipated by nurses and physicians. Also, a patient's need for postdischarge care (in an extended care facility or rehabilitation center) can be identified early by means of the preadmission assessment and education program.

Multidisciplinary collaboration identifies overutilization or underutilization of resources. This makes it possible to redirect personnel, time, fiscal, and physical plant resources as dictated by patient needs and case volume.

With a case management/clinical path model in place, expected or "standard" clinical outcomes can be identified in advance. This advantage reduces variation in treatment patterns, which in turn reduces cost and length of stay, enhances continuity of care, and maintains desired quality of service. Incorporating quality indicators and discharge criteria into the clinical path documentation process aids in assessing quality of care as well as systems by which care is administered.

Patient education is enhanced by initiating a teaching plan prior to admission. For example, the need for postop care at an extended care facility or rehabilitation center can be incorporated into the education process.

Job enrichment, ownership, and professional development have been fostered in all caregivers. In large part this is due to an increase in staff hours per patient day — the actual number of hours of patient care has increased without the addition of new employees.

Reduction in the number of off-unit patient trips has decreased time delays in the processes of care and, consequently, in time spent documenting care. Nursing time at the bedside has increased, and charting is more focused and timely. Finally, the smaller number of caregivers at the bedside has enhanced collaboration among all members of the health team.

Expectations were that deployment of this orthopedic model of focused patient care delivery would decrease lengths of stay by at least one day. Such a decrease would translate into an annual savings of $763,866 (based on January 1992 volume data). Surprisingly, the average length of stay for patients undergoing total joint replacements from July 1, 1992, through June 30, 1993, was eight days — three days shorter than the previous fiscal year. This improvement represented an annual savings of *$2,291,598.00* in gross patient room charges alone! Patients attending the preoperative assessment and education program had an average length of stay of 0.5 days less than those who did not attend the class. Patient, physician, and staff satisfaction have also increased with this new model of patient care delivery.

Conclusion

Based on experience in the orthopedic unit, the University of Pittsburgh Medical Center adopted clinical paths, primary nursing, and patient care management for all patient care areas, allowing for delivery of high-quality care at lower costs. This change has allowed the center to demonstrate medical appropriateness, document patient satisfaction, and use scarce resources more appropriately. In the future, as this model is implemented in other areas, many system variations can be discovered and immediate adjustments made through a team approach to continuous quality improvement.

CHAPTER TWELVE

Clinical Paths at Carondelet St. Joseph's Hospital

Vicky A. Mahn and Christopher Heller, MD

Motivated by changing reimbursement trends in 1992 and the agenda for change mandated by the Joint Commission on Accreditation of Healthcare Organizations (JCAHO) in 1986, hospitals are exploring innovative strategies for evaluating the quality of the services hospitals provide. Driven largely by entry into a capitated reimbursement structure, Carondelet St. Joseph's Hospital in Tucson adopted as its priority agenda concern for efficient resource utilization and quality of care.

Carondelet St. Joseph's Hospital is a nonprofit, 325-bed acute care hospital offering a full range of integrated continuum services, including high-risk maternal/child, cardiac surgical services, rehabilitation, transitional care, hospice, and community nurse case management. It serves the Tucson community of approximately 650,000 population, and is one of eight licensed hospitals providing tertiary services in the Tucson area.

History of Clinical Paths at Carondelet St. Joseph's

Hospital leaders initially viewed the implementation of critical pathways (hereafter called clinical pathways) as one means to reduce variation in the clinical care production process and ensure appropriate utilization of scarce resources. However, the mere introduction of clinical pathways into the nursing care system proved to have little effect. That is, unless the corporate culture is modified to support the potential advantages of such tools, they have no more value than a nursing documentation system disguised under a new name and format.

The major reason use of clinical pathways fell short of expectations was attributed not only to lack of medical staff participation in pathway development but also to a failure to integrate path implementation into an overall process of continuous quality improvement. In addition, pathways could not become meaningful guides for multidisciplinary clinical care management without consensus among clinicians on medical practice parameters.

Many hospital leaders launch total quality management (TQM) or continuous quality improvement (CQI) efforts at the staff level, their vision being that, as the philosophy and management skills required for these initiatives permeate the organization, the medical staff subsequently will be brought aboard. Hospitals that rely on this approach often experience limited success, largely because physician practice patterns remain unchanged. However, in an era when 80 percent of each patient's hospital costs are controlled by what the physician orders, changes in practice patterns that influence cost and quality can occur only with heightened physician awareness and multidisciplinary collaboration.[1]

At Carondelet St. Joseph's, practice improvements are reflected in *patient care guidelines,* which are an integration of clinical pathways and practice parameters. Here a *clinical pathway* is defined as a multidisciplinary plan designed to cross a time line with benchmarks for achievement of defined critical elements projected to affect resource consumption or outcome. *Practice parameters* are recommendations that reflect current practice patterns for the diagnosis, evaluation, and treatment of specific diseases.

To be effective, patient care guidelines need to be diagnosis or procedure specific, not physician specific. To implement a patient care guideline, it is necessary to measure current, local patient care practice patterns and critical elements. Although a nursing care plan is attached to the guidelines document, it is considered to be a separate component from patient care guidelines.

This chapter discusses Carondelet St. Joseph's experience in developing patient care guidelines, the achievement of which is the result of an integrated systems approach using CQI philosophy as the guiding framework. Actual guidelines for lumbar laminectomy will be used to illustrate the process components.

Key Barrier to Physician Support of Quality Efforts

The most significant barrier to overcome in integrating clinical paths into the CQI process was gaining physician support. In general, nonprofit community hospitals rely on physicians' voluntary participation in two areas. The first involves their input and support to hospital committees. The second relies on their commitment to implementing the six medical staff functions as outlined by the JCAHO:

1. Monitoring and evaluation
2. Surgical case review
3. Blood usage review
4. Drug usage review
5. Adverse drug reaction evaluation
6. Medical record documentation clinical pertinence review

Because physician committee time is donated voluntarily, often it is given less than enthusiastically because in the past this time was used ineffectively and with limited success. For their participation to be effective, physicians require significant education, exposure, and the desire to be productive members of the CQI process. Despite the large numbers of medical staff in the typical community hospital, only a few are willing to commit time and interest to assume the role of initiating physician facilitators of this process. Most hospitals are structured such that physicians are either elected or appointed to the major positions of authority—regardless of their interest in quality issues and resource management. Furthermore, these positions usually are limited to a one- or two-year rotation cycle. One technique used to enhance support was to forge a physician–administration alliance.

Physician–Administration Alliance as a Strategy

The first step in creating an environment conducive to the hospital's continuous quality management process was initiated by the quality resource management committee.

This committee, which reports to the medical executive committee, is charged with developing an effective utilization management process to reduce financial loss, increase profitability, and streamline the clinical production process to ensure consistent delivery of optimal patient care. The committee defines and integrates JCAHO requirements, practice guidelines, clinical pathways, and nursing case management approaches in order to provide for care across the continuum of Carondelet services. The quality resource management committee's central focus is to develop a value-driven, integrated health care delivery system.

The committee is composed of hospital administrators; medical and nursing staff; and personnel from the departments of medical records, human resources, infection control, pharmacy, safety, risk management, and quality resource management. Whereas in the past these essential components of hospital quality assurance functioned within individual committees, the cross-functional approach was taken for evaluating the level of quality both for the clinical delivery and the supporting operational systems. This coordination strategy alone resulted in a reduction of more than 132 annual meetings and a nonlabor cost savings of $6,000.

All members are voting members, with 15 members from medical staff and the remainder from administration, nursing and ancillary divisions. The committee is facilitated by a medical director appointed jointly by hospital administrators and the medical executive committee members.

The first half of each monthly meeting is devoted to pertinent operational issues brought to the committee from medical, nursing, and ancillary departments. All key areas provide a formal report on a quarterly basis. Figure 12-1 illustrates the organizational framework that supports Carondelet's quality resource management committee. The second half of the meeting is dedicated to a summary report on peer review activities. A large segment is devoted to analysis of preselected aspects of care,

Figure 12-1. Organizational Structure of Carondelet St. Joseph's CQI Program

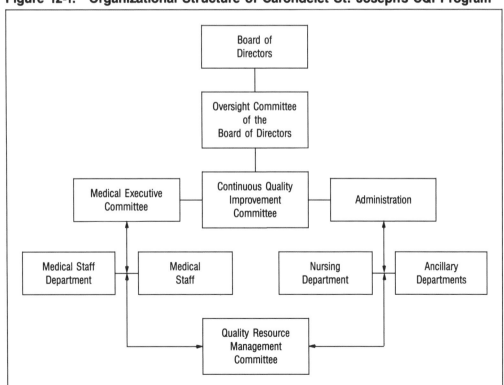

Reprinted, with permission, from Carondelet St. Joseph's Hospital, Tucson.

identified by the multidisciplinary team based on areas of concern that are high risk or problem prone or have significant economic implications for the hospital.

Aspects of care are not limited to a specific DRG. They include specific medical diagnoses (for example, pneumonia; operative procedures, such as lumbar laminectomy or coronary angioplasty; therapy related, such as total parenteral nutrition; or broader areas of concern regarding management of clinical responses, such as pain management). Operational or system issues are also reviewed, such as transcription processes and admission processes. Clinical pathways may be developed for specific diagnostic or procedural aspects; however, not all selected aspects will result in the development of a pathway. The outcome of reviewing selected aspects result in data driven improvement recommendations, and may be reflected in practice parameters, guidelines, and policies and procedures, as well as clinical pathways when appropriate.

Communication Flow in the CQI Process

The communication and information network through which care aspects are reviewed is reflected in figure 12-2. This configuration has yielded important new insights into care delivery systems, resulting in improvement recommendations for both clinical and operational systems. This process of analysis is systematic and data driven. Physicians, nurses, and ancillary support staff are presented with utilization information, practice patterns, and supporting literature in order to reach consensus on "best practice" for given aspects. Outcomes of the CQI process have resulted in improved utilization of preadmission testing for elective surgical cases, reduction in blood ordering practices in lumbar laminectomy, cesarean section, total knee arthroplasty, and cardiac surgery. Analysis of postoperative pain management has resulted in improved nursing assessment, development of a patient pain scale, and more consistent and effective administration of analgesia.

Ultimately, patient care guidelines are developed that reflect these improvements in the clinical delivery process for selected case types. The points along the network are tantamount to "steps" in which to organize meaningful data collection and arrive at multidisciplinary consensus in which to better manage care for the selected aspects.

Step 1: Define the Aspect of Care

As indicated, important aspects of care are selected on the basis of areas of concern, including high volume, high risk, and heavy economic impact. Typically, 9 to 13 important aspects of care are reviewed annually once they are identified by medical, nursing, and ancillary departments. Aspects selected during the first year were for the following case categories: myocardial infarction, coronary artery bypass graft (CABG), cesarean section, central lines, pneumonia, coronary angioplasty, breast cancer, total knee arthroplasty, abdominal hysterectomy, transurethral prostatectomy, and lumbar laminectomy.

Ultimately, patient care guidelines were developed for each aspect of care reviewed. Some clinical pathways, however, have been developed using a stand-alone approach by individual nursing departments. Although these pathways may appear similar in format, they tend to lack the specificity of patient care guidelines derived from the CQI process.

Step 2: Select CQI Teams

Comprised of nursing and ancillary hospital staff, CQI teams are responsible for analyzing an assigned aspect of care. Initially, Carondelet established nine CQI teams, staffed by recognized clinical experts within the various departments associated with the

Figure 12-2. CQI Communication Network

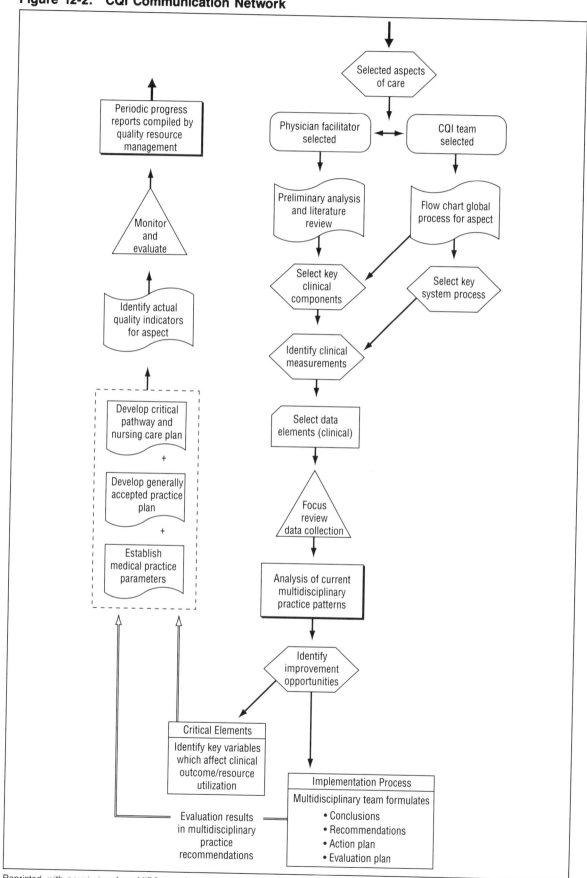

delivery of care. During the process, the team may call on "floating members" to provide greater detail on various aspects of the care delivery process. As experts closest to the bedside, team members research probable causes of problems or barriers to clinical excellence. Each member contributes recommendations for possible improvement opportunities. Actually, the team has a threefold responsibility: generating a flowchart of the process; selecting the key clinical components on which to measure the existing process; and, ultimately, developing recommendations for improvement. Each team selects one of its members to facilitate the CQI process. As the driving force behind the team, facilitators establish time frames and coordinate resources for the group. All facilitators and members are supported with ongoing training and education on the CQI process.

Team members for the lumbar laminectomy CQI team included nurses representing preadmissions testing, ambulatory surgery, the operating room, orthopedics, and neurosurgery. Floating members included a physical therapist and directors of nursing, pharmacy, quality resource management, and clinical case management.

Step 3: Select a Physician Facilitator

The purpose of the physician facilitator for each selected aspect of care is to assist the quality resource management committee and the CQI teams in developing a list of data elements to be collected so as to identify possible opportunities for improvement in medical staff functions. The physician facilitator supports the development of clinical pathways and medical practice parameters for each aspect. He or she then presents the findings that pertain to the subject aspect of care, along with the CQI team's recommendations for improvement, to the quality resource management committee. Physicians are requested to participate by the quality assurance medical director or quality assurance department director, based on expertise in the selected aspect, personal interest, and availability.

In addition, the physician facilitator assists in educating medical staff peers on current practices surrounding the selected aspect. Under the coordination of the medical director, individual physician performance is shown confidentially to each physician to show how his or her performance compares with that of peers. This educational approach results in physician behavior modification as each physician strives to provide the best care.

Step 4: Perform Preliminary Analysis and Literature Review

Beginning with what is already known about each aspect of care, a preliminary assessment of existing information and data found in the medical information system is made. Data categories include, for example, average length of stay, total number of cases per surgeon, total charges and costs, point of access information, payer distribution, risk stratification, and adverse medical outcomes. Figure 12-3 shows a sample of data accumulated in the preliminary analysis for the lumbar laminectomy; figure 12-4 illustrates current blood utilization data; and figure 12-5 is a summary analysis of lumbar laminectomy performed by each surgeon—total number of cases, average patient age, average length of stay, average time for surgery, and average charge by surgeon. In addition, a literature search for existing guidelines and clinical pathways is instituted. Community and national standards are reviewed whenever available.

Step 5: Flow Chart the Global Process

The CQI team begins to organize its efforts by flow charting the process by which patients enter into the health care setting (point of access) and progress through to discharge. Often this process begins with documenting the basic nature of the patient's

Figure 12-3. Sample Preliminary Analysis

N = 271

Demographics

Aspect of care	Lumbar laminectomy
Mean age	46
Age range	20–85
Mean LOS	3
CPT code	63030

Hospital Charges

Total charges	$1,633,485
Charges/case	$ 6,050

Admission Status

Inpatients	43
Emergency	1
AM admits	227

Adverse Medical Outcomes

		Rate
Mortality	0	0%
Urinary retention	52	19%
Injury DURA	5	2%
Febrile response	7	3%
Incisional infections	5	2%

Figure 12-4. Blood Usage Analysis

Surgeon	Number of Cases*	Type and Screen	Type/X-Match (not transfused)	Number of Patients Transfused
1	93	68		1
2	16	13		
3	38	0		
4	38	28		
5	10	3		
6	10	0		
7	9	1	1	
8	15	6		
9	18	7	2	1 4
Total Patients	271	133	3	8

*Physicians with more than 8 cases

6 received autologous   5 single units

2 received packed cells   1 single unit

Transfusion rate 2.9%

Figure 12-5. Efficiency Analysis Report

Surgeon	Number of Cases*	Average Age	Average LOS	Average OR Time	Average Total Charges
1	93	46	3	64	$4,783
2	16	54	3	80	5,406
3	38	45	3	105	5,845
4	38	46	3	104	5,898
5	10	45	3	132	6,267
6	10	44	4	72	6,810
7	9	42	3	143	8,206
8	15	52	4	114	8,268
9	18	44	5	112	8,757
Total Patients	271	46	3	89	$6,050

*Surgeons with more than 8 cases

episode of illness. Staff from each clinical area pertaining to the delivery process for the particular aspect of care participate in flow charting. In this manner, each department begins to understand the inner workings of other departments with which they interface. Once dialogue commences about mutual problems and complaints regarding system breakdowns, preliminary ideas to improve systems begin to surface.

The physician facilitator contributes to the prehospitalization phase of the diagnostic workup, an important procedure given that many costly preadmission and preoperative diagnostic tests are completed in outpatient settings and physician's offices. Therefore, ensuring efficient utilization of preadmission resources can make a critical difference both in Medicare and managed care contracts. Costs associated with an acute care admission are generally "rolled over" to the DRG reimbursement for Medicare patients, thus making for more efficient and more cost-effective preop diagnostics for patient and hospital alike. An equally important consideration is the potential lost charges associated with capitated managed care contracts that include preop diagnostics.

Figure 12-6 outlines the global flowchart process for lumbar laminectomy that reflects the preimprovement care delivery process. Flow charting allows the team to organize their work into meaningful and manageable sections before going on with the next steps in the CQI process. Flowcharting the process begins prior to the admission procedure, to include outpatient diagnostics and interfaces with the physician office when possible, and follows the patient through the "hospital continuum" to discharge. Some aspects may have additional flowchart process following discharge when postdischarge care is essential to the selected case type. An example would be home health and cardiac rehab following coronary artery bypass surgery.

As the team flowcharts out the patient's movement through the episode of care, preliminary ideas to improve systems and care begin to emerge. Improvement ideas are recorded by the team leader and will be discussed again by the team at the conclusion of the data analysis in step 11 (p. 202).

Step 6: Select Key Clinical Components

At this juncture the team can step back and identify the most important clinical components that relate to their assigned aspect of care. The team focuses valuable time and energy only on the most significant variables believed to have impact on outcomes of care, quality, and resource utilization. As a rule, key clinical components can be identified by applying the previously mentioned six JCAHO required medical staff functions and any other pertinent components identified (for example, quality concerns regarding urinary retention). Identifying key clinical components is essential to an organized, focused review so that a more complete analysis can delineate the current multidisciplinary practice patterns for each aspect of care.

Even with the initial focus on medical components, a credible and comprehensive picture of nursing care associated with each aspect begins to emerge. The medical focus provides the structure in which to organize data collection, and as the process unfolds nursing's impact on each aspect becomes evident. The results are improved

Figure 12-6. Sample Global Flowchart

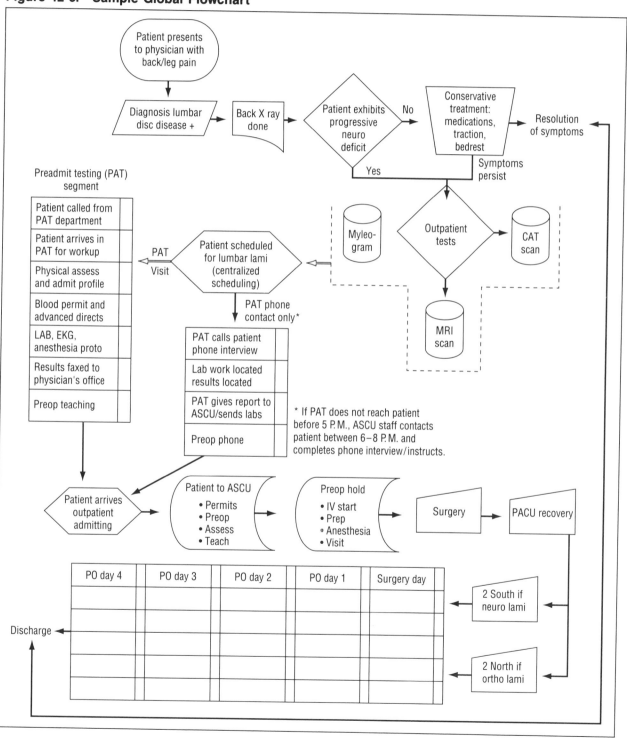

interdisciplinary collaboration, timely patient education and discharge plans, and consistent evaluation for potential problems. Multidisciplinary improvements are finally reflected in patient care guidelines, standard orders, and nursing care plans.

Step 7: Identify Clinical Measurements

Having identified key clinical components, the team can be even more specific in terms of which clinical components are to be measured. Team members select specific clinical interventions that define each key clinical component. Figure 12-7 outlines the clinical measurements selected to review the key component (drug usage) for lumbar laminectomy; the data elements necessary to define the specific clinical measurement are antibiotic prophylaxis and acute pain management. Clinical measurements are defined for each key clinical component, including documented outcomes of pain management, patient and family education, activity and diet tolerance, wound care, and efficacy of discharge plan.

Step 8: Select Clinical Data Elements

A list of data elements to be collected on focus review is completed by the CQI team, the physician facilitator, and the quality resource management department. Data collection instruments are developed so that data can be input directly into a computerized database as it is extracted during the focus review. Figure 12-8 illustrates this process.

Step 9: Perform a Focus Review

A focus review is initiated, at which a number of charts from the past six months or year are pulled for retrospective review by a quality resource management nurse specialist. All data elements developed by the multidisciplinary team and the physician facilitator are collected. In this case, all lumbar laminectomy patient charts with CPT-4 code 63030 for calendar year 1992 were reviewed for a total of 142 patients.

Step 10: Analyze Current Multidisciplinary Practice Patterns

Following a comprehensive focus review, a synthesis of information is prepared by the physician facilitator, the medical director, and the director of quality resource management. The result is a profile of current practice patterns that reflect critical components associated with the clinical management for each aspect of care.

Figure 12-7. Clinical Measurements (Lumbar Laminectomy)

I. Drug Usage (Key Clinical Component)

   A. Antibiotic prophylaxis (clinical measurement)

      1. Antibiotic (data element)

      2. Preoperative timing

      3. Postoperative doses

   B. Acute pain management

      1. Pain medicine

      2. Route

      3. Day of conversion to PO

Figure 12-8. Sample Clinical Data Elements (Lumbar Laminectomy)

CRITERIA	RESPONSE VALIDATION	SUB-CRITERIA
NAME: LAMINECTOMY FOCUS		
DOC. H/O BACK/LEG PAIN	YES/NO/NA	
DOC. ATTEMPT CONS. RX	YES/NO/NA	
INCREASE NEURO DEFICIT	YES/NO/NA	
DOC. PH DIABETES/CANCER	YES/NO/NA	
DOC. BACK EXAM	YES/NO/NA	
DOC. CARDIAC EXAM	YES/NO/NA	
DOC. RECTAL/PELVIC	YES/NO/NA	
DOC. PERIPH. PULSES	YES/NO/NA	
DOC. PERIPH. NEURO	YES/NO/NA	
DOC. BREAST EXAM	YES/NO/NA	
BACK X RAY RPT	YES/NO/NA	
DIAGNOSTIC	SELECT	CT BACK
		MRI
		MYELOGRAM
H/O SURG DIFF LEVEL	YES/NO/NA	
SURG REDO/FUSION	YES/NO/NA	
INTRA-OP MICROSCOPE	YES/NO/NA	
INTRA-OP MARKER X RAY	YES/NO/NA	
PRE-OP ANTIBIOTIC	SELECT	KEFZOL
		GENTAMICIN
		CEFAZOLIN
		OXACILLIN
		CEFUROXIME
		CEFTRIAXONE
		CEFOTAXIME
# POST-OP DOSES	NUMERIC	
POST-OP PAIN MED	SELECT	MORPHINE
		DEMEROL
		TORADOL
ROUTE	SELECT	PACA
		IV
		IM MEDS
		PO
		SUBCUTANEOUS
POST-OP DAY PO PAIN MED	NUMERIC	
POST-OP DAY AMBULATING	NUMERIC	
POST-OP DAY IV D/C	NUMERIC	
POST-OP FOLEY CATH	YES/NO/NA	
RETENTION VOLUME	NUMERIC	
HOURS POST-OP	NUMERIC	
FOLEY CONT./REPEAT REQ	YES/NO/NA	
POST-OP DAY BOWEL MOV.	NUMERIC	
POST-OP DAY DRESSING REMOVED	NUMERIC	

Figure 12-9 is a summary of 1992 practice patterns for lumbar laminectomy among nine surgeons. Numeric counts for each key component are presented in order to identify current practice patterns.

Data also are summarized for the key components selected for review within each aspect. Figure 12-10 illustrates the analysis of acute pain management for patients undergoing lumbar laminectomy. The analysis generally consists of simple descriptive statistics, although more comprehensive correlational statistics may be used when indicated. The purpose of the analysis is to identify patterns within each key component in preparation for medical peer review. (See figure 12-11.) Such a display becomes invaluable when presented to a group of physicians because it leads to consensus building among physicians on the most appropriate medical management for key components. Individual physician pathways fail to achieve this level of collaborative "best practice" standards throughout the institution.

Step 11: Identify Opportunities for Improvement

With analysis of current practice patterns in hand for each aspect of care, the multidisciplinary team reviews all data and begins to identify opportunities for improvement. Recommendations may revolve around an operational issue, such as how patients are routed through the hospital system, or they may relate to specific components of clinical management, such as antibiotic usage, acute pain management, or blood ordering practices. (See figure 12-12.)

Figure 12-9. Sample Practice Patterns (Physician Orders)

N = 142

Practice	Number of Key Components	Percentage of Patients for Each Component
1. History surgery at different level	8	6
2. History re-do or fusion	25	18
3. Use of intraoperative microscope	46	32
4. Intraoperative X ray to mark level	75	53
5. Preoperative antibiotics *	108	76
6. Patients who received only preop antibiotic	28	20
7. Postoperative pain control IV or PCA	49	35
8. Postoperative pain control morphine	70	49
9. Postoperative foley catheter	57	40

*Of those 108 patients who received preoperative antibiotics, 83 patients were given cefazolin

Figure 12-10. Sample Practice Patterns (Acute Pain Management)

Drug	Route			
	SC	IM	IV	PCA
Morphine	34(2)	10	9	17
Demerol		40	1	22
Toradol		7(1)		

1. All Toradol by 1 physician
2. 33/34 subcutaneous route by 1 physician
3. Only 31 patients not on p.o. pain medicines by postop day 1

Figure 12-11. Practice Patterns Analysis by Physician (Acute Pain Management)

Physician	Number of Cases	Pain Medication	Route
A	20	Demerol	PCA
	1	Morphine	PCA
B	8	Morphine	IV
	1	Morphine	SC
	1	Demerol	IV
C	4	Morphine	IM
	1	Morphine	PCA
D	33	Morphine	SC
	5	Morphine	PCA
	6	Demerol	IM
E	19	Demerol	IM
	1	Morphine	IM
	1	Morphine	PCA
F	1	Demerol	PCA
	1	Demerol	IM
G	5	Demerol	IM
H	5	Demerol	IM
	2	Morphine	PCA
I	7	Toradol	IM
	1	Demerol	IM
	1	Morphine	IV
J	2	Morphine	PCA
K	1	Morphine	PCA
	1	Demerol	PCA
	3	Demerol	IM
L	4	Morphine	PCA
	5	Morphine	IM

Figure 12-12. Opportunities for Improvement

1. Antibiotic prophylaxis
2. Acute pain management
3. Blood ordering practice
4. Urinary retention
5. Medical record documentation
6. Preadmission process
7. Medical record coding

Recommendations for improvement are presented to the quality resource management committee following approval from the physician facilitator, medical director, and the CQI team. Practice recommendations central to nursing service are reviewed and approved by the nursing executive council of shared governance. Action plans for implementing improvement recommendations are also presented, along with suggested evaluation plans. (See figures 12-13 and 12-14.)

Step 12: Identify Critical Elements

Prior to development of a patient care guideline, critical elements are identified for each selected aspect. *Critical elements* are the essential components of care believed to have a significant impact on clinical outcomes or resource utilization for each selected aspect. Each critical element includes a description of the desired intervention and the benchmark by which success of the intervention will be measured. Generally, only 5 to 10 critical elements are identified for each aspect and then incorporated into the patient care guideline document. Critical elements are readily identified in the patient care guideline by larger, bold type set within the document. Figure 12-15 specifies eight critical elements identified for lumbar laminectomy as having significant impact on quality of care, clinical outcomes, and resource utilization.

Clinical Pathway Format Design

Perhaps the greatest challenge to clinical path implementation is the creation of a user-friendly format. How the format will be used on the nursing units, who will use

Figure 12-13. Improvement Recommendations for Lumbar Laminectomy

1. Document back and/or leg pain
2. Document failure of conservative therapy or increasing neurologic deficit
3. Obtain standard PA and lateral back X ray
4. Document status of peripheral pulses
5. Document peripheral neurologic status
6. Document status breast exam in female
7. Document rectal exam
8. CT or MRI scan to document pathology
9. Preadmission process
10. Preadmission assessment for discharge planning
11. No routine blood component orders
12. Cefazolin 1GM IV 30–60 minute preop
13. Bladder sonography at discharge from PACU and 6 hours postop if not voided
14. Acute pain management with morphine IV or PCA
15. Oral pain control at 24 hours
16. Ambulate progressive day 1 postop
17. Diet as TOL day 1 postop
18. D/C IV day 1 postop
19. Remove dressing day 1 postop
20. Dulcolax suppository PRN

Figure 12-14. Action Plan and Evaluation Recommendation

Aspect of care: Lumbar laminectomy

Opportunity for improvement: Acute pain management

Conclusion: 91/40 (65%) patients the parental route of administration was IM or SC. 70/140 (50%) received morphine.

Recommendation: For acute pain management, the drug of choice is morphine IV or PCA.

Action: Mail out to physicians the results of focus study and the national guidelines. "Acute Pain Management: Operative or Medical Procedures and Trauma. Clinical Practice Guideline. AHCPR pub No. 92-0032. Rockville, MD: Agency for Health Care Policy and Research, Public Health Service, U.S. Department of Health and Human Services, Feb. 1992.

Evaluation: Follow-up 3 months after action implementation.

Figure 12-15. Sample Critical Elements with Recommended Interventions and Benchmark

Intervention	Benchmark
1. Preadmission process	Yes
2. Antibiotic prophylaxis	No postop dose
3. Acute pain management	Morphine IV/PCA
4. Oral pain management	Postop day 1 oral/control
5. Normal urinary voiding	No cath needed
6. IV management	D/C IV postop day 1
7. Diet	Regular diet postop day 1
8. Ambulation	Walking postop day 2

them, and how path documents will fit into existing and future documentation systems must be taken into account when designing a format.

Resistance to increased paperwork is a common phenomenon among health care workers. Therefore, it was essential for the Carondelet team to produce a document that would reduce documentation time as well as provide a meaningful tool to guide patient care. The traditional nursing care plan was relegated to a low-priority status, held by nursing clinicians to be little more than a task required to satisfy JCAHO requirements and of little value in guiding care.

Therefore, clinical path format had to encourage cooperation among nurses. Toward this end, an 18-member nurse steering committee was established to give design input: seven staff nurses, six nurse managers, one quality resource management nurse specialist, two clinical nurse specialists, and two professional nurse case managers. Based on existing attitudes about the value of the nursing care plan, the decision was made to create a format that would combine the nursing care plan with the patient care guideline or clinical path, thus eliminating the need for double documentation.

The steering committee reviewed in excess of 28 clinical pathway formats from all parts of the country before reaching consensus on a workable format. Following a series of pilots on critical care, telemetry, and orthopedics, the format was altered several times before being accepted. Figures 12-16 through 12-19 (pp. 207–211) show the forms currently used for lumbar laminectomy patient management.

As documentation systems continue to evolve, the format also may need to be altered. The potential for internal computerized documentation systems is another issue to address when designing format. The steering committee identified six format criteria geared to gain support from nursing staff *and* meet JCAHO documentation requirements:

1. Format design must economize documentation time.
2. Nursing care plans must incorporate nursing diagnosis that maintains focus on individual patient and family needs.
3. Design must be flexible, able to serve concurrently as a quality monitoring tool amenable to daily update as necessary.
4. Design must identify essential outcomes of care along a projected time frame based on medical practice parameters and standards of nursing care.
5. Design must allow for coordination of care from preadmission through discharge.
6. Design must be compatible with automated documentation systems.

Critical elements and expected outcomes were organized into the following categories: activity, treatments and assessments, diet, medications, diagnostics, education, and consults and discharge planning. Time frames within which to organize guidelines generally are constructed in terms of days; however, some case types may require varying increments of time. For example, guidelines for diabetic ketoacidosis were constructed in increments of half-days in order to maintain timely progression of treatment. Guidelines for less predictable case types, such as cerebrovascular accident or Guillain-Barré syndrome, might be appropriately managed in increments of phases, although to date no patient care guidelines have been constructed for such case types at St. Joseph's.

Initially, the draft layouts were done on a personal computer using WordPerfect 5.0, with output produced on a Hewlett-Packard Laser Jet with small font capability. Following a trial period of use to identify additional improvements in content, final drafts were typeset by the corporate print shop. All guidelines are kept on disk so that revisions are timely and cost-effective. To minimize the cost of printing forms in small volume, documents are reproduced on a Docutech digital printing system. Nursing departments can then order small quantities for approximately 18 cents per copy. Forms are currently printed on two sides and attached in a bifold format using 24-pound paper.

Currently, design of patient care guidelines using a computerized software program is being explored. This improvement would be integrated with the database used by the quality resource management department to track clinical outcomes.

Procedure for Using Patient Care Guidelines

To date, the primary users of patient care guidelines are the staff nurses. The document becomes a permanent part of the medical record and is kept with the medication sheets and nursing assessment record outside the patient's room. Nurses review guidelines during shift report, and essential components of care are evaluated between offgoing and oncoming nurses.

Nurse case managers, discharge planners, and quality resource management specialists may also review guidelines in order to evaluate a patient's progress during the hospital episode. Patient care guidelines are often a useful tool for managed care reviewers who share responsibility for discharge planning and utilization review with hospital staff. Although other disciplines (such as social work, physical therapy, and dietary services) may be incorporated into guideline content, their representatives generally do not document on the form—not that they are prohibited from doing so. Nursing is accountable for evaluating the patient's progress and revising the plan of care from a multidisciplinary perspective. The nursing care plan component shown in figure 12-16 is preprinted, using the most common nursing diagnosis that pertains to each case type. Problem resolution is documented by the appropriate caregiver, who dates and signs the front portion of the form. Additional problems can be logged on the care plan extension, located on the back of the document. (See figure 12-17, p. 208.)

In addition to essential aspects of discharge planning listed in the clinical pathway component, specific discharge criteria and expected outcomes are printed on the back of the form. These criteria are derived from Medicare utilization guidelines used by quality resource management and external managed care reviewers. This information was viewed as essential for staff nurses, who participate in daily discharge rounds for all patients on the nursing units.

Variance Tracking

The patient care guideline shown in figure 12-18 (p. 209) is reviewed by the staff nurse each shift. Outcomes not achieved are circled as *variances* (exceptions) unless it is reasonable to expect that the outcome will be met on the following shift. Variances imply neither good nor bad care; they simply identify whether the selected critical element has been achieved. Each critical element is essentially a benchmark for measuring

Figure 12-16. Nursing Care Plan Component for Lumbar Laminectomy

NURSING CARE PLAN — LUMBAR LAMINECTOMY • Developed By 2 South, Carondelet St. Joseph's

PROBLEMS	INTERVENTIONS	STATUS
1. Potential for alteration in CNS function.	1. Monitor vital signs and neurovascular checks. Include: color, sensation, movement, capillary refill, muscle power and skin temperature. Document peripheral pulses. Compare to baseline neuro assessment and notify physician for significant findings. 2. Inspect dressing and report excess drainage. Check serous drainage with glucose reagent strip and report the presence of glucose (indicated a CSF leak).	DATE INITIATED: _____ RN: _____ DATE RESOLVED: _____ RN: _____
2. Impaired physical mobility related to imposed physical limitations, pain and neurological impairment.	1. Follow medical directions for activity restrictions. 2. Assist patient with repositioning using Log roll method every 2 hours. 3. Head of bed flat or elevated 20 to 30 degrees as desired, unless otherwise ordered by physician.	DATE INITIATED: _____ RN: _____ DATE RESOLVED: _____ RN: _____
3. Potential alteration in elimination: bowel and bladder, related to anesthesia, swelling, immobility and the use of narcotics for post-op pain.	1. Identify patients normal elimination pattern. 2. Assess/palpate bladder for signs of distention and tenderness every 6-10 hours post op or as ordered by physician. Straight cath if unable to void or if output is insufficient. Encourage patient to attempt to void out of bed if activity permits. 3. Observe for abdominal distention, and auscultate bowel sounds every 8 hours. Restrict oral intake until peristalsis returns. 4. Encourage oral intake unless peristalsis has not returned, or medical condition requires restricted fluid intake i.e. CHF or renal disease. 5. Begin bowel regime when peristalsis returns. Maintain record of BM's and flatus. 6. Assist patient with dangling on edge of bed and ambulation to encourage peristalsis as ordered.	DATE INITIATED: _____ RN: _____ DATE RESOLVED: _____ RN: _____
4. Potential for infection related to surgical incision.	1. Monitor patient for signs and symptoms of infection. Consider temperature, pulse, drainage, wound appearance, secretions, appearance of urine, and skin condition. 2. Monitor lab values. Consider CBC, cultures, serum protein and albumin. 3. Assess for signs of meningeal irritation: Headache, photophobia, nuchal rigidity and Kernig's signs. 4. Administer antibiotics as prescribed.	DATE INITIATED: _____ RN: _____ DATE RESOLVED: _____ RN: _____
5. Alteration in comfort related to immobility, surgical manipulation, edema and inflammation.	1. Assess intensity, description and location/radiation of pain, changes in sensation. Rate pain on scale 1-5. 2. Assist patient to assume position of comfort if indicated. Reinforce importance of proper body alignment and need to log roll while in bed. Avoid use of large pillows. Teach patient how to get out of bed properly. 3. Provide backrub/massage avoiding operative site. 4. Administer prescribed analgesics, corticosteroids and throat lozenges. Evaluate response. Notify physician if pain unrelieved. 5. Assist with patient-controlled analgesia (PCA) and ensure patient demonstrates correct understanding and use of device. 6. Apply stabilizing devices as prescribed. 7. Reinforce importance of avoiding prolonged sitting and avoidance of straining with BM's. 8. Encourage and demonstrate relaxation techniques. 9. Document patient's response to comfort measures.	DATE INITIATED: _____ RN: _____ DATE RESOLVED: _____ RN: _____

CARONDELET ST. JOSEPH'S HOSPITAL

TUCSON, ARIZONA

NURSING CARE PLAN

LUMBAR LAMINECTOMY

ADDRESSOGRAPH

J-543 (NF 8/93)

Reprinted, with permission, from Carondelet St. Joseph's Hospital, Tucson.

Figure 12-17. Nursing Care Plan (Extension)

EXTENDED NURSING CARE PLAN				
DATE INITIATED	PROBLEMS	INTERVENTIONS	SIGNATURE	DATE RESOLVED

EXPECTED OUTCOMES TO BE MET AT TIME OF DISCHARGE

1. Wound without signs and symptoms of infection.
2. Vital and neuro signs within normal range for patient. Temperature <101 x 24 hours.
3. Patient reports pain control with oral analgesics.
4. Able to transfer in/out of bed, chair and ambulate.
5. Patient and family verbalize understanding of written discharge instructions, including medication with 100% accuracy.
6. Elimination pattern within normal limits for patient.
7. Patient taking prescribed diet without nausea/vomiting.

ANY VARIATION FROM EXPECTED OUTCOMES TO BE DOCUMENTED ON ACTION PLAN FOR EXCEPTIONS TO CARE

	ADDRESSOGRAPH
CARONDELET ST. JOSEPH'S HOSPITAL **TUCSON, ARIZONA** **EXTENDED NURSING CARE PLAN** **LUMBAR LAMINECTOMY**	

J-543 (NF 8/93)

Figure 12-18. Patient Care Guidelines (Lumbar Laminectomy)

PATIENT CARE GUIDELINES FOR LUMBAR LAMINECTOMY
CARONDELET ST. JOSEPH'S HOSPITAL • Revised August 1993

DAY	ACTIVITY	TREATMENTS & ASSESSMENTS	DIET	MEDICATIONS	DIAGNOSTICS	EDUCATION	CONSULTS & DISCHARGE PLAN
PRE-ADMIT DATE _____	• Pre-op ADL level and functional status documented	• Patient instructed to shower at HS with surgical soap • **DESCRIPTION OF CURRENT BACK/LEG PAIN DOCUMENTED** • Baseline neuro status and peripheral pulses documented	• Instructions for NPO given	• Instructed to take all routine a.m. meds on day of surgery *except* ASA and anti-coagulants. • Insulin dependent diabetics: instruct to take 1/2 dose long acting insulin if case before 1200 noon, 1/4 dose if case after 1200.	• Pre-op labs & tests as ordered and results reported to surgeon. • EKG if patient > 60 (if not done in past 6 months) • Serum K+ if patient on both digoxin and diuretics, or hemodialysis • ABC if patient has hx anemia, blood loss or renal failure • Type and screen not routine for laminectomy	• Routine hospital and post-op instructions provided. • PCA instruction completed if desired by surgeon • Diabetic patients instructed to bring vials of insulin with them on day of surgery	• Discharge needs assessed & referral to Social Work or Nursing Case Management if indicated • Primary Care MD notified of patient's pending admission
SURGERY DAY DATE _____	• Bedrest • Log rolled q 2 hours • HOB elevated as ordered • Incentive spirometer q 2 hours while awake	• Vital signs stable compared to baseline • Peripheral pulses unchanged from baseline • **BLADDER SONOGRAPHY AT DISCHARGE FROM PACU AND 4 HOURS AFTER RETURN TO UNIT** • **STRAIGHT CATH IF SONOGRAM VOLUME > 500 CC.**	• Ice chips and progressed to clear liquids without nausea and vomiting	• **CEFAZOLIN 1 GRAM IV 30-60 MINUTES PRE-OP** • **MORPHINE IV OR PCA FOR PAIN MANAGEMENT** (Unless morphine allergy) • Oxygen continued if pulse ox < 90% • Pre-op meds reordered • Peripheral IV maintained as ordered	• Hemoglobin > 10 if H&H ordered post op by surgeon	• Patient and family demonstrate understanding of log rolling, use of incentive spirometer and pain management techniques	• Preliminary discharge plan documented on chart
P.O. DAY #1 DATE: _____	• Patient dangles and stands with assistance • Log rolls with assistance • Uses Incentive spirometer	• **PATIENT VOIDING WITHOUT CATHETER** • Peripheral pulses unchanged from baseline • Dressing removed • Pulse ox > 90%	• **PATIENT TOLERATES REGULAR DIET WITHOUT NAUSEA AND VOMITING**	• **MAINTENANCE IV SOLUTION DISCONTINUED** (Heparin well prn) • **PAIN MANAGED WITH ORAL ANALGESIA** • Oxygen discontinued		• Patient demonstrates understanding of techniques for transferring out of bed	• Consider PT evaluation if mobility goals have not been achieved
P.O. DAY #2 DATE: _____	• **PATIENT AMBULATES IN HALLWAY WITH ASSISTANCE**	• Incision without redness, swelling or drainage	• Regular diet tolerated without nausea and vomiting	• Oral analgesics control pain as reported by patient • Dulcolox suppository given if no BM		• Patient demonstrates understanding of medications and activity plan	• Home health or SNF orders on chart if indicated • Social Work evaluation completed and documented.
P.O. DAY #3 DATE: _____	• **PATIENT AMBULATES IN HALLWAY INDEPENDENTLY**	• Incision without redness, swelling or drainage • Pulses unchanged from baseline • Neuro status unchanged or improved from baseline	• Regular diet taken without nausea and vomiting	• Oral analgesics control pain as reported by patient • Home medication prescriptions written by surgeon		• Patient verbalizes understanding of home medications, activity and follow up appointments	• **DISCHARGE FROM HOSPITAL**

Reprinted, with permission, from Carondelet St. Joseph's Hospital, Tucson.

the effectiveness of care as defined by *current* practice within the institution. As technology advances, systems improve, or practice patterns change, so may the critical elements change that benchmark the care process. These benchmarks do not hold care providers to a legal standard; they simply represent points along the continuum by which the institution measures the process of care for a given case type.

Variances are documented on the form represented in figure 12-19. Using brief, concise language, nurses identify the variance and corrective action taken in response to it. Actions may reflect independent, interdependent, or dependent nursing interventions.

A common question arises among users of patient care guidelines about how to manage patients who fall off the pathway. Not all patients are expected to stay on the projected course, and minor deviations can be addressed in the care plan extension shown in figure 12-17 (p. 208). Major deviations, such as an unexpected return to intensive care, may be addressed by placing the patient on a different patient care guideline that takes into account the complication. The traditional care plan format is used to guide care for patients with complex diagnoses or complications for which no appropriate patient care guideline has been written.

More important in addressing the management of complex cases or unexpected complications are the resources available to staff for managing the needs of such patients. The patient care guideline is only the tool for projecting and evaluating care. The power behind every documentation tool is the body of caregivers. Specifically, clinical staff nurses have access to nurse case managers and a wide variety of clinical specialists who assist in the management of patients with complex needs. Together, medical, nursing, and ancillary staff collaborate to plan, implement, and evaluate care.

Ongoing Monitoring: Quality Indicators

The major component of variance tracking is derived from the identification of *quality indicators* specific for each case type in which patient care guidelines are developed. Quality indicators, derived from the same CQI process that identified critical elements (discussed in step 6), are agreed-on indicators of performance for a particular case type. Some quality indicators may be the same as critical elements, although there may be additional indicators of performance the institution wishes to monitor on an ongoing basis. Figure 12-20 (p. 212) lists the quality indicators identified for lumbar laminectomy.

These indicators are monitored by quality resource management nurse specialists, and information is collected and entered into the medical informatics database. Monthly or quarterly summaries related to each aspect can then be generated for review by nursing departments, the quality resource management committee, or specific medical departments. The information obtained provides a performance profile for each selected case type.

Ongoing monitoring and evaluation can occur continuously or periodically using a focus review. Frequency depends on the data to be captured and the resources available for data collection.

Quality indicators, like critical elements, may evolve over time as changes in delivery systems and technology occur. In addition, the profile permits comparison with community and national standards. A composite of information provided by the tracking of clinical outcomes and quality indicators will be essential in the coming years, because Medicare reimbursement and managed care contract negotiations will hinge on such evaluative techniques.

Figure 12-19. Variance Reporting Form (Lumbar Laminectomy)

ACTION PLAN FOR EXCEPTIONS TO CARE — LUMBAR LAMINECTOMY
Carondelet St. Joseph's

EXCEPTIONS	ACTIONS	SIGNATURE	DATE RESOLVED

Reprinted, with permission, from Carondelet St. Joseph's Hospital, Tucson.

Figure 12-20. Quality Indicators

1. ALOS AM admissions
2. Percent mortality
3. Percent of patients with documented peripheral pulses
4. Percent of patients with orders for blood component
5. Percent of patients receiving postop antibiotic
6. Percent of patients with postop urinary retention = vol > 800 cc
7. Percent of patients with acute pain management = morphine IV/PCA
8. Percent of patients ambulatory on postop day 1
9. Percent of patients in preadmission process
10. Percent of patients with one diagnostic modality

Interface with Case Management

Since 1985 Carondelet has used a highly successful case management program modeled on the St. Mary's community-based professional nurse case management prototype.[2] Community nurse case managers facilitate discharge planning within the hospital and follow high-risk patient populations along the continuum of Carondelet and community services.

In addition to community nurse case managers, the role of the staff nurse has evolved to promote a greater emphasis on internal management of patients in the acute care setting. Patient care delivery has been restructured, providing greater nonnursing support for technical and task-oriented care. This way, the professional nurse can focus on clinical assessment, resource coordination, discharge planning, nurse–physician rounds, and patient/family education. The patient care guidelines currently in use serve as essential tools for development of the professional nurse at St. Joseph's, particularly for new graduates, orientees, and floating staff nurses.

Improvements in Operational Systems Using the CQI Approach

In all CQI teams involved with selected aspects of care, issues arise pertaining to the efficiency of hospital operational systems that support the clinical care delivery process. Following a similar process for evaluating the clinical management component, each CQI team selects one key hospital system to evaluate for potential improvement opportunities.

The improvements suggested by one CQI team will likely benefit functional areas related to many other aspects of care. For example, the flowchart for lumbar laminectomy (figure 12-6, p. 199) indicated a major interface with the preadmission testing department. While the CQI team for angioplasty also identified the preadmission testing segment as a critical part of the angioplasty process, the angioplasty team left improvement opportunities for the preadmission testing system to the laminectomy CQI team, so that the angioplasty CQI team could concentrate on scheduling systems in the cardiac cath lab. Keeping in mind that both CQI teams have a representative from the preadmission testing department, system improvement strategies are then developed across a wide range of services and systems within a short time. All teams were kept abreast of improvement recommendations from other teams, and all ultimately report their recommendations to the quality resource management committee.

Following a similar process used to identify opportunities for improvement for the clinical aspect of care, opportunities for improvement are identified for system processes. (See figure 12-2, p. 195.) The CQI team for lumbar laminectomy recommended seven opportunities for improvement for the preadmission testing component of care:

1. Increase the percentage of patients being admitted for elective surgical procedures.
2. Complete preop teaching with patient and family during the preadmission testing appointment. Include discussion of pain management techniques expected to be used during the acute care stay.
3. Assess potential discharge needs prior to admission and complete appropriate referrals to social work and/or nursing case management.
4. Coordinate operative permits and consents from physicians' offices, or complete consent forms during the preadmission testing appointment.
5. Provide patient and family with literature on advance directives and living wills during the preadmission testing appointment.
6. Coordinate preop labs and diagnostics as ordered by the admitting physician and anesthesia protocols.
7. Develop standard preop orders specific to case type, eliminating physician-specific orders.

Finally, the CQI analysis of preadmission process yielded significant information regarding the reimbursement structure associated with the preadmission testing department. A floating member from the accounting department joined the team's efforts in reviewing how different payer groups negotiated patients through the preadmission department. A significant number of patients who belonged to various managed care providers were undergoing repetitive preop labs and diagnostics in the hospital that previously had been obtained in outside laboratories and clinics. Communication barriers between the managed care providers and the hospital resulted in unnecessary utilization of costly resources—frequently tests were repeated because results from outside laboratories were not available on a timely basis.

The resulting analysis enabled the hospital to clarify the preop process with the managed care providers and, in one case, led to contract improvements that resulted in cost savings and enhanced quality of patient care.

Benefits and Drawbacks of Patient Care Guidelines

The single most apparent benefit from the development of patient care guidelines has been the cooperation and integration of patient care across all disciplines. Administrators, medical staff, and nursing staff have acknowledged communication as the missing link across hospital care delivery channels and are better able to collaborate toward the objective of more effective multidisciplinary practice.

Specific cost savings have been quantified for several areas of patient care at St. Joseph's. For example, improvements in blood ordering practices for cesarean section patients resulted in an annual cost savings of $5,406. A similar reduction was found for CABG procedures.[3] In addition, focusing on early, effective discharge planning, identifying patients for case management follow-up, and making changes in clinical delivery have resulted in lower costs, shorter lengths of stay, and fewer readmissions for selected case types. Cost savings cannot be attributed solely to the advent of patient care guidelines, but the effective implementation of a truly multidisciplinary CQI process undoubtedly has become the hallmark of success at Carondelet St. Joseph's.

One disadvantage is the complexity of the process of developing patient care guidelines. Intensive commitment is required on the part of medical staff, nursing staff, and quality resource management. This tool is not a quick fix for the complex challenges facing hospitals today. Top-down commitment must be undisputed in order to produce the paradigm shift necessary to create and sustain a value-driven integrated health care system.

References

1. Zander, K. Defining nursing . . . roots and wings. *Definition* 1(1):1–2, 1985.

2. Etheridge, P., and Lamb, G. Professional nursing case management improves quality, access, and costs. *Nursing Management* 20(3):30–35, 1989.

3. Mahn, V. Clinical nurse management: a service line approach. *Nursing Management* 24(9):48–50, 1993.

CHAPTER THIRTEEN

Clinical Paths and Lessons Learned at Alliant® Health System

Alice B. Keeling, Carol Fisher, Carla Sanders, Laura Sullivan, David T. Allen, MD, and Connie Anton

Alliant® Health System consists of three facilities—Kosair Children's Hospital, Norton Hospital, and Alliant Medical Pavilion. Kosair Children's Hospital is a 235-bed, full-service, tertiary care hospital for children; Norton Hospital is a 373-bed, tertiary, referral hospital providing care for patients from a multistate area; and Alliant Medical Pavillion is a 364-bed acute care and outpatient facility. All three facilities are located in Louisville, Kentucky.

The use of critical paths (referred to here as clinical paths) at Alliant Health System's three facilities has continued to be a learning experience since the organization took its first steps in 1989 to map the processes of health care services. As the program matured, several questions arose about the efficacy of path usage for the clinical management of patient care. Through the dedicated efforts of administrative staff, physicians, and other caregivers, Alliant is now developing among all three hospitals a second-generation clinical path strategy. By reevaluating clinical path applications in managing patient care, the organization hopes to better understand the relationship between care processes and patient outcomes. To demonstrate how the second generation of pathways began, it is necessary to relate Alliant's seminal experience with clinical path usage.

Historical Overview of First-Generation Activities

The Alliant Health System was introduced to the concept of clinical paths in 1989, when its corporate senior vice-president for nursing attended a lecture on nursing case management and clinical paths presented by the Center for Nursing Case Management (New England Medical Center, Boston). The speaker presented the clinical path as a master plan for nursing case managers, a way to standardize patient care while enhancing the utility of nursing care plans. Although Alliant's organizational structure did not lend itself to nursing case management, there was a vision of possibly using the path in some other way. The nursing vice-president, interested in developing an automated audit trail for the nursing process, asked the center to present an all-day seminar for Alliant nurse managers. In the fall of that year, the seminar was held, attended also by the vice-president for quality and managed care and the director of managed care. They saw the path as a tool to define the treatment process and to track clinical outcomes and costs. With this beginning, leadership was established and clinical pathway development, design, and deployment got under way.

Initial Leadership

One of the most important lessons Alliant learned from its early experience with clinical path development and implementation had to do with consensus among leaders. From the beginning, the purpose of initiating clinical paths at Alliant hospitals differed for the nursing departments and for the quality and managed care departments. At the time, however, the purposes were believed to be compatible and the nursing and managed care departments worked together to develop and implement paths.

Another lesson was related to direct physician involvement, accountability, and early "buy-in." For example, even though physicians worked with nurses at the outset, they served primarily as advisers to path development; there was no upfront requirement that physicians follow the paths. However, because hospital departments concurrently were attempting to define and improve their care processes as part of a total quality management philosophy, the need to define processes of clinical care also was recognized. The vice-president for clinical quality saw the clinical path as a tool to accomplish this end.

Following the on-site workshop presented that fall, a managed care organizational chart and a detailed action plan were developed for implementation of clinical pathways at Alliant's three hospitals. The chart and action plan are shown in figures 13-1 and 13-2, respectively.

The corporate *managed care council* provided direction, oversight, and coordination among the three hospitals. The council consisted of the vice-president for quality and managed care and his/her direct reports; the director of managed care and his/her hospital utilization management coordinators; the director of utilization management; the director of clinical quality improvement; and the vice-presidents of nursing for each hospital and their managers of nursing systems. Later, clinical ancillary service representatives were added to the council. Members who reported to the vice-president for quality and managed care provided data to hospital steering committees. Data included the Health Care Financing Administration's Medicare average length of stay, Alliant's Medicare average length of stay, its charges per case, and its top 50 diagnoses and procedure categories. This information was used to help identify target

Figure 13-1.   Alliant Health System's Managed Care Council: Organizational Chart

Alliant Health System Managed Care Council			Membership: Representation from nursing administration in each hospital, managed care department, clinical quality department
MEH Steering Committee	KCH Steering Committee	Norton Steering Committee	Membership: Vice-president for nursing, manager of nursing systems, product line manager, one head nurse, two critical path managers, and one clinical instructor
		Critical Path Management Team	Critical Path Management Team	Membership: Critical path manager, physician advisor, RNs from appropriate nursing units and representatives from appropriate ancillary departments

Reprinted, with permission, from Alliant Health System, Louisville, Kentucky. ©1990 Alliant Health System.

Figure 13-2. Critical Path: Nursing Managed Care Action Plan

Goal	Action
1. To establish a Steering Committee at the hospital and corporate levels to guide implementation of Critical Paths at the clinician level, whether that be the staff nurse, head nurse, or physician.	A. Appoint members of hospital and corporate Steering Committee(s). B. Establish roles/goals of Critical Path implementation through this structure. C. Develop meeting schedule for 1990.
2. To establish 1990 targets for numbers of Critical Paths by hospital and by corporation.	A. Evaluate data based on criteria of statistical significance, improvement opportunities, and Selective Contracting/Outcomes Management "targets." B. Apply 80/20 rule to overall volume of each hospital to arrive at required number of Critical Paths for 1990. C. Evaluate impact by applying volume per charge to impact per case. D. Develop "gain-sharing" proposal based on estimated impact and finance projections. E. Obtain approval of gain-sharing plan from administration.
3. To educate the medical staff, including the residents, new attendings, and existing staff about the overall concept of Managed Care and the specific intent of Critical Paths.	A. Provide a synopsis of the role of Managed Care at Alliant Health System and the crucial importance of Critical Paths. B. Incorporate Critical Path Status/Diagnosis/Procedure/DRG-specific discussion at each major medical staff section meeting.
4. To educate the nursing staff, including all new nurses and existing staff about the overall concept of Managed Care and, specifically, instruct them on skills development regarding Critical Paths and DRG/PM-DRG literacy.	A. Integrate an overview to Managed Care/Critical Path Process including DRG/PM-DRG Literacy Course at the nurse orientation. B. Provide the *Physicians DRG Guidebook for 1990* on each Nursing Unit at Norton and Methodist Evangelical hospitals. C. To revise the *NEMC DRG Self-Directed Study Course* (2.6 CEUs) to NH/MEH use, drafting a *PM-DRG* complement for KCH, and giving this course to every nurse with a follow-up test and *short* survey of most common DRGs/PM-DRGs on their unit. D. To present a 10-minute videotape giving an overview of Managed Care. To be presented to nursing during communication meeting. E. To involve as many nursing units as possible in creation of Critical Paths, through participation of Medical Management Teams and internal Managed Care Seminars. F. To educate ancillary departments regarding their role in Managed Care and the application of Critical Paths to their cost and discharge goals.
5. To integrate critical paths into the entire nursing process. This will be accomplished by gradually replacing the nursing care plans with a Critical Path for that diagnosis and using this as a joint medical staff/nursing care plan.	A. Integration of involvement and application of Critical Paths into each nurse's job description and evaluation. B. Replacement of the nursing care plan/standards of care with the Critical Path. C. Audit on use of the Critical Path/Variance Analysis approach under the JCAHO survey.

Alice B. Keeling, Carol Fisher, Carla Sanders, Laura Sullivan, David T. Allen, MD, and Connie Anton

patient populations for path development and to set length-of-stay goals. Council members reporting to the three vice-presidents for nursing were responsible for actual development and implementation of paths at their respective hospitals.

Each hospital named a *steering committee* to help implement paths at the respective hospitals. The committee consisted of the nursing vice-president, manager of nursing systems (a support position to nursing administration), a nursing education representative, head nurses and selected staff nurses, and a nurse liaison from corporate information systems. This early steering committee selected which paths to implement, planned the implementation schedule, and selected clinical path managers and physician advisers. It also planned and facilitated all education and facilitation required of nursing staff members.

Path Development and Design

The first paths selected for development from the top 50 diagnoses and procedures among the three hospitals were chosen for at least one of three reasons: (1) The categories or cases were clear-cut and easy to follow; (2) a physician champion would facilitate implementation; and (3) a problem had been identified with a particular diagnosis or procedure. The first paths selected for pilot testing at each hospital are listed below:

Kosair Children's Hospital:

- Newly diagnosed diabetes
- Diabetic ketoacidosis
- Asthma

Norton Hospital:

- Coronary artery bypass graft
- Cholecystectomy
- Elective PTCA
- Mastectomy
- Vaginal and abdominal hysterectomy

Alliant Medical Pavillion:

- Total cholecystectomy
- Total hip replacement
- Total knee replacement
- Mastectomy
- Diabetes
- Hysterectomy
- Chemotherapy

The action plan for the development and implementation of each path was very prescriptive, and a member of the hospital steering committee was assigned to guide and assist the clinical path management teams as delineated in figure 13-3. The value of educating the nursing staffs and maintaining open communication with and among them was another learning experience. To formalize this awareness, two *mandatory* continuing education programs were presented. Because mandatory programs were rare at Alliant, it was believed this policy would send a message about the importance of this topic and project. The first program addressed the status of health care in the United States; the definition, role, and future of managed care; and managed care applications specific to the Alliant system. The second program was devoted solely to clinical pathways—what they were, their purpose, how they were to be utilized, and the

Figure 13-3. Sample Clinical Path Development and Implementation Guidelines

The appropriate sequence to follow in the development and implementation of a critical path is outlined under the action plan on the form below. This form is to be utilized by the critical path manager as a guide and as a communication tool for his/her designated resource person on the steering committee.

When writing critical paths, consideration should be given to:

- The inclusion of both process and outcome criteria
- Criteria contributed by all appropriate members of the health care team (physicians, nursing staff, ancillary department)
- Medical advisor's preference as to extent and timing of participation
- Current length of stay, cost, and utilization

The assigned steering committee resource person will provide guidance and assistance as needed to the critical path manager and management team.

Diagnosis: _____ Date of update: _____

Development Team:

Critical Path Manager _____

Medical Advisor _____

Head Nurse (ex officio) _____

Other Members _____

Action Plan:

Norton Hospital Critical Path Implementation Plan

	Medical Advisor Agreement	Team Inserviced	Critical Path Developed	Medical Advisor Sign-Off	Section Sign-Off	Reservations Notified	Staff Inserviced	Implemented
Target Dates:								
Actual Dates:								

	Week of:			
Number of paths initiated				

Critical Path Manager: Your resource person is _____ at _____ number.

Send an updated copy of this form to her every Tuesday.

role of every position within the nursing department relative to path-based patient management. Following these initial education programs, a newsletter was circulated periodically to keep the staff informed, maintain enthusiasm, and acknowledge the achievements of individual staff members.

Physician orientation and education were provided at section meetings and at individual meetings with section chiefs and selected physician champions. Additionally, the initial group of nurses selected to be clinical path managers received in-depth education about their new role.

Clinical path managers assembled their own teams to develop, implement, and evaluate the effectiveness of their assigned paths. (See the team profile in figure 13-4.) Although each hospital had different managers (for example, head nurse or staff nurse), all were nurse experts in the diagnoses for which pathways were being developed.

Path managers and steering committee representatives met with each key physician individually to discuss what the paths were intended to accomplish and to solicit their input and support as physician advisers. In their advisory roles physicians were asked to validate or share with the team the informal treatment protocols and to communicate information about the project and share data with the appropriate medical staff group at each monthly meeting.

The procedure followed by the nursing staffs in using the clinical paths differed slightly among the hospitals. The one used at Norton Hospital is shown in figure 13-5. Other variations had to do with the pathway model itself, as explained in the next section.

Adaptation of the NEMC Model to Meet Alliant's Needs

The clinical pathway model used at the three Alliant hospitals was based on the New England Medical Center (NEMC) prototype promoted by its Center for Nursing Case Management. However, several amendments were adopted almost from the beginning. First, an integral part of NEMC's clinical path—the case management component—was omitted from Alliant's pathway. The attending staff nurse—not a case manager—assigned a clinical pathway upon admission of "path-bound" patients. Second, in accord with the NEMC prototype, every diagnosis initially had its own set of process criteria (activities) to guide the delivery of care. But Alliant teams quickly learned that in order to do comparative data analysis, activity categories needed to be standardized. Therefore, the following categories were agreed on:

- Assessments/evaluations
- Tests
- Consults
- Treatments
- Medications
- Diet
- Activity
- Elimination
- Education
- Discharge planning

In addition to NEMC's checkoff columns of "met" or "unmet" for each intervention on the path, Alliant incorporated a "not applicable" column. When this column was marked, the staff was asked to document the rationale (for example, complete blood count "N/A" on admission if it was done prior to admission in the physician's office). However, this provided an avenue to avoid compliance by physicians and nurses—a lesson learned.

Figure 13-4. Critical Path Management Team Profile

The critical path management team is led by the critical path manager and consists of selected staff nurses from relevant units and ancillary departments as appropriate. A physician serves as a medical adviser and medical staff liaison. Critical path management team members participate in developing, implementing, and monitoring the progress of their assigned critical paths by fulfilling the following responsibilities:

1. Completes team members' orientation.

2. Participates actively in Managed Care activities as assigned by case manager. Activities include:

   - Contributing to development of the critical path(s)
   - Reporting data results to staff
   - Encouraging staff compliance
   - Monitoring pathway compliance with clinical protocols

3. Serves as resource to staff for designated critical path.

4. Demonstrates positive attitude in all interactions.

5. Serves as team member for one year.

Figure 13-5. Critical Path Process Guidelines: Norton Hospital

1. A current critical path with the participating physicians are available in MIS [management information systems] under:

   Unit Entry
   > Additional entry
   >> Nursing information
   >>> Critical path participants

2. Copies of all current critical paths are available in each nursing unit.

3. The admitting nurse is to initiate a critical path on every patient whose diagnosis and physician is listed under "Critical Path Participants" in MIS (see #1). *Exception:* Some critical paths may be initiated in PAT, ER, or OPS and are to be continued by the admitting nurse.

4. The admitting nurse will communicate that a critical path has been implemented on the MCP (medical care plan) through the *Admission Assessment* pathway:

   Admission data
   > Critical path implemented?
   >> Yes or No?

5. A sticker on the patient's door chart will indicate the patient's participation in a critical path.

6. The nurse will review path daily with the attending physician and/or resident to obtain needed orders or explain variance.

7. The critical path will be discussed during shift report as an update on patient condition.

8. The critical path will be kept in the front of the door chart for easy access.

9. A variance occurs if an anticipated order is not met by 10:00 pm.

10. The nurse will document variances on the critical path.

11. As the patient moves from unit to unit as part of the planned pathway, the critical path follows and is continued by receiving nurses.

12. At the time of discharge, the completed critical path is separated from the patient's record and placed with the nursing service report.

13. The completed paths will be picked up for data analysis.

Instead of checking off nursing activities accomplished on the final day of anticipated length of stay as modeled by NEMC, nursing staff listed discharge criteria related to each activity. That is, the nurse checked whether the incision was "intact without redness or drainage" instead of "dressing changed." Staff nurses believed that it was more pertinent to ensure discharge readiness than simply to catalogue one final activity.

Finally, unlike the NEMC prototype, nurses were not allowed to combine clinical paths or to alter the preprinted path. To analyze variances at the three hospitals, it was necessary to keep the data diagnosis pure. Therefore, when a patient developed a complication that precluded following the designated path, the reason was documented on the path and the path was suspended. The final length of stay and cause of variation were recorded.

Variance Analysis

Initial attempts at variance tracking and analysis were cumbersome and bias prone. (See figure 13-6.) Due in part to physician concerns about risk liability, the decision was made to use the paths as tools to track variances manually and to keep data separate from the patient record. Because the nursing care plan was part of the permanent record, this decision created an additional step for nursing documentation and, in effect, devalued the clinical path.

The path was being used both as a tool to guide care and as a retrospective data analysis tool. The primary admitting diagnosis determined which path was initiated,

Figure 13-6. Data Analysis Guidelines

Data analysis or variance analysis refers to the separation of a whole into its component parts and using factual information to determine the relationship of one or more of those parts to each other or to the whole.

For our purposes, we will be analyzing the differences in both cost and quality (outcomes) of care between two groups:

- A pilot group (patients on a critical path) compared to a control group (patients with the same diagnosis not on a critical path) for the same time period.
- A category of patients on a critical path compared to the same category prior to critical path implementation (e.g., hysterectomies first quarter 1989 to first quarter 1990).
- Actual outcomes compared to targeted or goal outcomes and to national averages.

The differences, or variance, can be either positive or negative and can occur in or be caused by one of three overall categories:

- The system itself (our processes)
- The practitioner
- The patient

Based entirely on the staff nurses' written explanations on the critical path forms, deviations from critical paths are assigned to one of the above categories. The managed care research department is responsible for entering all information from the critical paths into a data bank.

The codes used on the variance reports are as follows:

Code	Cause of Variance
P100	Patient: Physical complication
P200	Patient: Social cause
M100	Physician: Compliance
S100	System: Scheduling
S200	System: Nursing compliance
S300	System: Ancillary departments
S400	System: Placement, discharge planning issues

Reprinted, with permission, from Alliant Health System, Louisville, Kentucky. ©1990 Alliant Health System.

but charges and length-of-stay information were driven by the discharge diagnosis. This drawback created tracking problems with pediatric and medical patients whose admitting and actual diagnoses frequently differed. Because the paths were tracked manually and variances were explained in narrative form on the path, the variance code was assigned retroactively on the basis of this narrative account. The lesson here was that this retroactive approach introduced an unknown error quantity.

Originally, three sources of pathway variation were identified: patient, practitioner/ physician, and system. *Patient-caused variances* might stem from physical complications such as adverse reactions to medication or from social causes such as education or language barriers that inhibit understanding of care requirements (for example, self-injected insulin therapies). A caregiver who deviates from path recommendations — either deliberately or inadvertently — creates a *practitioner/physician variance*. For example, a physician who orders a generic drug over a path-recommended drug creates a practitioner variance. A *system variance* might be due to nurse noncompliance, lack of support from ancillary departments, or problems with patient placement or discharge planning issues (for example, laboratory tests not performed within established time frames characterizes a system variance).

A fourth cause of variance, "undetermined," was added later when Alliant discovered that data were contaminated by "forcing" unknown causes into one of the three categories. For example, if blood gas should be drawn on day four and was not with no explanation given, the variance coder had no way to know the appropriate category to assign to the variance. Overall, aggregation and coding of this information did not easily support hypothesis testing.

Benefits Derived from First-Generation Critical Paths

The first two years of the clinical path program witnessed a number of drawbacks, as described in the preceding section. These were the bases for many of the lessons learned.

Those years also saw benefits emerge from clinical path development, design, and deployment. Many initial paths reduced length of stay and overall charges per case — due in large part to their original purpose, which was to serve as a guide for nursing care. Anticipated length of stay and status of key critical care process steps were clearly communicated on the paths, providing nurses (including "floats" and others unfamiliar with specific patient types) with a "formula" for delivering focused, consistent care throughout the patient's hospital stay.

Furthermore, the paths proved to be flexible in their applications and time frames. For example:

- Some paths initiated in Kosair Children's Hospital's emergency department were written in 15-minute segments, whereas portions of paths written for Norton Hospital's geriatric psychiatry unit were written in 7- to 10-day intervals. Others, such as burn unit paths, were written in sequential phases.
- The simple mastectomy clinical path was used by its physician adviser, a general surgeon, prior to admission to inform patients about the anticipated course and length of stay. This enabled patients to be informed, active participants in their care.
- The elective PTCA path was designed to encourage and track compliance with tests and activities that should have been accomplished prior to admission.
- Some physician practice groups discussed common methodologies for treatment as they assisted in path design. As a result of this collaboration, one CABG path was written for two practice groups of cardiovascular surgeons.
- Similarly, two orthopedic surgery groups also developed common paths for joint replacement, including the specific brand of prosthesis to be used. The total

joint paths are initiated in the preadmission testing department and in the Alliant Bone and Joint Center, where assessment and education are provided approximately one month prior to surgery.

- One orthopedic group also tracks its patients postoperatively for two years and evaluates the success of the surgery based on specific quality of life indicators. Alliant hopes to emulate this practice, with the collaboration of its medical staff, for additional diagnoses.
- The managed care department utilized the comparative length-of-stay and charges data to inform health care purchasers about potential benefits of managed care delivery.
- The physicians were also presented information on length of stay and charges for patients whose physicians had agreed to follow the paths, compared with patients having the same diagnoses whose physicians had not. This information stimulated interest among physicians in the monitoring of resource utilization and practice patterns related to as-yet-undefined quality of care indicators.

These successes grew out of a corporate culture that allowed for experimentation with tracking and mechanics of path usage as well as quality of care indicators prior to computerization.

Current Status and Future Plans

In 1992 Alliant Health System contracted with the 3M Company to design and install the HELP™ system for order entry and tracking of clinical data. Concurrent with computerization the clinical improvement department began working with the hospitals' medical staffs to determine the clinical significance of specific path content. This is being accomplished through a process Alliant calls focused process review.

Focused process review (FPR) allows medical staffs at all three hospitals to define for a select group of diagnoses certain process steps and specific diagnostic or treatment methodologies to be tested in study groups. In FPR, data required for analyses—for example, data on infection rate, blood usage, drug utilization, and the like—are pulled for the specific diagnosis under study and combined with the clinical path information for analysis by the medical staff's medical or surgical care appraisal committees. The paths are then revised to improve the outcomes of care as suggested by analysis of these studies. An example of a clinical path (figure 13-7) and the corresponding order set developed from this analysis (figures 13-8 and 13-9, pp. 226–227) are shown for Kosair Hospital's asthma critical path. Alliant, therefore, has changed its definition of clinical path from "those key events in the process of care which must be accomplished to achieve maximum quality at minimal costs" to "those key events in a process of care that are hypothesized to be required to achieve maximum quality at minimal costs." Inherent in this definition is the belief that the assumptions underlying care processes must be tested continuously.

In 1993 new specifications were established for future clinical paths. The original critical paths were used as tools for communication among the health care disciplines; they were not designed to test competing or alternative pathways against each other. The clinical path will become Alliant Health System's vehicle of choice for testing the adequacy and appropriateness of care plans.

Yearly goals will center around a few targeted studies. The organization's intent is to focus efforts on high-volume, high-cost, or problem-prone diagnoses. For each targeted diagnosis, a physician champion committed to patient care process improvement will be recruited. The physician champion's role will be to enlist an expert panel that will write an "ideal" order set (permanent chart document) identifying the critical minimal steps of each day's care under ideal circumstances. Additionally, the panel

Figure 13-7. Asthma Critical Path

Patient label:		ASTHMA CRITICAL PATH KOSAIR CHILDREN'S HOSPITAL PATH # K0006

Adm date: _____

Disc date: _____

Expected LOS: _____3_____

Actual LOS: _____

Treatment date: ___/___/___   ___/___/___   ___/___/___   ___/___/___

	DAY 1 (admit)	DAY 2	DAY 3	DAY 4 (discharge)
TESTS	Theo level Theo level 4° after drip started CBC chem6 UA CXR ABG or CBG &/or pulse eximeter	Theo level chem6	Theo level chem6	therapeutic Theo level (12–15)

TREATMENTS	Albuterol MN q1–2hrs initially—then
	  give MN q2–4°
	peak expiratory flow monitoring before
	  & after MN (>5yrs)
	CR monitor
	strict I&O
	02 (to maintain sat 02>94)
		MN q4–6°
		peak expiratory flow
		  monitoring before &
		  after MN (>5yrs)
		CR monitor
		strict I&O
			MN q4–6°
			peak expiratory flow
			  monitoring before &
			  after MN (>5yrs)
			CR monitor
			strict I&O
				MN q6°
				peak expiratory monitoring
				  before & after MN
				  (>5yrs)
				CR monitor
				strict I&O

MEDICATIONS	IV Aminophylline drip (for PO
	  Theophylline) (or bolus q6°)
	steroid IV or PO
		IV Aminophylline drip
		  (or PO Theophylline)
		  (or bolus q6°)
		steroid IV or PO
			d/c IV -> PO
			d/c IV -> PO
				tolerating PO medications

EDUCATION	Asthma handout
	Theophylline handout
	correct use of breathing treatment &
	  inhaler
	Asthma/Allergy Support Group handout
	Prednisone handout
	breathing treatment handout
		reinforce
		
		reinforce
		reinforce
		reinforce
		reinforce
			reinforce
			
			reinforce
			reinforce
			reinforce
			reinforce
				pt/SO voices understanding
				  of asthma
				SO voices understanding
				  of need for medications
				  and how to give

DISCHARGE PLANNING	reinforce hazards of smoking in
	  relation to asthma
	pulmonary function testing before d/c
	  or after for baseline or followup
	allergy/pulmonary consult
	Asthma/Allergy Support Group referral
				discharge instructions
				parents demonstrate use
				  of MN, nebulizer or
				  inhaler

VARIANCE CODES:

01 Inadequate PO intake
02 Febrile
03 Vomiting
04 Still wheezing
05 Transferred to PICU/TCU
06 Parents not available
07 Physician did not order
08 Chronic patient with multiple problems
09 Other (specify)

CIRCLE ANY AREAS NOT MET AND WRITE
APPROPRIATE CODE NEXT TO CIRCLED AREA

Alice B. Keeling, Carol Fisher, Carla Sanders, Laura Sullivan, David T. Allen, MD, and Connie Anton

Figure 13-8. Order Set for Asthma (Day I)

Alliant® Health System KOSAIR CHILDREN'S HOSPITAL	IMPRINT PATIENT'S NAME BELOW THIS LINE

IMP-K17 (1-93)

DATE	PHYSICIAN'S ORDERS	DISPENSING BY NON-PROPRIETARY NAME IS AUTHORIZED UNLESS CHECKED IN THIS COLUMN.
	ORDER SET FOR ASTHMA	**DAY I**
	Admit to _____ Service	Wt. _____
	Diagnosis Status Asthmaticus	Ht. _____
	Condition _____	BSA _____
	Allergies _____	
	_____ Diet _____	
	_____ Vital Signs _____	
	_____ *CXR (optional)	
	_____ Aminophylline—(Optional) (Complete aminophylline order sheet)	
	_____ Methyl Prednisolone (2 mg/kg/dose recommended) _____ mg IVQ _____ hrs.	
	OR	
	_____ Prednisone (1–2 mg/kg/day recommended) _____ mg q _____ hrs.	
	OR	
	_____ Prednisone (1–2 mg/kg/day recommended) _____ mg po q _____ hrs.	
	Complete Respiratory Care Order Sheet	
	_____ Albuteral minineb q 1–2hr initially (until PEFR is > or = 70% or predicted or if < 5 yr O_2 sats > or = 94 or CO_2 retention < or = then give minineb q 2–4 hours). rs).	
	_____ Peak expiratory flow monitoring before and after minineb (>5 yr.)	
	_____ CR monitor.	
	_____ *Theophylline level now (if on Theo at home).	
	_____ Chem 6 in a.m. (Optional)	
	_____ Theophylline level 4 hours after drip started.	
	_____ Theophylline level in a.m.	
	_____ *ABG ─┐	
	OR	
	_____ *CBG ──→ For baseline physician perference	
	AND/OR	
	_____ *Pulse Oximeter ─┘	
	_____ O_2 (To maintain Sat. O_2>94)	
	Signature	
	*DISREGARD IF DONE IN ED.	

ORDERS

Figure 13-9.   Order Set for Asthma (Day II)

	IMPRINT PATIENT'S NAME BELOW THIS LINE

Alliant® Health System
KOSAIR CHILDREN'S HOSPITAL

IMP-K17 (1-93)

DATE	PHYSICIAN'S ORDERS	DISPENSING BY NON-PROPRIETARY NAME IS AUTHORIZED UNLESS CHECKED IN THIS COLUMN.
	ORDER SET FOR ASTHMA	**DAY II**
	_____ ABG in a.m. (Optional)	
	OR	
	_____ CBG in a.m. (Optional)	
	_____ Theophylline level in a.m. (If indicated)	
	_____ Chem 6 in a.m. (Optional)	
	Complete Respiratory Albuteral minineb q 4–6 hours.	
	Care Order Sheet	
	_____ Allergy/Pulmonary consult (Optional)	
	_____ Pulmonary function testing before dc or after for baseline or F/U. (Optional but preferred for > 5 yrs.)	
	Signature	

ORDERS

Reprinted, with permission, from Alliant Health System, Louisville, Kentucky.

Alice B. Keeling, Carol Fisher, Carla Sanders, Laura Sullivan, David T. Allen, MD, and Connie Anton

will describe defining characteristics of a patient outlier for purposes of determining which patients should be excluded from future comparative studies. To make this determination, the panel must ask: What are the conditions under which it would be inappropriate to include a patient in a test population? Finally, the expert panel will be asked to use the order set for their patients, with the expectation that all other patients admitted by other physicians with the same diagnosis will be the control group.

The first measurement will be the frequency with which each individual order on the prototype order set is appropriate for patients in that test group. The operative premise will be that the physician is always right. The order set should be evaluated continuously for appropriateness of the predetermined treatments, tests, and procedures. The second set of data will be the comparison of quality outcome measures as outlined by the expert panel for test and control patients. The third set of measurements will be for resource utilization, average length of stay, and total costs for the test group versus the control group.

Physicians' concerns about "cookbook medicine," an issue emphasized throughout this book, must be confronted. There are many instances where predetermined protocols enhance care. Two are heparin protocols and antibiotic regimens. There are undisputed instances where a physician was protected against liability claims when evidence confirmed that the physician followed a prereviewed guideline in the delivery of care. Nonetheless, today's physicians must ask: Is the predetermined care plan for the *average patient* with this diagnosis appropriate for *this unique patient?*

Conclusion

The first-generation steps of clinical path development and implementation were critical to Alliant's understanding of the mapping of care plans and enhanced communication among the various disciplines. The first few years also revealed limitations of the organization's approach to variance reporting. These experiences, however, were invaluable lessons that helped lay the groundwork for development of second-generation paths.

The primary lesson learned is that a clear consensus on the purposes for using clinical pathways must be arrived at for all prospective users before design, development, or deployment activities begin. Also, the proper tools must be selected for each purpose.

A clinical path may be a tool for nursing case management, incorporating independent standards of nursing practice. It may be a physician practice guideline, consisting of predetermined order sets for the "average" patient with a particular diagnosis. Mixing these purposes at the beginning promoted confusion and frustration among nurse and physician caregivers. As knowledge, experience, and sophistication increase with growing usage and with computer-assisted data and variance tracking, it may be possible to accomplish both purposes through the same mechanism. Always the questions must be asked: Why are we doing this? How can we make it better?

PART THREE

Case Studies: Spanning the Continuum of Care

Clinical Path Development by Phases within an Episode of Illness: Acute Myocardial Infarction

Carol A. Huttner, Karen A. Doran, Marc R. Pritzker, MD, and Cathy K. Ahern

Historically, the provision of inpatient hospital care has been a fragmented process with various health care providers working autonomously and anonymously under the general guidelines of a physician's day-by-day orders. At its best, this system provided highly individualized care that could be very good, depending on the expertise and intuition of the providers. In less fortunate circumstances, the care was deficient and difficult to systematize into a program that lent itself to retrospective review or rapid introduction of therapeutic modalities.

The underpinning of clinical pathways at Abbott Northwestern Hospital in Minneapolis is a multidisciplinary approach that draws on the expertise of individual component providers to define a consistent therapeutic plan for patients with similar diagnoses. This approach is a system of care provision and evaluation that creates a series of expectations among providers so that specific predefined patient care outcomes can be reached. Patients whose disease courses deviate from predefined outcome variables are identified early in their care to promote constructive intervention. Rather than static, "cookbook" medical and nursing care, the pathway illustrates a dynamically evolving series of evaluative and therapeutic algorithms that promote the best care for all patients.

A Philosophical Perspective

Under traditional models of health care, identification of critical junctures in the patient's course frequently is difficult. For example, the provision of preventive care and home care may be as uneven as the symptoms with which a patient presents; consequently, responsibilities may be ambiguously defined or their assignment omitted altogether. Likewise, in this era of exposé journalism, the public's perception of the expertise and efficiency of health care provision has been eroded by anecdotal horror stories. Unfortunately, traditional patterns of hospital and outpatient care do little to restore patient confidence. This is because, in addition to indistinctly drawn lines of responsibility, information may be withheld or incomplete (after all, only the attending physician may have authority to provide information) or consensus among caregivers may be lacking. Consequently, the patient is left to wonder—and wander—in a vacuum.

In traditional hospital delivery systems, elements of care also are obscurely defined, making it difficult to distinguish variation in practice patterns from system inefficiencies. Not only must the correct information be obtained and appropriate therapies provided, the proper information must be transmitted to the appropriate place at the appropriate time once the therapeutic intervention is completed. Inability to differentiate between practitioner-related versus system-related inefficiencies makes continuous performance improvement a difficult task.

By introducing a clinical pathway program, health care service content and responsibility become more clearly defined. Resources necessary to provide optimal care can be identified, measured, and cost accounted on a prospective basis. A provider's case mix experience can be readily identified and appropriate care provision and cost containment initiatives can be quantified to facilitate direct contract bidding. Once individual health care components are identified, the real power of clinical paths comes into play: Elements of care can be extracted and analyzed for their individual performance and contribution to the overall goals of the care plan; patients and their families can know what to expect from service delivery (and therefore participate in the process); variance reporting and analysis can equip the health care team to identify, circumvent, and/or resolve potential and actual system breakdowns.

Clinical Pathways and Centers of Excellence

Abbott Northwestern's philosophy on the value of clinical pathways guided program development and implementation at the facility, where development was linked to key product lines called *centers of excellence*. During the late 1980s, each center of excellence was challenged to improve quality and reduce costs in the managed care environment that characterized health care provision in the metropolitan Minneapolis/St. Paul area.

At first, each center of excellence approached these challenges from a different perspective, without a central oversight committee to monitor the process. Separate teams in the cardiovascular, oncology, behavioral care, orthopedics, and rehabilitation services departments were creating their own processes, working independently to develop patient-specific pathways. Some teams were multidisciplinary in their makeup; others were composed primarily of nurses. There was no formal mechanism for the teams to interact and share key points of learning.

The first teams focused on high-volume, high-cost diagnosis categories, eventually sharing information with one another informally. Over time, this informal process led to the formation of a central, multidisciplinary team that identified key elements each team had to follow in order to develop and implement clinical pathways. The most significant elements were a standardized format, systemwide guidelines for variance analysis, and standardized use of functional health patterns and nursing diagnoses for each pathway.

The center of excellence approach to developing and implementing clinical pathways revolves around cardiovascular services at Abbott Northwestern Hospital. First and foremost to remember is that the implementation of clinical paths is not an event but an evolutionary process that promotes continuous improvement in patient care. Second, this chapter represents a snapshot in time—a bit of hindsight intermixed with plans for future evolution.

Development of Cardiovascular Clinical Pathways

The cardiovascular team was one of the first at Abbott Northwestern to implement clinical paths. A cardiovascular continuous quality improvement (CQI) initiative was undertaken in late 1989 in an attempt to reduce costs and improve patient outcomes. An outside consultant was hired to guide the CQI initiative. The cardiovascular program is the largest revenue center at Abbott Northwestern and has the highest patient volume of any program in the hospital. At the initiation of this project, Abbott Northwestern was known for its high-quality cardiovascular program and for having the second-highest patient charges in the Twin Cities area.

The project began by looking at the highest-volume cardiovascular patient categories by diagnosis-related group (DRG). With patient discharge data showing 1,300 open-heart surgeries, 1,200 PTCAs, and 6,000 catheterization laboratory procedures in 1989 alone, it was clear where the focus belonged. Therefore, reams of utilization and quality data about these patient groups were analyzed; nurses were sent to clinical pathway conferences; and teams were convened to develop strategies to improve patient outcomes and decrease costs.[1]

A team lead by a cardiovascular surgical clinical nurse specialist developed and implemented the first pathway for open-heart surgery, which applied to all patients who undergo coronary artery bypass or heart valve procedures. The development and implementation process took nine months and focused only on the nursing components of patient care. The process was painstakingly slow, and enormous team learning occurred. One by one, caregivers from key disciplines who interact with this patient population became more involved and began to work collaboratively to streamline the patient care process. This first clinical pathway – and subsequent cardiovascular paths – soon reflected the interdisciplinary nature of the patient's experience.

The open-heart surgery team initially had targeted a length-of-stay reduction of 1.5 days. Over the course of a year, that target was exceeded, and length of stay for this patient category was reduced by 2.3 days. The net effect of these improvements yielded an annual savings of $3.5 million in hospital charges.

Creating Cardiovascular Clinical Pathways for Medical Patients

The considerable success of cardiovascular clinical paths for surgical patients led to more challenging work with medical cardiovascular patient groups. Clinical path-based management for patients admitted with an uncomplicated myocardial infarction (MI) was developed in 1990. It was used by staff to discuss various aspects of the care plan for individual patients but did not become a useful tool for concurrent patient care management. Unlike the cardiac clinical pathway, the MI progression did not integrate well with the process of care. This was due to a number of reasons:

1. Because it was not designed as a true multidisciplinary patient care tool, all members of the team did not address the same issues. For example, the cardiac rehabilitation staff did not understand the importance of assessing the patient's activity needs by day two. The physician did not communicate reasons for delaying or duplicating certain laboratory tests. Because the pathway was not designed collaboratively, team members did not appreciate the impact of their individual contributions on the larger system of care delivery.
2. There was no formal mechanism to collect data variances or follow up on recurring issues that inhibited a patient's progress.
3. No data were gathered to show that use of the MI clinical path positively influenced the efficient and effective use of resources.
4. There was no assurance, once a patient was started on the pathway by the admitting nurse, that it would be used by all staff, especially when the patient transferred to other hospital units.
5. The patient admitted for treatment of an MI followed numerous paths and did not necessarily advance according to one path. For example, some MI patients had a coronary angiogram and were then treated medically or underwent another intervention that might include PTCA, atherectomy, or CABG.

6. The MI pathway was based on a seven-day length of stay, although the current average LOS for MI patients was five days.

The cardiac surgery pathways continued to show benefits, whereas the success of the MI clinical progression was stymied. Not only did the surgical pathways reduce length of stay and costs, they improved patient outcomes. In addition, all health care team members involved with cardiac surgery patients and families knew the plan of care. It became apparent that, to attain the same benefits that the surgical cardiac clinical paths had achieved, the medical-oriented pathways needed to be revised. This realization laid the foundation for changes in the clinical progression for patients with uncomplicated MI.

Revising the Myocardial Infarction Clinical Pathway

A health care team representing physicians and other cross-discipline caregivers for patients admitted for MI treatment was organized by the cardiovascular clinical nurse specialist. The team was charged with developing an MI clinical path that would be a viable working document for all disciplines. The lessons learned during the surgical pathway project were incorporated into the revised MI project. (See figure 14-1.)

The first step in developing the path was to identify current patient management practices, costs, length of stay, and admitting physicians for patients with an acute, uncomplicated myocardial infarction. Data were obtained from three sources. One source, a study by the department of internal medicine's quality management work group entitled Level of Care Decisions in Patients Admitted to "Rule Out" Myocardial Infarction, supplied important information about practices at Abbott Northwestern.[2] The study reported that the majority of patients admitted with chest pain to the emergency department were triaged to the appropriate inpatient unit, but after 12 and 24 hours they were not transferred out of the coronary care unit (CCU) to a telemetry unit in a timely manner.

A second study, Acute Myocardial Infarction Descriptive Study, was initiated by the CCU unit joint practice council to determine practice patterns relative to the treatment of patients with proven myocardial infarctions.[3] Closed hospital records of 200 consecutive patients with a discharge diagnosis of acute MI were selected for the study. Data were gathered to determine the patient length of stay, outcome, pharmacologic treatments, use of thrombolytic therapy, interventional diagnostic and therapeutic treatments, use of invasive monitoring, and initiation of preventive strategies prior to discharge. The most revealing finding from this study was that 70 percent of MI patients were transferred from primary and secondary hospitals.

A third study determined the extent of duplication of laboratory, electrocardiogram (ECG), and chest X rays for patients transferred to Abbott Northwestern from other hospitals.[4] Thirty cases were reviewed, and data showed that more than 40 percent of

Figure 14-1. Points of Learning Applied to MI Clinical Path Development

1. Involve all members of the health care team (acute and progressive care staff) who provide care/service for the MI patient/family.

2. Develop a formal mechanism to collect variance data and link the information to continuous quality improvement activities.

3. Provide financial and descriptive data to show improvement in efficiency and effectiveness.

4. Emphasize the clinical path as a tool to support managed care.

5. Develop a mechanism to adapt the MI clinical path to medical or interventional treatments.

6. Base the MI clinical pathway on a five-day length of stay.

tests done by the transferring facility were duplicated after transfer despite the fact there had been no change in the patient's status.

Stakeholders for MI Clinical Pathway

All stakeholders involved in caring for the patient with acute MI were asked to join the MI clinical pathway task force. Physician representation included not only a cardiologist, but also internal medicine and family practice physicians. Other clinical input was provided by nursing staff from the three units that provided care for patients with acute MI, the emergency department, cardiac rehabilitation, nutritional services, clinical social work, respiratory therapy, laboratory, and home health care. Nonclinical support was offered to the team by representatives from staff education, finance, hospital information services (HIS), and quality management.

Team Objectives

The MI patient clinical path team started off by defining their charter, which clarified their purpose, as quoted in the following.

Problem Identification

There is a lack of coordination among the various professionals involved in establishing the plan of care for the MI patient. Consequently, there are inconsistencies and delays that could result in inadequate discharge preparation of patient/family, extended length of stay, preventable readmissions, and patient/family/hospital staff dissatisfaction.

Goal Statement

To define and implement an MI clinical path that will delineate the multidisciplinary plan of care and discharge outcomes based on a five-day length of stay. The path format will be based on functional health patterns.

Measures of Success

- MI patient/family satisfied with hospitalization process and discharge preparation
- Multidisciplinary team informed of patient progress and plan of care
- Decrease in length of stay for MI patient
- Decrease in costs for MI patient
- No increase in unplanned readmissions

Team Parameters

Additional membership and projects may need to be added based on further development of the clinical path.

Expectations

The MI clinical progression task force will meet every other week for one hour. Agenda items and minutes will be sent to all members within one week. Working group meetings will occur between these meetings. Active participation by all committee members, openness to a team approach, and willingness to modify current procedures is essential to the success of this initiative.

Once their charter was clear, team members were given the opportunity to determine what information was needed to complete the clinical path. Small groups were established to accomplish the following tasks:

1. Revise the coronary care unit orders to reflect current practice guidelines and provide easy access to the results of diagnostic tests performed by transferring hospitals.
2. Update the cardiac rehabilitation exercise protocols for MI patients to reflect a five-day length of stay. Differentiate the protocols for patients being treated medically and for patients undergoing surgical interventions.
3. Develop a mechanism to adapt the MI clinical path to patients who receive medical treatment with the use of medications, PTCA, or surgery.
4. Write department- and discipline-specific discharge outcomes for MI patients.

The information from all members and small groups was used to develop the uncomplicated MI clinical pathway for a five-day length of stay.

Individualizing the MI Clinical Pathway

The greatest challenge was to create an MI path that could be individualized according to the patient's plan of care. For example, a different path was followed by the patient who underwent surgical intervention rather than medical treatment only. To address the issue of various studies or treatments (that is, with or without angiogram, with or without PTCA or atherectomy), overlays were designed for the path. The basic MI clinical path was patterned after the typical MI inpatient. This included a coronary angiogram, PTCA and/or atherectomy, and discharge within five days. Several overlays were designed for days two and three for the patient treated medically with or without interventional therapy. These overlays could be taped to the generic uncomplicated path on day two or three to show the differences in progression steps. Currently, changing the pathway via these overlays is done manually; however, the process could easily be computerized at a later date.

A sample of the uncomplicated MI clinical path for patients undergoing angiography is shown in figure 14-2 (pp. 238–239). Figure 14-3 (p. 240) represents the overlay for days two and three, used for those patients who do not undergo diagnostic studies.

Implementing the Multidisciplinary MI Clinical Pathway

The latest utilization data show that length of stay for the MI patient at Abbott Northwestern has been reduced by 0.8 days, with a corresponding reduction in cost of care. A study is under way to determine what impact the revised CCU standing orders have on the number of diagnostic studies completed by the transferring hospital but are redone unnecessarily upon the patient's admission to Abbott Northwestern.

Expanding the MI Clinical Pathway

Once the in-hospital portion of the MI path was completed, questions regarding post-discharge care were addressed by an interregional group comprised of administrative and clinical nursing staff from Abbott Northwestern Hospital and Health Bond, a consortium of hospitals in south central Minnesota. The group discussed the possibility of defining MI health care services that cover a patient's entire episode of illness. Members further envisioned the restoration of care delivery to a more patient-centered, cost-effective system, one that satisfied patients and providers alike. To determine the present health care processes for cardiovascular patients transferring interregionally, patient/family interviews and closed record reviews were undertaken. During the patient/family interviews, questions centered on five areas of experience:

1. General reflections (environment, physicians, nurses)
2. Provider behaviors (empathy, expertise, patient wait, personalization and continuity of service, presence, regard for patient autonomy)

3. System issues (interregional transfer, cost and insurance issues)
4. Education (information, timing, dispelling anxiety, need to know)
5. Discharge (postdischarge contacts, planning, concerns, compliance)

The closed record reviews showed a need to reduce duplication of tests, use standardized language, improve documentation practices, provide continuity for patients who traveled to multiple hospital units, and improve communication among interregional sites. Based on study results, an interregional MI clinical path was developed to illustrate patient care during the entire illness episode.

Phases of the Interregional MI Clinical Pathway

To address health promotion and treatment, the MI clinical pathway spans an entire year to enable promotion of suggested lifestyle changes. The four phases of this progression are as follows:

1. *Acute phase:* The acute phase starts at the patient's entry into the health care system and continues until the day of discharge from the acute care setting. It may involve transfer through three hospitals or clinics. Based on current data, the acute phase usually runs from day one to day nine.
2. *Recovery/posthospital phase:* The posthospital phase starts on the day after discharge and ends on the day the patient begins cardiac rehabilitation. This phase usually lasts from day 10 to day 16.
3. *Recovery/rehabilitation phase:* During this period the patient participates in cardiac rehabilitation as the cardiac myocardium recovers from the infarction. This recovery phase usually spans days 17 to 45.
4. *Enhancement/maintenance phase:* This phase starts when the patient is discharged from cardiac rehabilitation and/or when the attending physician permits the patient to return to all preillness activities without restrictions. The enhancement phase, which ends a year from the date the patient first entered the acute phase, usually lasts from day 46 to day 365.

Functional Health Patterns in the Interregional MI Clinical Pathway

Structure of the interregional clinical path is based on functional health patterns (FHPs) (designed by Marjorie Gordon, RN, PhD, FAAN) that provide a holistic approach to patient care.[5] The 11 FHPs used in the interregional MI clinical path (in place of key events) include:

1. Health perception/health management
2. Nutritional/metabolic status
3. Elimination
4. Activity/exercise
5. Sleep/rest patterns
6. Cognitive/perceptual abilities
7. Self-perception/self-concept
8. Role/relationship issues
9. Sexuality/reproduction concerns
10. Coping/stress tolerance
11. Value/belief systems

Outcomes Measurement for Interregional Clinical Pathways

The team incorporated a valid and reliable outcomes measurement system that is user-friendly, objective, holistic in approach, adaptable to the continuum of care, adaptable

Figure 14-2. MI with Angiography Pathway

CARDIAC CHEST PAIN: MI WITH ANGIO/PTCA

NURSING DIAGNOSIS / COLLABORATIVE PROBLEM	DATE INITIALED	R LAST NOTE	DATE RESOLVED / INITIALS
Alteration in cardiac output related to myocardial ischemia/death.			
Alteration in comfort related to myocardial ischemia/death.			

KEY EVENTS/ DISCHARGE OUTCOMES

- Day 1:
- Day 2: Resolved cardiac chest pain. Angio/PTCA without complications.
- Day 3: Transferred to telemetry. IV Meds to PO. IV to Saline Lock. Nursing Home referral initiated as needed.
- Day 4:
- Day 5: Patient/family receives: • Plan for emergency • Prescribed meds • Prescribed activity • Prescribed diet • Follow-up appointment

DISCHARGE PLANNING
Assess needs re:
DC home assessment
- Stairs ☐ Yes ☐ No
- Main floor bath ☐ Yes ☐ No
Equipment
Transportation
Meds
Teaching need for DC
Discussed in discharge rounds/care conference

Living Situation: With whom
☐ House ☐ Apartment
☐ Room ☐ Health Care Facility
Provide patient/family with anticipated plan.
Assess need for Social Service/ Home Health Care

- Day 3: Can patient return to current living situation? ☐ Yes ☐ No
Prior use of home health care services? ☐ Yes ☐ No
- Day 4: Complete nursing part of referral form, prn.
- Day 5: Complete referral form as needed.

LAB/ DIAGNOSTIC/ PROCEDURES/ MEDS
- Day 1: ECG, SMA-7, PCXR, CK/MB, Hgb or CBC, PT (on anticoagulants) PTT (on Heparin)
- Day 2: ECG, CK/MB (if #2 not done Day 1) Angio PTCA
- Day 3: IV Meds to PO.

HEALTH MANAGEMENT
- Compliance
- Safety
- Potential for injury
- Potential for infection
- Physical & emotional

Assess for high-risk patients:
- Falls/restraints
- Suicidal
- Vulnerable adult (call SS)

Isolation:

NUTRITIONAL/ METABOLIC
- Diet
- Fluids
- Tolerance
- Skin Integrity
- I.V.'s
- Weight
- IV → po
- Surgical incision

- Day 1: Lo Chol, NAS full liquid diet, Advance as tolerated. I & O q shift. Daily weight (type)
- Day 2: Dietary Consult
- Day 3: I & O (discontinue upon transfer or IV fluids D/C) Weight IV to Saline Lock Dietary Instruction

ELIMINATION
- Bowel
- Bladder
- Abdomen/girth

- Day 1: Urinary Continence: ☐ Yes ☐ No ☐ Foley LBM:
- Day 2: LBM:
- Day 3: Assess for Foley removal. LBM:
- Day 4: LBM:
- Day 5: LBM:

ACTIVITY/EXERCISE
- ADL's
- Tolerance
- Cardiovascular
- Respiratory/O₂

- Day 1: Oxygen 2-6 LPM Cardiac monitor Head to toe assessment q shift & prn. CV/Resp assessment & VS q 4 hr WA & PRN Bedrest with commode
- Day 2: O₂ D/C for Oximetry on RA >92% & pain free. Post angio assessments Post PTCA assessments Obtain order for Cardiac Rehabilitation
- Day 3: Sheath removal protocol Telemetry Assessment BID & PRN VS BID & PRN Cardiac Rehab initiated Protocol: Activity:
- Day 4: Cardiac Rehab Activity
- Day 5: Met guidelines for Out Patient Cardiac Rehab/Home Program Activity

SLEEP/REST
• Sleep Patterns

COGNITIVE / PERCEPTUAL
• Neuros
  – Compare with baseline
  – Motor / power of ext.
  – Sensation
  – Mental status
  – Hearing, speech , vision
  – Level of consciousness
  – Orientation
  – Swallowing
• Pain Management
• Teaching needs for hospital care

Neuro assess per post Thrombolytic	Neuro assessment BID post-thrombolytic on telemetry unit.	Obtain prescriptions or take home meds
CCU/MI/Angina information		
Give patient/family CV folder		Send NTG (SL) bottle with patient if appropriate
Videos:	Videos:	Mediminder as needed
• "Preparing for Your Coronary Angiogram"	• "Your Heart Attack and Your Future"	Out Patient Cardiac Rehab/Home Program
• PTCA Video	• "Signals for Action"	CV Folder
	MI/Angina information/teaching	
Pre and post Angio/PTCA information/teaching		
Med cards/instruct	Coumadin Video, PRN	
•	Med cards/instruct	Med cards/instruct
•	•	•
•	•	•
	•	•

SELF-PERCEPTION/SELF-CONCEPT
Concerns About:
• Illness
• Body Image
• Anxiety/Fear

Assess level of anxiety/fear

Provide reassurance and comfort

Refer to SS prn

ROLE/RELATIONSHIP
• Dependents
• Family Dynamics
• Social Isolation
• Changes in Roles

Dependents: ☐ Yes ☐ No   Ages _____

Any with disabilities: ☐ Yes ☐ No

Who can assist you after discharge _____   Times available for teaching _____

Length of medical leave _____

SEXUALITY
• Changes/Concerns re: Illness

Allow patient/family to vocalize concerns

Enlist resources as necessary

Refer to SS prn

COPING/STRESS TOLERANCE
• Emotional Status
• Effectiveness of Coping
• Support Groups
• Coping Skills of Patient/Family

Need for referral to:
☐ Behavioral Med
☐ Psych
☐ CNS
☐ Social Services
☐ Pastoral Care
☐ Other

Support system: ☐ Yes ☐ No

Identify: _____

Assess needs for referral to support groups:	Yes	No	Information

Reinforce info. received on support groups

VALUES/BELIEFS
• Spiritual / cultural
• Importance to pt. / family
• Goals of care

Chaplaincy is consulting with: ☐ patient ☐ family ☐ staff
Spirituality is a source of strength/comfort: ☐
Patient is struggling with spiritual issues: ☐
Priest called - Sacrament   Date: _____

RECOPIED _____   _____, HUC   CHECKED BY _____   _____, RN

239

Figure 14-3. Sample Overlay

CARDIAC CHEST PAIN: MI WITHOUT ANGIO/PTCA

DAY 2	DATE	DAY 3	DATE
Resolved cardiac chest pain. Transferred to telemetry IV Meds to PO IV to Heparin Lock		Nursing Home referral initiated as needed.	
		Can patient return to current living situation? ☐ Yes ☐ No Prior use of home health care services? ☐ Yes ☐ No	
ECG, CK/MB (if #2 not done Day 1) IV Meds to PO			
→ I & O (discontinue upon transfer or IV fluids D/C) → Weight IV to Saline Lock Dietary Consult		Dietary Instruction	
Assess for Foley removal. LBM:		LBM:	
O₂ D/C for Oximetry on RA > 92% & pain free. Telemetry Assessment BID & PRN VS BID & PRN Obtain order for Cardiac Rehabilitation		Cardiac Rehab initiated _____ Protocol: _____ Activity: _____	
Neuro assessment BID post-thrombolytic on telemetry unit.			
		Videos: • "Your Heart Attack and Your Future" • "Signals for Action"	
Med cards/instruct • • •		Med cards/instruct • • •	

for computer analysis, and accommodating of nursing diagnoses. The method chosen for documenting patient outcomes was an adaptation of the Omaha Visiting Nurses Association methodology,[6,7] which seemed to fit with the functional health patterns used as key events on the interregional MI clinical path.

The Omaha system, designed initially for home health and public health service systems, was believed to adapt easily to the episode of illness for the MI patient given that the majority of time both patient and family are in the community, outside the acute care setting. The Omaha system includes a problem classification scheme with 44 problems that can be coded as health promotion, potential, deficit/impairment/actual, and patient or family. The rating scale for outcomes is a five-point Likert-type scale, which assesses knowledge, behavior, and status. With the Omaha system, outcomes for each functional health pattern on the clinical path were developed by interregional team members. The functional health pattern, activities/functions, and the outcomes for each phase of care in this functional health pattern are shown in figure 14-4. Following the Omaha model, interventions are categorized into four broad areas including health teaching, guidance and counseling, treatments and procedures, and case management and surveillance. These are further described by 62 activities or objects of nursing action.[8]

Interregional Pathway Variances

Variances from the clinical progression provide the health care team with meaningful information for evaluating and improving the processes of care. A *variance* is defined as any deviation between what happened and what was expected to happen. These variations are classified according to suspected cause—patient situation, system/hospital, or staff. In addition, all deviations from expected outcome scores on the path for each phase are noted as variances. Variances, either positive or negative, are categorized in the same manner as deviations from the planned interventions.

Variance data are collected concurrently by the case manager for the interregional MI clinical path project. All variances are stratified according to the functional health patterns and phases of care. A group of clinical specialists and caregivers experienced in variance analysis will evaluate interregional MI clinical path variances and

Figure 14-4. Interregional MI Clinical Pathway Phases

Health Pattern	Dates _____ Acute (day 1–9)	Dates _____ Recovery: Post hosp. (day 10–16)	Dates _____ Recovery: Rehabilitation (day 17–45)	Dates _____ Recovery: Enhancement/ Maintenance (day 46–365)
Activity/ Exercise	1. Patient performs self care and begins exercise routine (37 B-2) and (37 K-2). See teaching folder. Scores _____ Intervention scheme:	1. Patient performs self care, ADLs and follows home instructions. (37 B-4) and (37 K-3). Scores _____ Intervention scheme:	1. Patient will be independent in ADLs and follows exercise program. (37 B-4) and (37 K-4). Scores _____ Intervention scheme:	1. Patient will participate in regular exercise program based upon physical condition. (37 B-5) and (37 K-5). Scores _____ Intervention scheme:

B = Behavior Scale 1–5 (never appropriate to consistently appropriate)

K = Knowledge Scale 1–5 (no knowledge to superior knowledge)

©Interregional Cardiovascular Collaborative Project, Aug. 1993. Adapted from Omaha System. (This example was made possible by the efforts of the representatives from Health Bond and Abbott Northwestern Interregional Cardiovascular Collaboration Project team whose participation was funded in part by the Robert Wood Johnson Foundation–PEW Charitable Trust national initiative, Strengthening Hospital Nursing: A Program to Improve Patient Care. The names and addresses of individual members of that team are available from the authors.

determine their impact on patient outcomes. Given that these efforts are new, no data are available.

Conclusion

Clinical pathways are an important case management tool for physicians and staff in tracking the direction and movement of care. They help ensure patient progress by outlining the optimal sequencing, timing, and coordination of care delivery. Pathways identify benchmarks of care that aid in determining the success of patient management practices. Furthermore, they provide a vehicle for shared expectations, quality control for data collection, identification of variances, data analysis, and continuous improvement. At Abbott Northwestern, the clinical path has become an important patient care reference for physicians, nurses, and other providers.

Myocardial infarction represents a brief moment in a patient's lifetime, and yet the adaptive healing process for patients and their families requires significantly more time. Implementation of a clinical path that transcends the patient's acute episode of illness and links with follow-up care helps ensure a seamless health care system that leads to patient/family-specific outcomes for an adaptive, healing process. This chapter presented an actual acute MI clinical path model that links the acute episode with follow-up care.

At Abbott Northwestern, teams of clinical and nonclinical caregivers came together with a common goal to produce cost-effective, improved patient outcomes. This led to an overall cardiovascular program savings of more than $8 million over four years and increased patient and family satisfaction. The power of these outcomes stems from the dedication and effort of participants in the team process. Shared learning through this process can enhance care for patients in other medical centers throughout the United States.

References

1. Walton, M. *The Deming Management Method.* New York City: Putnam Publishing Group, 1986.

2. Abbott Northwestern Hospital Department of Internal Medicine Quality Assurance Work Group. Level of Care Decisions in Patients Admitted to "Rule Out" Myocardial Infarction. Unpublished report, Mar. 1992.

3. Abbott Northwestern Hospital Station 45 Joint Practice Council. Acute Myocardial Infarction Descriptive Study. Unpublished report, May 1993.

4. Abbott Northwestern Hospital Station 45 Joint Practice Council. Duplication of Tests for Transferred MI Patients. Unpublished report, Jan. 1993.

5. Gordon, M. *Nursing Diagnosis: Process and Application.* New York City: McGraw-Hill, 1987.

6. Martin, K. S., and Scheet, N. J. *The Omaha System: Application for Community Health Nursing.* Philadelphia: W. B. Saunders Company, 1992.

7. Martin, K. S., and Scheet, N. J. *The Omaha System: A Pocket Guide for Community Health Nursing.* Philadelphia: W. B. Saunders, 1992.

8. Martin and Scheet. *The Omaha System: Application for Community Health Nursing.*

CHAPTER FIFTEEN

A Regional Approach to the Development of Clinical Paths that Span the Continuum of Care

Kathleen Ciccone and Tina Gerardi

Overhauling the health care system has become a priority at state and national levels. Among the many reform plans proposed, a common theme is the quality of care and increased provider accountability for patient outcomes. As a result, virtually all reform plans call for the development of better measures of quality: clinical guidelines to better evaluate performance; indicator data to better monitor patient outcomes; and uniform, systematic interpretations of quality data to better inform patients, communities, payers, and regulators. An emphasis on total quality management and variation reduction in provider practice and patient outcomes is inherent in these plans. The focus of the Agency for Health Care Policy and Research (AHCPR), of physician groups on the development of clinical practice guidelines, of the Joint Commission on Accreditation of Healthcare Organizations' (JCAHOs') indicator monitoring system, as well as the shift in focus from case review to systems improvement by peer review organizations, and the many state and regional data and quality initiatives, all underscore the unequivocal nature of these changes.

Quality Improvement in an Era of Health Care Reform

Several trends are evident upon observing this evolving health care environment. These concern the expanded availability of consumer information in the media; enhancement of data systems for quality management; development of practice guidelines; research and regulatory initiatives to reduce variation and improve outcomes; the importance of hospital–physician partnerships; and the emergence of value-based purchasing as defined by health care payers.

Against the backdrop of these activities, hospitals are challenged more and more to continue meeting the changing needs of their patients and communities. They look for innovative ways to redesign, restructure, and retool their care delivery systems and to flourish in this highly competitive and chaotic environment.

Clinical pathways, the step-by-step sequencing of patient care for specific diagnoses or DRGs, are one approach that can help hospitals meet patient, provider, and payer needs. A clinical pathway introduces a more rational and systematic process of care that benefits all parties through improvements in practice patterns and efficiency indexes. Because the pathway extends to care provided outside the hospital, it can stimulate productive discussions among a wide array of health care providers and social organizations, resulting in much more effective and efficient care at a regional level. Pathway development incorporates clinical practice guidelines, best practice models, interdisciplinary discussion, consensus building, process and outcome measurements, and patient feedback. Furthermore, clinical pathways are effective tools for achieving quality, efficiency, and satisfaction standards.

This chapter focuses on the implications for hospitals and other providers as they design and redesign patient care processes. In particular, it highlights the development of group clinical pathway teams that span multiple providers and include whole continuums of service. As health care professionals envision the future of patient care (and for some the future is now), these groups are seen as reaching beyond traditional medical care into local communities, linking up with other providers and community organizations. Examples of community partnerships are illustrated throughout the chapter.

Northeastern New York Hospital Council's Experience

The Northeastern New York Hospital Council (NNYHC) is a voluntary membership and service organization representing 28 member hospitals that serve a 17-county region of northeastern New York State. The council's mission is to promote an effective and efficient health care system through the coordination of educational forums, cooperation in the development of clinical programs, promotion of opportunities for the improvement of hospital operations, and regional advocacy.

In 1991 the NNYHC board of directors began to emphasize collaboration and cooperation in the development of clinical and quality improvement programs. The board formed the Iroquois Healthcare Consortium (IHC) to accomplish this goal. Unlike many hospital alliances, the IHC is a regionally based alliance involving hospitals that are direct competitors. Although the New York State health care system is one of the most tightly regulated in the nation, state reimbursement policies have created a highly competitive hospital marketplace.

Despite competitive barriers to cooperation and collaboration, the IHC agreed to pursue the development of a regional quality improvement project. The consortium selected the publication *Continuous Performance Improvement through Integrated Quality Assessment: IQA-2*, written by the Hospital Association of New York State (HANYS), as its guide.[1] At the direction of its board, HANYS (a statewide membership organization representing more than 300 voluntary, nonprofit health care organizations in the state) had developed a formal quality initiative in 1986 and *IQA-2* is one in a series of membership-based quality management tools. As a result of educational programs sponsored by a HANYS affiliate, the Hospital Education and Research Fund, all of the hospitals in New York State were familiar with the concepts and approaches of *IQA-2*.

Project Overview and Methodology

The cornerstone of the *IQA-2* approach is the development of clinical pathways. A clinical pathway encompasses all aspects of patient care around a particular diagnosis or diagnosis-related group (DRG) and spans the period from the time the decision is made to admit a patient for hospitalization through, and including, discharge to appropriate follow-up care. The IHC enlisted the support of the *IQA-2* authors, one of whom was a nationally recognized physician consultant with substantial experience in clinical pathway development, to facilitate project development and group training. A full-time coordinator was secured shortly after the project was initiated.

Sixteen hospitals participated in the development, implementation, and evaluation of clinical pathways relating to four specific DRGs. The DRG or procedure selection was based on identified high-volume, high-cost services, as well as clinical issues previously identified through research or past experience. The four diagnoses chosen for the initial phase of the project were cardiac chest pain, total hip replacement, cerebral vascular accident (CVA), and laparoscopic cholecystectomy. Hospitals were clustered based on their DRG or procedure preference.

The following project objectives were identified:

- Develop collaborative working partnerships within and among participating hospitals.
- Improve patient care management from preadmission through postdischarge through the linkage of the quality improvement process with clinical management decision making.
- Improve patient and staff satisfaction levels.
- Encourage innovative and creative initiatives for efficient resource utilization.
- Assist hospitals in their transition from traditional quality assurance (QA) to continuous quality improvement (CQI).
- Strengthen trustee oversight for quality of care and hospital performance.

To accomplish these objectives, the 16 hospital participants (project team) engaged in a number of activities that ultimately led to clinical path development. Activities included organizing a team structure within which to work, identifying and assessing their needs, reaching consensus on key processes and important aspects of care, ensuring education of prospective path users, overcoming resistance, pilot testing clinical paths, and devising systems for variance analysis.

Project Team Profile and Structure

The project team reflected the diverse characteristics of the region and included small rural and large community hospitals. The number of inpatient beds ranged from 20 to 442. Several hospitals also had long-term care and psychiatric beds and were affiliated with other providers. Some participated in medical teaching programs, but none were academic medical centers.

The council sponsored several meetings with the hospitals and medical staffs to explain the project, its objectives, and responsibilities of all parties involved. This forum was also an opportunity to educate the participants about continuous quality improvement (CQI) and the clinical pathway as a tool for facilitating the CQI process.

The chief executive officer of each hospital signed a formal memorandum of understanding to participate in the project and meet deliverable time frames. A strong commitment from each CEO and hospital board of trustees was essential because of the significant staff time involved. Without commitment, cooperation, and collaboration among competing hospitals, the project would not have been possible.

Hospital trustees were briefed about the project and became involved in monitoring pathway development. The consortium encouraged each participating hospital individually to educate and involve its board of trustees in project objectives. From the hospitals' perspective these objectives were as follows:

- To assist in the transition to CQI
- To increase focus on systems issues
- To improve databases
- To encourage physician participation
- To improve patient outcomes
- To build teams and promote collaboration

- To provide education to multiple hospital levels (from trustees to line staff)
- To influence cost of care positively
- To meet community service requirements

Each hospital designated two individuals to serve on the Northeastern New York Hospital regional quality improvement task force, made up mostly of quality management directors and medical directors. This group met every other month and served as the overall steering committee for the project. Individual participants managed the clinical pathway development processes within their respective hospitals, but before they could do this, they first had to identify and assess their needs.

Needs Assessment

To address the project team's primary needs and develop effective partnerships for sharing information and data, the four DRG work groups met for one hour every four to six weeks to focus on development of the individual pathway for the identified DRG or procedure. Although each hospital developed its own clinical pathway, the work group provided a forum for sharing ideas, successes and setbacks in process development, and clinical outcomes data and for supporting the clinical pathway team leaders.

Each hospital had its own clinical pathway team whose members included medical, nursing, and other professional staff, as well as ancillary staff. For example, the 10 members of one hospital team for CVA included an internist, a family practitioner, a neurologist, a staff nurse, a physical therapist, a discharge planner, a financial officer, a nurse executive, a psychologist, and a dietitian. The psychologist was added to assist with team building and group dynamics, as well as to contribute to pathway development.

Hospital trustee boards monitored the functioning of these groups and reported to the hospital's quality management committee. A number of hospitals also solicited board members' recommendations for clinical pathway projects and kept them involved as the process unfolded, which served multiple purposes, including:

- Maintenance of strategic goal alignment
- High project exposure
- Continued trustee and administrative support
- Increased pathway credibility within the organization

Also, after being asked for educational assistance by several hospitals, IHC staff conducted orientation sessions for board members to introduce them to the tenets of continuous quality improvement. Hospitals also needed assistance in learning to use the basic monitoring and evaluation tools that apply in the hospital setting.

Four workshops addressed the following areas: an overview of CQI, CQI for the board and CEOs, team building and group facilitation, and data analysis and display. A sample agenda (teams and facilitation) is shown in figure 15-1. Each hospital identified its learning needs with respect to CQI principles and clinical pathway development, and the workshops assisted in meeting these needs. The next activity was to pinpoint key processes of care.

Important Aspects of Care

Internal hospital clinical pathway development began with identification of key processes and important aspects of care. When selecting a pathway for development, the hospital focused first on high-volume, high-cost, or problem-prone DRGs or diseases. It was also important to pick an area not clouded by controversy, one for which early "buy-in" could be obtained. Once a particular DRG or disease was identified,

Figure 15-1. Sample Agenda for Education Session

1. Introduction
   a. Expectations and goals
   b. Overview of the workshop
2. Characteristics of effective teams
3. Process observation
4. Team development and group facilitation
5. Meeting skills and facilitation
6. Alternative methods of team decision making
7. Ensuring success: Implementing change
   a. Action planning
   b. Next steps
8. Overview and summary

the following background information about each process was assembled at the hospital level:[2]

- Community need and projected service demand
- Key participants in all aspects of the process
- Historical volume, length-of-stay data, and outcomes data
- Benchmark results, practice guidelines, and current research findings from the literature
- Existing standards or quality indicators
- Patient satisfaction information (if available)

One hospital developed a pathway for laparoscopic cholecystectomy, which was a new service. Because the hospital had no experience with this procedure, it obtained utilization, financial, quality, and outcomes information from the literature on the procedure and from discussions with other hospitals and physicians performing the procedure. At the time, laparoscopic cholecystectomy was an emerging technology in nonteaching hospitals, and concerns were being raised about potential risk liability. In fact, during the course of the project, the New York State Department of Health promulgated detailed guidelines for physician credentialing programs for laparoscopic procedures.

The clinical pathway approach to designing a new service was appropriate, but difficulties arose due to lack of "organizational" experience with the process. For example, a hospital developing a pathway for a new service should try to team up with experienced providers, so that difficulties associated with a learning curve can be avoided. In a highly competitive market area, it may be necessary to seek support from organizations outside the immediate market area.

Once baseline data were assembled, a hospital clinical pathway team was formed, consisting of key participants in the delivery of care. Active participation of the medical and nursing staff was essential to success. Lack of participation or acceptance of this approach to care by either the physicians or nurses needed to be addressed immediately and participation secured. One medical director met with resistance from the medical staff when he first introduced the concept of clinical pathway development for pneumonia patients. Subsequent to this initial response, he formulated a history and physical for a patient presenting to the emergency department with suspected pneumonia. The medical director presented this case study at the next department of medicine and family practice meeting and asked physicians present to write initial admitting orders for the patient. He then collected the orders and presented results at the next staff meeting. The results showed a great deal of physician variation in orders and in the timing of orders. The medical staff was surprised by this inconsistency in practice patterns, noting that most things were ordered but not necessarily in a timely manner in all instances.

A pulmonologist also gave a brief educational session on the care and treatment of pneumonia and used this example of variation as a reintroduction to the concept of clinical pathways. The medical staff, armed with this new understanding of process variation, agreed that clinical pathways could assist in establishing best practice standards and a more coordinated sequence of care within the facility. Thus, medical staff buy-in of the clinical pathway concept probably began at that session.

Benefits Derived from Clinical Pathways

The function of the clinical pathway team was to map out each step of care, beginning with the initial physician contact, through hospitalization, and on to the postdischarge phase. The basic intent was to identify the optimal way to deliver and coordinate every step of care. The results were individual hospital clinical pathways that operated within the hospital's program goals, identified fiscal and personnel resources, and established relationships with external providers.

Patient expectations and feedback are critical to pathway success, and patient input was solicited by each hospital during development and throughout evaluation. For example, one hospital invited former patients who had undergone total hip replacement to breakfast with the intent of sharing with them the clinical pathway developed. The patients were pleased with the pathway but recommended that new patients have an opportunity to speak with former patients who had undergone total hip replacement. Although the education and support received from the medical and nursing staff was excellent, it was not the same as patients speaking as peers. As a result of this discussion, a program was developed that pairs new total hip replacement patients with former ones, either via telephone or in person, thus establishing a total hip replacement support group.

Another hospital incorporated a brief formal patient teaching program into the preadmission testing program that gives patients and staff the opportunity to discuss the upcoming hospitalization and posthospitalization program. The teaching program is offered by nursing education staff, although clinical nurse specialists, unit nurses, and/or residents or other medical staff members could provide this education.

Initially, certain physicians and nurses feared that patients would misinterpret events if their care varied from the pathway. Quite the opposite has been the case: Hospitals found that patients understand that the pathway is a general plan and that modifications may be needed. Being informed about the general sequence of care helps alleviate patient anxiety, gives patients a better sense of participation in the delivery of care, and helps prepare them for discharge.

Pilot Test Findings

Once preliminary pathway components were established, they were tested by being introduced to other participating hospitals in the DRG work groups. Hospitals shared their experiences, thereby benefiting from the group knowledge. Key clinicians for the specific pathway being developed were encouraged to participate in these discussions. As a result of hospitals sharing their data among each other, one facility reduced its length of stay for cardiac chest pain patients by half a day even before beginning the full pathway development process. While sharing current practices, all but one facility was found to rule out myocardial infarction by doing serial EKGs and serial enzymes every 8 hours, thus ruling out MI within 24 hours. The facility that varied in this practice did the same diagnostic testing; however, the tests were ordered every 12 hours, thus ruling out MI within 36 hours. By sharing this information with the medical staff, the hospital changed its standing policy to perform these tests every 8 hours, thereby reducing length of stay by 12 hours.

Quality Indicators and Variance Analysis

Following completion of the internal hospital and external work group review, objective clinical data elements were established for measuring the effectiveness of each of the four pathways. During the pilot test period, the following elements were evaluated at each hospital:[3]

- Patient satisfaction
- Frequency rates of pathway variance and their causes
- Process efficiency
- Patient outcomes
- Practitioner perceptions
- Ability of coordinators to collect data

Variances are categorized as patient-related, system-related, or practitioner-related and are documented on the form shown in figure 15-2. Variance analysis based on these three categories assists in identifying areas in which further education is needed. It also discloses the need to make changes in the pathway or the need for further system analysis.

Patient outcome criteria have been identified for each pathway. Some of these criteria are listed for the specific DRG being evaluated:

- *Cardiac chest pain:* Readmission within 30 days for cardiac diagnosis, inpatient mortality, length of stay in the intensive care unit, on a telemetry unit, and on a medical floor
- *Laparoscopic cholecystectomy:* Conversion to an open procedure, significant intraabdominal bleed, common bile duct injury, leak from liver bed, clinical indications for surgery
- *Cerebrovascular accident:* Complications of anticoagulation or antiplatelet therapy, nosocomial pneumonia, readmissions within 30 days, length of stay
- *Total hip replacement:* Harris Hip Scores obtained preoperatively, at discharge, and six months postoperatively; length of stay and discharge destination (home, rehabilitative facility, nursing home); complications including deep venous thrombosis, hip dislocation, infection, anesthesia issues; and urinary tract management (see figure 15-3, pp. 252–253)

Patient and staff satisfaction surveys were developed through the consortium (see figures 15-4 and 15-5, pp. 254–257). Hospitals have handled completion of survey documents in a variety of ways. For example, some have a patient representative or discharge planner conduct a personal interview with the patient on the day of discharge. Others have found it beneficial to call the patient one or two days after discharge and incorporate the survey questions into the discussion.

Progress Measurement

There are two important components of data collection in this program. The first is measurement of current practice and outcomes; the second is measurement of what has changed as a result of pathway implementation. Hospitals addressed the issue of data collection in several different ways. A few institutions incorporated the collection of variance data into the work of the quality management staff, who reviewed the medical records for quality and utilization issues. The majority, however, split duties among several members of the pathway team. For example, the nursing staff monitored pathway compliance daily as part of the shift-to-shift report, which created the opportunity to address variances concurrently. Aggregate variance data were also collected and analyzed by pathway team members at designated intervals (usually monthly).

Care must be taken in identifying data elements to be collected, with concentration only on those aspects that will have an impact on care delivery or processes of care. Too much data can be cumbersome, prove difficult to control, and have little meaning for process improvement.

The quality management staff monitored data elements such as length of stay and cost information. All hospitals collected data manually, although several looked to incorporate variance collection into computerized programs. Because the pathways were considered works in progress and subject to ongoing modification, most hospitals believed computerization to be premature at this phase. Several facilities, however, did use management programs for data analysis.

Patient and staff satisfaction data were also collected manually and sent to the consortium, which had an agreement with a private vendor to perform the data analysis. The results were sent to each hospital and shared with other hospitals in the same pathway group. Based on findings, the team made several decisions regarding educational needs for practitioners and/or patients, pathway modifications, data collection issues, and information dissemination activities. The timing of these decisions, which depended on the volume of patients served at each hospital, ranged from monthly to quarterly.

Once the pilot testing phase was completed, IHC groups met to discuss their findings, share their results, and, if deemed necessary, modify their pathways. Once again, the pathway was pilot tested and evaluated based on the criteria noted above and on other performance indicators developed by each hospital and its governing body. Most facilities used similar formats for their pathways, mimicking existing care plans and defining care based on segments of days. One hospital, in the process of embracing CQI philosophy, created a pictorial pathway to supplement its written total hip replacement pathway (figure 15-6, p. 258). Members of the management team also have used this graphics program to outline possible obstacles that could throw the organization "off track" in the implementation of CQI (figure 15-7, p. 259).

When the clinical pathway for a particular DRG was in the pilot testing phase, hospital groups selected a second DRG or service line and followed the same process outlined above. Further refinements are an ongoing component of each hospital's continuous quality improvement activities.

Pathway Implementation

This section provides a composite description of clinical pathway implementation activities. Although activities occurred in all 16 hospitals, a single facility is identified for illustration purposes only.

Quality Hospital is a 352-bed acute care community hospital with an 82-bed skilled nursing facility. It has been actively involved in CQI for five years, a background that proved useful because a methodology was already in place that was common to all hospital departments. Furthermore, there was a shared value belief that clinical care process improvements were critical to hospital survival. The hospital chose the total hip replacement (THR) pathway, based on the high volume of cases among this patient segment and the relatively low risk associated with the procedure. Development of the THR pathway also was seen as an opportunity to concentrate on systemwide process improvements.

As part of its strategic planning process, the hospital continually focused on improving medical staff relations and involving physicians in decisions related to patient care delivery systems. Administrators felt that the consortium's clinical pathway project would complement this effort. Because of the amount of preliminary work identified, the hospital set a nine-month time frame for pathway completion.

Figure 15-2. Total Hip Replacement Clinical Pathway Data Collection Sheet (Variance Reporting Document)

MEDICAL RECORD #_____ PHYSICIAN I.D._____

ADMISSION DATE_____ DISCHARGE DATE_____

EXPECTED LOS (days)_____

ACTUAL LOS (days)_____

(MM/DD/YY)   (MM/DD/YY)

ADDRESSOGRAPH

DATE	CP DAY	*CODE 1	VARIANCE DESCRIPTION	**CODE 2	CAUSE DESCRIPTION	ACTION TAKEN	INITIALS

ANY ADVERSE PATIENT OUTCOMES, NOT PREVIOUSLY ADDRESSED:
_____

ANY PROBLEMS WITH DATA COLLECTION IDENTIFIED:
_____
_____

*VARIANCE CODE 1:
A   NOT DONE
B   DONE EARLY ***
C   DONE LATE
D   SUBSTITUTE
E   NOT DOCUMENTED ***
F   OTHER
*** May not require additional action.

**VARIANCE CAUSE CODE 2:
SYSTEM
S1 NO NH OR REHAB BED AVAILABLE
S2 INSURANCE DOES NOT COVER HOME CARE/SUPPLIES
S3 INTERNAL BED NOT AVAILABLE FOR TRANSFER
S4 UNABLE TO SCHEDULE TEST/PROCEDURE WITH DEPARTMENT
S5 OR TIME NOT AVAILABLE
S6 TEST/PROCEDURE RESULTS NOT AVAILABLE
S9 OTHER (SPECIFY)

CLINICIAN
C1 RESPONSE TIME
C2 CONSENSUS NEED AMONGST CONSULTANTS BEFORE DISCHARGE
C3 TIME ORDER WRITTEN
C4 DISCHARGE PRESCRIPTIONS NOT WRITTEN
C5 NOT DOCUMENTED
C6 CONSENSUS NEED AMONGST TEAM
C9 OTHER (SPECIFY)

PATIENT/FAMILY
P1 PATIENT CONDITION OR COMPLICATION
P2 UNABLE TO RETURN TO PREADMISSION ENVIRONMENT
P3 NOT INDICATED FOR PATIENT
P4 UNABLE TO LEARN SKILLS NEED FOR HOME CARE
P5 INADEQUATE SOCIAL SUPPORT OR ASSISTANCE AT HOME
P6 LACK OF TRANSPORTATION HOME
P9 OTHER (SPECIFY)

Source: Northeastern New York Hospital Council.

Figure 15-3. Data Collection Form: Total Hip Replacement

TOTAL HIP REPLACEMENT DATA COLLECTION FORM

1.   MEDICAL RECORD NUMBER: _____

2.   PHYSICIAN NUMBER: _____

3.   ADMISSION DATE: _____   4.   DISCHARGE DATE: _____

5.   AGE: _____   6.   SEX: __M   __F

7.   MARITAL STATUS: 1. ___ Single   2. ___ Married   3. ___ Widowed   4. ___ Divorced

8.   ASA SCORE: _____   9.   ACUTE LENGTH OF STAY:
       (See Anesthesia Record)

                                              1.   ALOS to home: _____ (days)

                                              2.   ALOS to rehab: _____ (days)

                                              3.   ALOS to nursing home: _____ (days)

10.   READMISSION: 1. ___ no   2. ___ yes

11.   HARRIS HIP SCORE: _____ (numerical score)

12.   COMPLICATIONS: 1. ___ no (go to #14)   2. ___ yes (check all that apply)

       ___   1.   TEMP >101° AFTER 72 HOURS POST-OP

       ___   2.   DVT OR PE PER DIAGNOSTIC TESTS

       ___   3.   DISLOCATION OF HIP REPLACEMENT

       ___   4.   RETURN TO THE OPERATING ROOM

       ___   5.   INFECTION:

                     ___   1.   RESPIRATORY

                     ___   2.   WOUND (go to #13)

                     ___   3.   URINARY TRACT

                     ___   4.   SKIN (other than wound)

                     ___   5.   SEPSIS

                     ___   6.   OTHER (specify)   _____

Figure 15-3. (Continued)

13.   WOUND INFECTION DESCRIPTION (all infections treated):

      ___   1.   SUPERFICIAL

      ___   2.   DEEP WOUND

      ___   3.   REQUIRES SURGICAL MANAGEMENT

14.   ANESTHESIA COMPLICATIONS: ___ 1. no (go to #15) ___ 2. yes (check all that apply)

      ___   1.   ASPIRATION PRE- OR POST-INTUBATION

      ___   2.   HYPOTENSION (< 80 SYSTOLIC) TREATED DURING SURGERY

      ___   3.   REINTUBATION

      ___   4.   HEART FAILURE

      ___   5.   LOSS OF TEETH

      ___   6.   TACHYCARDIA/BRADYCARDIA REQUIRING TREATMENT

      ___   7.   OTHER (specify) _____

15.   URINARY TRACT MANAGEMENT ISSUES: ___ 1. none (go to #16) ___ 2. foley
        ___ 3. straight catheterization

      ___   1.   FOLEY CATHETER IN > 24 HOURS

      ___   2.   STRAIGHT CATHETERIZATION > 2 TIMES

      ___   3.   GU STUDIES ORDERED (ie., cysto)

16.   STAT INTERVENTIONS REQUIRED: ___ 1. no (go #17)   ___ 2. yes

      ___   1.   NEED TO CALL HEALTH CARE PROVIDER FOR STAT STUDIES (other than those mentioned above)

      ___   2.   NEED FOR EMERGENCY CONSULTATION

      ___   3.   TRANSFER TO SPECIAL CARE UNIT

17.   AMBULATING BY THIRD POST-OPERATIVE DAY: ___ 1. no   ___ 2. yes

18.   DAY DISCHARGE PLAN COMPLETED: _____ (hospital bed day that tentative discharge plan is defined in record)

19.   TOTAL HOSPITAL STAY CHARGES: _____ (dollar amount rounded to nearest full number)

Source: Northeastern New York Hospital Council.

Figure 15-4. Patient Satisfaction Survey

ID# [ ][ ][ ][ ]

PATIENT SATISFACTION SURVEY:
TOTAL HIP REPLACEMENT

GENDER:
Man. 1
Woman 2

OUR HOSPITAL IS PARTICIPATING IN A PROJECT TO EVALUATE THE QUALITY OF CARE DELIVERED TO PATIENTS WHO ARE HOSPITALIZED FOR TOTAL HIP REPLACEMENT. YOUR OPINIONS ABOUT THE CARE YOU HAVE RECEIVED, INCLUDING YOUR EVALUATION OF THE INFORMATION AND INSTRUCTIONS YOU HAVE BEEN GIVEN DURING YOUR HOSPITAL STAY, ARE VERY IMPORTANT.

1) DID YOU HAVE ANY PRE-ADMISSION TESTING OR OTHER INTERACTION WITH HOSPITAL STAFF BEFORE YOU WERE ADMITTED TO THE HOSPITAL? *(If No Skip To Question 4)*

Yes 1
No. 0
No Opinion/Don't Know 8

THINKING ABOUT THE CARE YOU RECEIVED DURING YOUR PRE-ADMISSION TESTING...

2) HOW SATISFIED ARE YOU WITH THE INFORMATION YOU RECEIVED TO PREPARE YOU FOR YOUR HOSPITAL STAY? *(Read Choices)*

VERY SATISFIED. 1
SOMEWHAT SATISFIED 2
NOT SATISFIED AT ALL 3
No Opinion/Don't Know 8

3) HOW SATISFIED ARE YOU WITH THE CARE YOU RECEIVED FROM THE HOSPITAL STAFF WHO CONDUCTED YOUR PRE-ADMISSION TESTING OR INSTRUCTIONS? *(Read Choices)*

VERY SATISFIED. 1
SOMEWHAT SATISFIED 2
NOT SATISFIED AT ALL 3
No Opinion/Don't Know 8

NOW REFERRING TO THE CARE YOU RECEIVED DURING THIS HOSPITAL STAY...

4) HOW WOULD YOU RATE THE OVERALL QUALITY OF THE CARE YOU RECEIVED DURING YOUR STAY AT THIS HOSPITAL? *(Read Choices)*

EXCELLENT 1
GOOD. 2
FAIR. .3
OR POOR 4
No Opinion/Don't Know 8

5) OVERALL, HOW WOULD YOU RATE THE CARE YOU RECEIVED FROM THE NURSING STAFF? *(Read Choices)*

EXCELLENT 1
GOOD. 2
FAIR. .3
OR POOR 4
No Opinion/Don't Know 8

6) OVERALL, HOW WOULD YOU RATE THE CARE YOU RECEIVED FROM YOUR DOCTORS? *(Read Choices)*

EXCELLENT 1
GOOD. 2
FAIR. .3
OR POOR 4
No Opinion/Don't Know 8

THE FOLLOWING QUESTIONS ARE ABOUT THE VARIOUS HOSPITAL STAFF WHO CARED FOR YOU <u>DURING THIS STAY</u>, INCLUDING DOCTORS, NURSES, NURSING AIDES, RESPIRATORY, OCCUPATIONAL AND PHYSICAL THERAPISTS, X-RAY TECHNOLOGISTS, ETC.

7) HOW MANY OF THE VARIOUS HOSPITAL STAFF WHO CARED FOR YOU WERE WELL INFORMED ABOUT YOU AND YOUR PROGRESS? *(Read Choices)*

MOST OF THEM 1
SOME OF THEM 2
NONE OF THEM 3
No Opinion/Don't Know 8

8) HOW WELL DID THE VARIOUS HOSPITAL STAFF WORK TOGETHER AS A TEAM TO PROVIDE YOU WITH THE CARE YOU NEEDED? *(Read Choices)*

VERY WELL 1
FAIRLY WELL 2
NOT WELL AT ALL. 3
No Opinion/Don't Know 8

9) DID YOUR DOCTORS AND NURSES INVOLVE YOU IN DECISIONS ABOUT THE CARE YOU RECEIVED? *(Read Choices)*

Yes 1
No. 0
No Opinion/Don't Know 8

10) HOW SATISFIED ARE YOU WITH THE AMOUNT OF TIME DOCTORS, NURSES AND THERAPISTS SPENT TALKING WITH YOU ABOUT YOUR CARE? *(Read Choices)*

VERY SATISFIED. 1
SOMEWHAT SATISFIED 2
NOT SATISFIED AT ALL 3
No Opinion/Don't Know 8

Figure 15-4. (Continued)

11) **DURING YOUR HOSPITAL STAY, DID STAFF PROVIDE YOU WITH INFORMATION ABOUT** *(Read Factor, Mix Order)*

FACTOR:		YES	NO	DON'T KNOW
A)	YOUR DIAGNOSIS	.1	0	8
B)	TESTS TO BE PERFORMED.	.1	0	8
C)	MEDICATIONS YOU RECEIVED	.1	0	8
D)	SPECIAL DIET CHOICES	.1	0	8
E)	ACTIVITIES YOU COULD DO SAFELY	.1	0	8

12) **OVERALL, HOW SATISFIED ARE YOU THAT THE STAFF HAS GIVEN YOU THE INFORMATION YOU NEEDED DURING YOUR HOSPITAL STAY?** *(Read Choices)*

VERY SATISFIED. .1
SOMEWHAT SATISFIED 2
NOT SATISFIED AT ALL 3
No Opinion/Don't Know 8

13) **DID YOU EXPERIENCE ANY PAIN DURING YOUR HOSPITAL STAY?** *(If No Skip To Question 16)*

Yes 1
No. 0
No Opinion/Don't Know 8

14) **HOW WOULD YOU RATE THE EFFORTS OF THE HOSPITAL STAFF TO CONTROL THE PAIN WHICH YOU FELT?** *(Read Choices)*

EXCELLENT. 1
GOOD. 2
FAIR. 3
OR POOR 4
No Opinion/Don't Know 8

15) **HOW SUCCESSFUL WERE THE HOSPITAL STAFF IN CONTROLLING THE AMOUNT OF PAIN THAT YOU FELT?** *(Read Choices)*

VERY SUCCESSFUL. 1
SOMEWHAT SUCCESSFUL. 2
NOT SUCCESSFUL AT ALL. 3
No Opinion/Don't Know 8

THE NEXT QUESTIONS REFER TO THE INSTRUCTIONS YOU HAVE RECEIVED IN PLANNING FOR YOUR DISCHARGE FROM THE HOSPITAL...

16) **HAVE STAFF PROVIDED YOU WITH INSTRUCTIONS ABOUT** *(Read Factor, Mix Order)*

FACTOR:		YES	NO	DON'T KNOW
A)	WHICH MEDICATIONS TO TAKE AND WHEN TO TAKE THEM.	.1	0	8
B)	WHEN TO CALL THE DOCTOR AFTER YOU RETURN HOME	.1	0	8
C)	ANY LIFESTYLE CHANGES WHICH MAY BE NECESSARY	.1	0	8
D)	ANY LIMITATIONS ON EXERCISING.	.1	0	8
E)	MEDICAL APPOINTMENTS WHICH HAVE BEEN OR SHOULD BE MADE FOR FOLLOW-UP CARE	.1	0	8
F)	REHABILITATION PROGRAM OR SERVICE OPTIONS	.1	0	8

17) **OVERALL, HOW SATISFIED ARE YOU THAT THE STAFF HAS GIVEN YOU THE INSTRUCTIONS YOU NEED FOR USE AFTER YOUR DISCHARGE FROM THE HOSPITAL?** *(Read Choices)*

VERY SATISFIED. 1
SOMEWHAT SATISFIED 2
NOT SATISFIED AT ALL 3
No Opinion/Don't Know 8

18) **BASED ON YOUR EXPERIENCE DURING THIS HOSPITAL STAY, WHICH CHANGES, IF ANY, WOULD YOU RECOMMEND TO IMPROVE THE QUALITY OF CARE PROVIDED TO YOU?**

_____

_____

19) **AND FINALLY, WHAT IS YOUR AGE:**

Record Years. . . . . ____

Source: Northeastern New York Hospital Council.

Figure 15-5. Staff Evaluation Form

```
3 i 3 7
```

STAFF EVALUATION: PATIENT CARE FOR TOTAL HIP REPLACEMENT

Prior to the implementation of a clinical pathway for total hip replacement we would like to know your perceptions about caring for patients hospitalized with this diagnosis. Please complete this survey with reference only to patients with total hip replacement.

Your responses are confidential; all data analysis is being coordinated by the Iroquois Healthcare Consortium. Your participation in this project is appreciated as your responses are an integral part of our evaluation process.

Thank you very much for your time.

Referring to services provided to total hip replacement patients, how satisfied are you with the...

	Very Satisfied 1	Somewhat Satisfied 2	Not Satisfied 3
Timeliness of diagnostic tests and reports			
Time you have available to provide discharge planning			
Time you have available to provide patient/family education			
Degree to which patients (and their families) are included in decisions about their care			

How satisfied are you with the...

	Very Satisfied 1	Somewhat Satisfied 2	Not Satisfied 3
Time required to document patient care and/or orders			

Regarding communication among the many health professionals and departments in the hospital, how would you rate the...

	Excellent 1	Good 2	Fair 3	Poor 4
Efficiency of procedures for documenting patient care and/or orders				
Communication between the attending M.D. and other consulting M.D.'s				
Communication between the attending M.D. and you and your colleagues				
Communication between the nursing staff and other hospital staff members				
Communication about patient care issues among all hospital departments				
Contributions to the care plan from the entire team of health care professionals caring for the patient				
Cooperation among the entire team of health care professionals caring for the patient				

How would you rate the organization of the patient information which you use to plan your daily workload?

EXCELLENT 1 GOOD 2 FAIR 3 POOR 4

Thinking about your own satisfaction in performing your job, how satisfied are you with...

	Very Satisfied 1	Somewhat Satisfied 2	Not Satisfied 3
Your ability to participate in clinical decisions about care the patient receives	Very Satisfied 1	Somewhat Satisfied 2	Not Satisfied 3
The levels of respect of other health professionals for your clinical expertise	Very Satisfied 1	Somewhat Satisfied 2	Not Satisfied 3
The authority you have to organize your own workload	Very Satisfied 1	Somewhat Satisfied 2	Not Satisfied 3

How would you rate the overall quality of the care patients with total hip replacement receive during their stays at this hospital?

EXCELLENT 1 GOOD 2 FAIR 3 POOR 4

Have you received information about the project to develop clinical pathways to guide the treatment and care of patients with total hip replacement?

YES 1 NO 2

What one change, if any, would you recommend to improve the quality of care delivered to patients hospitalized for total hip replacement?

_____
_____
_____
_____
_____
_____
_____
_____
_____
_____

Surveys from all participating hospitals are being sent to the Iroquois Healthcare Consortium. For data analysis purposes, please fill in the following:

Date of Birth_____   Job Title_____

Number of Years in
Your Current Position_____   Male/Female_____

PLEASE RETURN COMPLETED SURVEY TO:
_____

Figure 15-6. Sample Pictorial Pathway: Total Hip Replacement

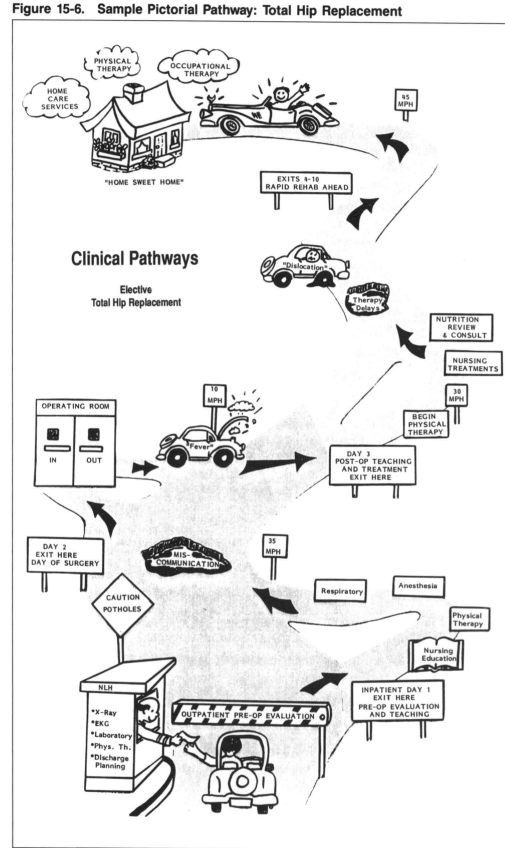

Source: Nathan Littauer Hospital. ©Collins, Hodlin, Burek.

Figure 15-7. Sample Pictorial Pathway: The CQI Track

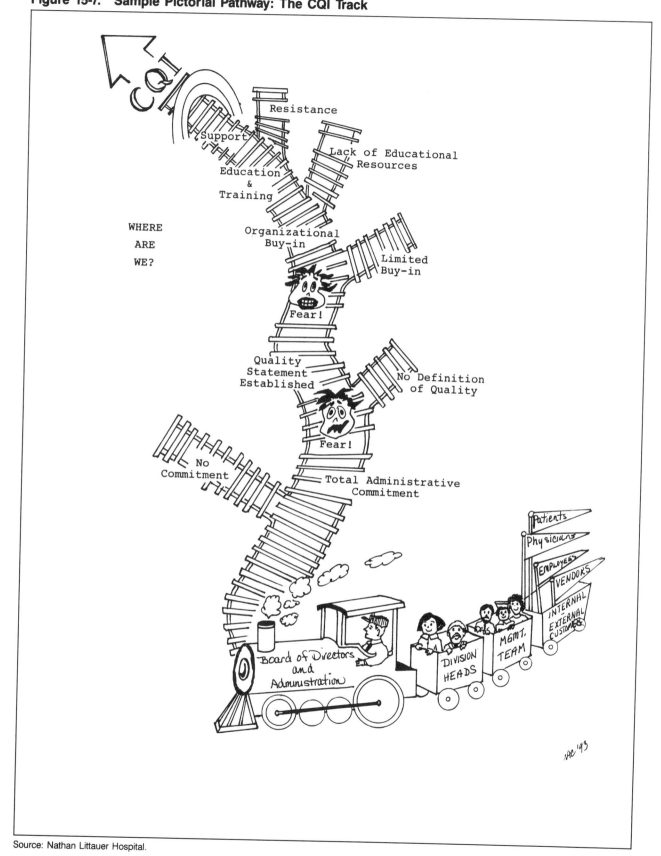

Source: Nathan Littauer Hospital.

From the outset, Quality Hospital secured the medical director's commitment to promoting the concept of clinical pathways as a CQI methodology among the medical staff. It was believed that staff support could be garnered by building on their interest in being involved in research, kept abreast of the current literature, and educated about current practice models.

The medical director sought the involvement and support of the orthopedic surgery chief, who eventually became the physician champion for the THR pathway. The approach taken with the medical staff—in addition to the emphasis on education and research—was that a THR path would allow the medical staff to assist the hospital in its management practices around this particular service line. In return, the hospital would support the medical staff in publishing any articles related to outcomes from the project.

One-hour team meetings were scheduled every other week. A core group of 10 members consisted of two orthopedic surgeons, an anesthesiologist, the medical director, an operating room nurse, a staff nurse, the nursing director, a discharge planner, and two physical therapists. Ancillary service personnel were added as necessary. The orthopedic nurse manager was the team leader, and the director of health care resource management was the quality improvement coach.

The team spent its first few meetings establishing a mission statement, goals, realistic time frames, and ground rules. Their approach was "go slow to go fast"; that is, by being very deliberate in its planning and early evaluation phase, the hospital was able to make significant and lasting improvements in its patient care process. The team had identified preadmission testing as a major system issue and worked on correcting that system prior to implementing the total hip pathway. Subgroups were assigned to address specific issues, such as postanesthesia care unit discharge, and were given "just-in-time" training on CQI methods and tools. A great deal of homework and out-of-meeting work was assigned. Reports of team progress were made regularly to the medical staff, nursing staff, administration, quality council, and board of trustees. Storyboards were posted on the orthopedics unit so that the team's progress could be followed.

As initial team meetings progressed, the medical staff, discharge planning staff, and quality improvement coach met with area home care agencies to discuss the project and ascertain their opinion of what, from the physician and hospital perspective, they felt THR patient needs were for home care services. In addition, they were asked to consider whether the goals and objectives established by physicians could meet patient needs in the time frames established. Despite competition among agencies, their shared response to the need for improved communitywide health care prevailed. In the end, all agencies committed to the delivery of services in the time frames established. Consequently, daily home physical therapy programs—regardless of day of discharge—were established. In return, Quality Hospital committed to notifying the agencies of projected discharge dates at the time of preadmission testing and to keeping the agencies advised of changes.

The team next approached the area's long-term rehabilitation center, which offered a 21-day THR inpatient therapy program. Because the hospital's medical staff was sure that many patients would benefit from a shorter stay, the rehabilitation center established a seven-day short-stay program. In return, the hospital developed a schedule for communicating with the home care agencies and rehabilitation center at the time of patient scheduling and a phone call on inpatient hospital day four to confirm discharge plans. A discharge date was built into the pathway. The nurse manager and utilization review coordinators monitor patient progress along the path and make reminder calls to physicians and staff as necessary. Increased communication about therapy needs has improved scheduling and eliminated unnecessary downtime for inpatient therapy that contributed to a longer length of stay.

Patient input to the process was critical. As changes to care options, education, and time sequences were considered by the pathway team, physicians consulted with former patients and their families for input and suggested changes. Enhanced communication and education helped alleviate patient and family anxiety.

Given that Quality Hospital staff were more experienced in CQI methods and tools than others in the consortium, they led in sharing their expertise with the work group. Members also benefited from hearing other approaches and suggestions for ways to involve team members.

Using the patient and staff satisfaction surveys as models, the hospital tailored a feedback instrument to meet the specific needs of each DRG work group. The surveys were designed to be used during prepathway and postpathway implementation. Quality Hospital chose to collect additional data to assist with process and outcome analysis. Information was collected manually by designated persons. For example, nursing collected patient and employee satisfaction data, the quality management staff collected technical data (such as length of stay), and pathway variances were collected at the unit level by the nursing staff. Once collected on paper, the data were entered into a D-base program by the quality management staff and sent to the consortium for analysis.

Approximately nine months into the process, the total hip replacement pathway was ready for implementation. (Figure 15-8 is an excerpt of the total hip replacement pathway; excluded are postop days 3 through 6.) After being used for four patients, the pathway earned the approval of the orthopedic physicians, who were ready to develop standing orders. As patterns emerged, issues were identified and brought back to the team for whatever changes were warranted. Hospital and medical staff perceived this as a dynamic process that required continual refinement.

Preliminary data demonstrated an increase in both patient and staff satisfaction. Length of stay decreased by 2.5 days, a cost savings of $1,500 per case. The hospital is working with the local Visiting Nurses Association to develop a program for at-home preadmission testing. This strategy is expected to cut costs, improve patient awareness, and minimize patient anxiety.

Lessons Learned

Implementation of the consortium's clinical pathway project met with many obstacles, but the strategy (from the consortium's perspective) was to adhere to Deming's principle of "drive out fear."[4] Whenever problems surfaced that were related to market share or competition, the work groups were refocused on patient care outcomes and improved health care for the community. Other lessons learned as a result of the project can be summarized briefly:

- *Active involvement and champion leaders:* Without "hands-on" participation from administrators and medical staff, and without physician champions, a pathway program cannot be effective. Physicians' schedules must be accommodated — which often means early morning meetings while physicians are on site for rounds or early evening meetings following office hours. Meetings must be well planned and structured so that all members feel that their time is well spent. One person should be designated clinical pathway champion so that it is clear who is responsible for moving the project forward to meet institutional timetables and deadlines. Also, as already indicated, a champion can help secure commitment from medical staff and overall organizational enthusiasm.
- *Unit nurse, bedside caregivers:* Hospitals should always include on the team staff who actually work with the patients. For example, one issue identified well

Figure 15-8. Clinical Pathway: Total Hip Replacement (Excerpt)

	PRE-ADMISSION	PRE-OP: DAY OF ADMISSION	ADMIT/SURGERY DAY	POST-OP DAY 1	POST-OP DAY 2
NURSING	Pathway review/teaching Tour of unit Vital Signs Nursing History and Assessment Pre-post op teaching Labs/tests as needed Pre-anesthesia teaching Pain control teaching (Buhrmaster) 2 DAY POST PAT ASSESSMENT OF ALL DATA	Review of Nursing Assessment Routine Patient Prep Vital Signs Review Pre-op teaching Review of Pain Control	Neuro checks q̄ 2° × 3 then q̄ 4° VS every 4 hrs and prm I&O Physical Assessment q̄ 8 DVT Prevention: Ankle Flexion q̄ q pt. Intervention; Equipment as ordered Drains: Quantify, check patency, reinfuse 02 × 24 hrs post Deep breathe with every PT intervention Dressing: Reinforce PRN Mobility: Bedrest o HOB↑, Position as ordered (Hip Precautions)	Neuro checks q̄ 4° and PRN VS every 4 hrs and prm I&O d/o Physical Assessment q̄ 8° DVT Prevention—Same as Day 1 Exercises—Quad & Gluteal Sets Drain—Same as Day 1 No Reinfuse 02—D/C unless otherwise needed Deep Breathe & Incentive Device Bedrest o HOB↑, Position as ordered Drsg—Reinforce PRN D/C foley catheter if in place (except if GU history check with MD)	Neuro checks q̄ 4° VS every 4 hrs and prm Physical Assessment q̄ 8° DVT Precautions Exercises—glut and quad sets Drain & dressing D/C Check wound q̄ 8° Resp—Deep Breath. & Incent. D Mobility—OOB to chair 2 × D Supply HI-JOHN
TEACHING	See Nursing, MD, PT., and Discharge Planning Anesthesia RN to education on the options and usage of PCA	See Nursing	Pain Control Reinforce Pre-Op Training	Pain Control Total hip precautions/Nrsg & PT Anticipatory Guidance Reinforce Deep Breathing & Incentive Device Tx	Reinforce Day #2 teaching Pivot transfer teaching
PHYSICAL THERAPY	(A) Teaching and exercise plans set up 6 weeks PTA —outpatient PT set up if needed —Harris Scale completed (B) Follow-up teaching/reinforcement done on PAT day		Sling Review Teaching	Sling Quad & Gluteal Sets Update Assessment Reassurance Ensure teaching of significant family × 1 by 3rd Post-op Day	Transfer/Ambulate PT 2 × D Sling Plan OT Consult
MEDICATIONS		Start 1 GM ancef IV upon transfer from Day Surgery to O.R. suite (open it up) to meet the goal of written 1 hr. prior to incision	PCA if ordered or Pain Regime Anticoagulant-majority c̄ Coumadin Antibiotics—Ancef (IV)	PCA Anticoagulants cont. Antibiotics cont. (IV) Bowel Regime (Colace PRN 2 × D MOM PRN)	PCA d/c begin P.O. meds D/C hepwell p̄ checking H&H results D/C antibiotic—1 dose 8 hrs. after drain removal Anticoagulant Bowel regime Start Fe
NUTRITION		NPO	IV until tolerating PO Diet as tolerated	Advancing to regular (pre-op diet) If lunch tolerated d/o IV to hepwell Encourage Fluids	Encourage Fluids Assess food intake
DISCHARGE PLANNING	Decision/Sched. of Sunnyview PTA as feasible Help pt./family with hotel if needed Do Anticipatory Guidance and Plan for getting house, equip., services in place Do Anticipatory Guidance and Plan for PHCP as feasible guidance Make decision about F/U agency Call, schedule agency F/U		Refer to liaison RN Confirm agency scheduled case	Reintroduction Family contact—Ensure F/U with PT. Review of D/C Planning Expectations	Check with patient & Nsg. to see how patient did. Ensure walker for in-patient Rx
OTHER-MD PAT	Methods: Identify Patients/ Schedule for Surgery/ Teach/Prepare Get Consults/Get Clearance Internist/FP/Specialists Anesthesiologist to see in PAT's PAT: Get anesthesia orders		Post-op anesthesia assessment (PCA)	Physical assessment by MD Post-op anesthesia assessment Medical consultant/attending assessment as needed GU Consult	PCA D/C
TEST/RX	PAT:CBC Urine C/S Cath Urine (Female) 4 wks PTA Joint X-rays C X R SMA-12 PT/PTT Sed Rate MD will bring Hip X-rays with them Type and Screen	Send bed to the O.R. Draw H&H STAT 6:30 AM Call to O.R. suite Type and Cross Match × 2-3 weeks Blood ready by 7:30 am in the O.R.	H&H in Recovery Room results to H.O. X-Ray in Recovery Room	H&H in AM—report to H.O. PT/PTT in AM—report to H.O.	PT/PTT ⌐ Results to H&H ⌐ H.O.
OR/PACU		Catheterization as per guidelines		02 × 24 hrs. then D/C unless otherwise needed	Post-op anesthesia assessment Physical Assessment

OR / PACU	**ADMIT/SURGERY DAY (ADDENDUM)**

	DISCHARGE CRITERIA FROM PACU
	I. No unexplained blood or drainage on dsg.
	II. Vital Signs
	   Temp—97 rectally—change to 98.5 with skin trunk to 96
	   BP—as preop for 1 hr—+ preop baseline
	   P—as preop for 1 hr—+ 20% preop baseline
	   RR—unlabored, easy not shallow.
	   O2 titrated from 98% face shield to 40% face shield to room air with the O2 saturation maintaining in the 90's. Preop saturation or better (97%) with O2 or s O2 90% for 15 min. or longer
	III. Mental Status
	  A) awake—alert
	  B) preop baseline
	  C) need report of baseline
	  ??Admit Criteria in Nursing Assessment
	IV. Fluid Management
	  A) Drainage—amt. different for knee than hip. No set # of cc's to call H.O. at present.
	  B) Reinfusion done if needed. IV Team called as soon as pt. arrives in PACU, then recalled if infusion is needed.
	  C) IV infusion—primarily to keep patient stable then titrated to ordered rate for 1 hour.
	  D) Urine output—cath prn, void, must have evidence of urine output of at least 100cc's or greater.
	  E) OR: fluid/blood management will be based on the individual.
	V. Pain Management
	  A) Mechanism—PCA/Intermittent
	  B) Warmth/comfort
	  C) Patient showing signs of pain relief.
	  D) Patient should have an empty bladder based on evidence of voiding 100cc and no distention.
	VI. PACU Score
	  A) Sensation, Mobility, Circulation
	  B) Sensation of extremities as preop or better.
	  C) Mobility for extremities for functional capacity as preop.
	  D) Circulation—pedal pulses, capillary refill.
	VII. Foley: If foley to be inserted, it should be done in the O.R. The need will be determined by the surgeon/anesthesiologist.
	  (or) if procedure, skin to skin will be → 3 hours.
	  (or) Total Hip Revision
	  (or) Anesthesiologist feels very strongly.

into the data collection process was a documentation tool used to measure total hip patient functional status. Each hospital's physical therapy department developed a unique process for integrating the tool into their practice, resulting in data that could not be compared or shared from hospital to hospital. If a physical therapist had been on the data collection portion of the team, this issue could have been addressed prior to pathway implementation.

- *Resistance to change:* Hospitals should expect some passive-resistant behavior. Patient shifting may occur among hospitals sharing one medical staff. For example, one hospital developed a clinical pathway for CVA patients, with the emergency department physicians championing the project. This hospital was one of three local facilities that shared the same medical staff. After implementation of the pathway, there was a marked decrease in CVA admissions to the pathway hospital, even though the medical staff had indicated support for the project. To avoid similar shifts, the three local hospitals decided to collaborate on developing a joint clinical pathway for pneumonia. Similar alliances among hospitals that share a medical staff have also been developed in other areas of the region.

- *Open communication channels:* By securing involvement of physicians' office staff, home care agencies, vendors, and other facilities early in the process, repetition and redundancy can be curtailed. Streamlined communication helps make for a smooth patient transition. Many facilities established patient education materials as a priority during pathway development (certain outside agencies and vendors already had developed these materials). Early networking and information sharing can save time and rework in the long run.

- *Community education and outreach:* Through patient and family participation, community education and outreach activities can be identified. Hospitals can then use this information on community service initiatives or partnering with community agencies. For example, health maintenance and illness prevention can be promoted in senior citizen centers, health maintenance organizations, health groups (for example, diabetes or cancer), and social agencies (such as correctional facilities). Managed care organizations may find it beneficial to standardize approaches to care through the use of pathways, especially when their patient mix extends beyond community lines.

- *Definition of data elements:* Data elements should be established early in the process. This activity helps to focus and bond team members, especially because this is a nonthreatening pursuit. Several participating hospitals pulled the same charts to examine current practice patterns and collect data. Had data elements been established, this rework could have been avoided.

- *Patient sophistication:* Physicians and other caregivers should be prepared to deal with better educated patients. Despite their early involvement with the pathway program and with patient education, physicians were not always equipped to answer patients' questions. For example, one orthopedic physician who had been the physician champion for one of the THR projects became frustrated at the depth of questions posed by one patient based on information received during the preadmission assessment program. The physician admitted that the questions were appropriate and addressed points that would have been shared during the course of hospitalization and therapy. However, because in the past there had been no standardized method or sequence for communicating with patients, the physician felt at a loss during the initial meeting. The physician now has a more formal plan for patient communication and education that dovetails with the clinical pathway program.

These and other lessons have proved instrumental in helping the hospital move forward with its program. Each lesson has been the impetus for further opportunity.

Benefits of Project Participation

All participants – patients, physicians, hospitals, and the consortium – have realized several benefits from participation in the clinical pathway project and in collaborating with other health care facilities. *Patients* enjoy increased satisfaction with and understanding of care processes related to their hospitalization. They also are involved more actively and more autonomously in decisions affecting the health care they receive.

Physicians created a stimulating environment in which to advance education, knowledge, and research. By bolstering hospital responsiveness to physician and patient needs they drew the medical staff more closely into participation in the hospital's decision-making processes. Physicians also developed their own ability to influence the design of multisystem processes that influence patient care.

Hospitals broke down competitive barriers and freely shared information about their respective hospital systems and clinical data. This information exchange led to improvements in overall hospital operations. Each hospital became more advanced in the concepts of continuous quality improvement and, by sharing what it learned, furthered the advancement of others less knowledgeable in CQI principles.

By widening the communication channels within and among key departments and services, caregivers have more ready access to collaborative team approaches. This access facilitates delivery of patient-centered care that is quality-effective *and* cost-effective. The net effect is improved patient outcomes, shorter length of stay, less "rework," and better relationships with outside providers.

For the *consortium,* benefits have been profound. The IHC established for itself a leadership role in clinical pathway development and gained a level of respect and trust among member hospitals that is evidenced by increased cooperation, collaboration, and participation in other consortium projects. The role of the IHC is not to be underrated. In its role as group facilitator, educator, and coordinator, the consortium became the chief champion for the project. Council staff acknowledged and praised individual hospital efforts and has since dedicated one full-time staff person to coordinate and oversee this project.

Finally, economies of scale were achieved. Staff conducted literature searches and created a small library of resources that were made available to all participants. The hospitals also relied on council resources to obtain regional data, conduct analyses, and compile summary information that assisted the group in setting its direction.

Conclusion

The Northeastern New York Hospital Council regional quality improvement demonstration project on clinical pathway development has proved to be a valuable experience for its provider and patient community. Member hospitals have simultaneously improved patient care by systematizing processes of care, drawing on the expertise of the group as a whole, and developing stronger collaborative relationships among the many health care providers and agencies. The council's experience with this project and view of the future, with increased development of alliances, networks, and managed care plans, suggests that the benefits of this type of collaborative clinical consensus development will become evident to all types of patient care providers.

References

1. Ciccone, K. R., and Lord, J. T. *IQA-2: Continuous Performance Improvement through Integrated Quality Assessment.* Chicago: American Hospital Publishing, 1992.

2. Ciccone and Lord, p. 43.

3. Ciccone and Lord.

4. Walton, M. *The Deming Management Method.* New York City: Dodd, Mead & Company, 1986, p. 35.

Additional Books of Interest

Nursing Leadership: Preparing for the 21st Century
edited by the American Organization of Nurse Executives

Explores important trends and issues as well as the skills needed by nursing management to promote organizational and personal excellence, inspire creativity, and achieve success. Practical strategies are provided to help nursing leaders manage change and reduce stress.
Catalog No. E99-154152 (must be included when ordering)
1993. 150 pages, 12 figures, 3 tables.
$45.00 (AHA members, $35.00)

Outpatient Case Management
edited by Michelle Regan Donovan and Theodore A. Matson

This book presents a framework for implementing case management strategies in the outpatient arena. General guidelines on case management are provided and the importance of this tool in a changing health care delivery system is examined. Examples are provided of sixteen different successful programs of all types.
Catalog No. E99-027100 (must be included when ordering)
1994. 298 pages, 20 figures, 8 tables.
$58.95 (AHA members, $48.95)

Medical Staff Credentialing: A Practical Guide
by Fay A. Rozovsky, J.D., Lorne E. Rozovsky, LL.B., and Linda M. Harpster, J.D.

Medical Staff Credentialing is designed for administrators and physicians who are either directly involved in the credentialing process or need to know how that process works. The book focuses on the basic practical problems of determining whether, and to what extent, a physician will be permitted to practice within the hospital. It covers the credentialing process, from initial application and clinical privilege delineation, through periodic reassessment, to reappointment and reprivileging.
Catalog No. E99-145102 (must be included when ordering)
1993. 132 pages, 8 figures.
$49.00 (AHA members, $39.00)

To order, call TOLL FREE
1-800-AHA-2626